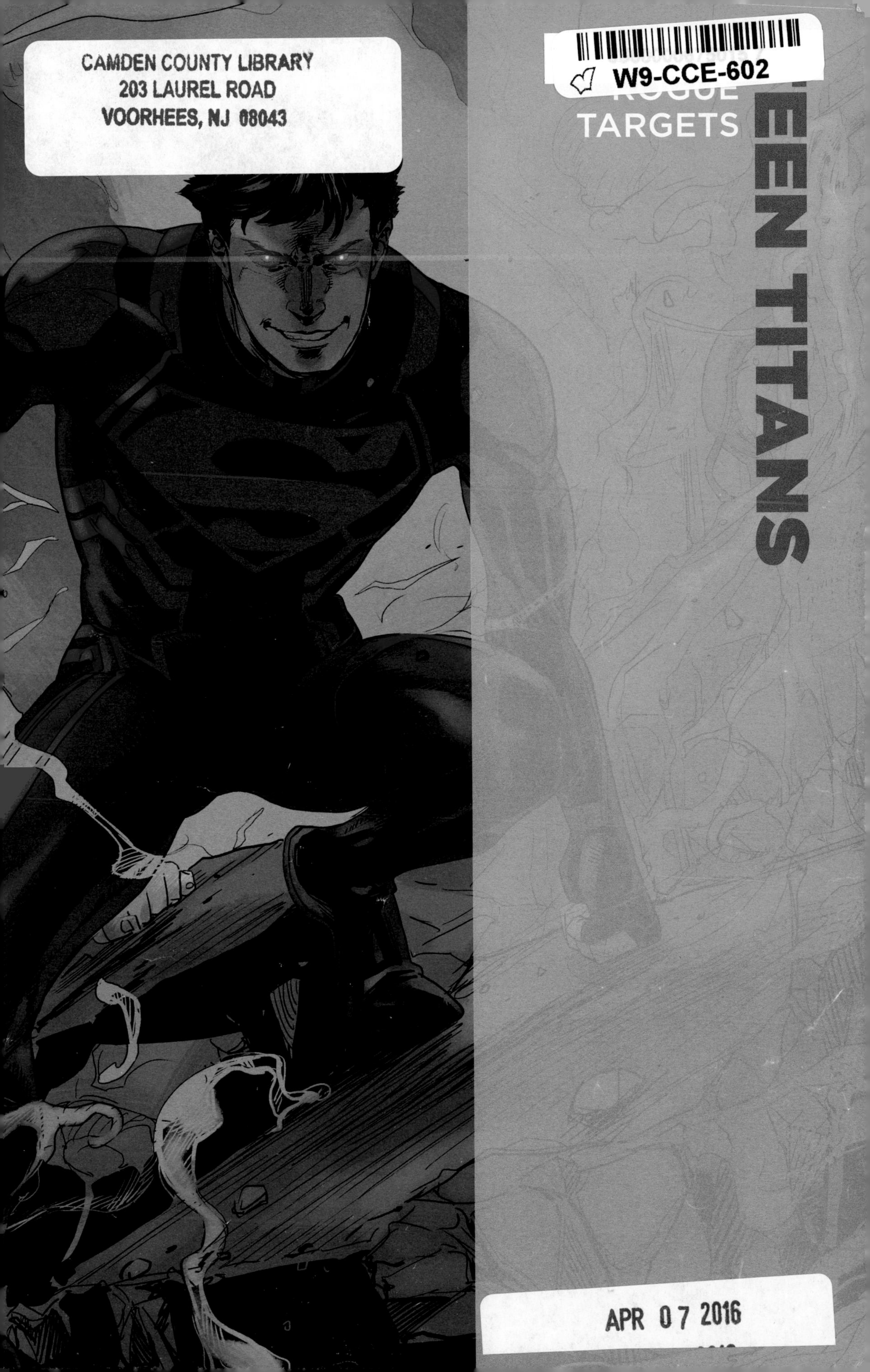
ROGUE
TARGETS
EEN TITANS

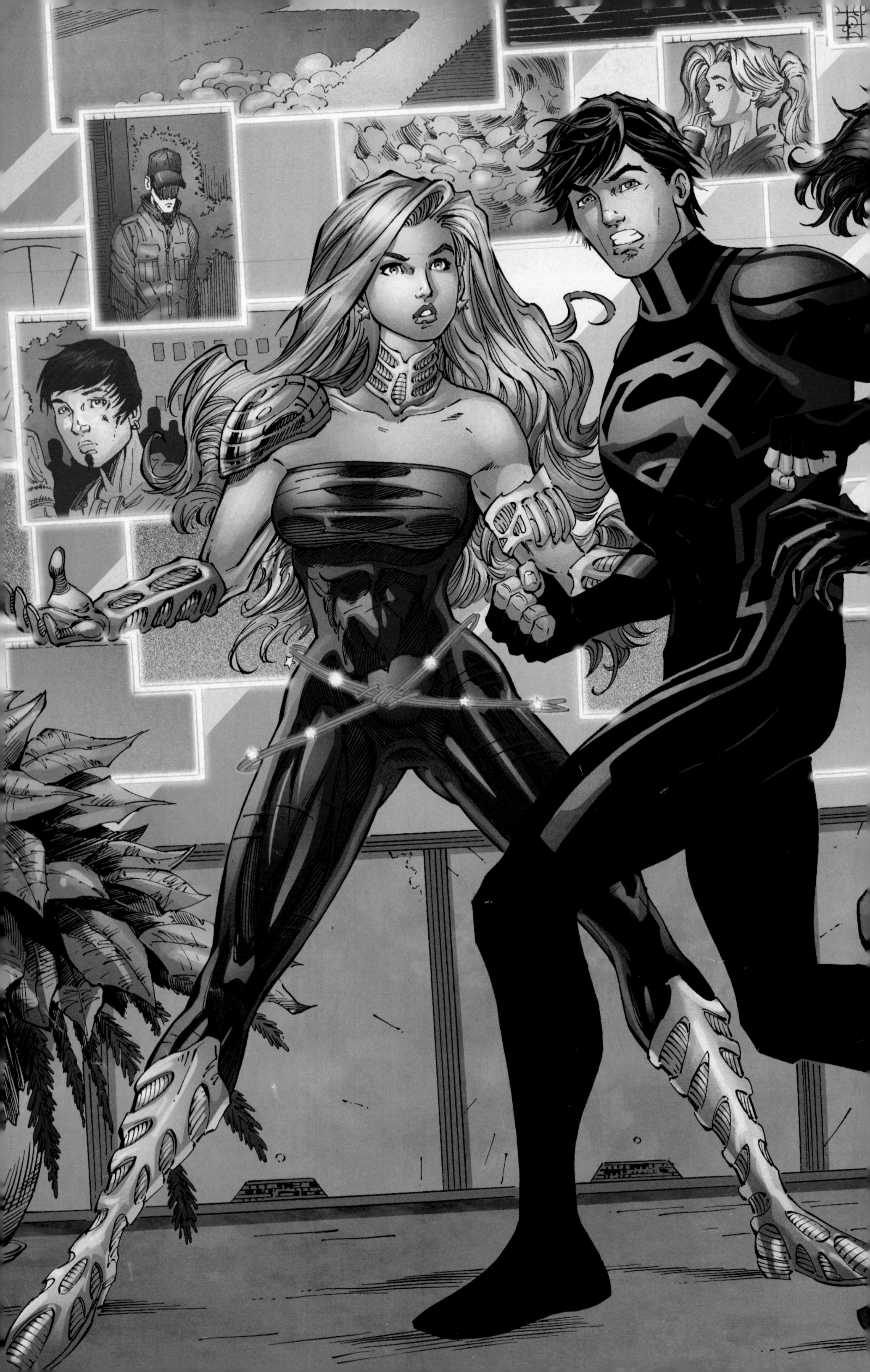

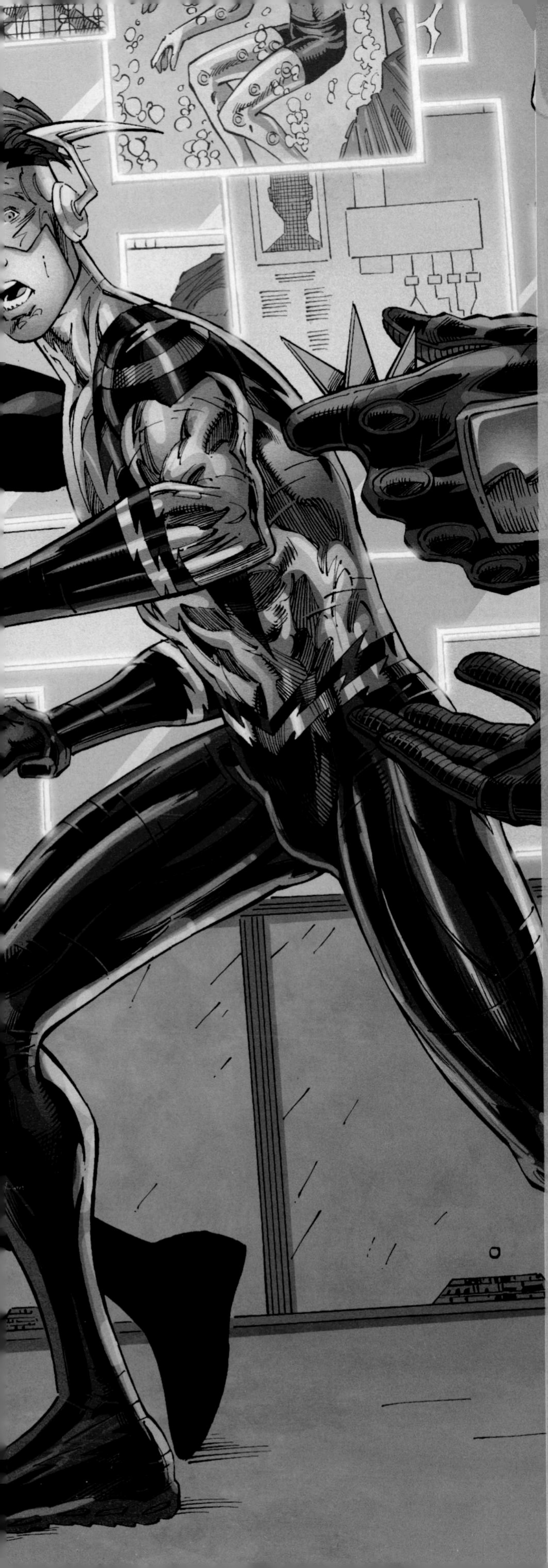

TEEN TITANS

VOLUME 2
ROGUE TARGETS

WRITTEN BY
WILL PFEIFER
TOM KING
SCOTT LOBDELL

BREAKDOWNS BY
RICKEN
SCOTT McDANIEL

PENCILS BY
KENNETH ROCAFORT
ALISSON BORGES
WES ST. CLAIRE
FELIPE WATANABE
RICKEN
IAN CHURCHILL
PAOLO PANTALENA
NOEL RODRIGUEZ

INKS BY
KENNETH ROCAFORT
ALISSON BORGES
WAYNE FAUCHER
TREVOR SCOTT
RICKEN
NORM RAPMUND
JOHNNY DESJARDINS
PAOLO PANTALENA

COLOR BY
BLOND
DAN BROWN
MATT YACKEY
TONY AVIÑA

LETTERS BY
JOHN J. HILL
COREY BREEN

COLLECTION COVER ART BY
BENGAL

SUPERBOY CREATED BY
JERRY SIEGEL
BY SPECIAL ARRANGEMENT
WITH THE JERRY SIEGEL FAMILY

MIKE COTTON Editor - Original Series
PAUL KAMINSKI RICKEY PURDIN Associate Editors - Original Series
JEREMY BENT Assistant Editor - Original Series
JEB WOODARD Group Editor - Collected Editions
LIZ ERICKSON Editor - Collected Edition
STEVE COOK Design Director - Books
DAMIAN RYLAND Publication Design

BOB HARRAS Senior VP - Editor-in-Chief, DC Comics

DIANE NELSON President
DAN DIDIO and JIM LEE Co-Publishers
GEOFF JOHNS Chief Creative Officer
AMIT DESAI Senior VP - Marketing & Global Franchise Management
NAIRI GARDINER Senior VP - Finance
SAM ADES VP - Digital Marketing
BOBBIE CHASE VP - Talent Development
MARK CHIARELLO Senior VP - Art, Design & Collected Editions
JOHN CUNNINGHAM VP - Content Strategy
ANNE DEPIES VP - Strategy Planning & Reporting
DON FALLETTI VP - Manufacturing Operations
LAWRENCE GANEM VP - Editorial Administration & Talent Relations
ALISON GILL Senior VP - Manufacturing & Operations
HANK KANALZ Senior VP - Editorial Strategy & Administration
JAY KOGAN VP - Legal Affairs
DEREK MADDALENA Senior VP - Sales & Business Development
JACK MAHAN VP - Business Affairs
DAN MIRON VP - Sales Planning & Trade Development
NICK NAPOLITANO VP - Manufacturing Administration
CAROL ROEDER VP - Marketing
EDDIE SCANNELL VP - Mass Account & Digital Sales
COURTNEY SIMMONS Senior VP - Publicity & Communications
JIM (SKI) SOKOLOWSKI VP - Comic Book Specialty & Newsstand Sales
SANDY YI Senior VP - Global Franchise Management

TEEN TITANS VOLUME 2: ROGUE TARGETS

DC Comics, 2900 West Alameda Ave., Burbank, CA 91505
Printed by RR Donnelley, Salem, VA, USA. 2/5/16. First Printing.
ISBN: 978-1-4012-6162-7

Library of Congress Cataloging-in-Publication Data is Available.

PEFC Certified
Printed on paper from sustainably managed forests and controlled sources
PEFC/29-31-75
www.pefc.org

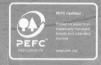

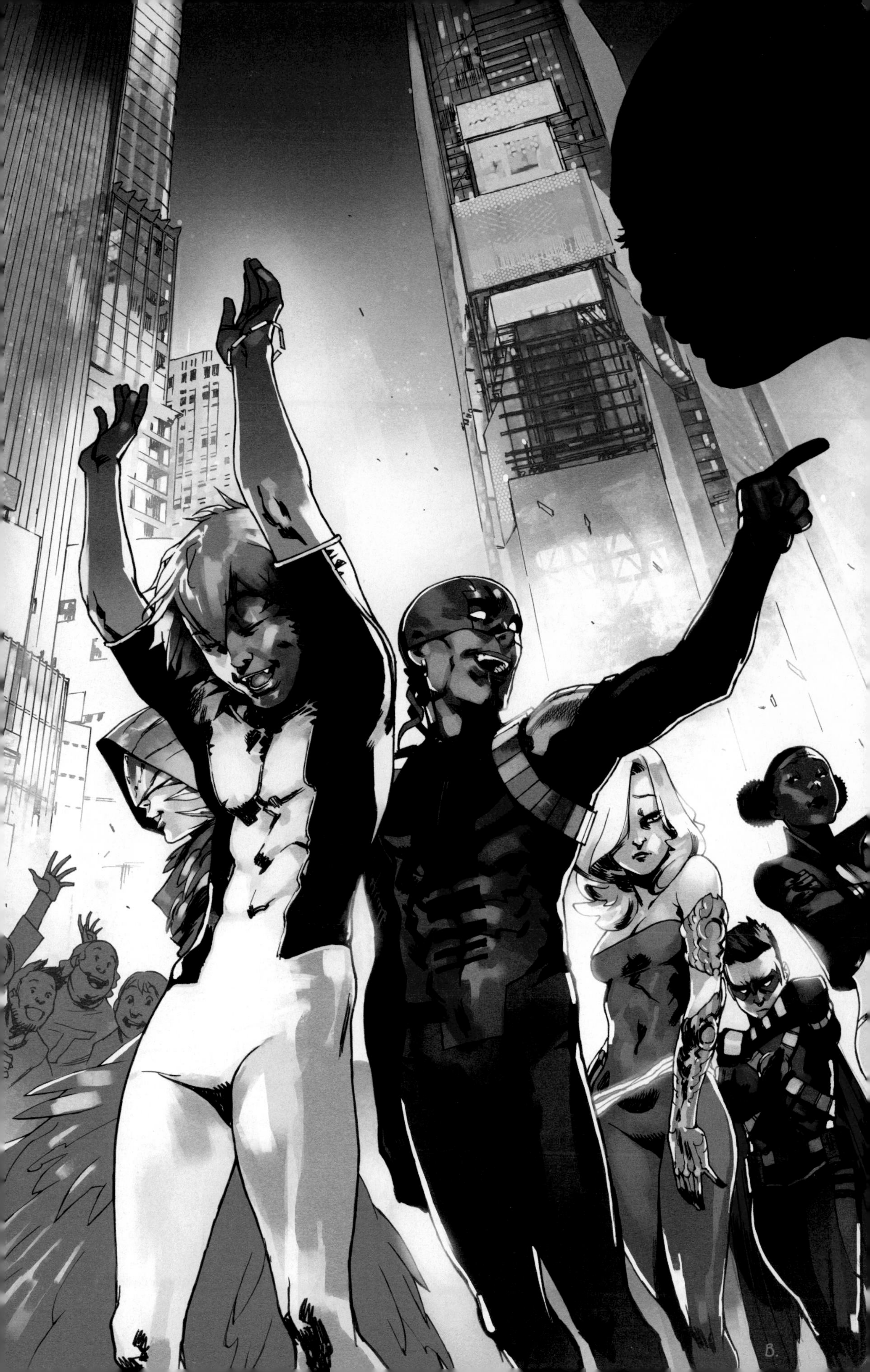

ONE BRIEF, SHINING MOMENT

WILL PFEIFER writer KENNETH ROCAFORT artist BLOND colorist JOHN J. HILL letterer cover art by BENGAL

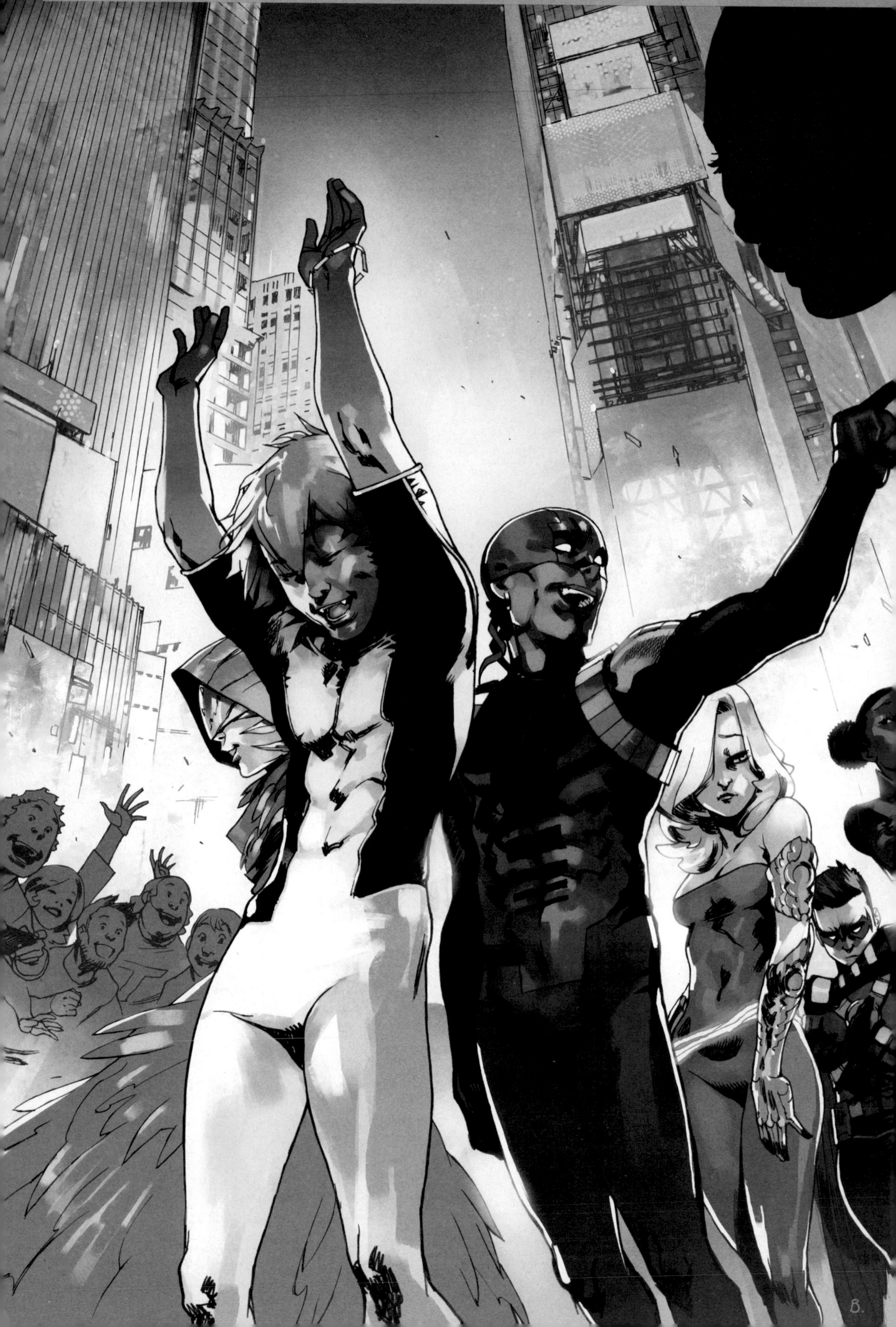

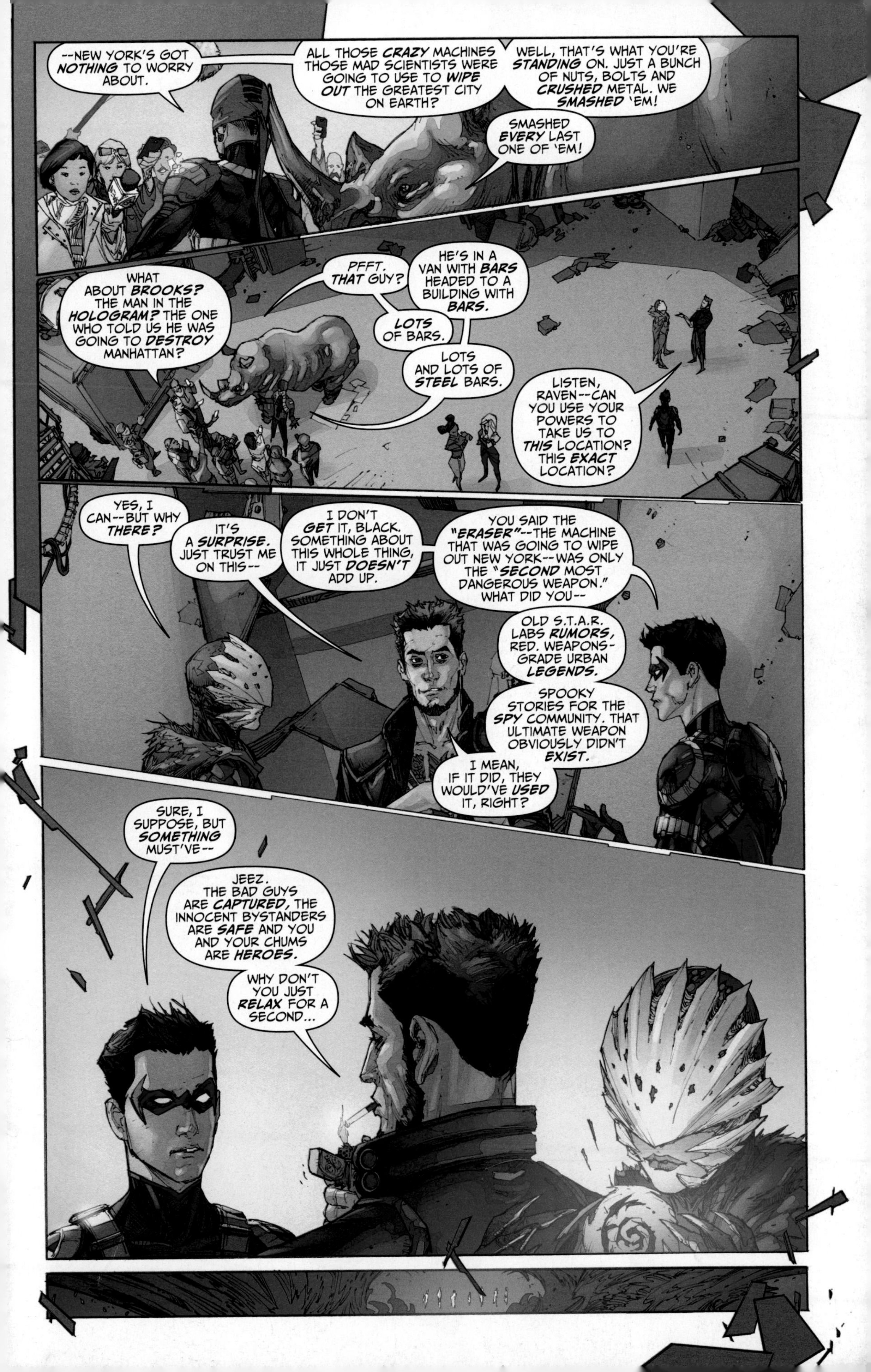
--NEW YORK'S GOT NOTHING TO WORRY ABOUT.
ALL THOSE CRAZY MACHINES THOSE MAD SCIENTISTS WERE GOING TO USE TO WIPE OUT THE GREATEST CITY ON EARTH?
WELL, THAT'S WHAT YOU'RE STANDING ON. JUST A BUNCH OF NUTS, BOLTS AND CRUSHED METAL. WE SMASHED 'EM!
SMASHED EVERY LAST ONE OF 'EM!
WHAT ABOUT BROOKS? THE MAN IN THE HOLOGRAM? THE ONE WHO TOLD US HE WAS GOING TO DESTROY MANHATTAN?
PFFT. THAT GUY?
HE'S IN A VAN WITH BARS HEADED TO A BUILDING WITH BARS.
LOTS OF BARS.
LOTS AND LOTS OF STEEL BARS.
LISTEN, RAVEN--CAN YOU USE YOUR POWERS TO TAKE US TO THIS LOCATION? THIS EXACT LOCATION?
YES, I CAN--BUT WHY THERE?
IT'S A SURPRISE. JUST TRUST ME ON THIS--
I DON'T GET IT, BLACK. SOMETHING ABOUT THIS WHOLE THING, IT JUST DOESN'T ADD UP.
YOU SAID THE "ERASER"--THE MACHINE THAT WAS GOING TO WIPE OUT NEW YORK--WAS ONLY THE "SECOND MOST DANGEROUS WEAPON." WHAT DID YOU--
OLD S.T.A.R. LABS RUMORS, RED. WEAPONS-GRADE URBAN LEGENDS.
SPOOKY STORIES FOR THE SPY COMMUNITY. THAT ULTIMATE WEAPON OBVIOUSLY DIDN'T EXIST.
I MEAN, IF IT DID, THEY WOULD'VE USED IT, RIGHT?
SURE, I SUPPOSE, BUT SOMETHING MUST'VE--
JEEZ. THE BAD GUYS ARE CAPTURED, THE INNOCENT BYSTANDERS ARE SAFE AND YOU AND YOUR CHUMS ARE HEROES.
WHY DON'T YOU JUST RELAX FOR A SECOND...

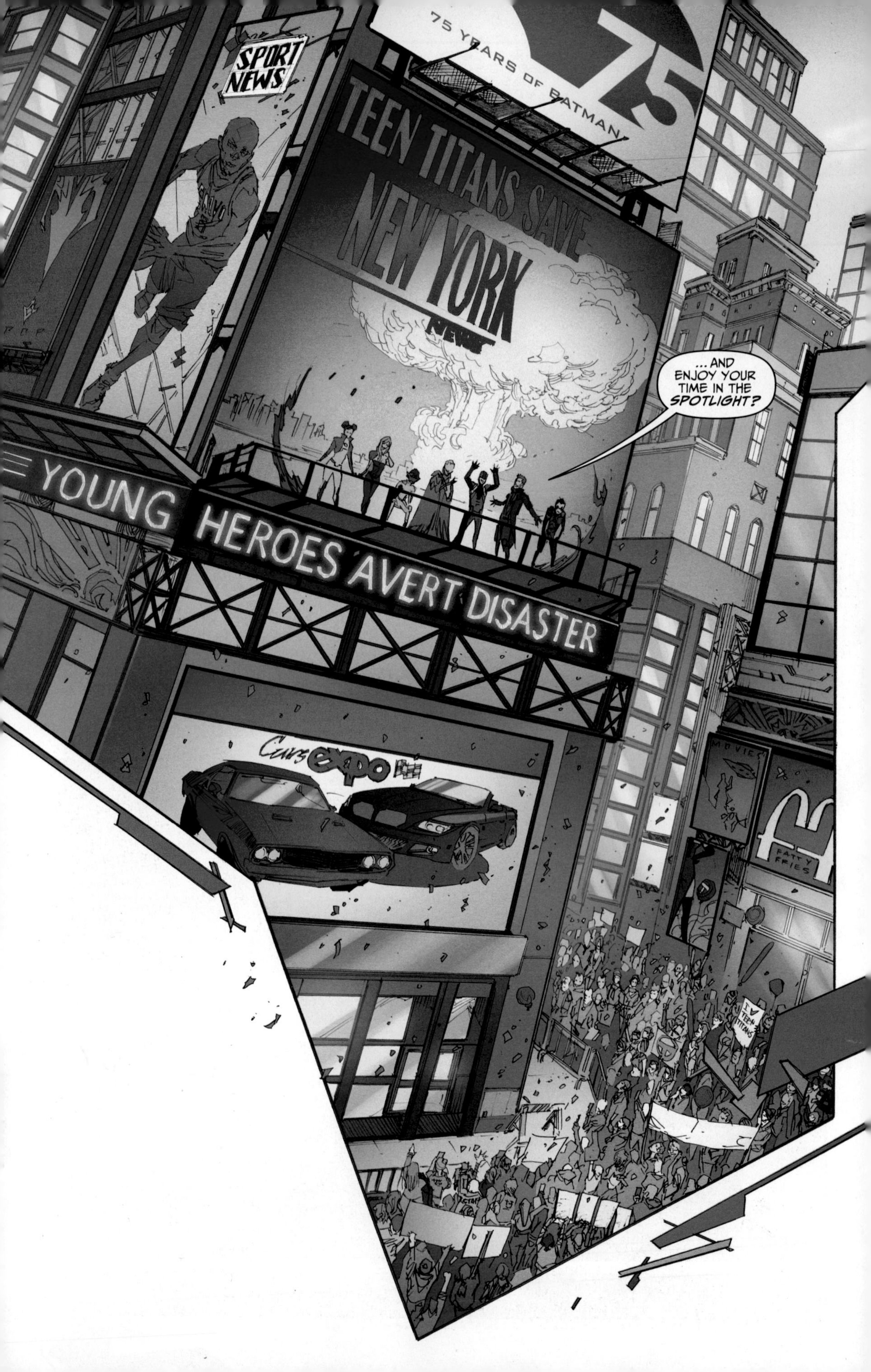
75 YEARS OF BATMAN
75
SPORT NEWS
TEEN TITANS SAVE NEW YORK
YOUNG HEROES AVERT DISASTER
...AND ENJOY YOUR TIME IN THE SPOTLIGHT?
Cars expo
MOVIES
FATTY FRIES

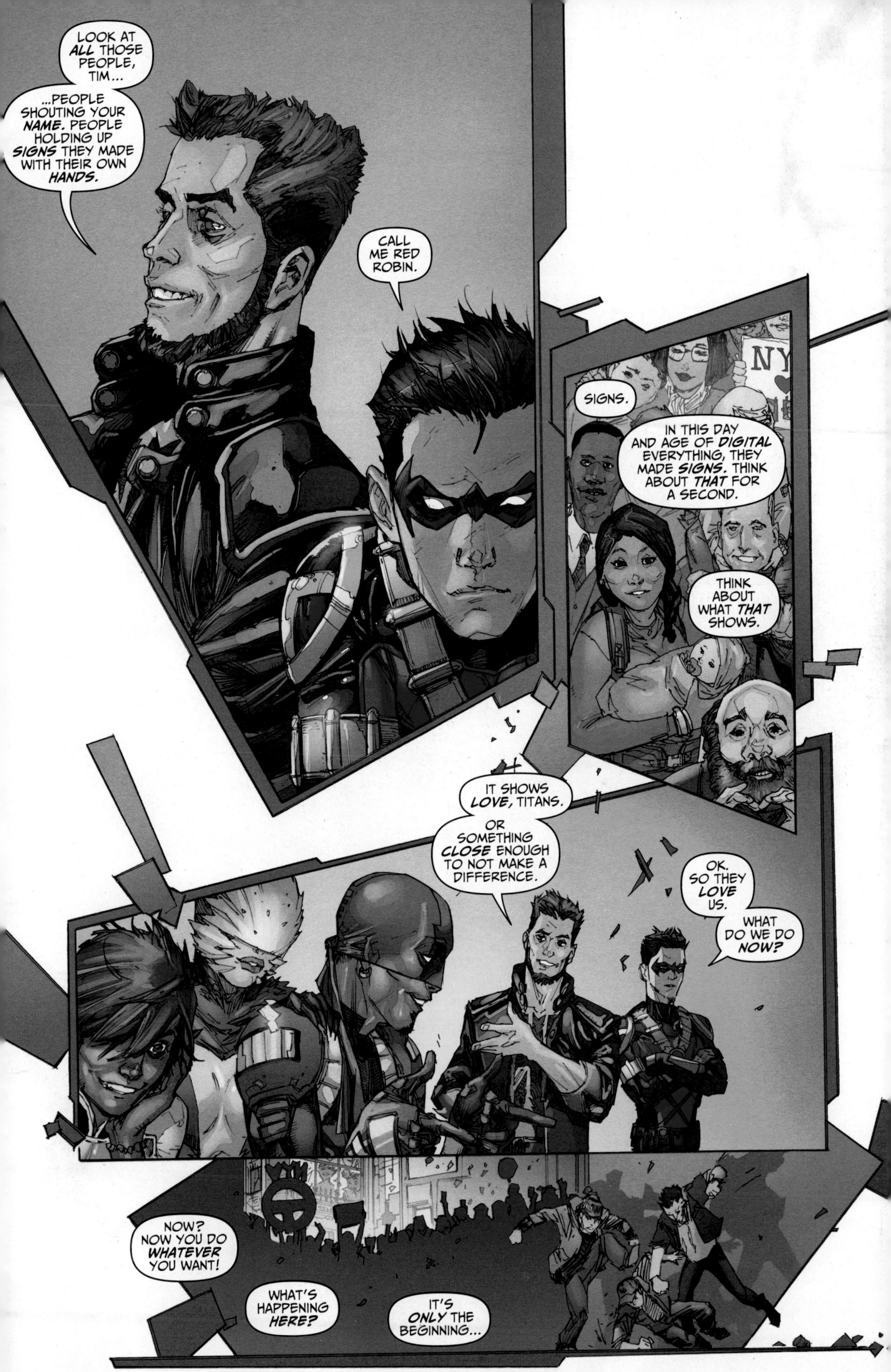

LOOK AT ALL THOSE PEOPLE, TIM...
...PEOPLE SHOUTING YOUR NAME. PEOPLE HOLDING UP SIGNS THEY MADE WITH THEIR OWN HANDS.
CALL ME RED ROBIN.
SIGNS.
IN THIS DAY AND AGE OF DIGITAL EVERYTHING, THEY MADE SIGNS. THINK ABOUT THAT FOR A SECOND.
THINK ABOUT WHAT THAT SHOWS.
NY
IT SHOWS LOVE, TITANS.
OR SOMETHING CLOSE ENOUGH TO NOT MAKE A DIFFERENCE.
OK. SO THEY LOVE US.
WHAT DO WE DO NOW?
NOW? NOW YOU DO WHATEVER YOU WANT!
WHAT'S HAPPENING HERE?
IT'S ONLY THE BEGINNING...

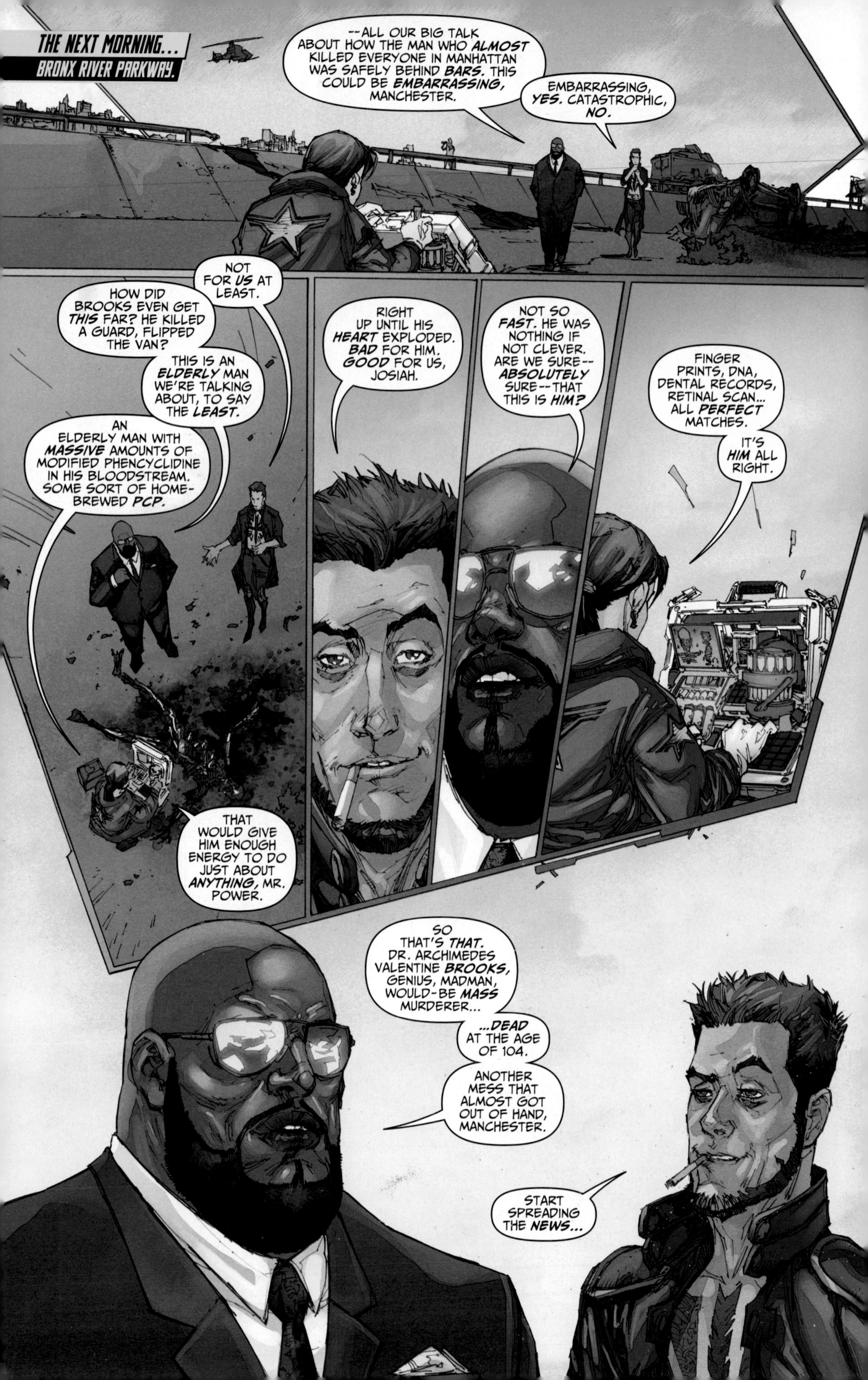
THE NEXT MORNING...
BRONX RIVER PARKWAY.
--ALL OUR BIG TALK ABOUT HOW THE MAN WHO ALMOST KILLED EVERYONE IN MANHATTAN WAS SAFELY BEHIND BARS. THIS COULD BE EMBARRASSING, MANCHESTER.
EMBARRASSING, YES. CATASTROPHIC, NO.
HOW DID BROOKS EVEN GET THIS FAR? HE KILLED A GUARD, FLIPPED THE VAN?
NOT FOR US AT LEAST.
THIS IS AN ELDERLY MAN WE'RE TALKING ABOUT, TO SAY THE LEAST.
AN ELDERLY MAN WITH MASSIVE AMOUNTS OF MODIFIED PHENCYCLIDINE IN HIS BLOODSTREAM. SOME SORT OF HOME-BREWED PCP.
THAT WOULD GIVE HIM ENOUGH ENERGY TO DO JUST ABOUT ANYTHING, MR. POWER.
RIGHT UP UNTIL HIS HEART EXPLODED. BAD FOR HIM. GOOD FOR US, JOSIAH.
NOT SO FAST. HE WAS NOTHING IF NOT CLEVER. ARE WE SURE--ABSOLUTELY SURE--THAT THIS IS HIM?
FINGER PRINTS, DNA, DENTAL RECORDS, RETINAL SCAN... ALL PERFECT MATCHES.
IT'S HIM ALL RIGHT.
SO THAT'S THAT. DR. ARCHIMEDES VALENTINE BROOKS, GENIUS, MADMAN, WOULD-BE MASS MURDERER...
...DEAD AT THE AGE OF 104.
ANOTHER MESS THAT ALMOST GOT OUT OF HAND, MANCHESTER.
START SPREADING THE NEWS...

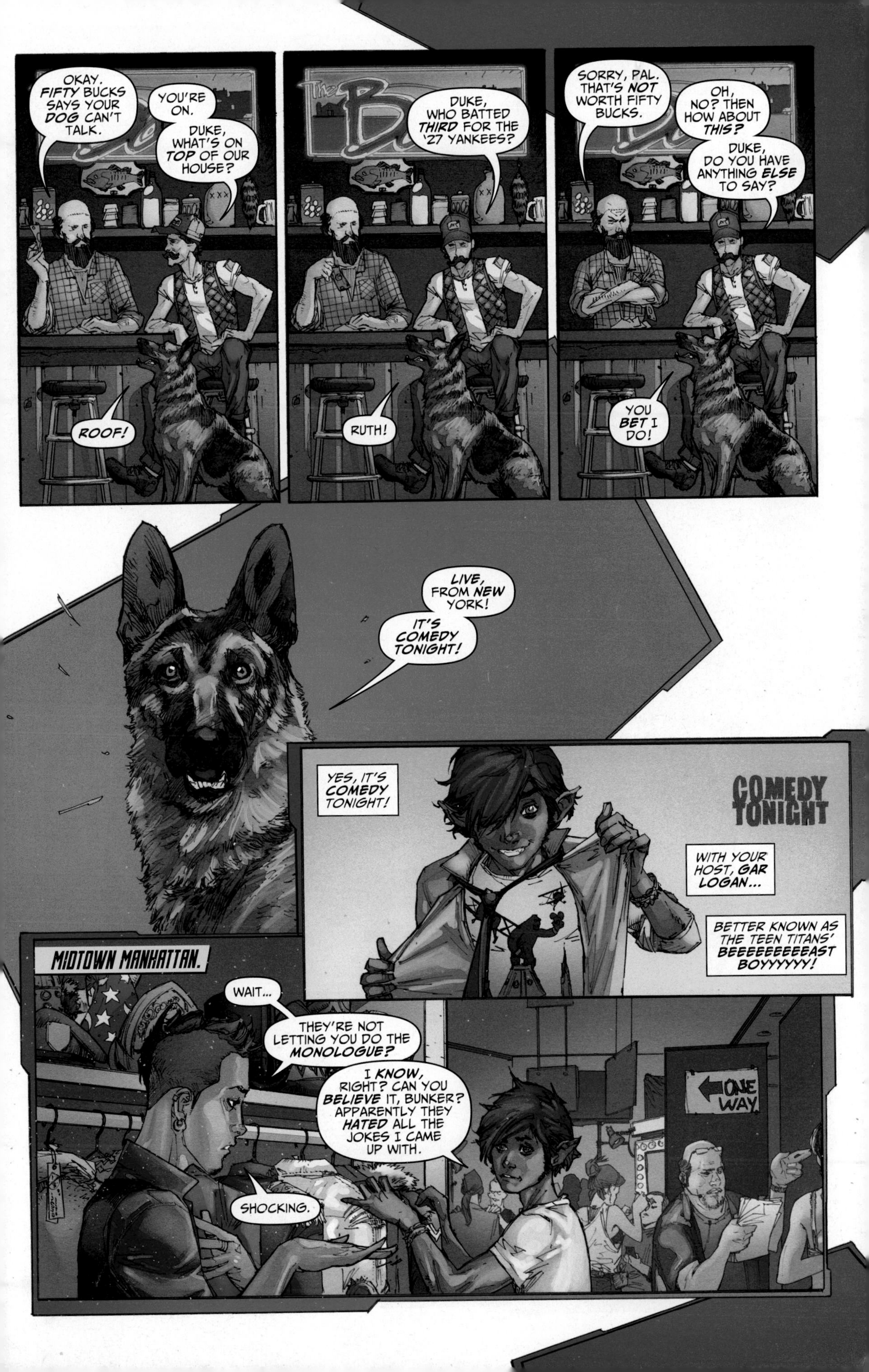
OKAY. FIFTY BUCKS SAYS YOUR DOG CAN'T TALK.
YOU'RE ON.
DUKE, WHAT'S ON TOP OF OUR HOUSE?
ROOF!
DUKE, WHO BATTED THIRD FOR THE '27 YANKEES?
RUTH!
SORRY, PAL. THAT'S NOT WORTH FIFTY BUCKS.
OH, NO? THEN HOW ABOUT THIS?
DUKE, DO YOU HAVE ANYTHING ELSE TO SAY?
YOU BET I DO!
LIVE, FROM NEW YORK!
IT'S COMEDY TONIGHT!
YES, IT'S COMEDY TONIGHT!
COMEDY TONIGHT
WITH YOUR HOST, GAR LOGAN...
BETTER KNOWN AS THE TEEN TITANS' BEEEEEEEEEAST BOYYYYYY!
MIDTOWN MANHATTAN.
WAIT...
THEY'RE NOT LETTING YOU DO THE MONOLOGUE?
I KNOW, RIGHT? CAN YOU BELIEVE IT, BUNKER? APPARENTLY THEY HATED ALL THE JOKES I CAME UP WITH.
SHOCKING.
ONE WAY

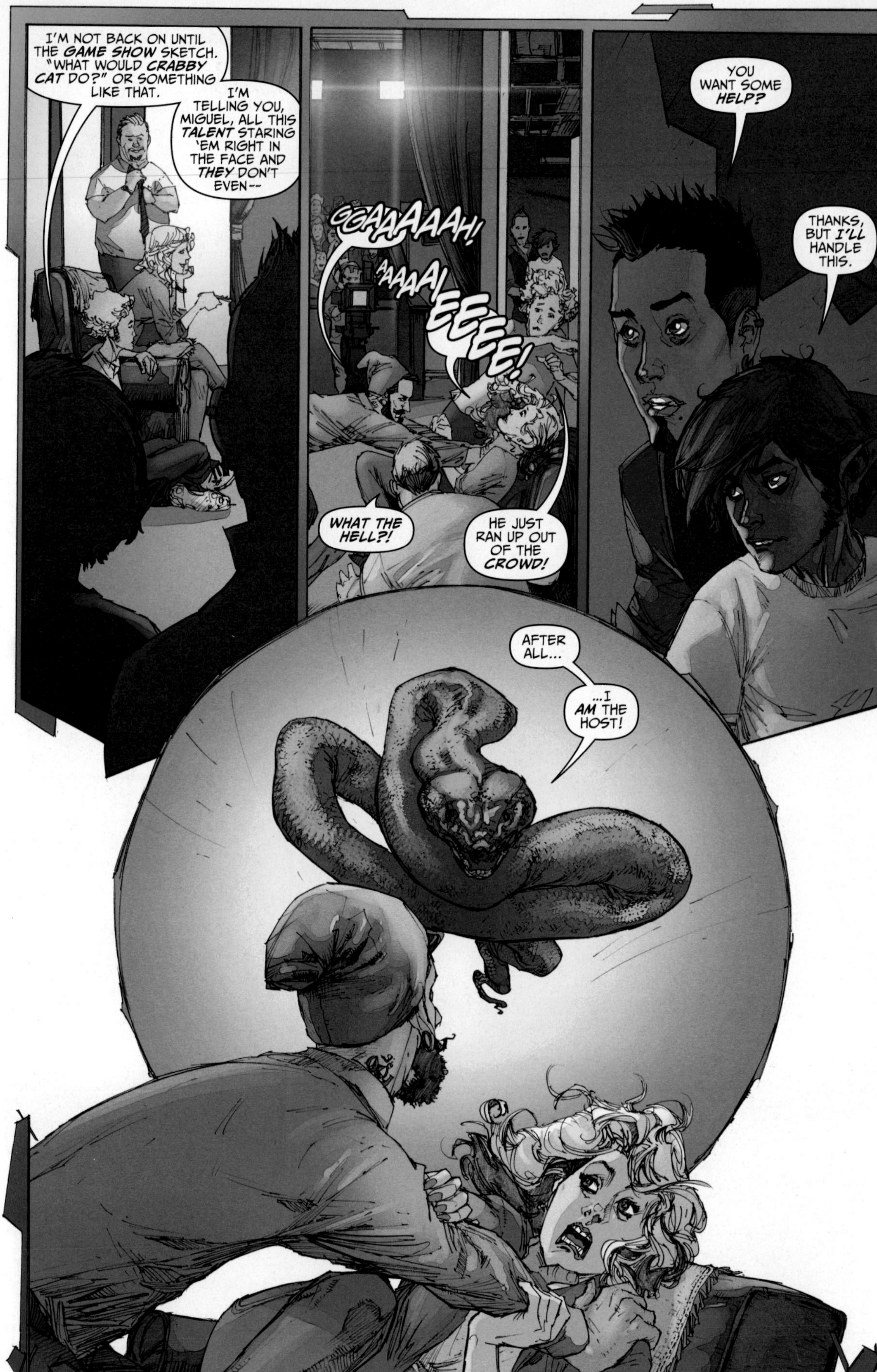

I'M NOT BACK ON UNTIL THE GAME SHOW SKETCH. "WHAT WOULD CRABBY CAT DO?" OR SOMETHING LIKE THAT.
I'M TELLING YOU, MIGUEL, ALL THIS TALENT STARING 'EM RIGHT IN THE FACE AND THEY DON'T EVEN--
GGAAAAAAH!
AAAAAIEEEEE!
WHAT THE HELL?!
HE JUST RAN UP OUT OF THE CROWD!
YOU WANT SOME HELP?
THANKS, BUT I'LL HANDLE THIS.
AFTER ALL...
...I AM THE HOST!

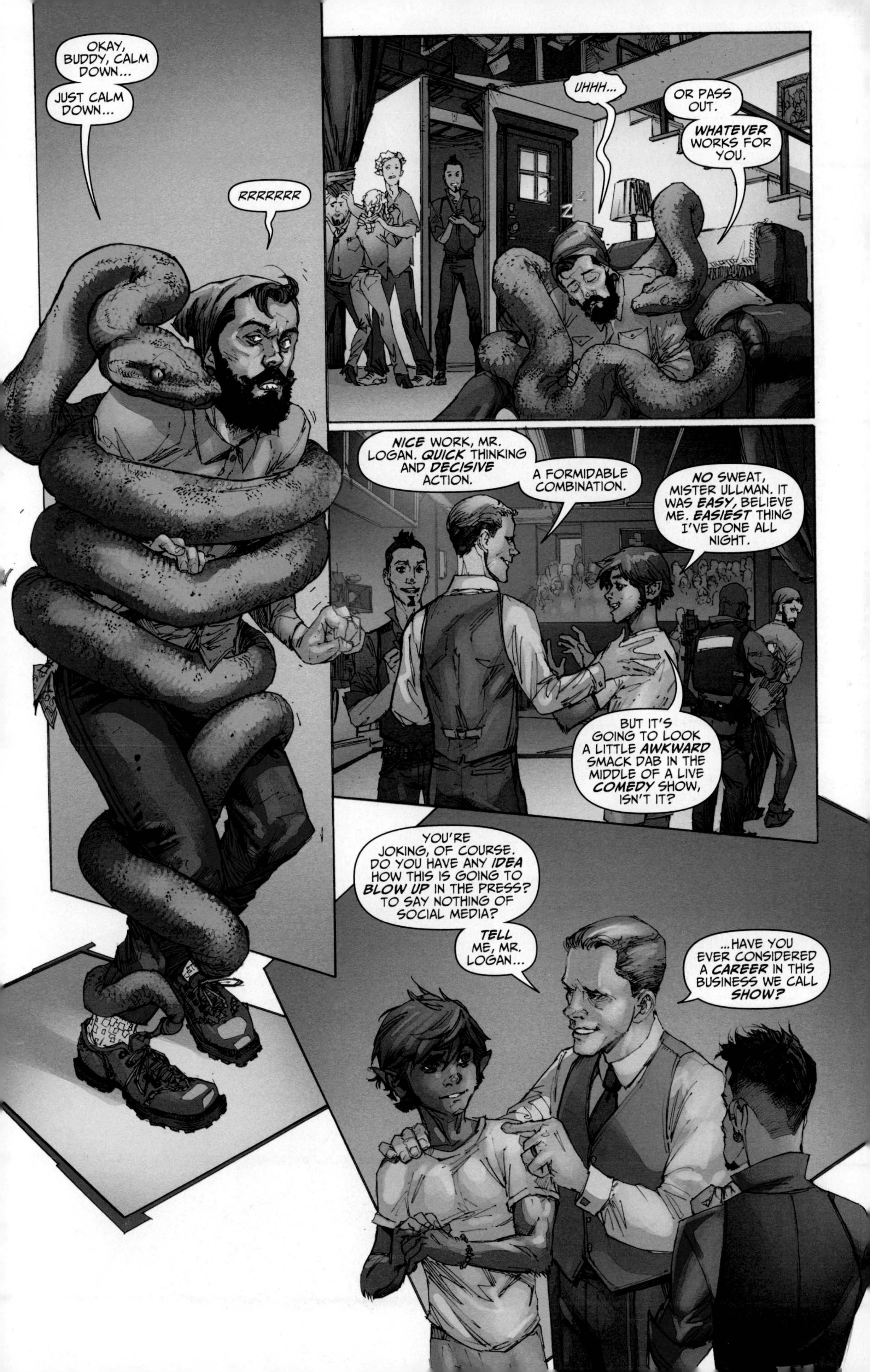
OKAY, BUDDY, CALM DOWN...
JUST CALM DOWN...
RRRRRRR
UHHH...
OR PASS OUT.
WHATEVER WORKS FOR YOU.
NICE WORK, MR. LOGAN. QUICK THINKING AND DECISIVE ACTION.
A FORMIDABLE COMBINATION.
NO SWEAT, MISTER ULLMAN. IT WAS EASY, BELIEVE ME. EASIEST THING I'VE DONE ALL NIGHT.
BUT IT'S GOING TO LOOK A LITTLE AWKWARD SMACK DAB IN THE MIDDLE OF A LIVE COMEDY SHOW, ISN'T IT?
YOU'RE JOKING, OF COURSE. DO YOU HAVE ANY IDEA HOW THIS IS GOING TO BLOW UP IN THE PRESS? TO SAY NOTHING OF SOCIAL MEDIA?
TELL ME, MR. LOGAN...
...HAVE YOU EVER CONSIDERED A CAREER IN THIS BUSINESS WE CALL SHOW?

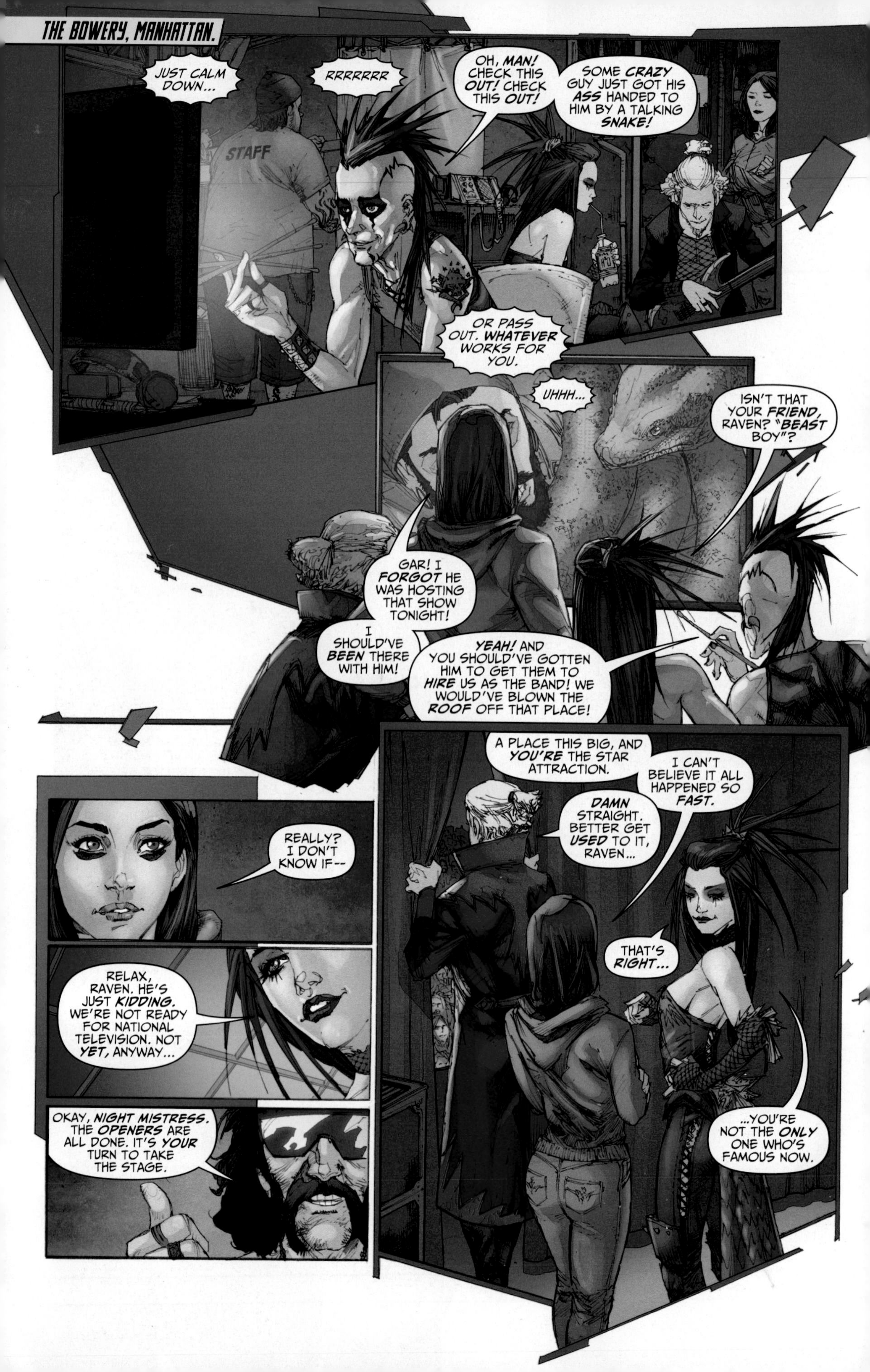
THE BOWERY, MANHATTAN.
JUST CALM DOWN...
RRRRRRR
OH, MAN! CHECK THIS OUT! CHECK THIS OUT!
SOME CRAZY GUY JUST GOT HIS ASS HANDED TO HIM BY A TALKING SNAKE!
OR PASS OUT. WHATEVER WORKS FOR YOU.
UHHH...
ISN'T THAT YOUR FRIEND, RAVEN? "BEAST BOY"?
GAR! I FORGOT HE WAS HOSTING THAT SHOW TONIGHT!
I SHOULD'VE BEEN THERE WITH HIM!
YEAH! AND YOU SHOULD'VE GOTTEN HIM TO GET THEM TO HIRE US AS THE BAND! WE WOULD'VE BLOWN THE ROOF OFF THAT PLACE!
REALLY? I DON'T KNOW IF--
RELAX, RAVEN. HE'S JUST KIDDING. WE'RE NOT READY FOR NATIONAL TELEVISION. NOT YET, ANYWAY...
OKAY, NIGHT MISTRESS. THE OPENERS ARE ALL DONE. IT'S YOUR TURN TO TAKE THE STAGE.
A PLACE THIS BIG, AND YOU'RE THE STAR ATTRACTION.
I CAN'T BELIEVE IT ALL HAPPENED SO FAST.
DAMN STRAIGHT. BETTER GET USED TO IT, RAVEN...
THAT'S RIGHT...
...YOU'RE NOT THE ONLY ONE WHO'S FAMOUS NOW.

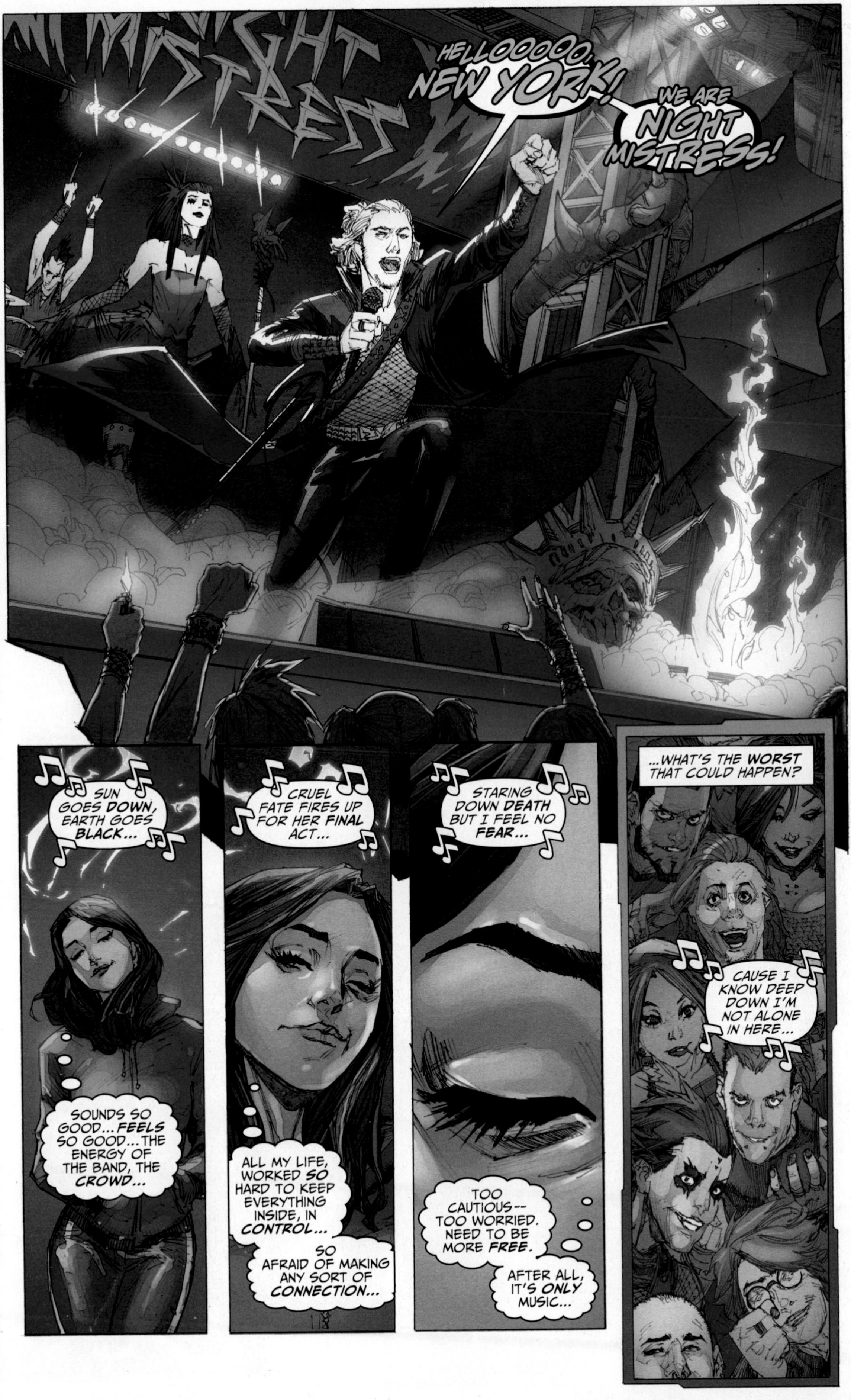
NIGHT MISTRESS
HELLOOOOO, NEW YORK!
WE ARE NIGHT MISTRESS!
SUN GOES DOWN, EARTH GOES BLACK...
SOUNDS SO GOOD...FEELS SO GOOD...THE ENERGY OF THE BAND, THE CROWD...
CRUEL FATE FIRES UP FOR HER FINAL ACT...
ALL MY LIFE, WORKED SO HARD TO KEEP EVERYTHING INSIDE, IN CONTROL...
SO AFRAID OF MAKING ANY SORT OF CONNECTION...
STARING DOWN DEATH BUT I FEEL NO FEAR...
TOO CAUTIOUS-- TOO WORRIED. NEED TO BE MORE FREE.
AFTER ALL, IT'S ONLY MUSIC...
...WHAT'S THE WORST THAT COULD HAPPEN?
CAUSE I KNOW DEEP DOWN I'M NOT ALONE IN HERE...

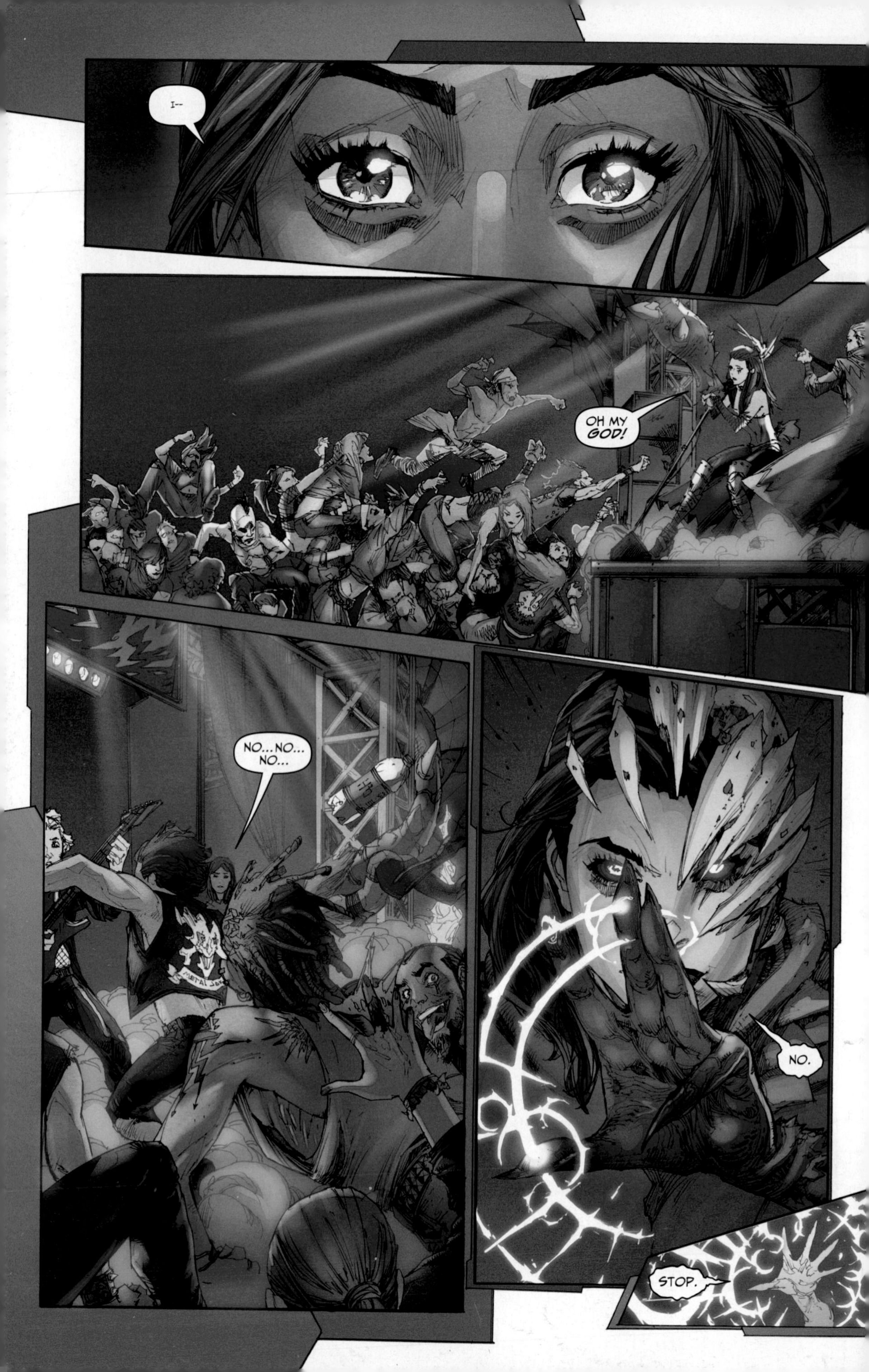
I--
OH MY GOD!
NO...NO... NO...
NO.
STOP.

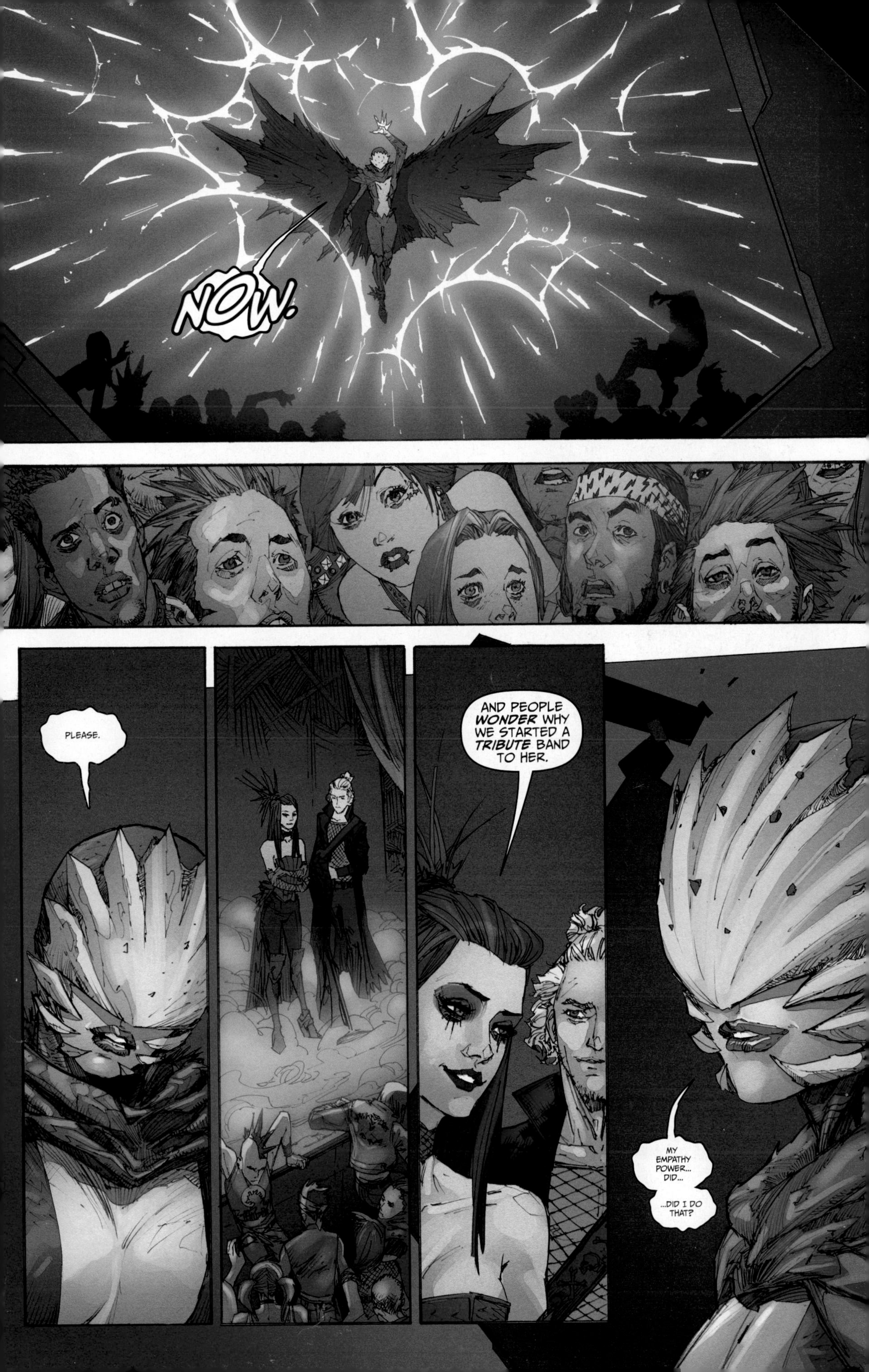
NOW.
PLEASE.
AND PEOPLE WONDER WHY WE STARTED A TRIBUTE BAND TO HER.
MY EMPATHY POWER... DID...
...DID I DO THAT?

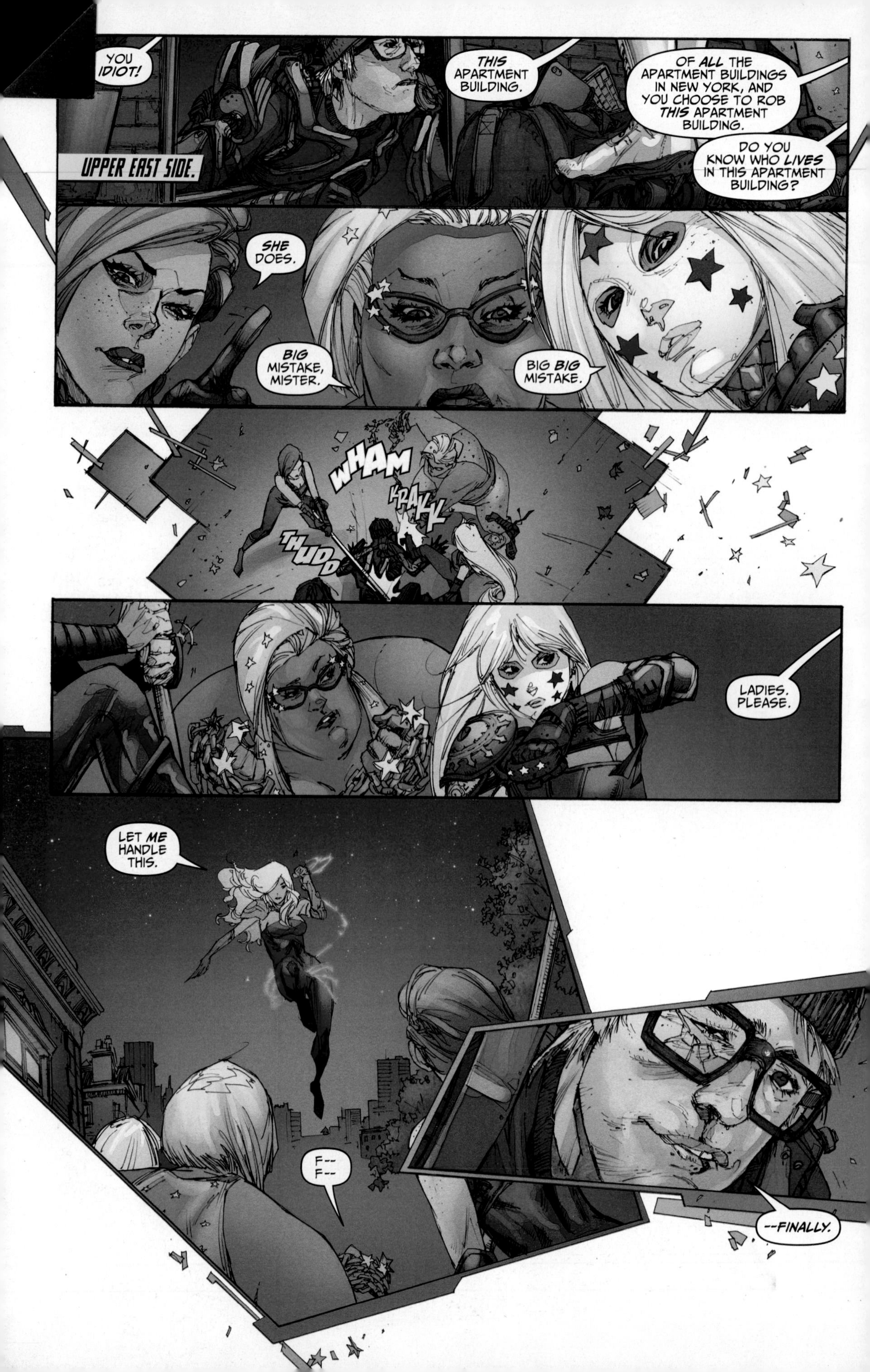

YOU IDIOT!
UPPER EAST SIDE.
THIS APARTMENT BUILDING.
OF ALL THE APARTMENT BUILDINGS IN NEW YORK, AND YOU CHOOSE TO ROB THIS APARTMENT BUILDING.
DO YOU KNOW WHO LIVES IN THIS APARTMENT BUILDING?
SHE DOES.
BIG MISTAKE, MISTER.
BIG BIG MISTAKE.
WHAM
KRAKK
THUDD
LADIES. PLEASE.
LET ME HANDLE THIS.
F-- F--
--FINALLY.

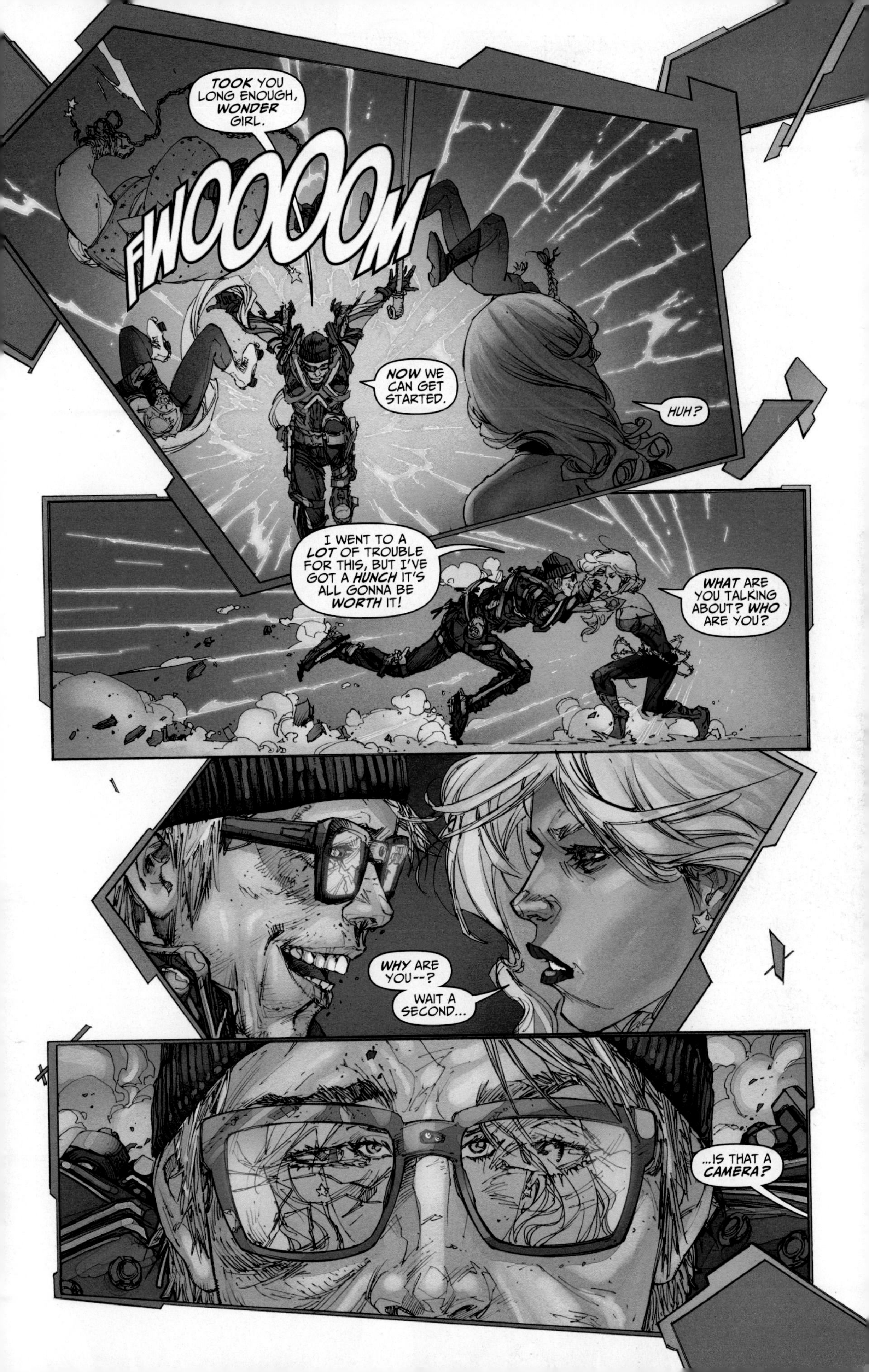

TOOK YOU LONG ENOUGH, WONDER GIRL.
FWOOOOM
NOW WE CAN GET STARTED.
HUH?
I WENT TO A LOT OF TROUBLE FOR THIS, BUT I'VE GOT A HUNCH IT'S ALL GONNA BE WORTH IT!
WHAT ARE YOU TALKING ABOUT? WHO ARE YOU?
WHY ARE YOU--?
WAIT A SECOND...
...IS THAT A CAMERA?

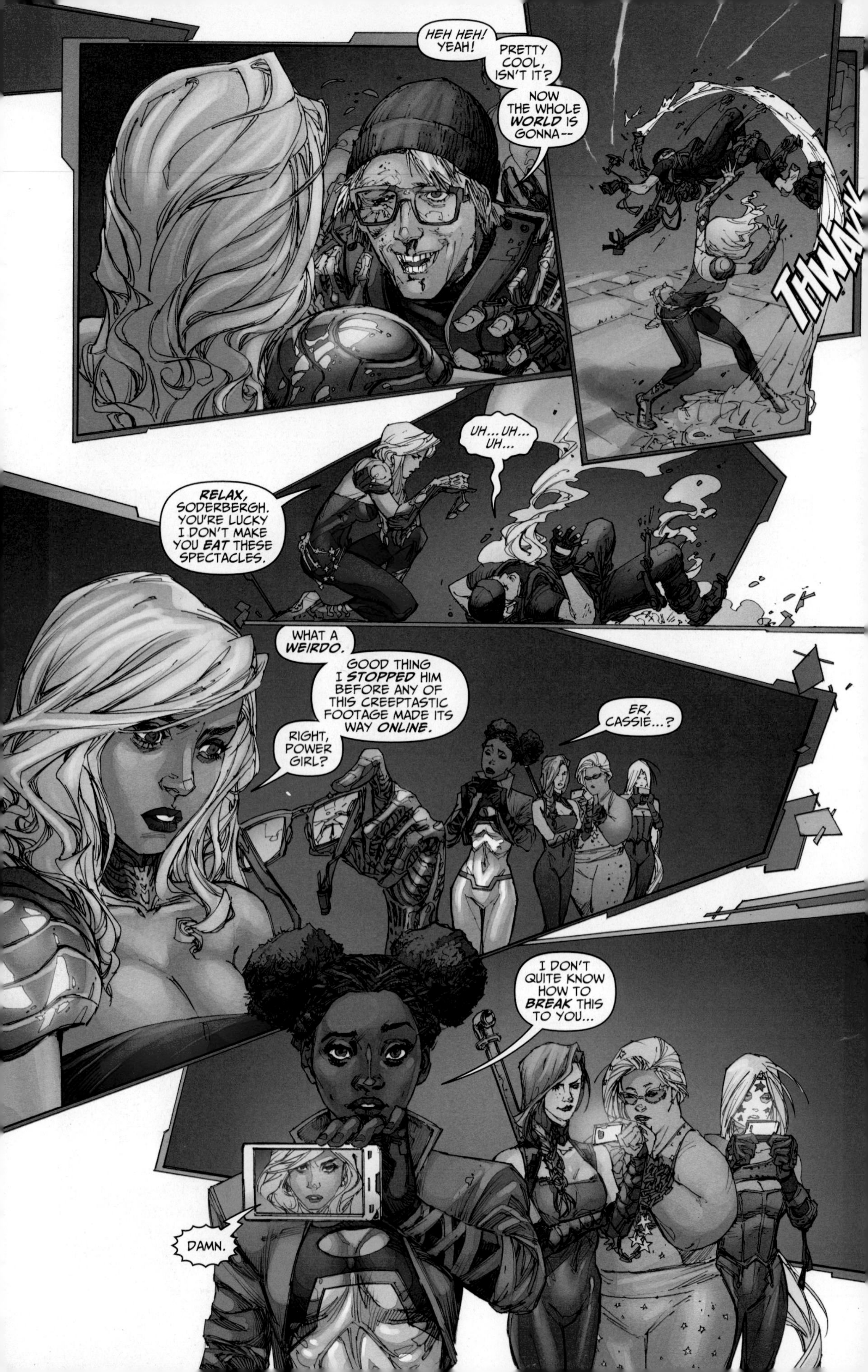
HEH HEH! YEAH!
PRETTY COOL, ISN'T IT?
NOW THE WHOLE WORLD IS GONNA--
THWAK
UH... UH... UH...
RELAX, SODERBERGH. YOU'RE LUCKY I DON'T MAKE YOU EAT THESE SPECTACLES.
WHAT A WEIRDO.
GOOD THING I STOPPED HIM BEFORE ANY OF THIS CREEPTASTIC FOOTAGE MADE ITS WAY ONLINE.
RIGHT, POWER GIRL?
ER, CASSIE...?
I DON'T QUITE KNOW HOW TO BREAK THIS TO YOU...
DAMN.

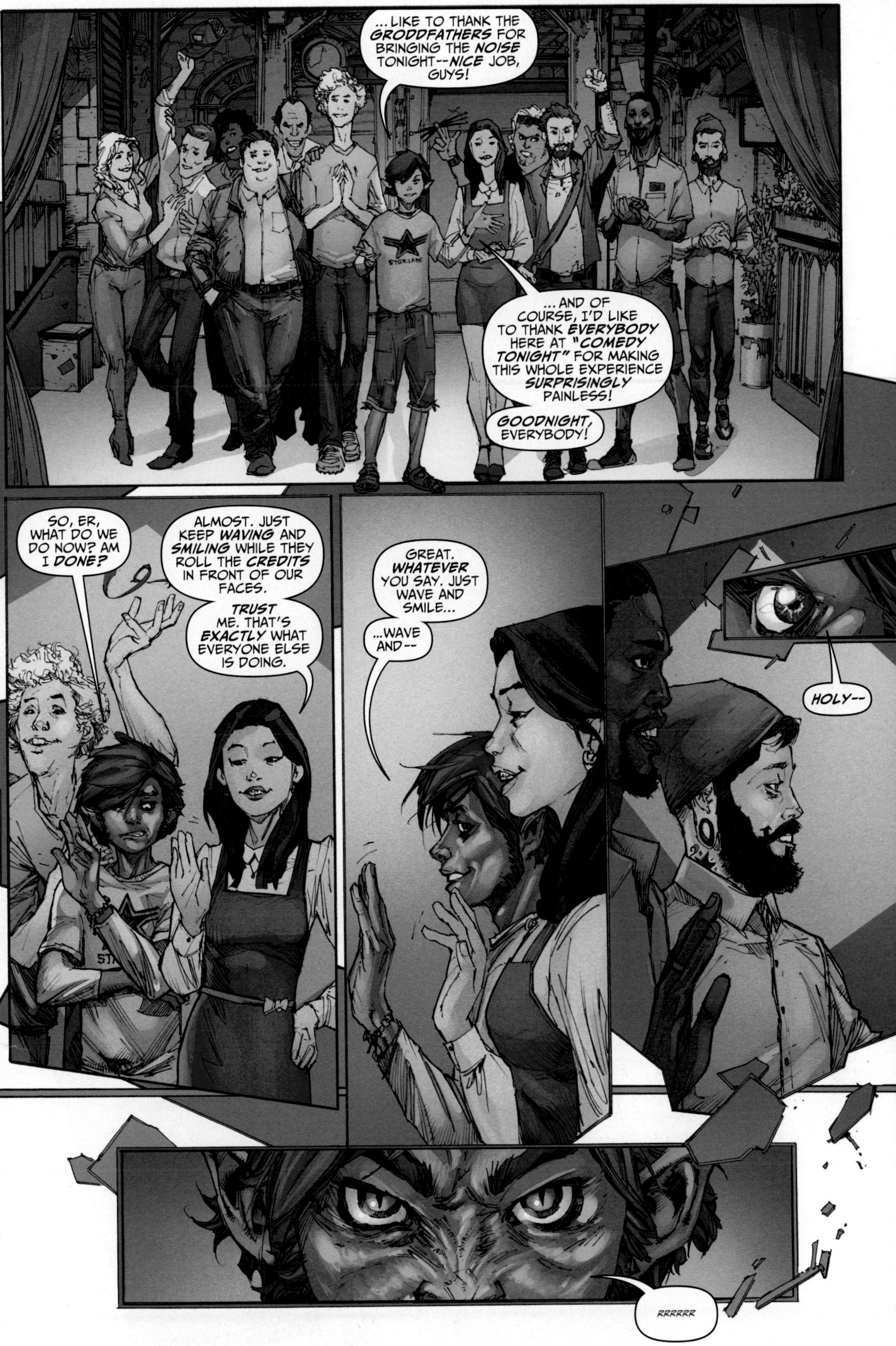
...LIKE TO THANK THE GRODDFATHERS FOR BRINGING THE NOISE TONIGHT--NICE JOB, GUYS!
...AND OF COURSE, I'D LIKE TO THANK EVERYBODY HERE AT "COMEDY TONIGHT" FOR MAKING THIS WHOLE EXPERIENCE SURPRISINGLY PAINLESS!
GOODNIGHT, EVERYBODY!
SO, ER, WHAT DO WE DO NOW? AM I DONE?
ALMOST. JUST KEEP WAVING AND SMILING WHILE THEY ROLL THE CREDITS IN FRONT OF OUR FACES.
TRUST ME. THAT'S EXACTLY WHAT EVERYONE ELSE IS DOING.
GREAT. WHATEVER YOU SAY. JUST WAVE AND SMILE...
...WAVE AND--
HOLY--
RRRRRR

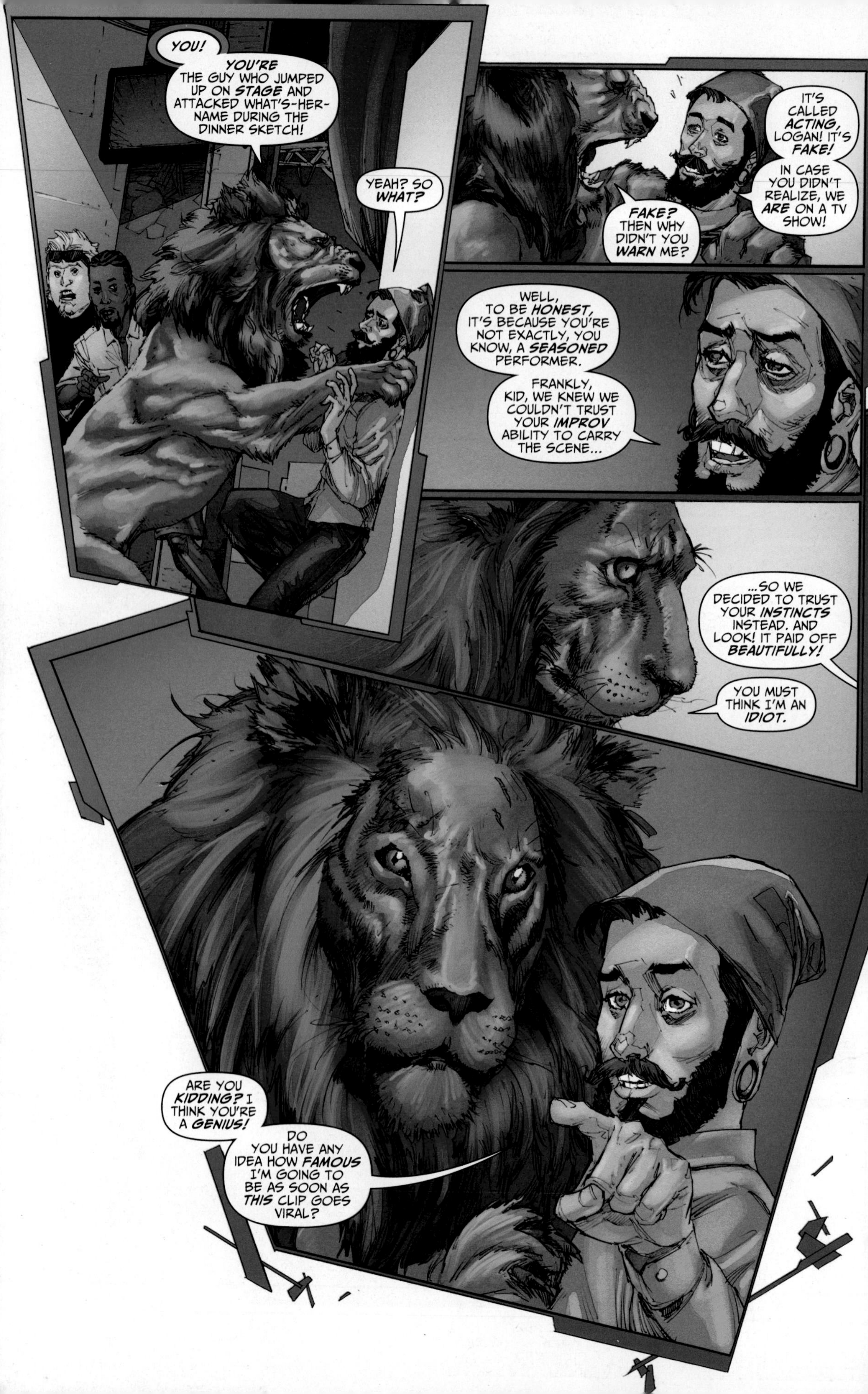
YOU!
YOU'RE THE GUY WHO JUMPED UP ON STAGE AND ATTACKED WHAT'S-HER-NAME DURING THE DINNER SKETCH!
YEAH? SO WHAT?
IT'S CALLED ACTING, LOGAN! IT'S FAKE!
IN CASE YOU DIDN'T REALIZE, WE ARE ON A TV SHOW!
FAKE? THEN WHY DIDN'T YOU WARN ME?
WELL, TO BE HONEST, IT'S BECAUSE YOU'RE NOT EXACTLY, YOU KNOW, A SEASONED PERFORMER.
FRANKLY, KID, WE KNEW WE COULDN'T TRUST YOUR IMPROV ABILITY TO CARRY THE SCENE...
...SO WE DECIDED TO TRUST YOUR INSTINCTS INSTEAD. AND LOOK! IT PAID OFF BEAUTIFULLY!
YOU MUST THINK I'M AN IDIOT.
ARE YOU KIDDING? I THINK YOU'RE A GENIUS!
DO YOU HAVE ANY IDEA HOW FAMOUS I'M GOING TO BE AS SOON AS THIS CLIP GOES VIRAL?

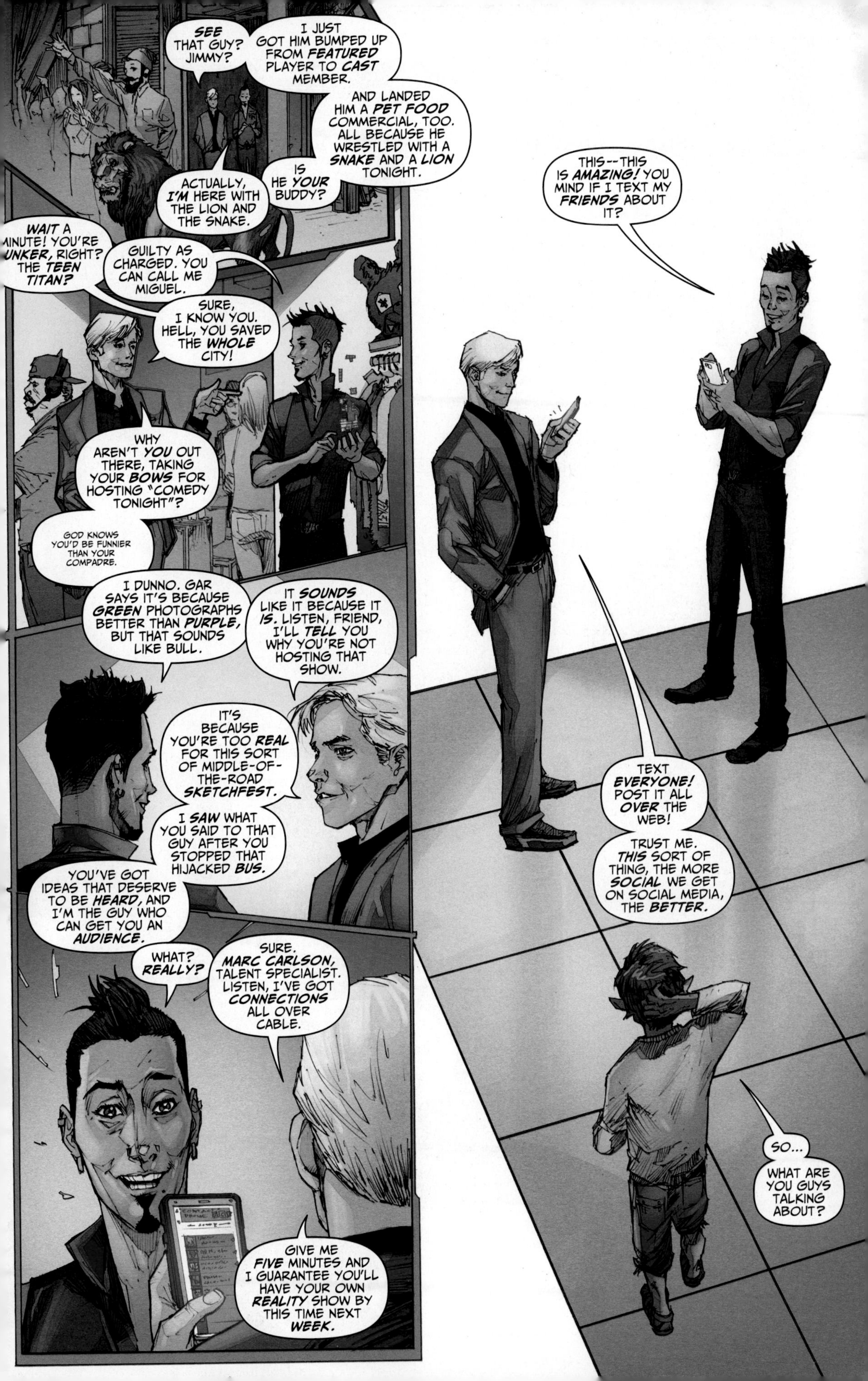
SEE THAT GUY? JIMMY?
I JUST GOT HIM BUMPED UP FROM FEATURED PLAYER TO CAST MEMBER.
AND LANDED HIM A PET FOOD COMMERCIAL, TOO. ALL BECAUSE HE WRESTLED WITH A SNAKE AND A LION TONIGHT.
IS HE YOUR BUDDY?
ACTUALLY, I'M HERE WITH THE LION AND THE SNAKE.
WAIT A MINUTE! YOU'RE UNKER, RIGHT? THE TEEN TITAN?
GUILTY AS CHARGED. YOU CAN CALL ME MIGUEL.
SURE, I KNOW YOU. HELL, YOU SAVED THE WHOLE CITY!
WHY AREN'T YOU OUT THERE, TAKING YOUR BOWS FOR HOSTING "COMEDY TONIGHT"?
GOD KNOWS YOU'D BE FUNNIER THAN YOUR COMPADRE.
I DUNNO. GAR SAYS IT'S BECAUSE GREEN PHOTOGRAPHS BETTER THAN PURPLE, BUT THAT SOUNDS LIKE BULL.
IT SOUNDS LIKE IT BECAUSE IT IS. LISTEN, FRIEND, I'LL TELL YOU WHY YOU'RE NOT HOSTING THAT SHOW.
IT'S BECAUSE YOU'RE TOO REAL FOR THIS SORT OF MIDDLE-OF-THE-ROAD SKETCHFEST.
I SAW WHAT YOU SAID TO THAT GUY AFTER YOU STOPPED THAT HIJACKED BUS.
YOU'VE GOT IDEAS THAT DESERVE TO BE HEARD, AND I'M THE GUY WHO CAN GET YOU AN AUDIENCE.
WHAT? REALLY?
SURE. MARC CARLSON, TALENT SPECIALIST. LISTEN, I'VE GOT CONNECTIONS ALL OVER CABLE.
GIVE ME FIVE MINUTES AND I GUARANTEE YOU'LL HAVE YOUR OWN REALITY SHOW BY THIS TIME NEXT WEEK.
THIS--THIS IS AMAZING! YOU MIND IF I TEXT MY FRIENDS ABOUT IT?
TEXT EVERYONE! POST IT ALL OVER THE WEB!
TRUST ME. THIS SORT OF THING, THE MORE SOCIAL WE GET ON SOCIAL MEDIA, THE BETTER.
SO...
WHAT ARE YOU GUYS TALKING ABOUT?

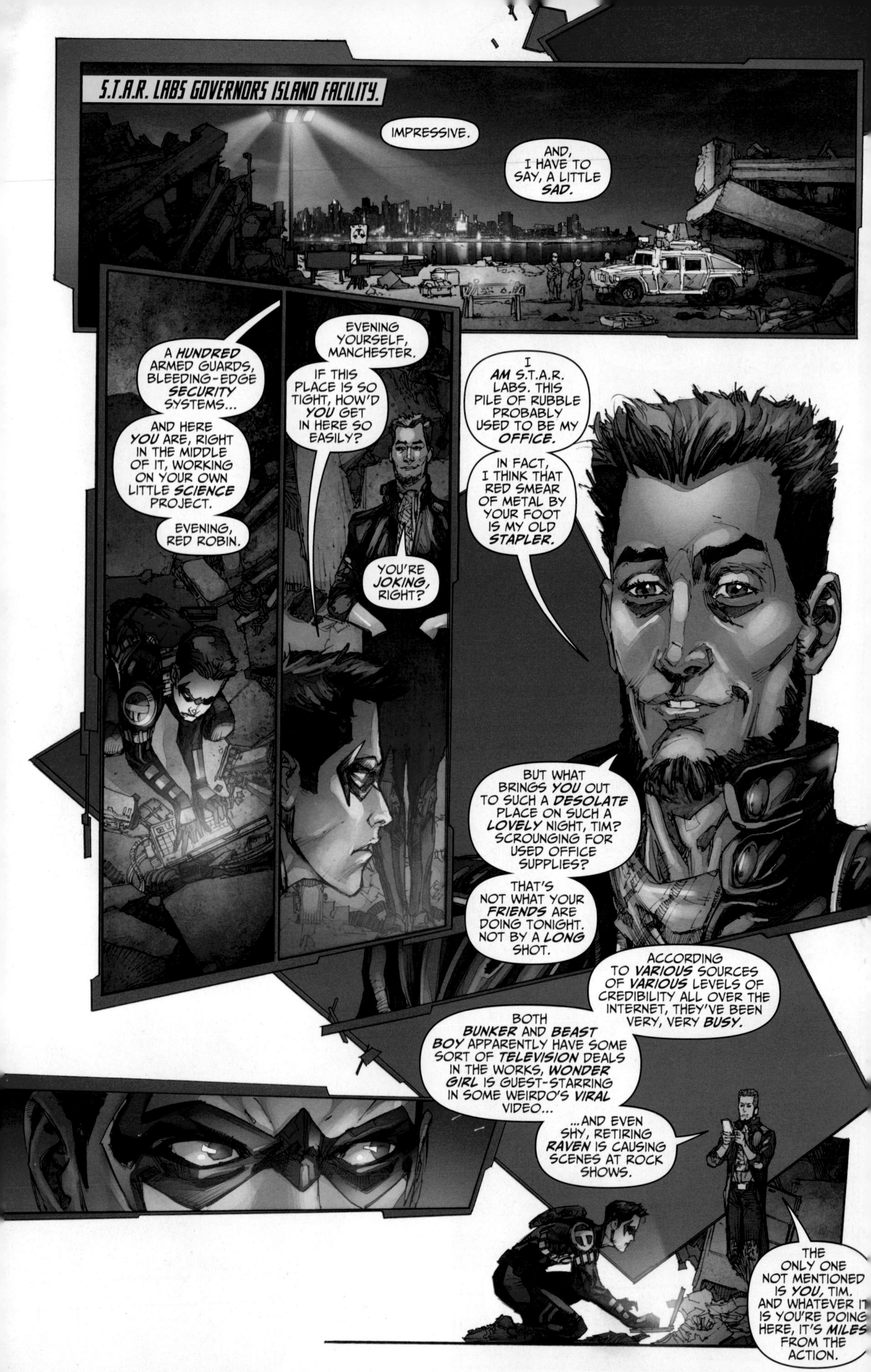
S.T.A.R. LABS GOVERNORS ISLAND FACILITY.
IMPRESSIVE.
AND, I HAVE TO SAY, A LITTLE SAD.
A HUNDRED ARMED GUARDS, BLEEDING-EDGE SECURITY SYSTEMS...
AND HERE YOU ARE, RIGHT IN THE MIDDLE OF IT, WORKING ON YOUR OWN LITTLE SCIENCE PROJECT.
EVENING, RED ROBIN.
EVENING YOURSELF, MANCHESTER.
IF THIS PLACE IS SO TIGHT, HOW'D YOU GET IN HERE SO EASILY?
I AM S.T.A.R. LABS. THIS PILE OF RUBBLE PROBABLY USED TO BE MY OFFICE.
IN FACT, I THINK THAT RED SMEAR OF METAL BY YOUR FOOT IS MY OLD STAPLER.
YOU'RE JOKING, RIGHT?
BUT WHAT BRINGS YOU OUT TO SUCH A DESOLATE PLACE ON SUCH A LOVELY NIGHT, TIM? SCROUNGING FOR USED OFFICE SUPPLIES?
THAT'S NOT WHAT YOUR FRIENDS ARE DOING TONIGHT. NOT BY A LONG SHOT.
ACCORDING TO VARIOUS SOURCES OF VARIOUS LEVELS OF CREDIBILITY ALL OVER THE INTERNET, THEY'VE BEEN VERY, VERY BUSY.
BOTH BUNKER AND BEAST BOY APPARENTLY HAVE SOME SORT OF TELEVISION DEALS IN THE WORKS, WONDER GIRL IS GUEST-STARRING IN SOME WEIRDO'S VIRAL VIDEO...
...AND EVEN SHY, RETIRING RAVEN IS CAUSING SCENES AT ROCK SHOWS.
THE ONLY ONE NOT MENTIONED IS YOU, TIM. AND WHATEVER IT IS YOU'RE DOING HERE, IT'S MILES FROM THE ACTION.

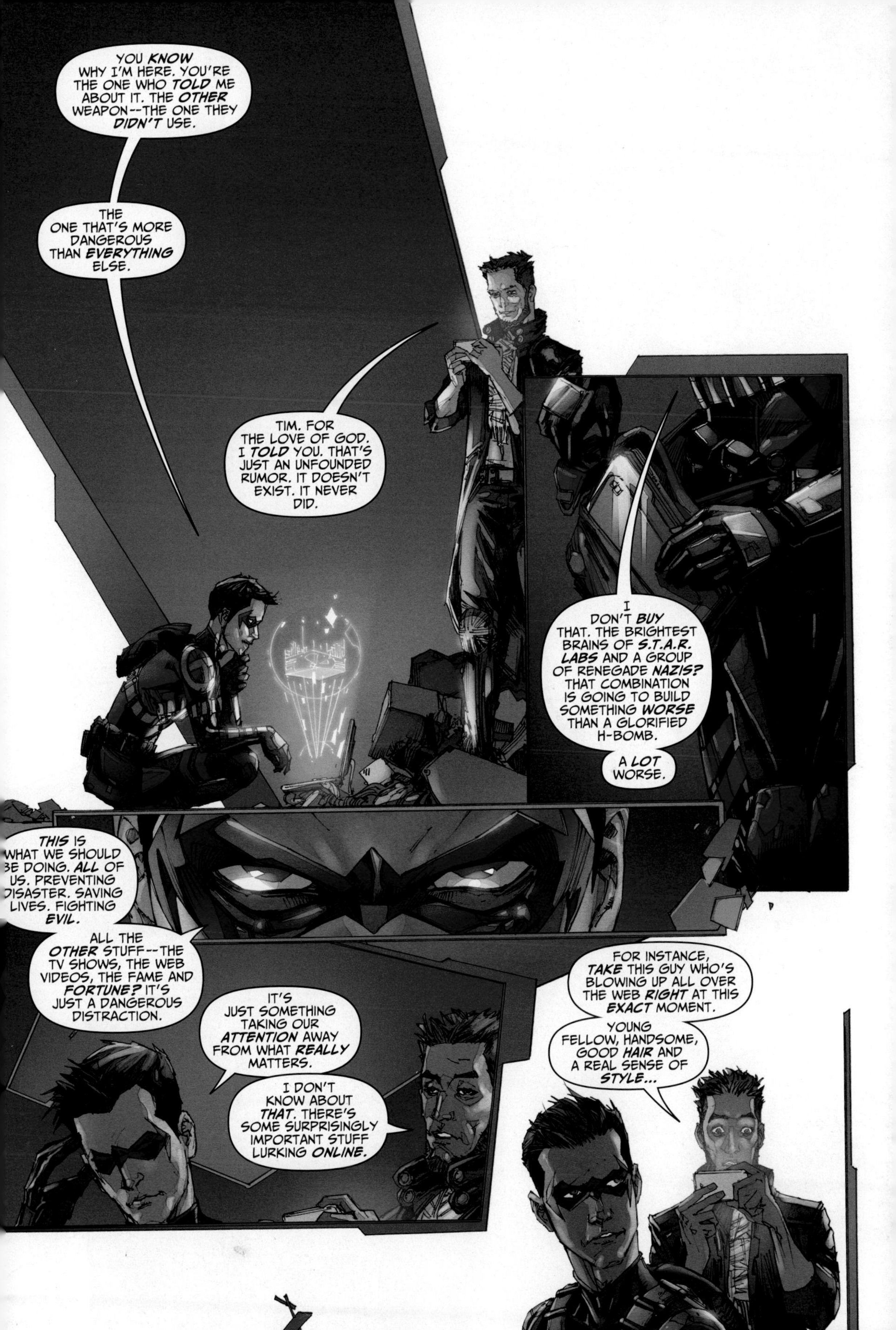
YOU KNOW WHY I'M HERE. YOU'RE THE ONE WHO TOLD ME ABOUT IT. THE OTHER WEAPON--THE ONE THEY DIDN'T USE.
THE ONE THAT'S MORE DANGEROUS THAN EVERYTHING ELSE.
TIM. FOR THE LOVE OF GOD. I TOLD YOU. THAT'S JUST AN UNFOUNDED RUMOR. IT DOESN'T EXIST. IT NEVER DID.
I DON'T BUY THAT. THE BRIGHTEST BRAINS OF S.T.A.R. LABS AND A GROUP OF RENEGADE NAZIS? THAT COMBINATION IS GOING TO BUILD SOMETHING WORSE THAN A GLORIFIED H-BOMB.
A LOT WORSE.
THIS IS WHAT WE SHOULD BE DOING. ALL OF US. PREVENTING DISASTER. SAVING LIVES. FIGHTING EVIL.
ALL THE OTHER STUFF--THE TV SHOWS, THE WEB VIDEOS, THE FAME AND FORTUNE? IT'S JUST A DANGEROUS DISTRACTION.
IT'S JUST SOMETHING TAKING OUR ATTENTION AWAY FROM WHAT REALLY MATTERS.
I DON'T KNOW ABOUT THAT. THERE'S SOME SURPRISINGLY IMPORTANT STUFF LURKING ONLINE.
FOR INSTANCE, TAKE THIS GUY WHO'S BLOWING UP ALL OVER THE WEB RIGHT AT THIS EXACT MOMENT.
YOUNG FELLOW, HANDSOME, GOOD HAIR AND A REAL SENSE OF STYLE...

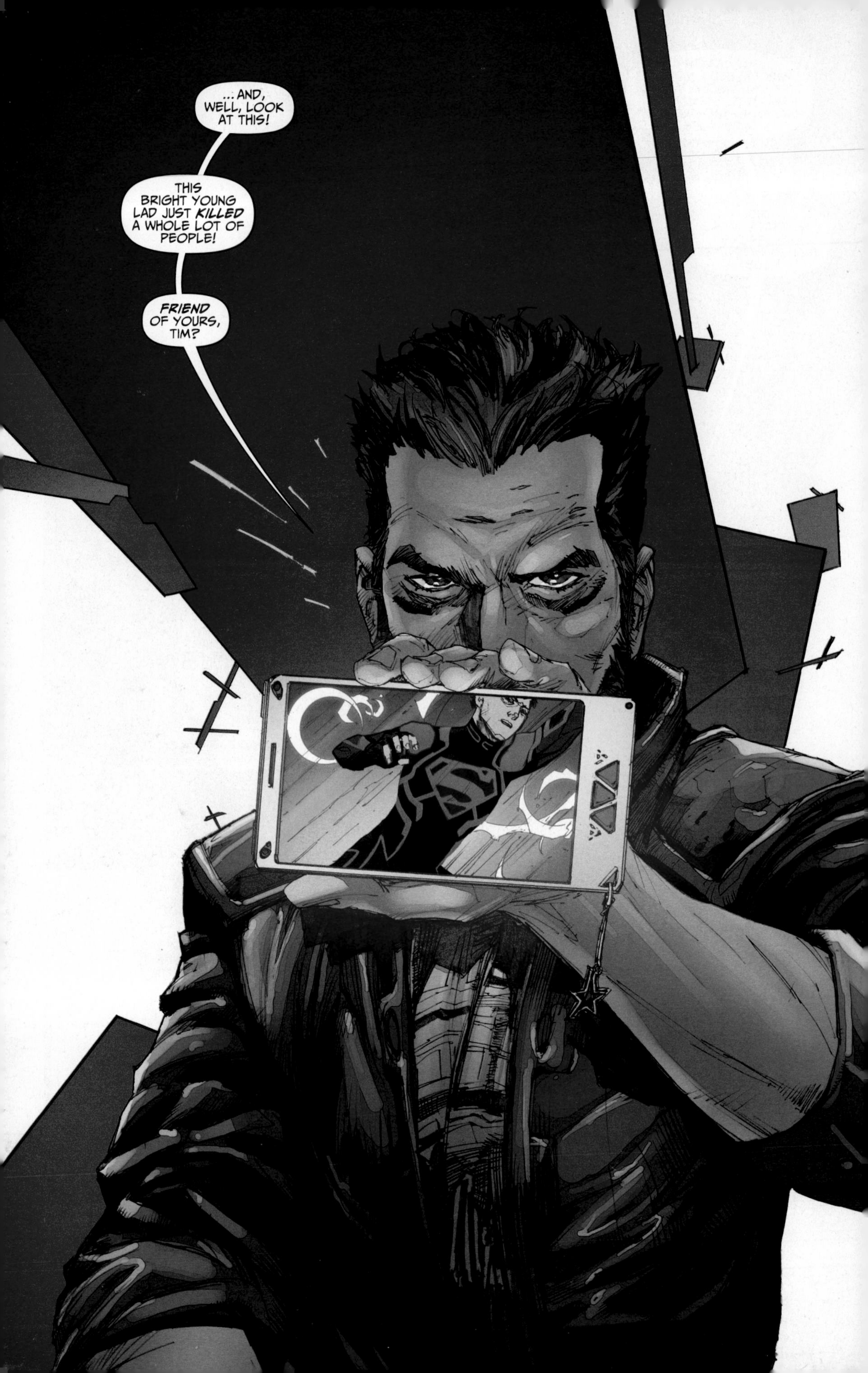
...AND, WELL, LOOK AT THIS!
THIS BRIGHT YOUNG LAD JUST KILLED A WHOLE LOT OF PEOPLE!
FRIEND OF YOURS, TIM?

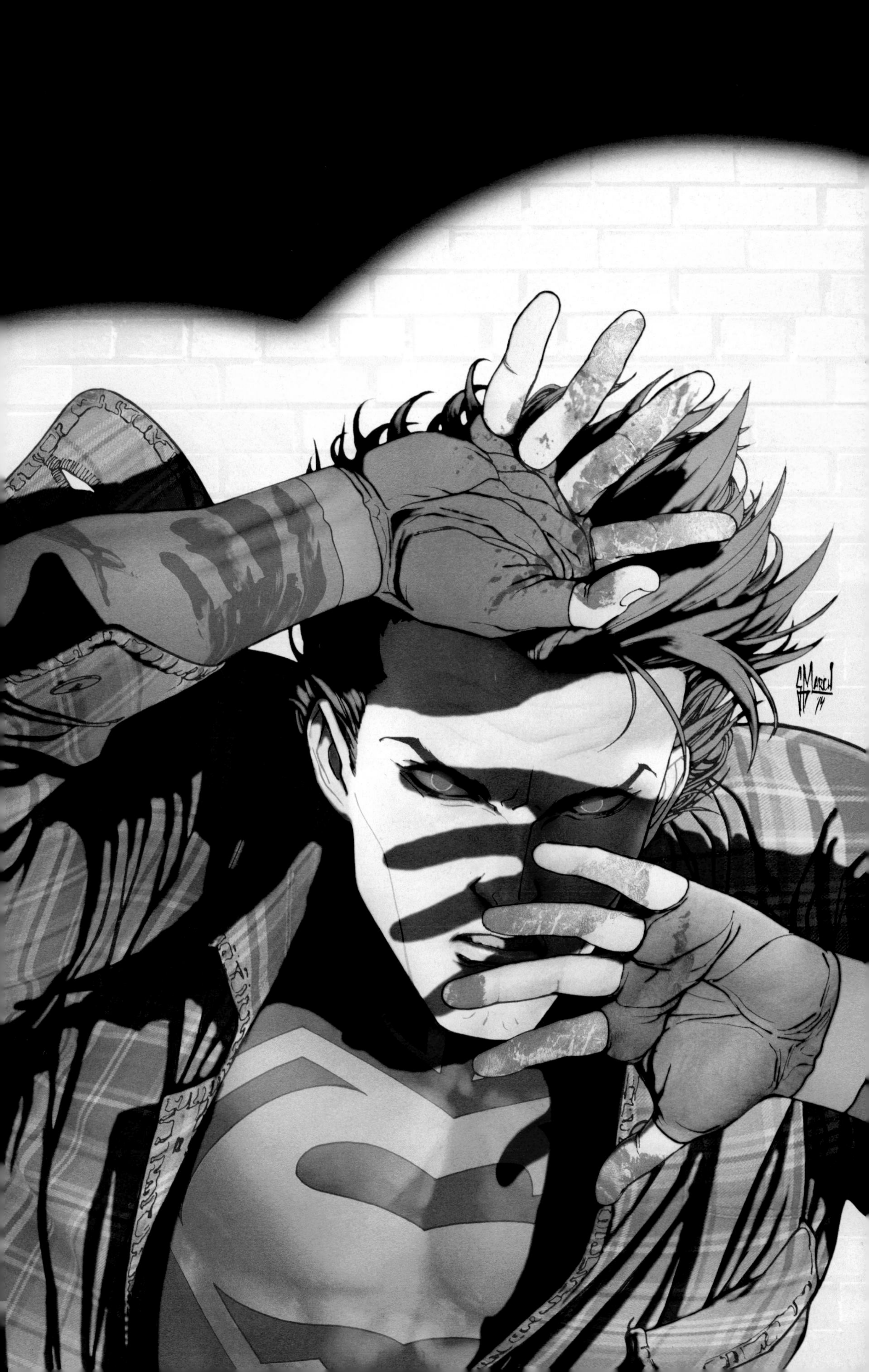

THE SOURCE OF MERCY

TOM KING WILL PFEIFER writers ALISSON BORGES WES ST. CLAIRE pencillers ALISSON BORGES WAYNE FAUCHER inkers MATT YACKEY colorist JOHN J. HILL letterer cover art by GUILLEM MARCH

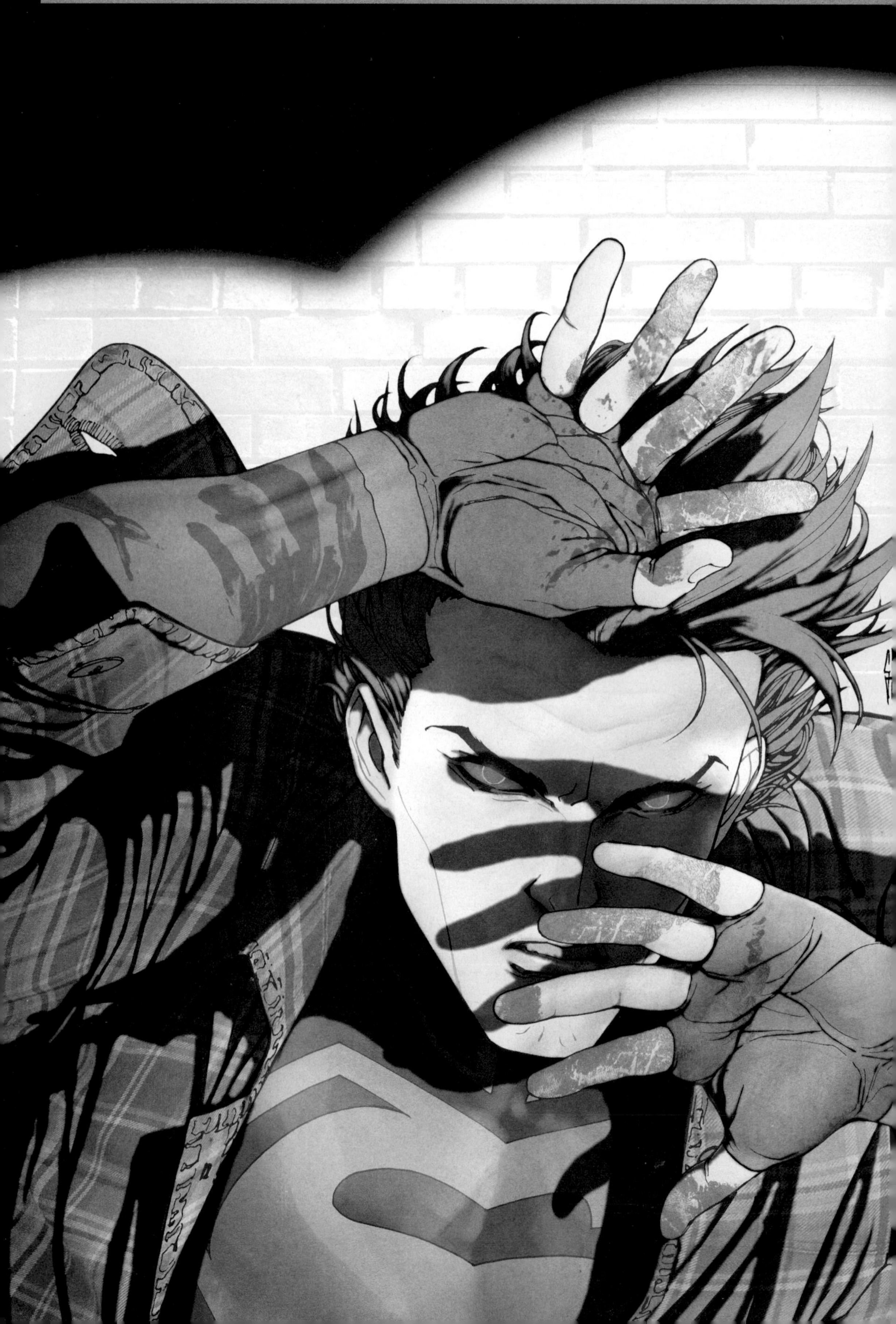

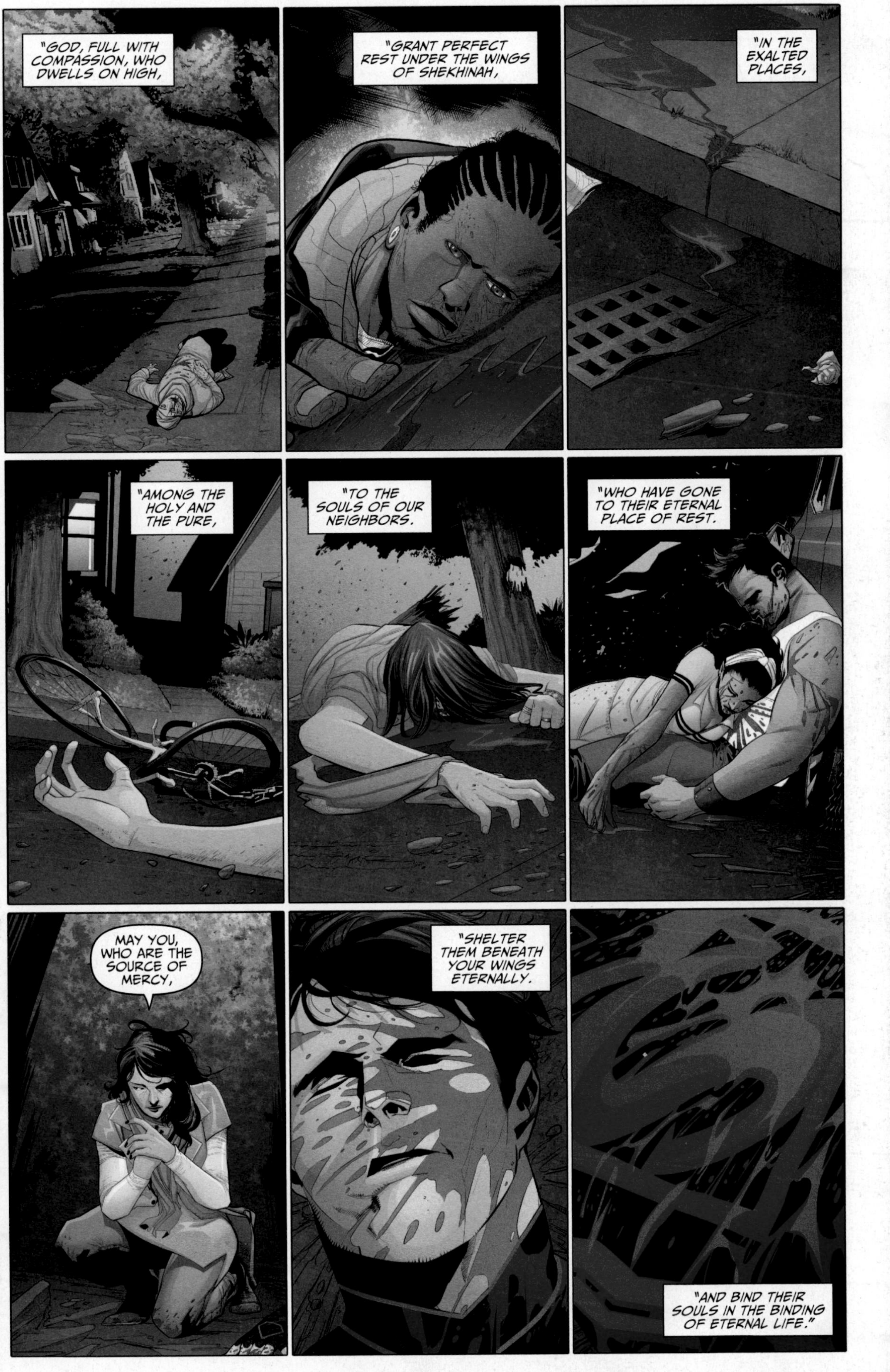
"GOD, FULL WITH COMPASSION, WHO DWELLS ON HIGH,
"GRANT PERFECT REST UNDER THE WINGS OF SHEKHINAH,
"IN THE EXALTED PLACES,
"AMONG THE HOLY AND THE PURE,
"TO THE SOULS OF OUR NEIGHBORS.
"WHO HAVE GONE TO THEIR ETERNAL PLACE OF REST.
MAY YOU, WHO ARE THE SOURCE OF MERCY,
"SHELTER THEM BENEATH YOUR WINGS ETERNALLY.
"AND BIND THEIR SOULS IN THE BINDING OF ETERNAL LIFE."

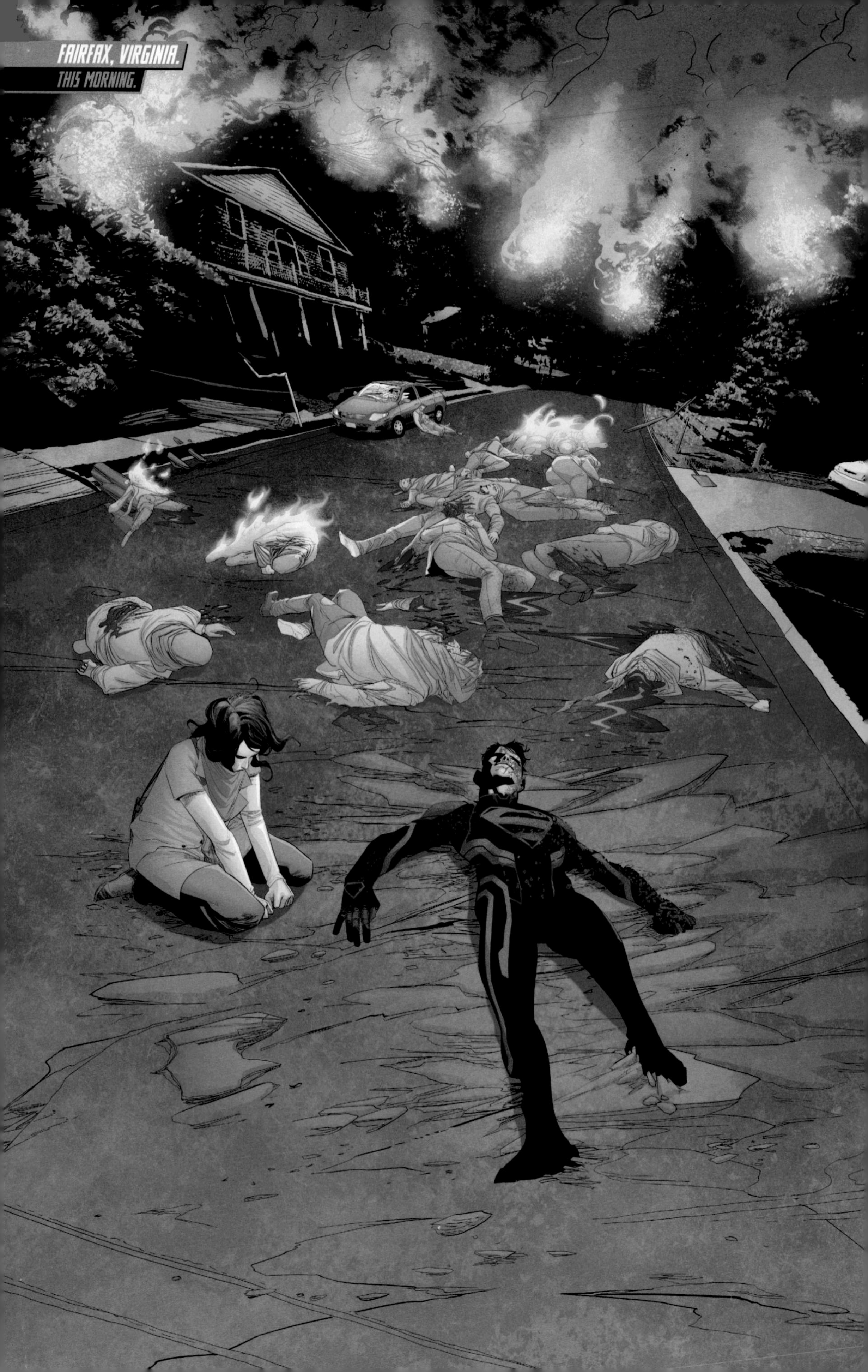
FAIRFAX, VIRGINIA.
THIS MORNING.

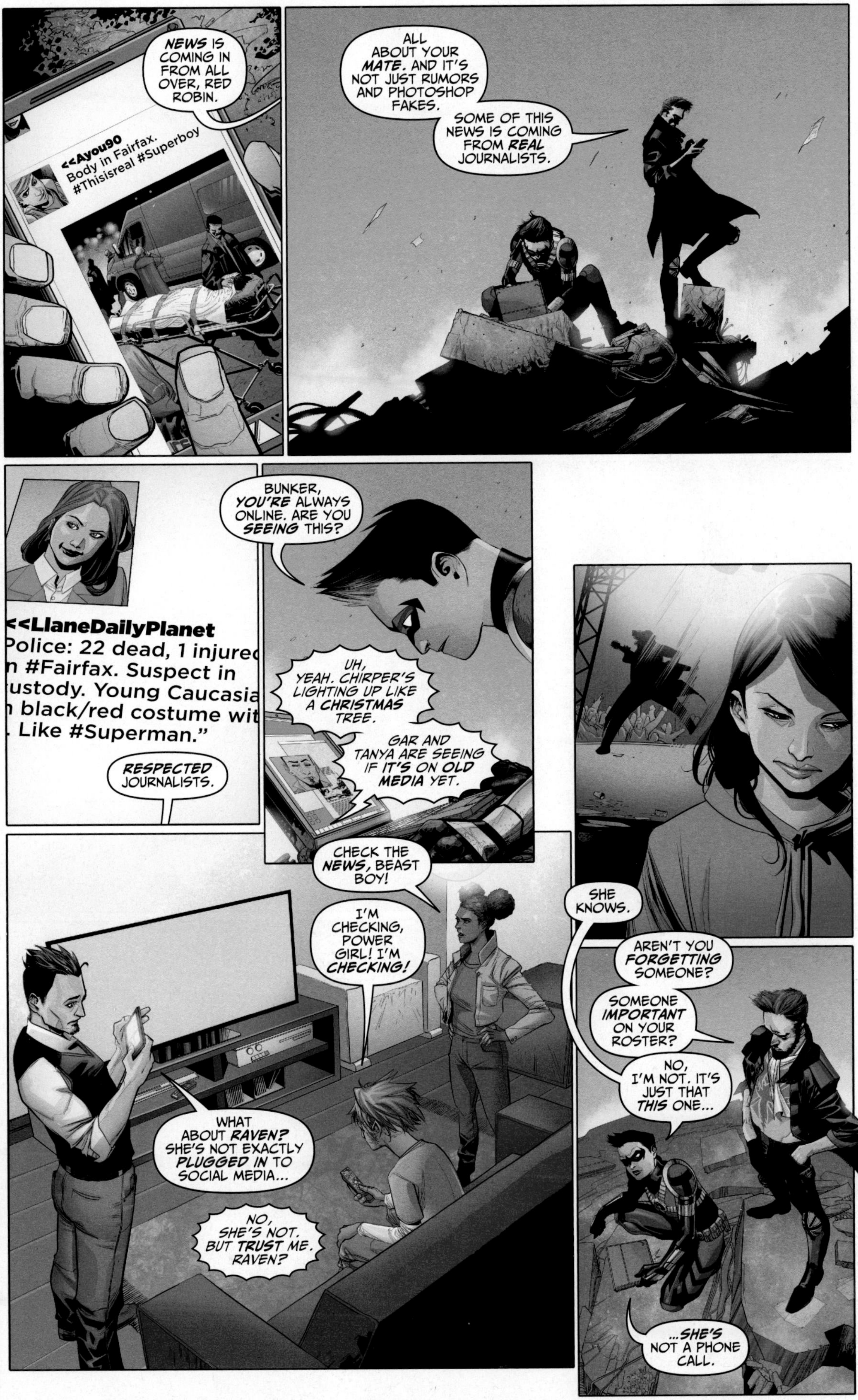
NEWS IS COMING IN FROM ALL OVER, RED ROBIN.
<<Ayou90
Body in Fairfax.
#Thisisreal #Superboy
ALL ABOUT YOUR MATE. AND IT'S NOT JUST RUMORS AND PHOTOSHOP FAKES.
SOME OF THIS NEWS IS COMING FROM REAL JOURNALISTS.
<<LlaneDailyPlanet
Police: 22 dead, 1 injured
n #Fairfax. Suspect in
ustody. Young Caucasia
n black/red costume wit
. Like #Superman."
RESPECTED JOURNALISTS.
BUNKER, YOU'RE ALWAYS ONLINE. ARE YOU SEEING THIS?
UH, YEAH. CHIRPER'S LIGHTING UP LIKE A CHRISTMAS TREE.
GAR AND TANYA ARE SEEING IF IT'S ON OLD MEDIA YET.
CHECK THE NEWS, BEAST BOY!
I'M CHECKING, POWER GIRL! I'M CHECKING!
WHAT ABOUT RAVEN? SHE'S NOT EXACTLY PLUGGED IN TO SOCIAL MEDIA...
NO, SHE'S NOT. BUT TRUST ME. RAVEN?
SHE KNOWS.
AREN'T YOU FORGETTING SOMEONE?
SOMEONE IMPORTANT ON YOUR ROSTER?
NO, I'M NOT. IT'S JUST THAT THIS ONE...
...SHE'S NOT A PHONE CALL.

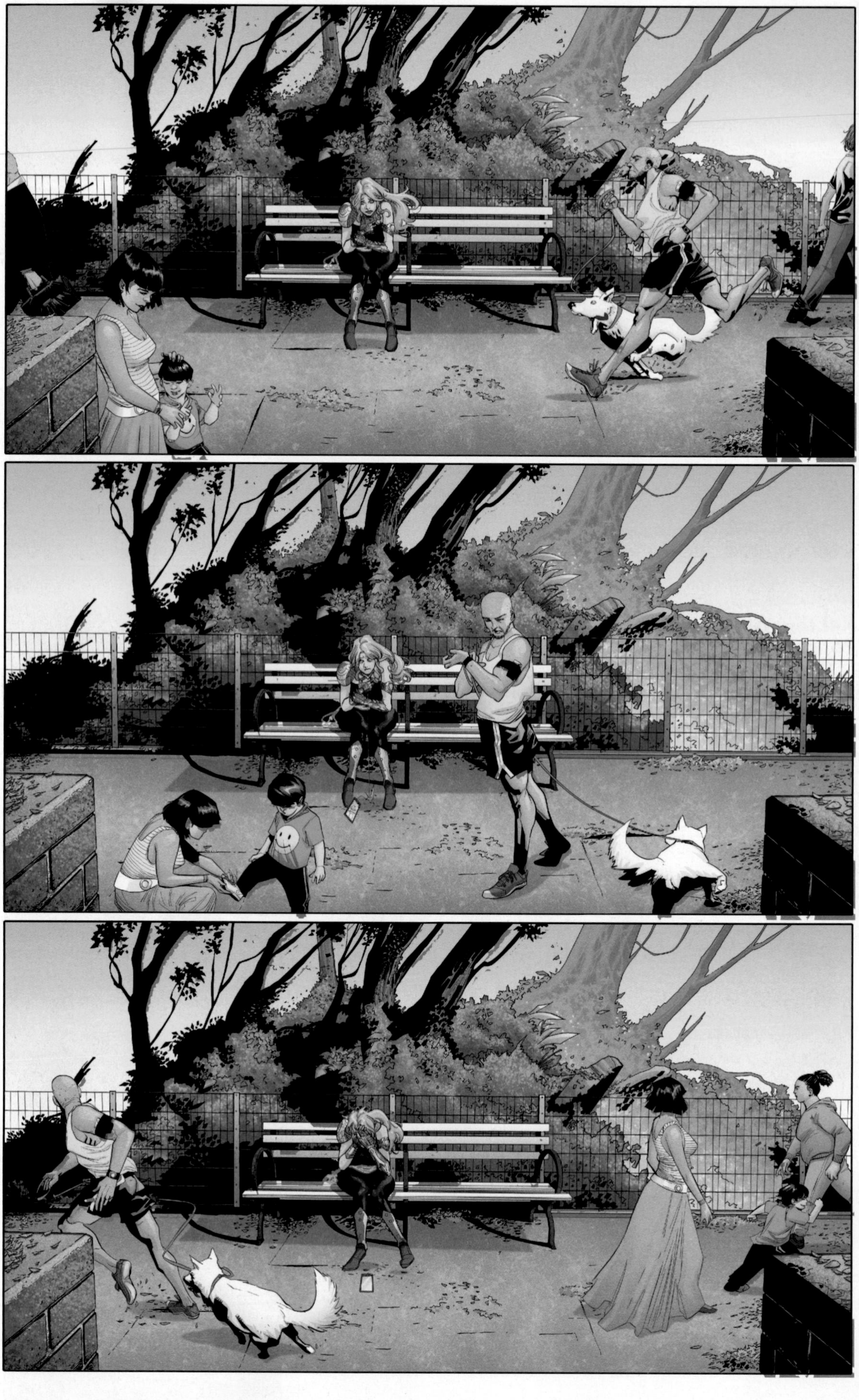

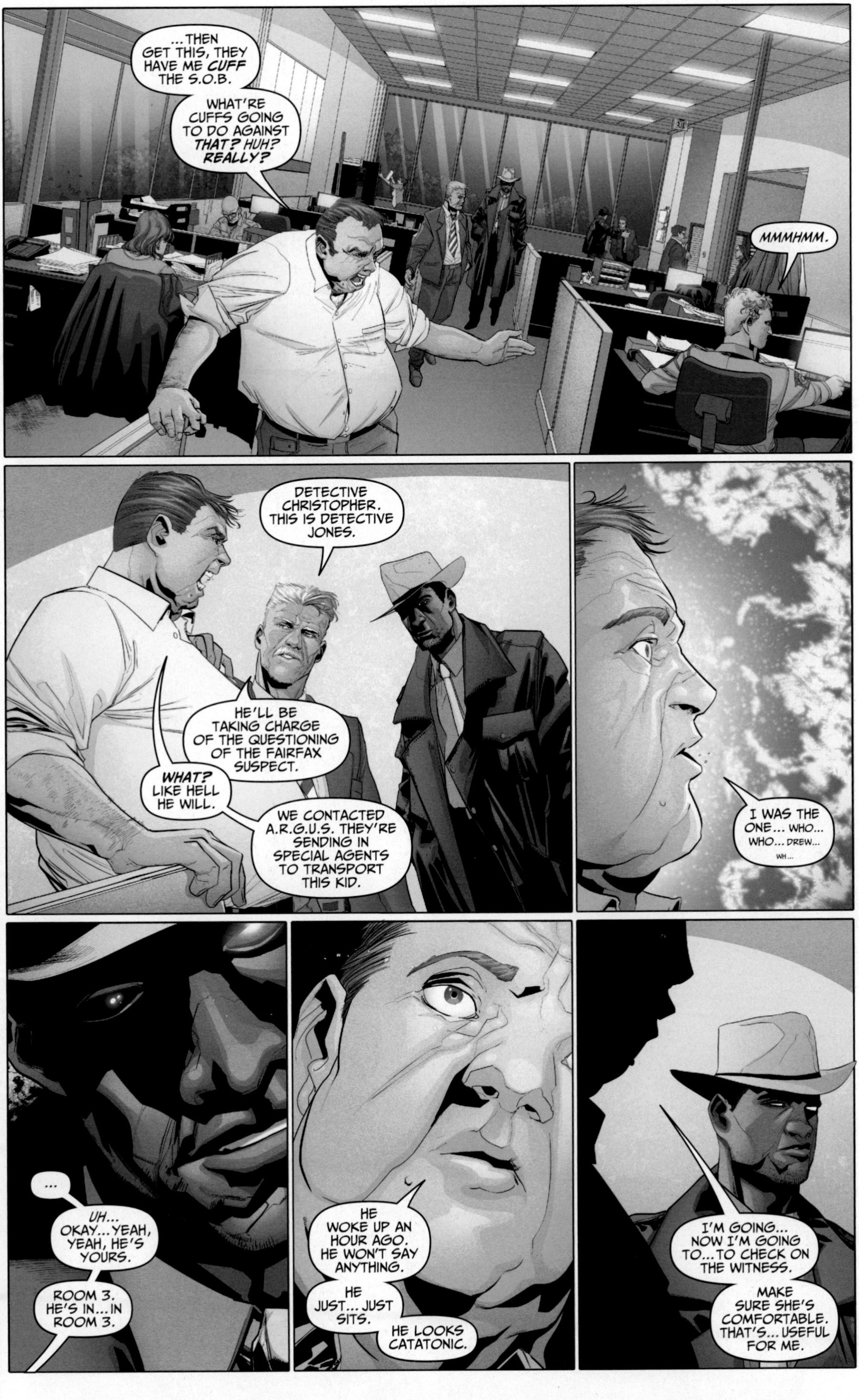
...THEN GET THIS, THEY HAVE ME *CUFF* THE S.O.B.
WHAT'RE CUFFS GOING TO DO AGAINST *THAT? HUH? REALLY?*
MMMHMM.
DETECTIVE CHRISTOPHER. THIS IS DETECTIVE JONES.
HE'LL BE TAKING CHARGE OF THE QUESTIONING OF THE FAIRFAX SUSPECT.
WHAT? LIKE HELL HE WILL.
WE CONTACTED A.R.G.U.S. THEY'RE SENDING IN SPECIAL AGENTS TO TRANSPORT THIS KID.
I WAS THE ONE... WHO... WHO... DREW... WH...
...
UH... OKAY...YEAH, YEAH, HE'S YOURS.
ROOM 3. HE'S IN...IN ROOM 3.
HE WOKE UP AN HOUR AGO. HE WON'T SAY ANYTHING.
HE JUST... JUST SITS.
HE LOOKS CATATONIC.
I'M GOING... NOW I'M GOING TO...TO CHECK ON THE WITNESS.
MAKE SURE SHE'S COMFORTABLE. THAT'S... USEFUL FOR ME.

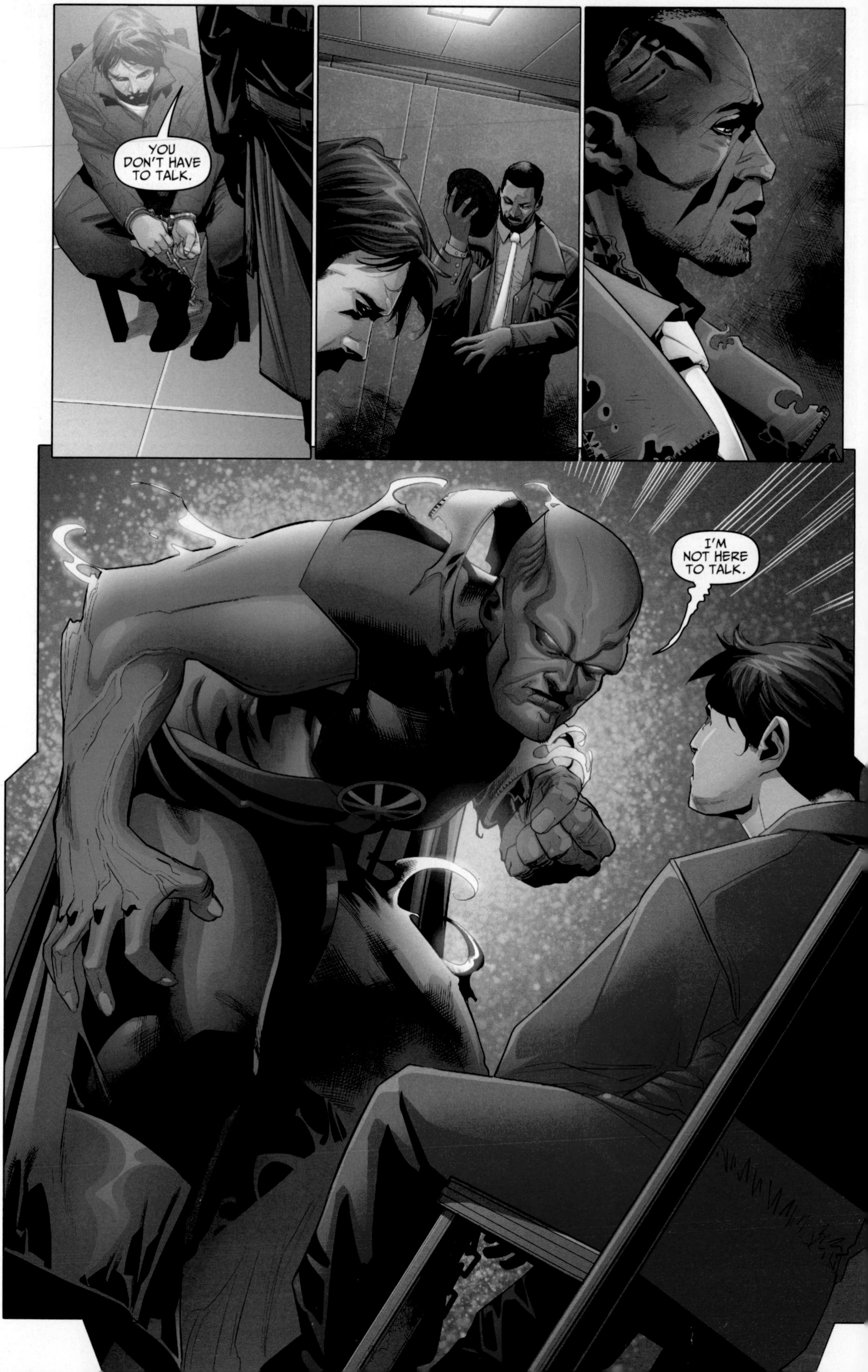
YOU DON'T HAVE TO TALK.
I'M NOT HERE TO TALK.

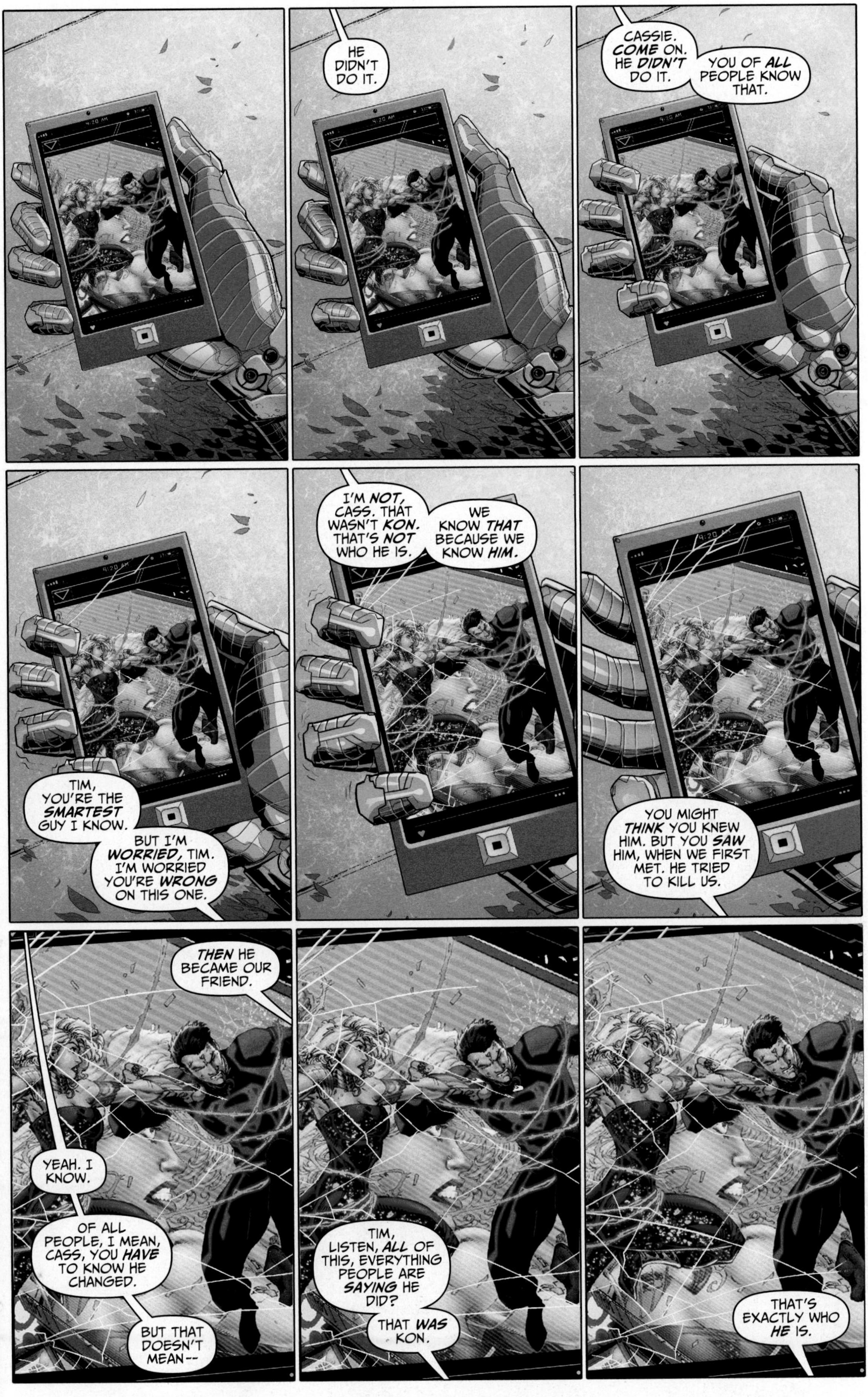
HE DIDN'T DO IT.
CASSIE. COME ON. HE DIDN'T DO IT.
YOU OF ALL PEOPLE KNOW THAT.
TIM, YOU'RE THE SMARTEST GUY I KNOW.
BUT I'M WORRIED, TIM. I'M WORRIED YOU'RE WRONG ON THIS ONE.
I'M NOT, CASS. THAT WASN'T KON. THAT'S NOT WHO HE IS.
WE KNOW THAT BECAUSE WE KNOW HIM.
YOU MIGHT THINK YOU KNEW HIM. BUT YOU SAW HIM, WHEN WE FIRST MET. HE TRIED TO KILL US.
THEN HE BECAME OUR FRIEND.
YEAH. I KNOW.
OF ALL PEOPLE, I MEAN, CASS, YOU HAVE TO KNOW HE CHANGED.
BUT THAT DOESN'T MEAN--
TIM, LISTEN, ALL OF THIS, EVERYTHING PEOPLE ARE SAYING HE DID?
THAT WAS KON.
THAT'S EXACTLY WHO HE IS.

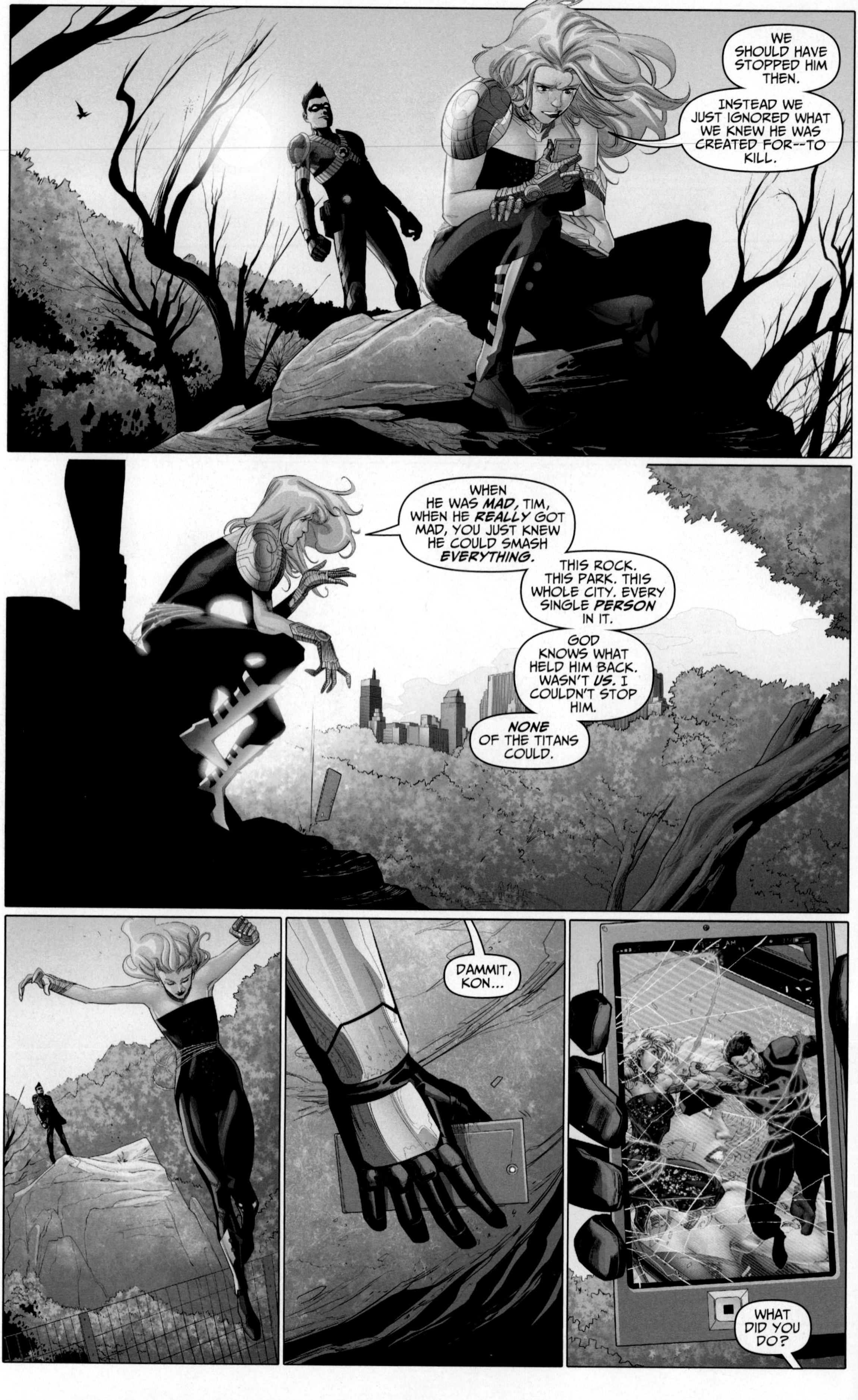
WE SHOULD HAVE STOPPED HIM THEN.
INSTEAD WE JUST IGNORED WHAT WE KNEW HE WAS CREATED FOR--TO KILL.
WHEN HE WAS *MAD,* TIM, WHEN HE *REALLY* GOT MAD, YOU JUST KNEW HE COULD SMASH *EVERYTHING.*
THIS ROCK. THIS PARK. THIS WHOLE CITY. EVERY SINGLE *PERSON* IN IT.
GOD KNOWS WHAT HELD HIM BACK. WASN'T *US.* I COULDN'T STOP HIM.
NONE OF THE TITANS COULD.
DAMMIT, KON...
WHAT DID YOU DO?

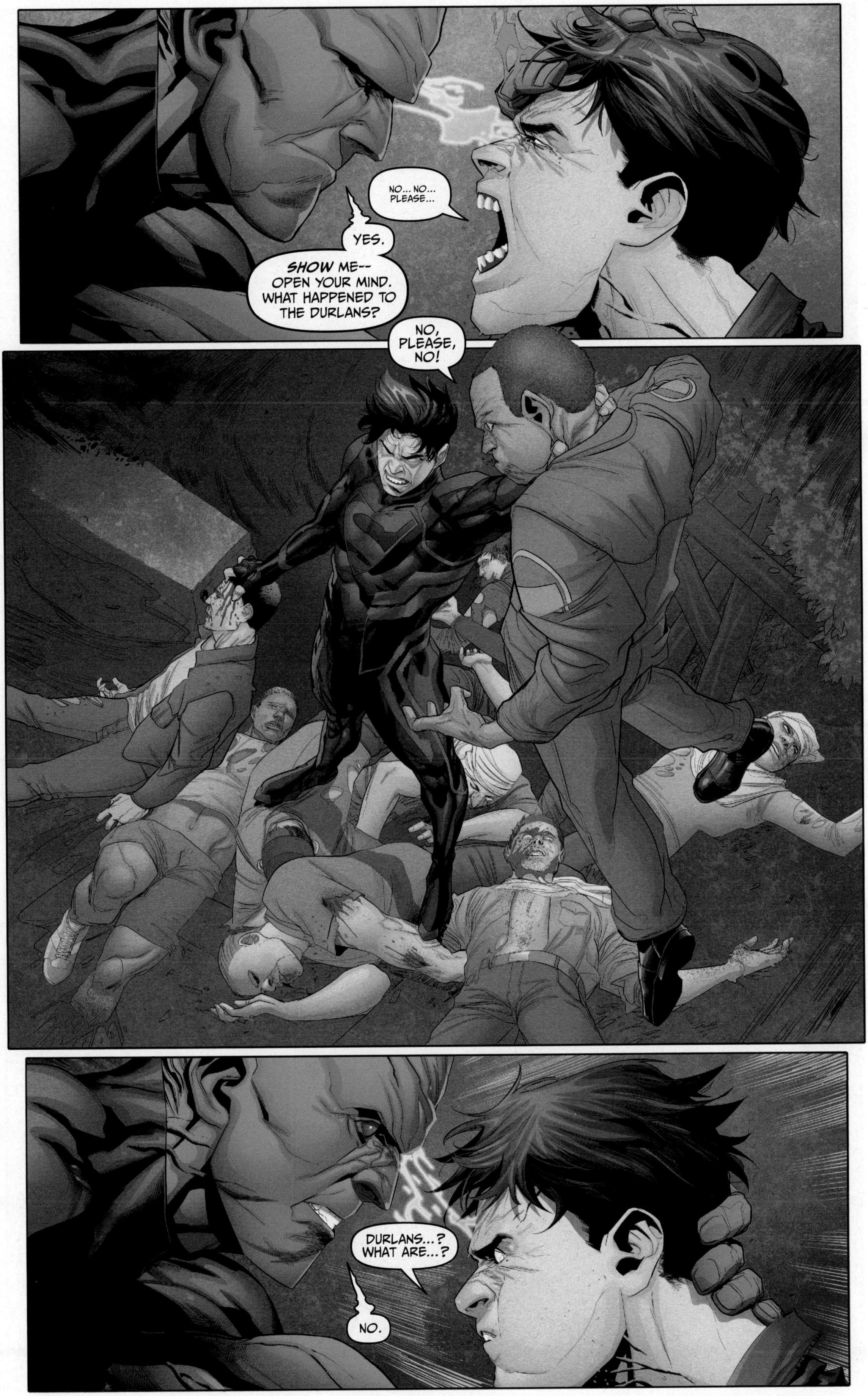
NO... NO... PLEASE...
YES.
SHOW ME-- OPEN YOUR MIND. WHAT HAPPENED TO THE DURLANS?
NO, PLEASE, NO!
DURLANS...? WHAT ARE...?
NO.

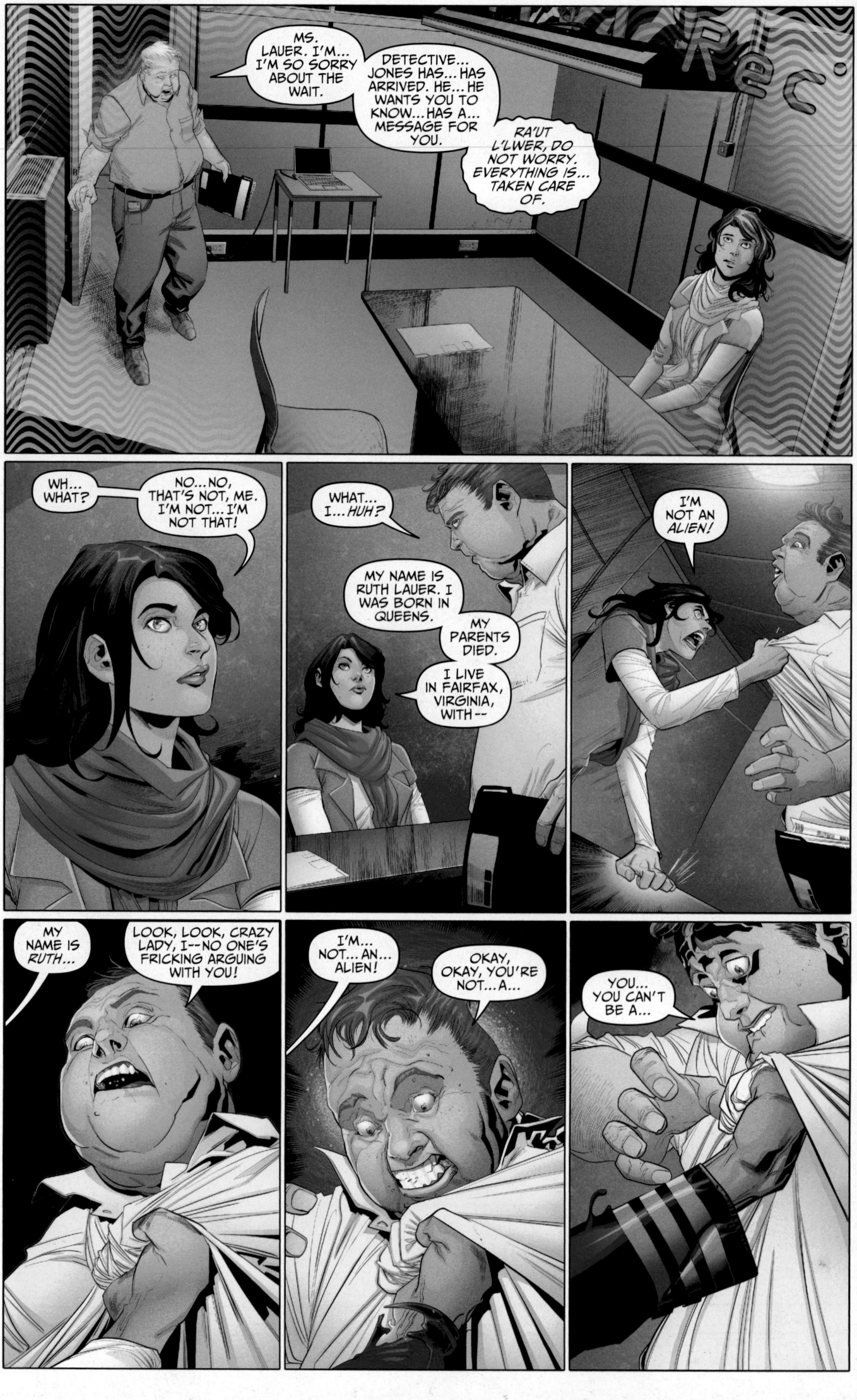

MS. LAUER. I'M... I'M SO SORRY ABOUT THE WAIT.
DETECTIVE... JONES HAS... HAS ARRIVED. HE... HE WANTS YOU TO KNOW... HAS A... MESSAGE FOR YOU.
RA'UT L'LWER, DO NOT WORRY. EVERYTHING IS... TAKEN CARE OF.
WH... WHAT?
NO...NO, THAT'S NOT, ME. I'M NOT... I'M NOT THAT!
WHAT... I... HUH?
MY NAME IS RUTH LAUER. I WAS BORN IN QUEENS.
MY PARENTS DIED.
I LIVE IN FAIRFAX, VIRGINIA, WITH--
I'M NOT AN ALIEN!
MY NAME IS RUTH...
LOOK, LOOK, CRAZY LADY, I--NO ONE'S FRICKING ARGUING WITH YOU!
I'M... NOT... AN... ALIEN!
OKAY, OKAY, YOU'RE NOT... A...
YOU... YOU CAN'T BE A...

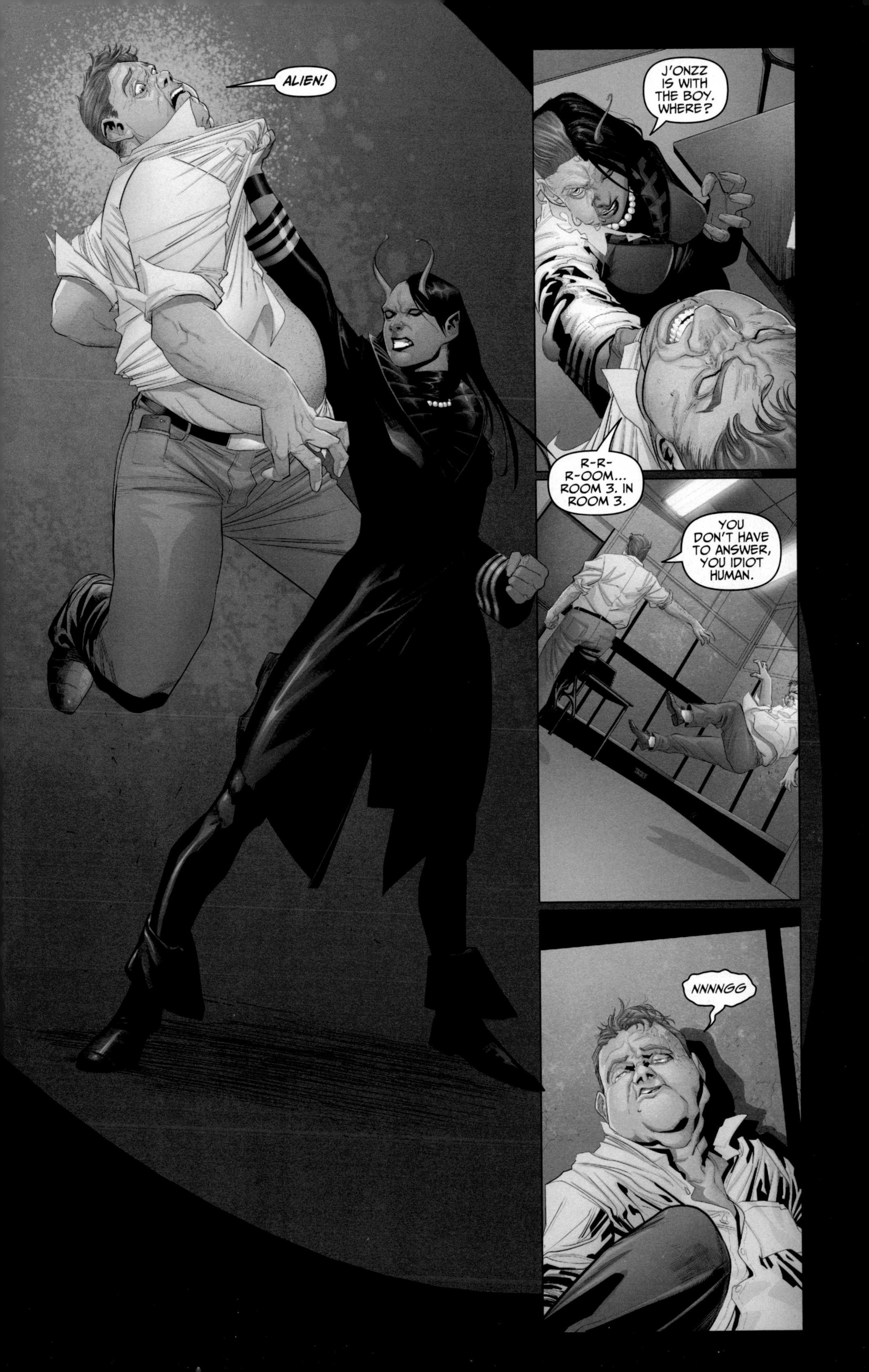
ALIEN!
J'ONZZ IS WITH THE BOY. WHERE?
R-R-R-OOM... ROOM 3. IN ROOM 3.
YOU DON'T HAVE TO ANSWER, YOU IDIOT HUMAN.
NNNNGG

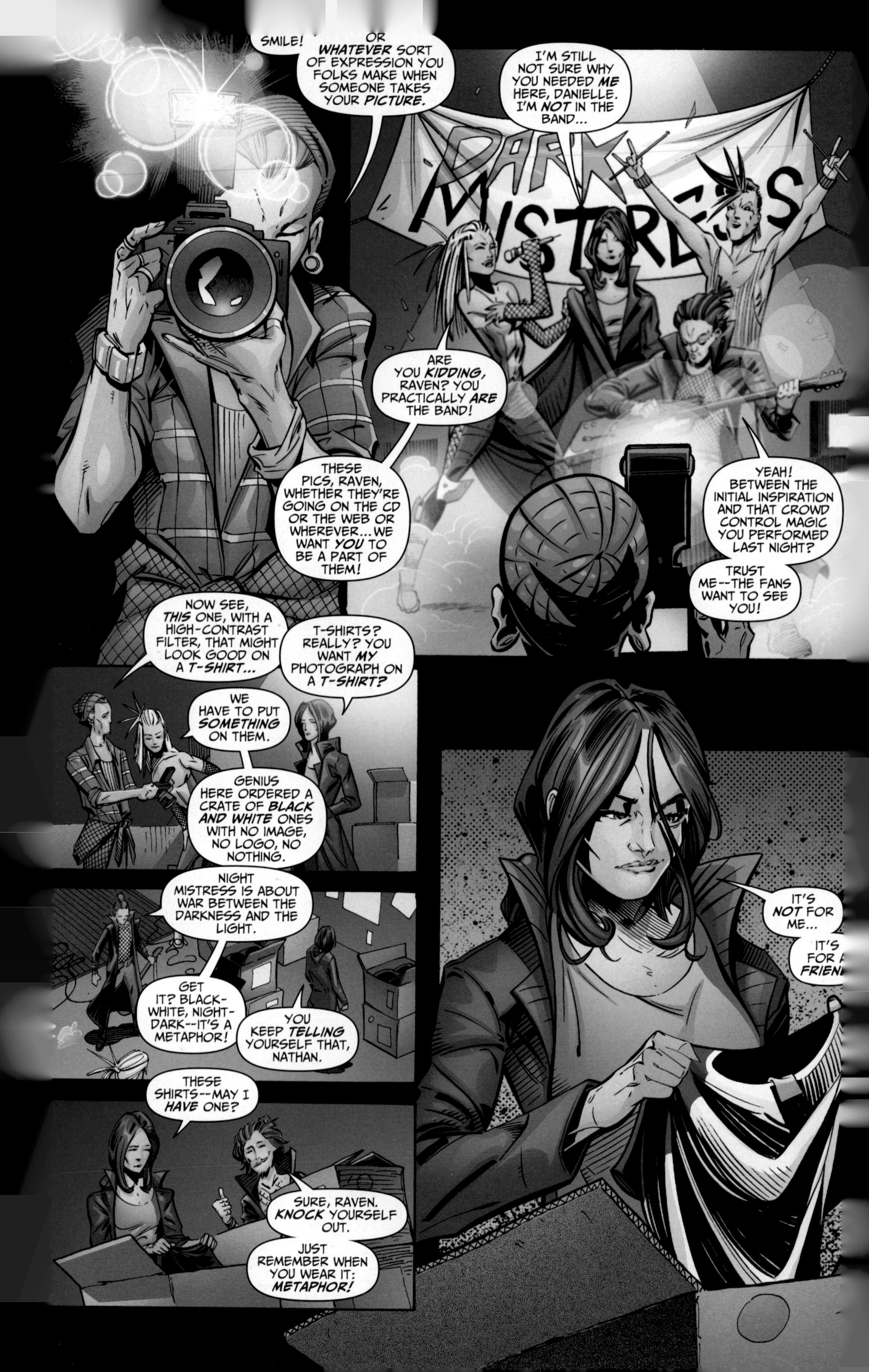
SMILE!
OR WHATEVER SORT OF EXPRESSION YOU FOLKS MAKE WHEN SOMEONE TAKES YOUR PICTURE.
I'M STILL NOT SURE WHY YOU NEEDED ME HERE, DANIELLE. I'M NOT IN THE BAND...
DARK MISTRESS
ARE YOU KIDDING, RAVEN? YOU PRACTICALLY ARE THE BAND!
THESE PICS, RAVEN, WHETHER THEY'RE GOING ON THE CD OR THE WEB OR WHEREVER... WE WANT YOU TO BE A PART OF THEM!
YEAH! BETWEEN THE INITIAL INSPIRATION AND THAT CROWD CONTROL MAGIC YOU PERFORMED LAST NIGHT?
TRUST ME--THE FANS WANT TO SEE YOU!
NOW SEE, THIS ONE, WITH A HIGH-CONTRAST FILTER, THAT MIGHT LOOK GOOD ON A T-SHIRT...
T-SHIRTS? REALLY? YOU WANT MY PHOTOGRAPH ON A T-SHIRT?
WE HAVE TO PUT SOMETHING ON THEM.
GENIUS HERE ORDERED A CRATE OF BLACK AND WHITE ONES WITH NO IMAGE, NO LOGO, NO NOTHING.
NIGHT MISTRESS IS ABOUT WAR BETWEEN THE DARKNESS AND THE LIGHT.
GET IT? BLACK-WHITE, NIGHT-DARK--IT'S A METAPHOR!
YOU KEEP TELLING YOURSELF THAT, NATHAN.
THESE SHIRTS--MAY I HAVE ONE?
SURE, RAVEN. KNOCK YOURSELF OUT.
JUST REMEMBER WHEN YOU WEAR IT: METAPHOR!
IT'S NOT FOR ME...

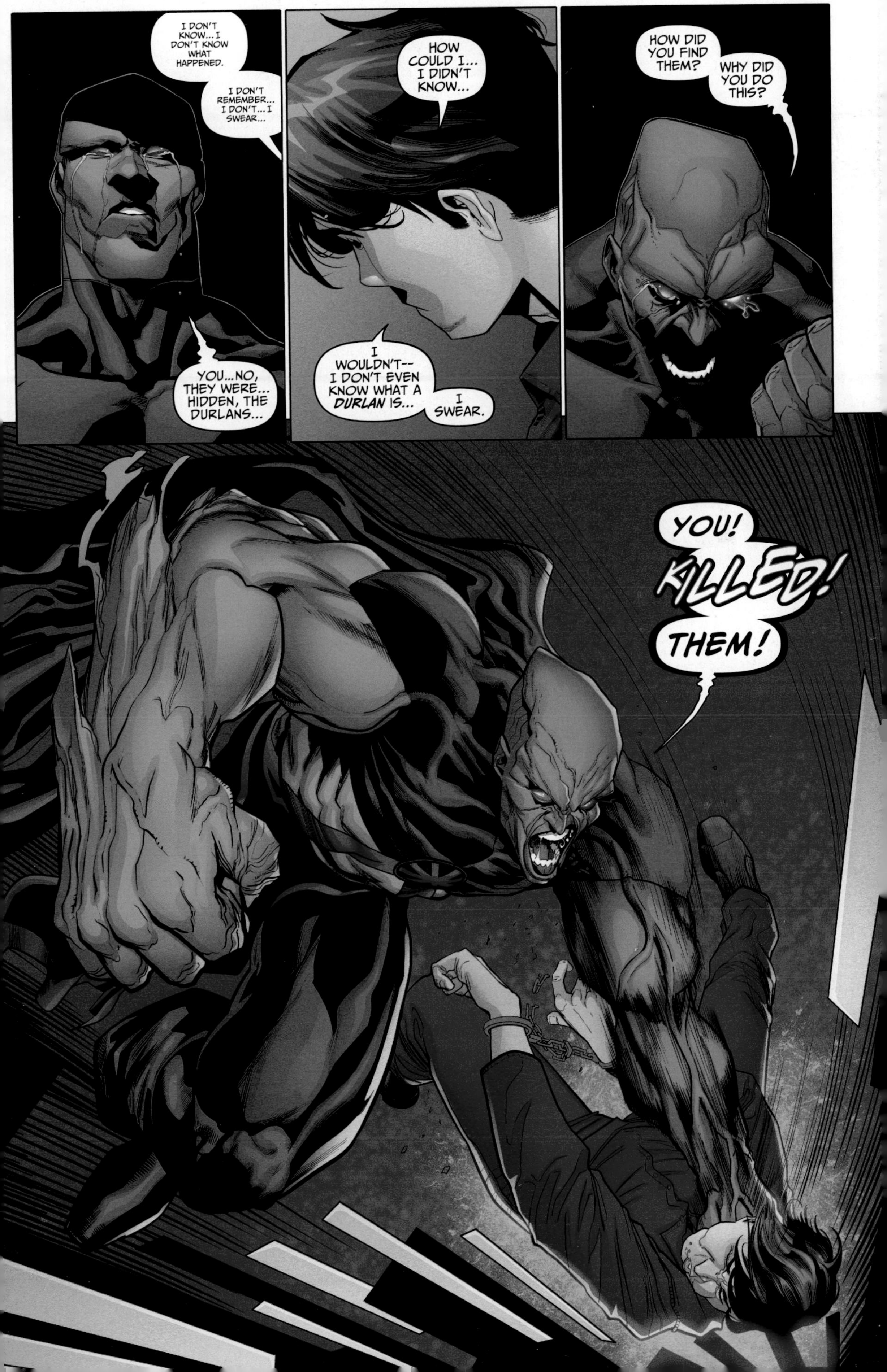
I DON'T KNOW... I DON'T KNOW WHAT HAPPENED.
I DON'T REMEMBER... I DON'T... I SWEAR...
YOU...NO, THEY WERE... HIDDEN, THE DURLANS...
HOW COULD I... I DIDN'T KNOW...
I WOULDN'T-- I DON'T EVEN KNOW WHAT A DURLAN IS...
I SWEAR.
HOW DID YOU FIND THEM?
WHY DID YOU DO THIS?
YOU!
KILLED!
THEM!

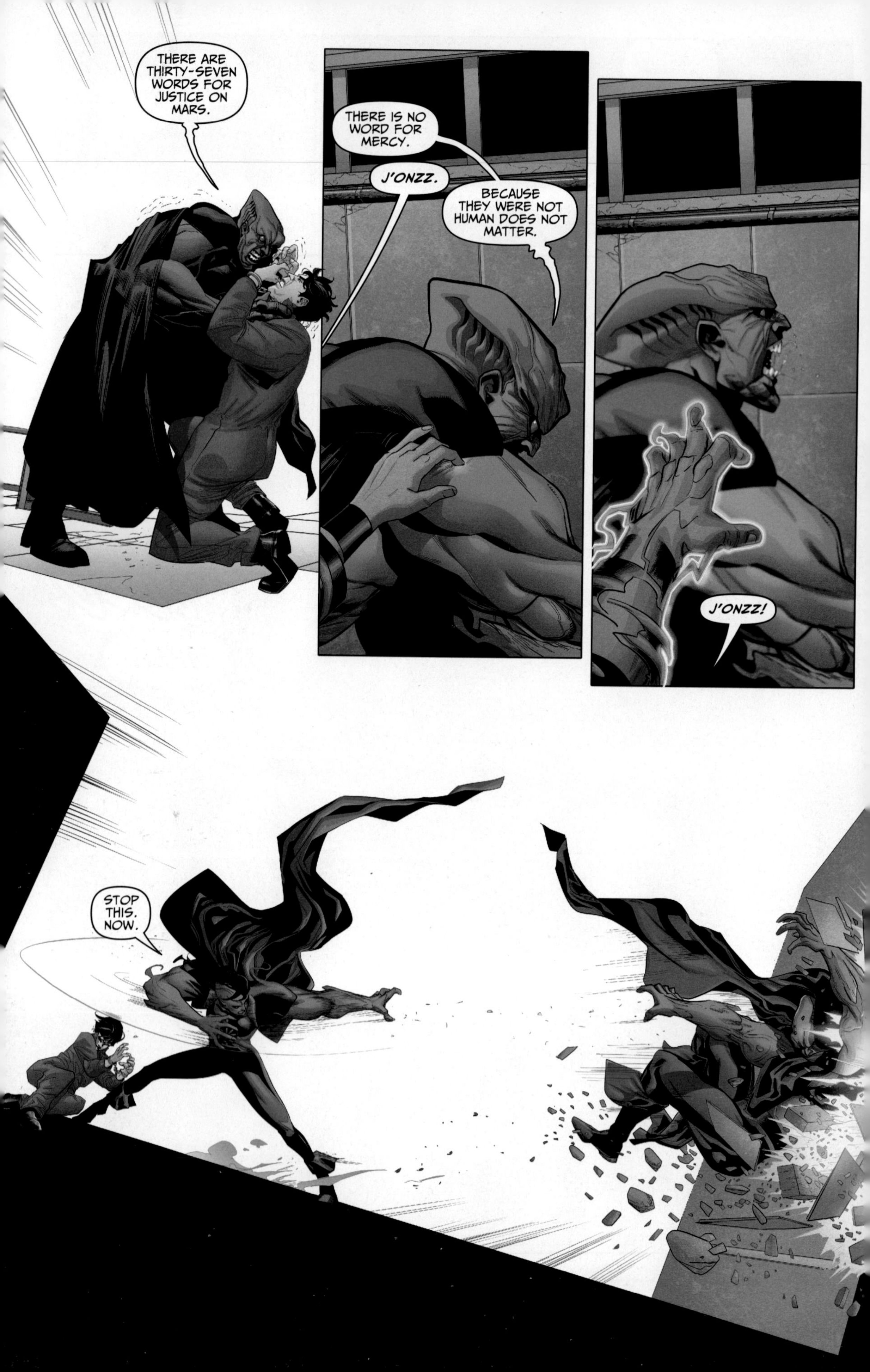
THERE ARE THIRTY-SEVEN WORDS FOR JUSTICE ON MARS.
THERE IS NO WORD FOR MERCY.
J'ONZZ.
BECAUSE THEY WERE NOT HUMAN DOES NOT MATTER.
J'ONZZ!
STOP THIS. NOW.

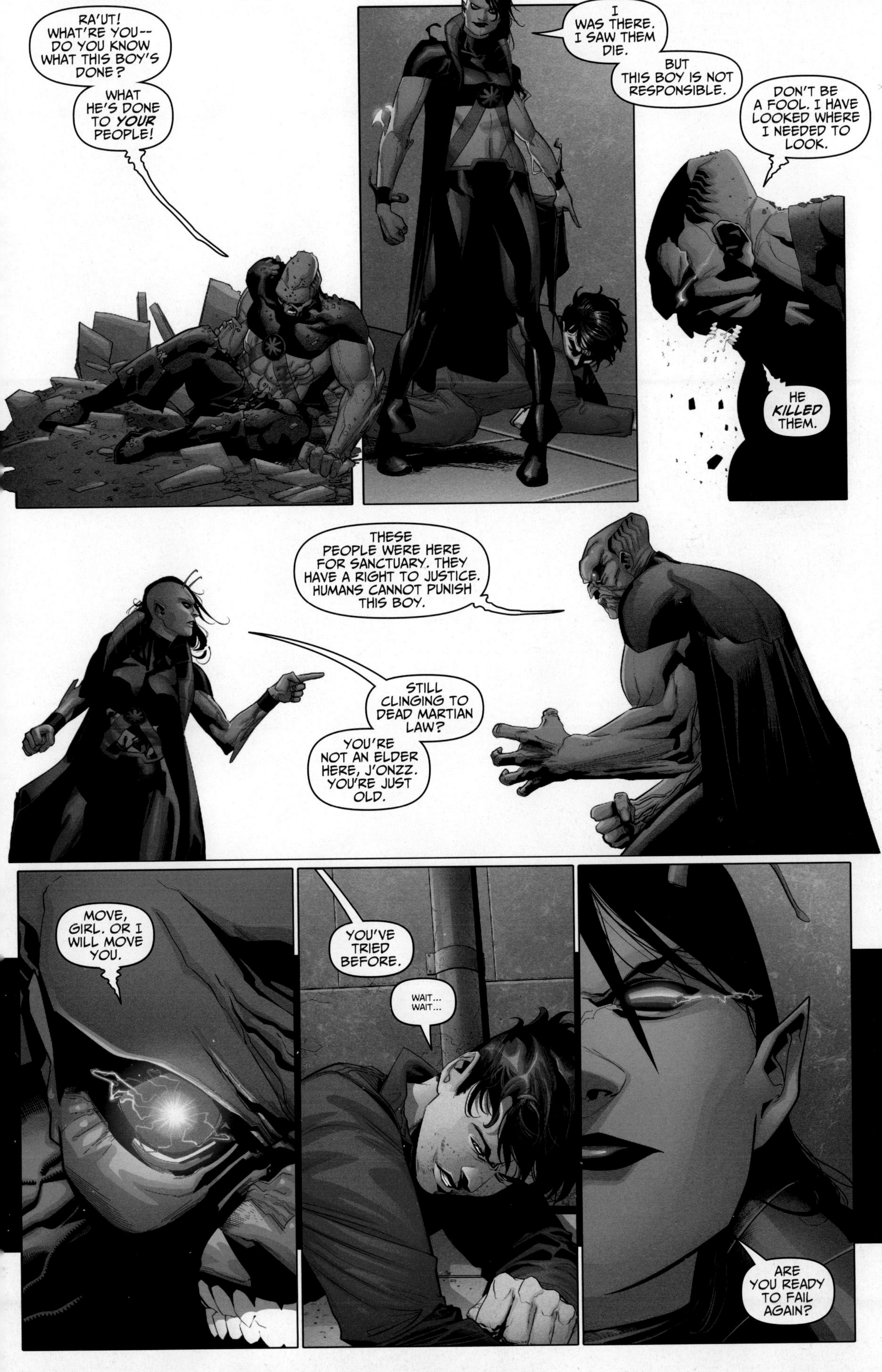
RA'UT! WHAT'RE YOU-- DO YOU KNOW WHAT THIS BOY'S DONE?
WHAT HE'S DONE TO *YOUR* PEOPLE!
I WAS THERE. I SAW THEM DIE.
BUT THIS BOY IS NOT RESPONSIBLE.
DON'T BE A FOOL. I HAVE LOOKED WHERE I NEEDED TO LOOK.
HE *KILLED* THEM.
THESE PEOPLE WERE HERE FOR SANCTUARY. THEY HAVE A RIGHT TO JUSTICE. HUMANS CANNOT PUNISH THIS BOY.
STILL CLINGING TO DEAD MARTIAN LAW?
YOU'RE NOT AN ELDER HERE, J'ONZZ. YOU'RE JUST OLD.
MOVE, GIRL. OR I WILL MOVE YOU.
YOU'VE TRIED BEFORE.
WAIT... WAIT...
ARE YOU READY TO FAIL AGAIN?

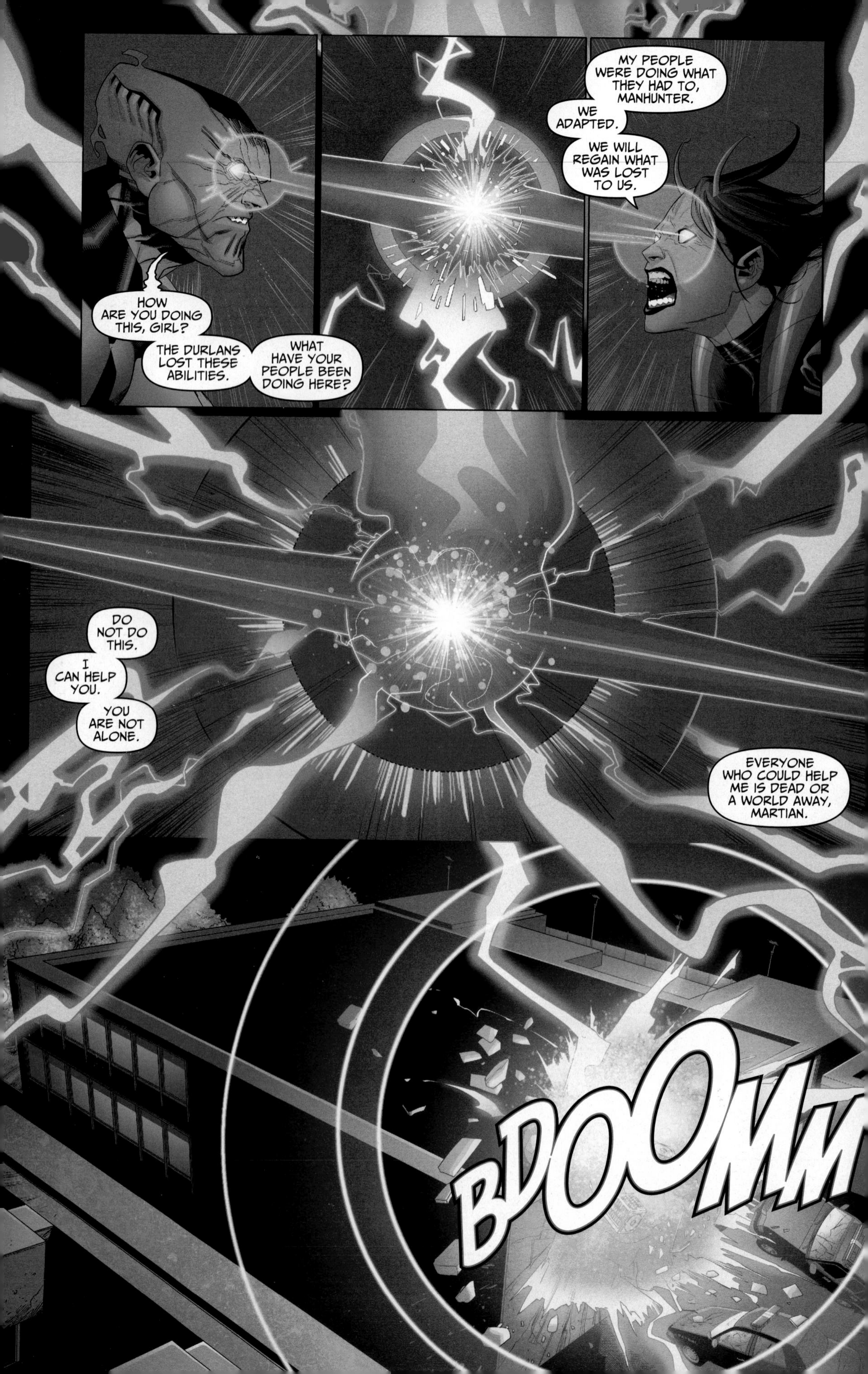
HOW ARE YOU DOING THIS, GIRL?
THE DURLANS LOST THESE ABILITIES.
WHAT HAVE YOUR PEOPLE BEEN DOING HERE?
MY PEOPLE WERE DOING WHAT THEY HAD TO, MANHUNTER.
WE ADAPTED.
WE WILL REGAIN WHAT WAS LOST TO US.
DO NOT DO THIS.
I CAN HELP YOU.
YOU ARE NOT ALONE.
EVERYONE WHO COULD HELP ME IS DEAD OR A WORLD AWAY, MARTIAN.
BDOOMM

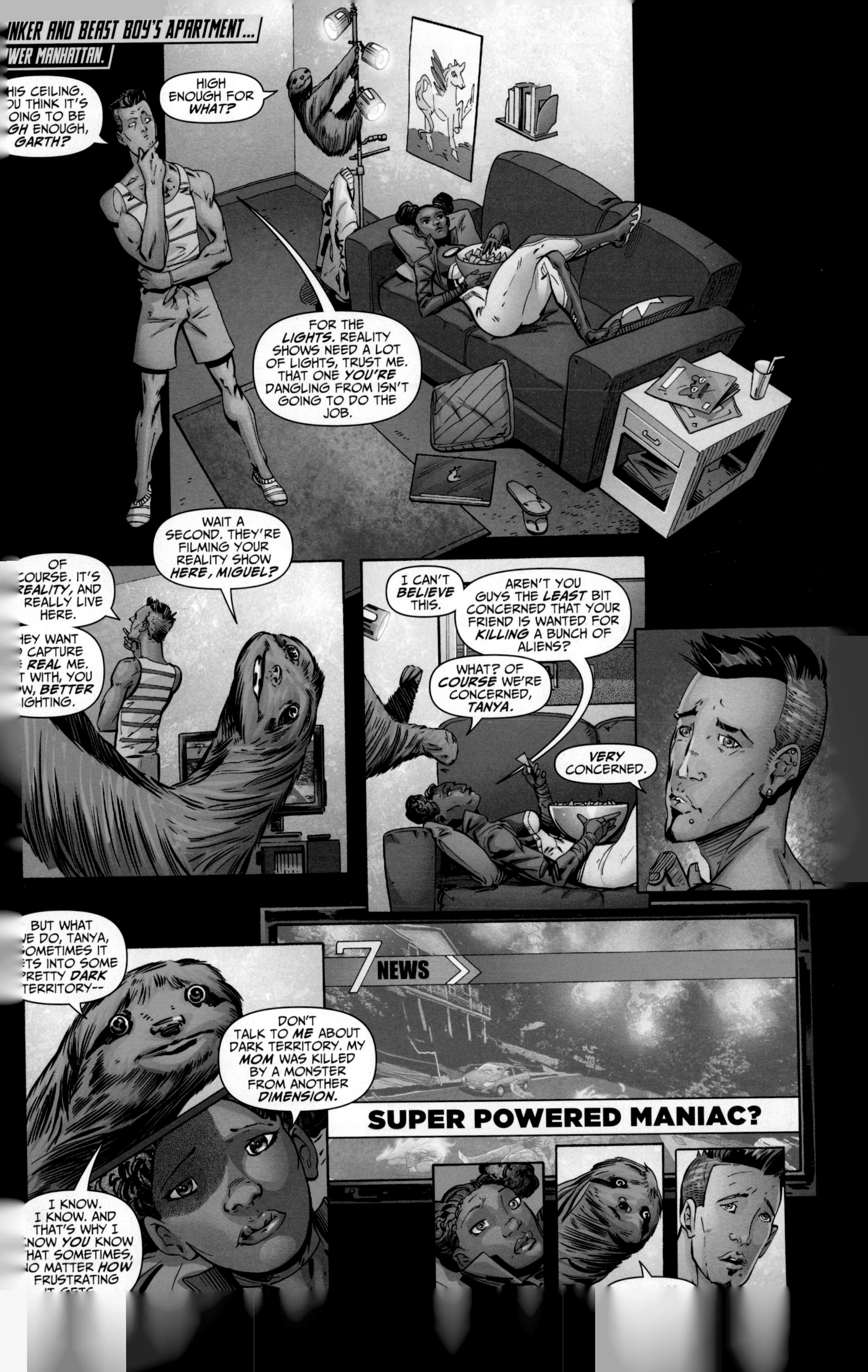
INKER AND BEAST BOY'S APARTMENT...
WER MANHATTAN.
HIS CEILING. DU THINK IT'S OING TO BE GH ENOUGH, GARTH?
HIGH ENOUGH FOR WHAT?
FOR THE LIGHTS. REALITY SHOWS NEED A LOT OF LIGHTS, TRUST ME. THAT ONE YOU'RE DANGLING FROM ISN'T GOING TO DO THE JOB.
WAIT A SECOND. THEY'RE FILMING YOUR REALITY SHOW HERE, MIGUEL?
OF COURSE. IT'S REALITY, AND REALLY LIVE HERE.
HEY WANT CAPTURE REAL ME. T WITH, YOU W, BETTER IGHTING.
I CAN'T BELIEVE THIS.
AREN'T YOU GUYS THE LEAST BIT CONCERNED THAT YOUR FRIEND IS WANTED FOR KILLING A BUNCH OF ALIENS?
WHAT? OF COURSE WE'RE CONCERNED, TANYA.
VERY CONCERNED.
BUT WHAT E DO, TANYA, OMETIMES IT ETS INTO SOME PRETTY DARK TERRITORY--
DON'T TALK TO ME ABOUT DARK TERRITORY. MY MOM WAS KILLED BY A MONSTER FROM ANOTHER DIMENSION.
7 NEWS
SUPER POWERED MANIAC?
I KNOW. I KNOW. AND THAT'S WHY I NOW YOU KNOW HAT SOMETIMES, O MATTER HOW FRUSTRATING

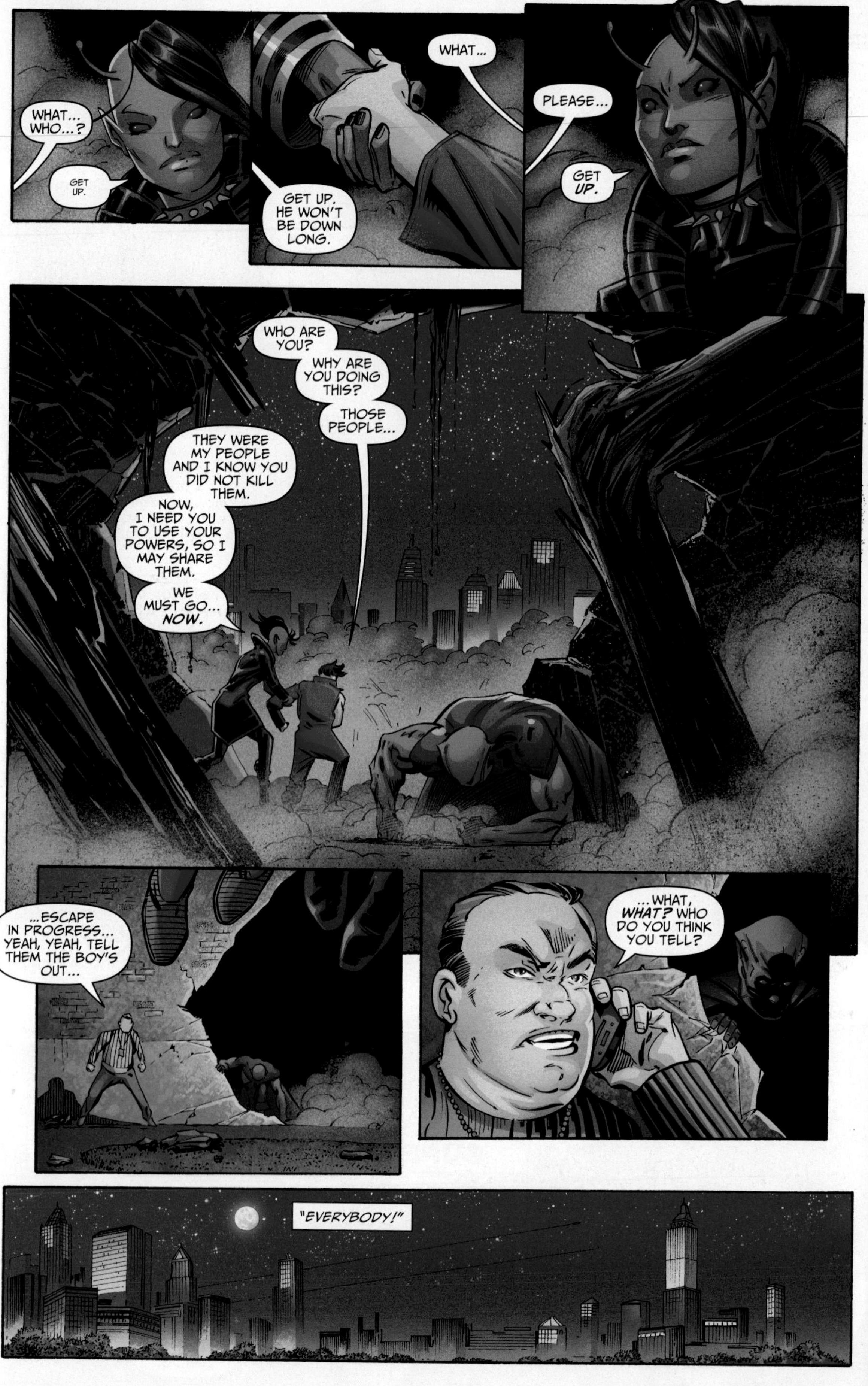
WHAT... WHO...?
GET UP.
WHAT...
GET UP. HE WON'T BE DOWN LONG.
PLEASE...
GET UP.
WHO ARE YOU?
WHY ARE YOU DOING THIS?
THOSE PEOPLE...
THEY WERE MY PEOPLE AND I KNOW YOU DID NOT KILL THEM.
NOW, I NEED YOU TO USE YOUR POWERS, SO I MAY SHARE THEM.
WE MUST GO... NOW.
...ESCAPE IN PROGRESS... YEAH, YEAH, TELL THEM THE BOY'S OUT...
...WHAT, WHAT? WHO DO YOU THINK YOU TELL?
"EVERYBODY!"

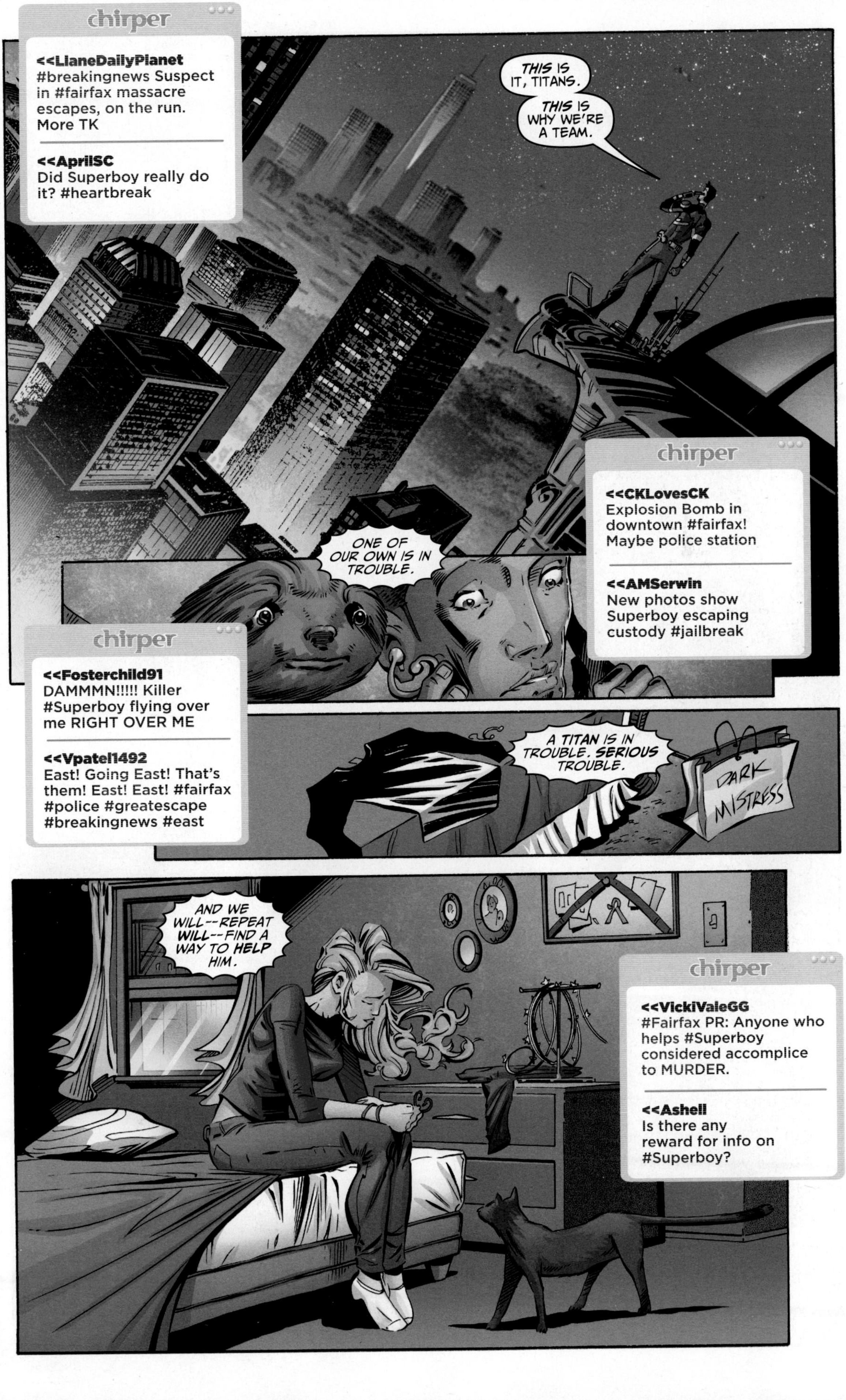
chirper
<<LianeDailyPlanet
#breakingnews Suspect in #fairfax massacre escapes, on the run. More TK
<<AprilSC
Did Superboy really do it? #heartbreak
THIS IS IT, TITANS.
THIS IS WHY WE'RE A TEAM.
chirper
<<CKLovesCK
Explosion Bomb in downtown #fairfax! Maybe police station
<<AMSerwin
New photos show Superboy escaping custody #jailbreak
ONE OF OUR OWN IS IN TROUBLE.
chirper
<<Fosterchild91
DAMMMN!!!!! Killer #Superboy flying over me RIGHT OVER ME
<<Vpatel1492
East! Going East! That's them! East! East! #fairfax #police #greatescape #breakingnews #east
A TITAN IS IN TROUBLE. SERIOUS TROUBLE.
DARK MISTRESS
AND WE WILL--REPEAT WILL--FIND A WAY TO HELP HIM.
chirper
<<VickiValeGG
#Fairfax PR: Anyone who helps #Superboy considered accomplice to MURDER.
<<Ashell
Is there any reward for info on #Superboy?

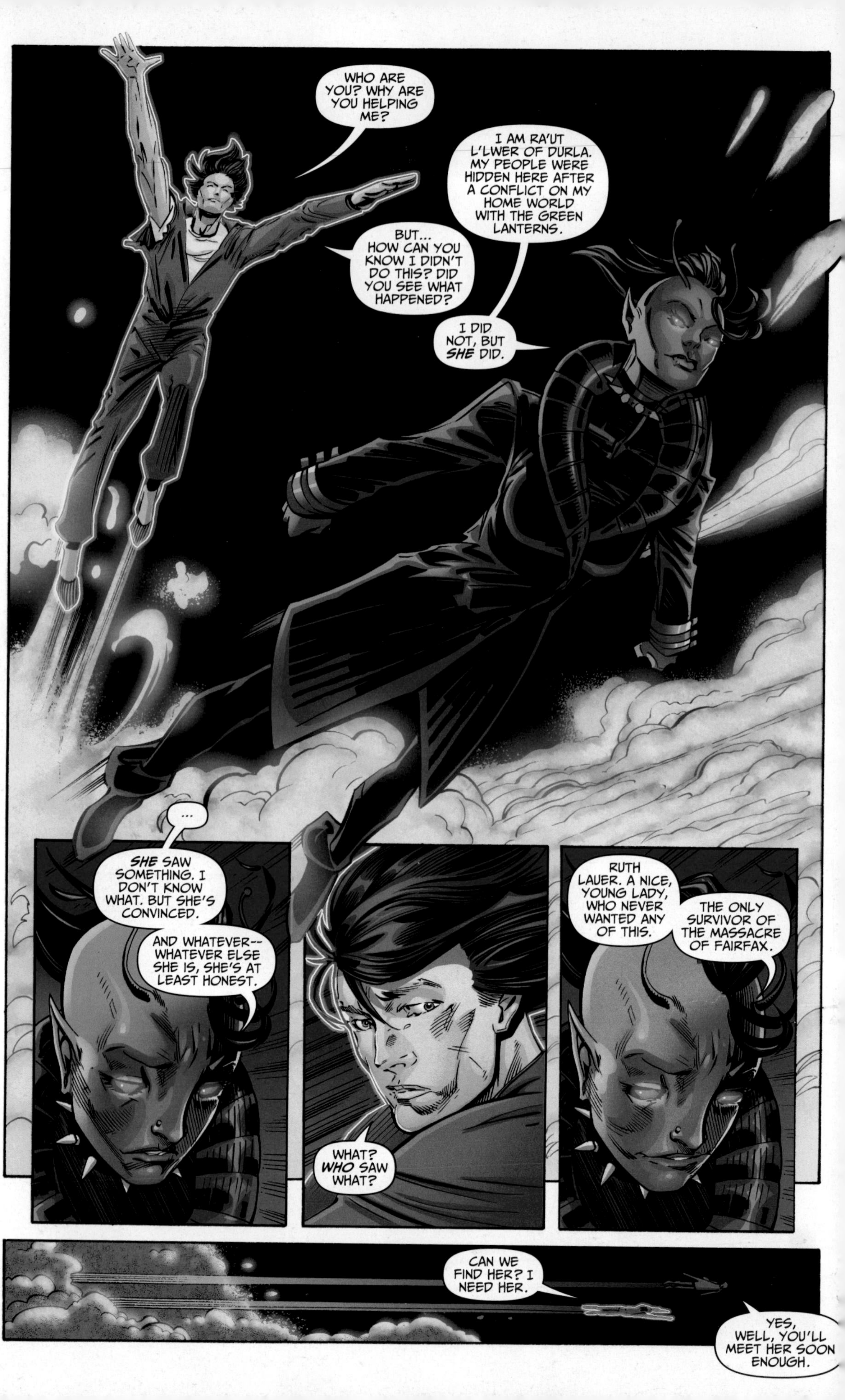
WHO ARE YOU? WHY ARE YOU HELPING ME?
I AM RA'UT L'LWER OF DURLA. MY PEOPLE WERE HIDDEN HERE AFTER A CONFLICT ON MY HOME WORLD WITH THE GREEN LANTERNS.
BUT... HOW CAN YOU KNOW I DIDN'T DO THIS? DID YOU SEE WHAT HAPPENED?
I DID NOT, BUT *SHE* DID.
...
SHE SAW SOMETHING. I DON'T KNOW WHAT. BUT SHE'S CONVINCED.
AND WHATEVER-- WHATEVER ELSE SHE IS, SHE'S AT LEAST HONEST.
WHAT? *WHO* SAW WHAT?
RUTH LAUER. A NICE, YOUNG LADY, WHO NEVER WANTED ANY OF THIS.
THE ONLY SURVIVOR OF THE MASSACRE OF FAIRFAX.
CAN WE FIND HER? I NEED HER.
YES, WELL, YOU'LL MEET HER SOON ENOUGH.

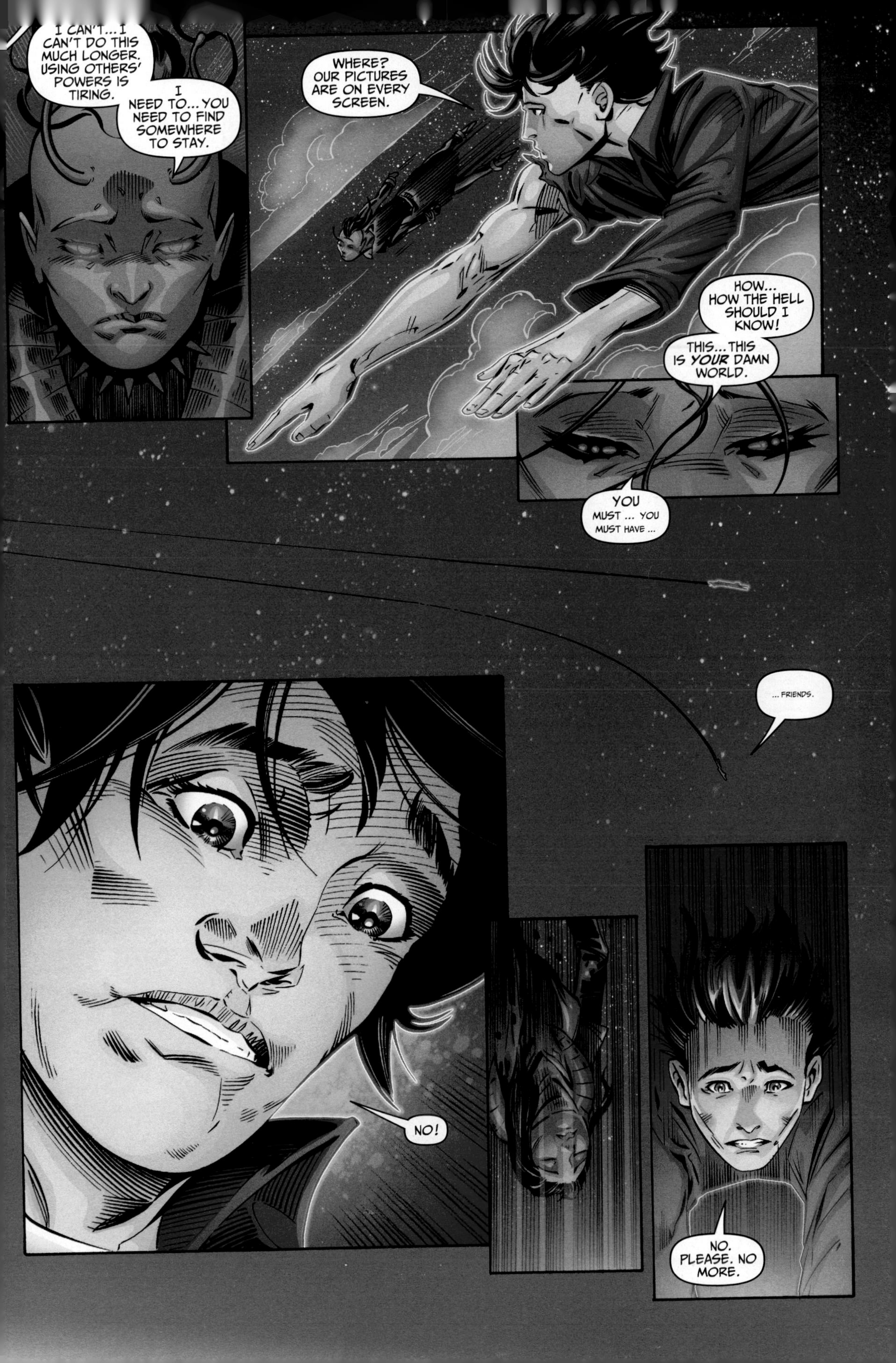
I CAN'T... I CAN'T DO THIS MUCH LONGER. USING OTHERS' POWERS IS TIRING.
I NEED TO... YOU NEED TO FIND SOMEWHERE TO STAY.
WHERE? OUR PICTURES ARE ON EVERY SCREEN.
HOW... HOW THE HELL SHOULD I KNOW!
THIS... THIS IS YOUR DAMN WORLD.
YOU MUST ... YOU MUST HAVE ...
... FRIENDS.
NO!
NO. PLEASE. NO MORE.

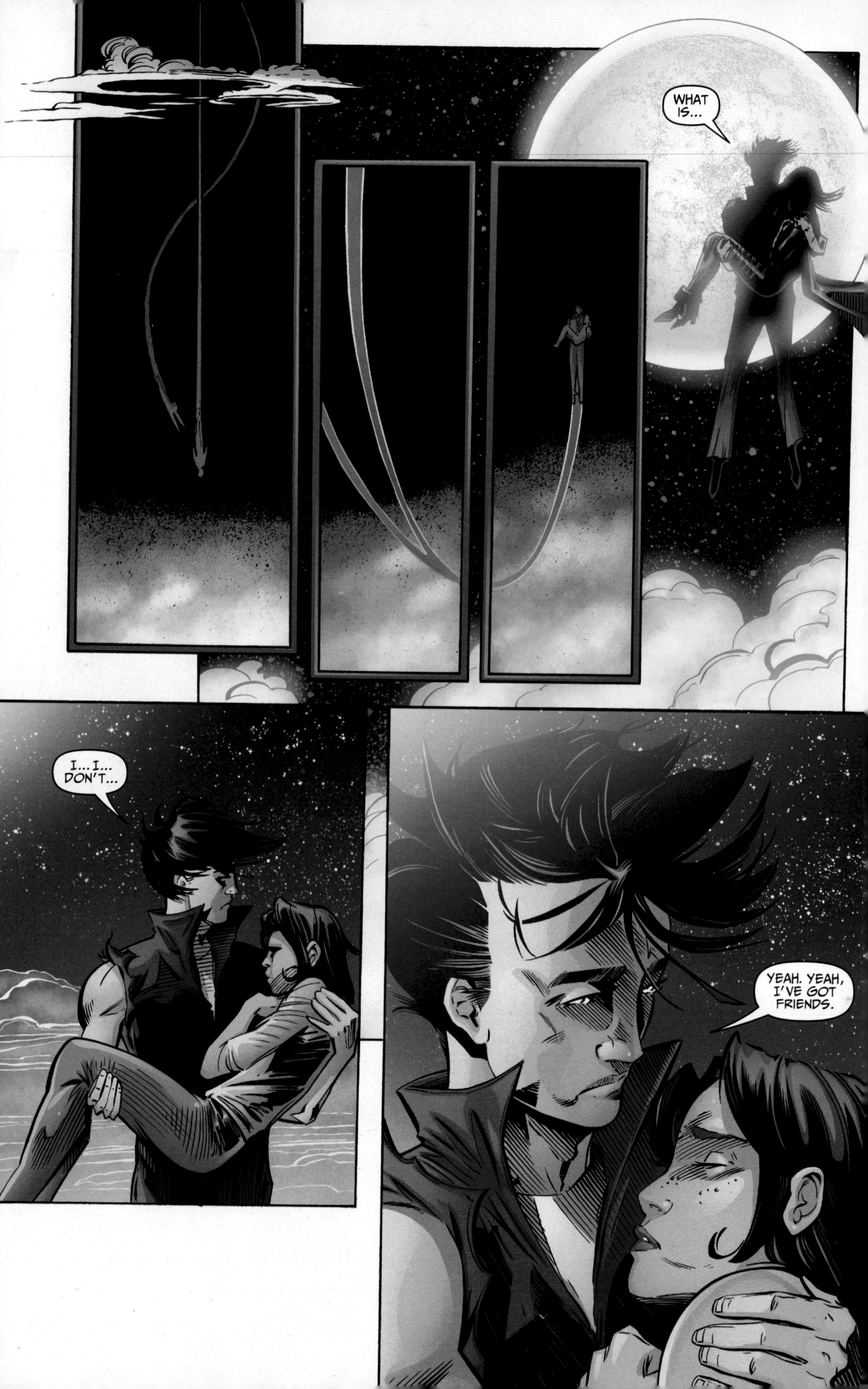
WHAT IS...
I... I... DON'T...
YEAH. YEAH, I'VE GOT FRIENDS.

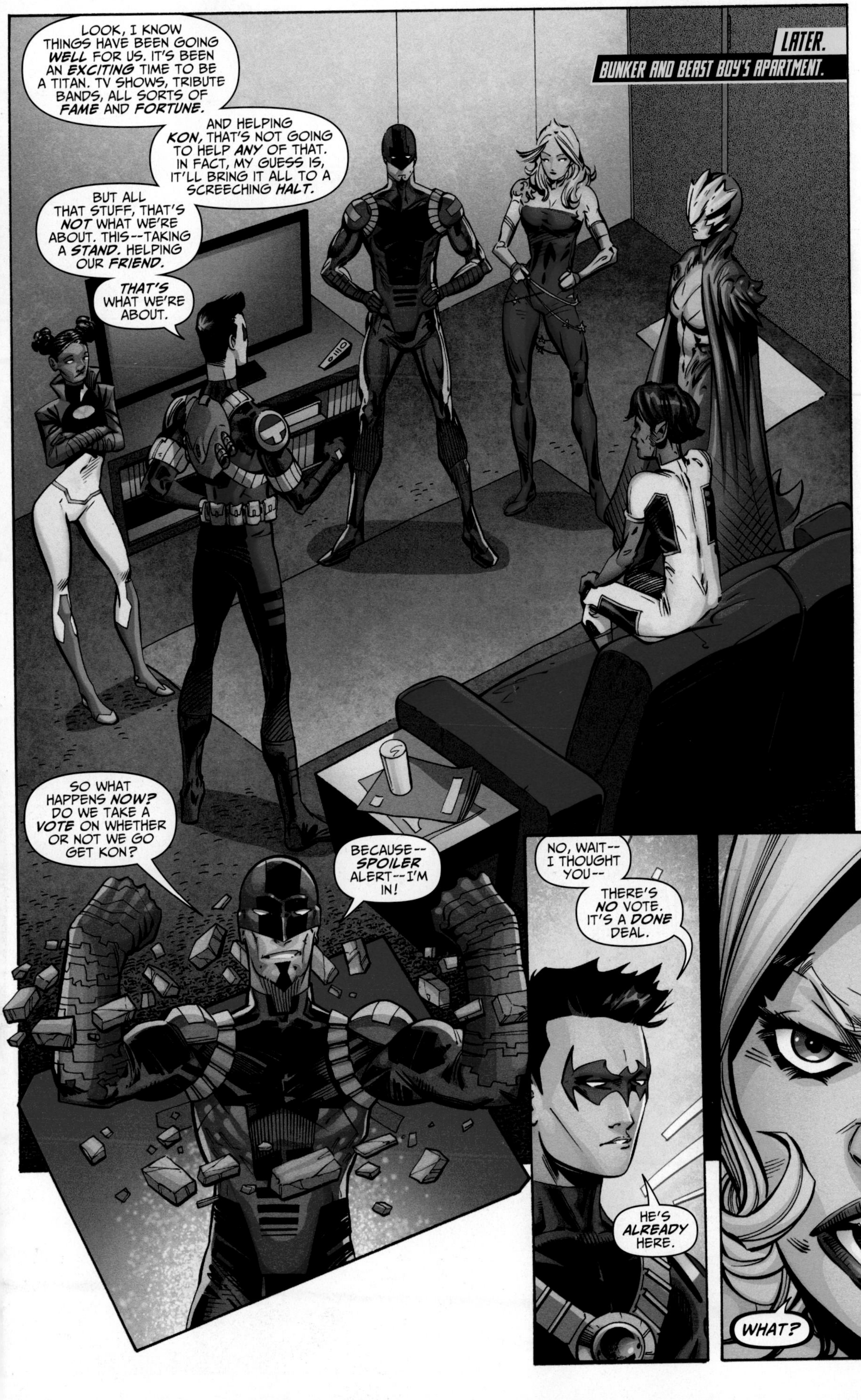
LATER.
BUNKER AND BEAST BOY'S APARTMENT.
LOOK, I KNOW THINGS HAVE BEEN GOING WELL FOR US. IT'S BEEN AN EXCITING TIME TO BE A TITAN. TV SHOWS, TRIBUTE BANDS, ALL SORTS OF FAME AND FORTUNE.
AND HELPING KON, THAT'S NOT GOING TO HELP ANY OF THAT. IN FACT, MY GUESS IS, IT'LL BRING IT ALL TO A SCREECHING HALT.
BUT ALL THAT STUFF, THAT'S NOT WHAT WE'RE ABOUT. THIS--TAKING A STAND. HELPING OUR FRIEND.
THAT'S WHAT WE'RE ABOUT.
SO WHAT HAPPENS NOW? DO WE TAKE A VOTE ON WHETHER OR NOT WE GO GET KON?
BECAUSE-- SPOILER ALERT--I'M IN!
NO, WAIT-- I THOUGHT YOU--
THERE'S NO VOTE. IT'S A DONE DEAL.
HE'S ALREADY HERE.
WHAT?

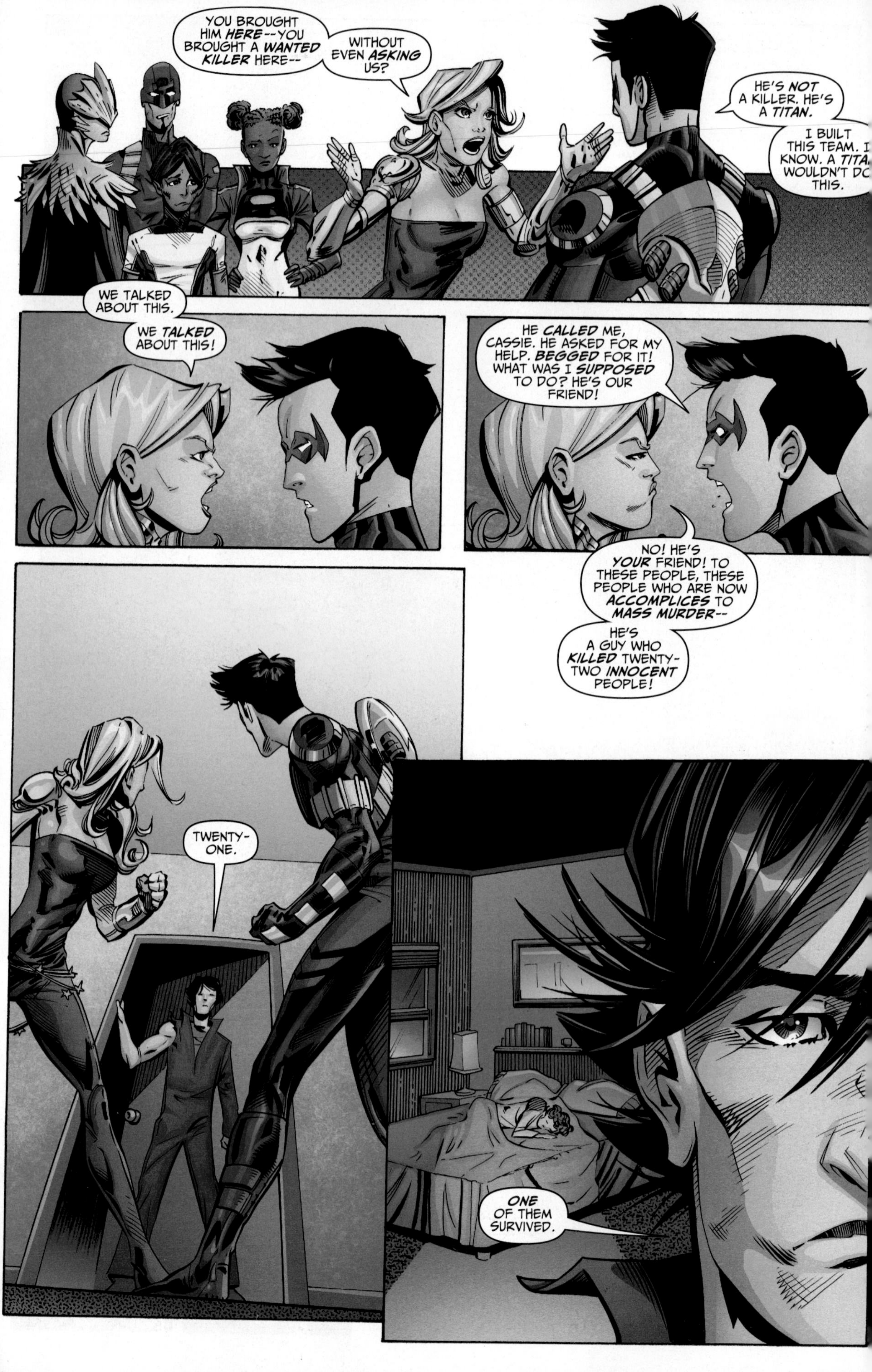
YOU BROUGHT HIM HERE--YOU BROUGHT A WANTED KILLER HERE--
WITHOUT EVEN ASKING US?
HE'S NOT A KILLER. HE'S A TITAN.
I BUILT THIS TEAM. I KNOW. A TITAN WOULDN'T DO THIS.
WE TALKED ABOUT THIS.
WE TALKED ABOUT THIS!
HE CALLED ME, CASSIE. HE ASKED FOR MY HELP. BEGGED FOR IT! WHAT WAS I SUPPOSED TO DO? HE'S OUR FRIEND!
NO! HE'S YOUR FRIEND! TO THESE PEOPLE, THESE PEOPLE WHO ARE NOW ACCOMPLICES TO MASS MURDER--
HE'S A GUY WHO KILLED TWENTY-TWO INNOCENT PEOPLE!
TWENTY-ONE.
ONE OF THEM SURVIVED.

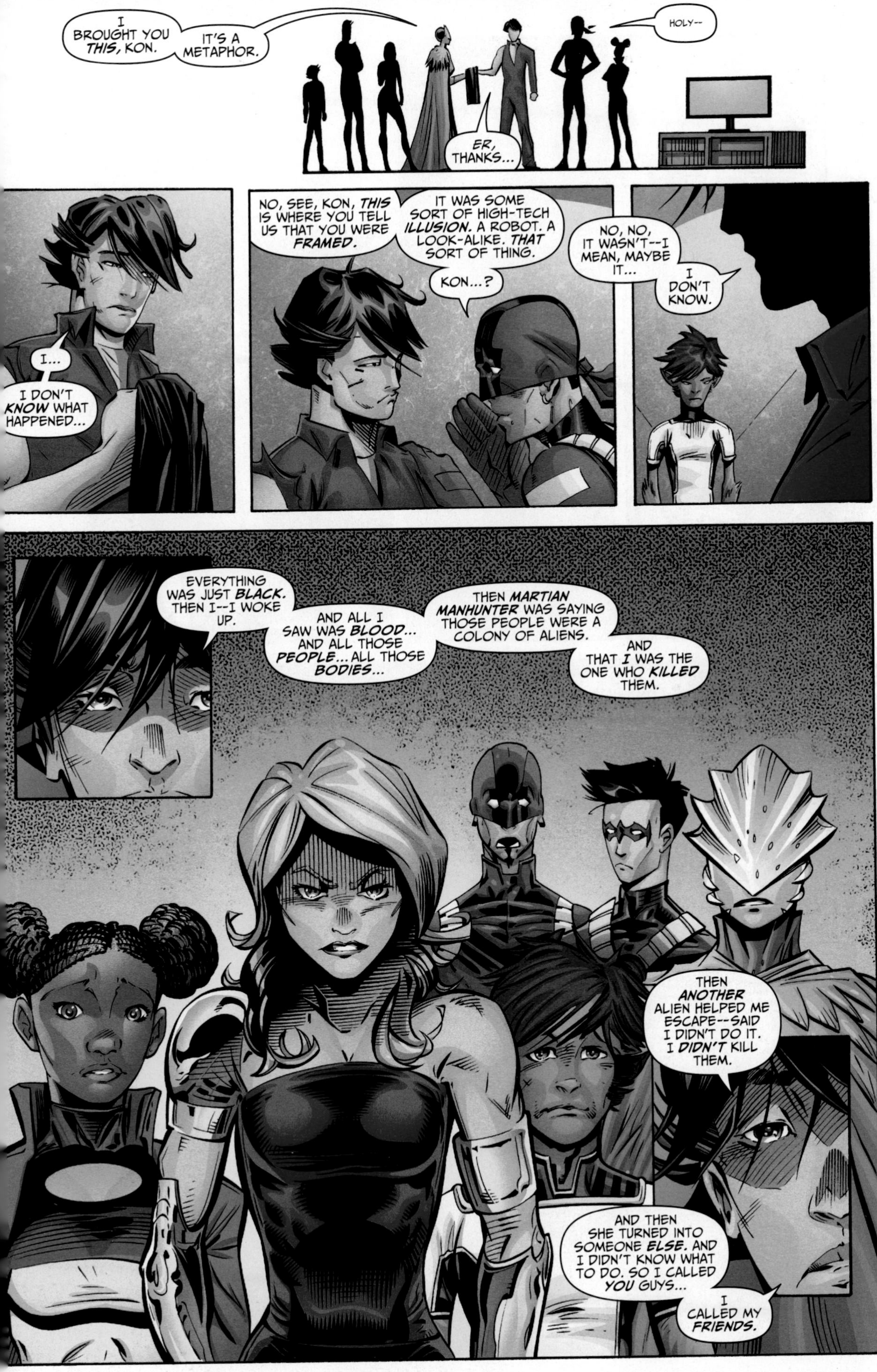
I BROUGHT YOU *THIS*, KON.
IT'S A METAPHOR.
ER, THANKS...
HOLY--
I... I DON'T *KNOW* WHAT HAPPENED...
NO, SEE, KON, *THIS* IS WHERE YOU TELL US THAT YOU WERE *FRAMED*.
IT WAS SOME SORT OF HIGH-TECH *ILLUSION*. A ROBOT. A LOOK-ALIKE. *THAT* SORT OF THING.
KON...?
NO, NO, IT WASN'T--I MEAN, MAYBE IT...
I DON'T KNOW.
EVERYTHING WAS JUST *BLACK*. THEN I--I WOKE UP.
AND ALL I SAW WAS *BLOOD*... AND ALL THOSE *PEOPLE*... ALL THOSE *BODIES*...
THEN *MARTIAN MANHUNTER* WAS SAYING THOSE PEOPLE WERE A COLONY OF ALIENS.
AND THAT *I* WAS THE ONE WHO *KILLED* THEM.
THEN *ANOTHER* ALIEN HELPED ME ESCAPE--SAID I DIDN'T DO IT. I *DIDN'T* KILL THEM.
AND THEN SHE TURNED INTO SOMEONE *ELSE*. AND I DIDN'T KNOW WHAT TO DO. SO I CALLED *YOU* GUYS...
I CALLED MY *FRIENDS*.

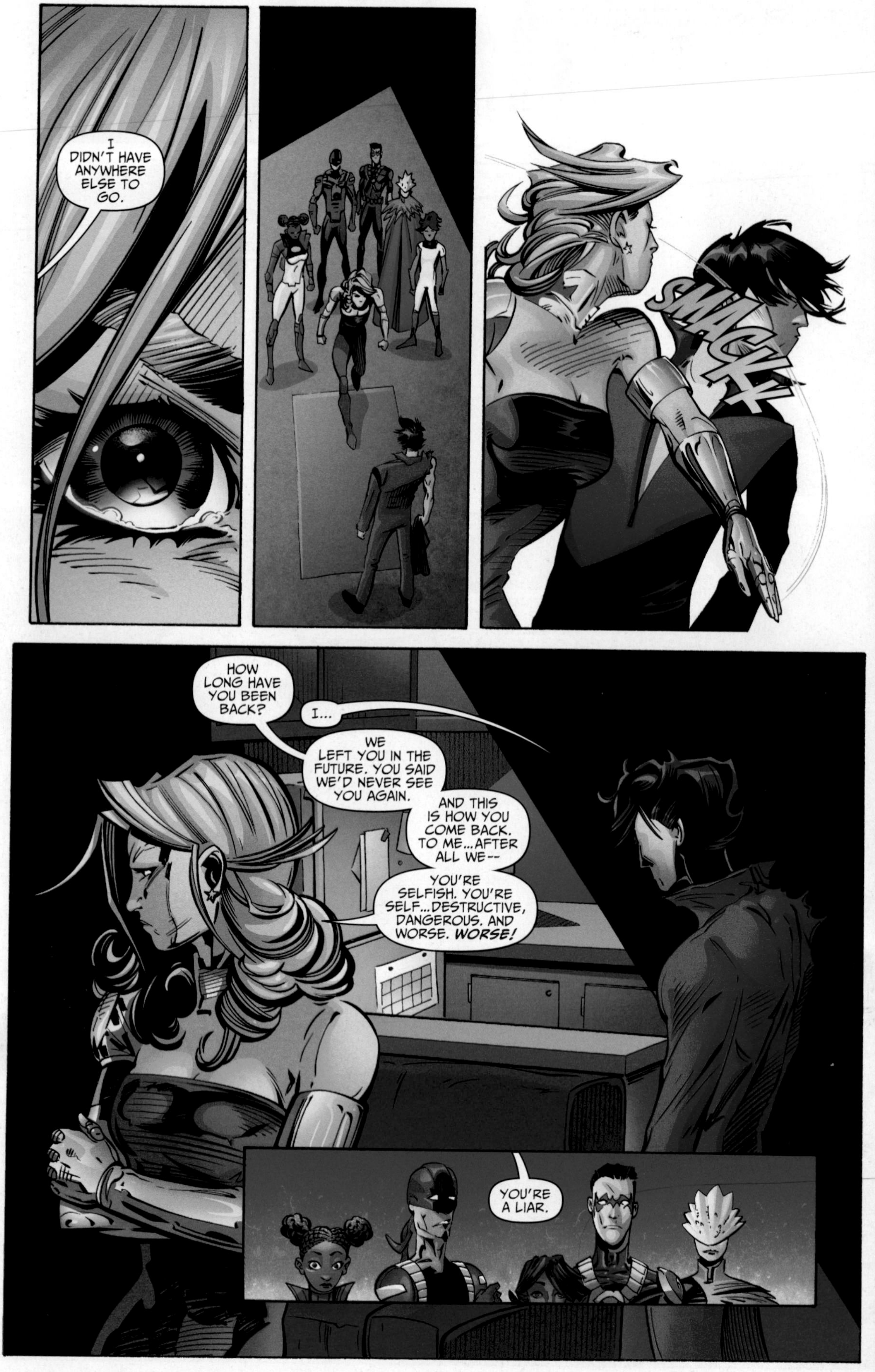
I DIDN'T HAVE ANYWHERE ELSE TO GO.
SMACK!
HOW LONG HAVE YOU BEEN BACK?
I...
WE LEFT YOU IN THE FUTURE. YOU SAID WE'D NEVER SEE YOU AGAIN.
AND THIS IS HOW YOU COME BACK. TO ME...AFTER ALL WE--
YOU'RE SELFISH. YOU'RE SELF...DESTRUCTIVE, DANGEROUS. AND WORSE. ***WORSE!***
YOU'RE A LIAR.

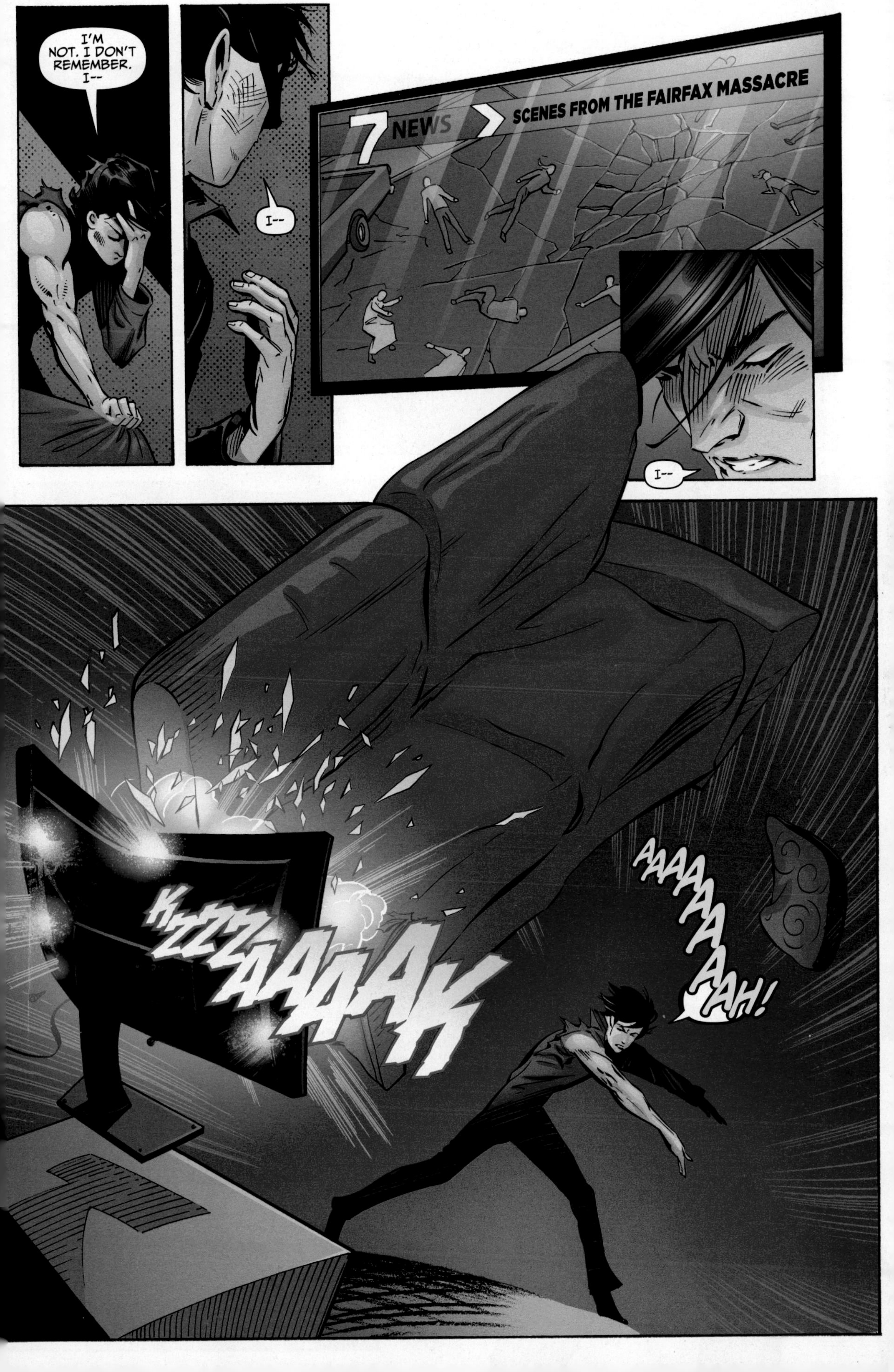
I'M NOT. I DON'T REMEMBER. I--
I--
7 NEWS
SCENES FROM THE FAIRFAX MASSACRE
I--
KZZZAAAAK
AAAAAAAAH!

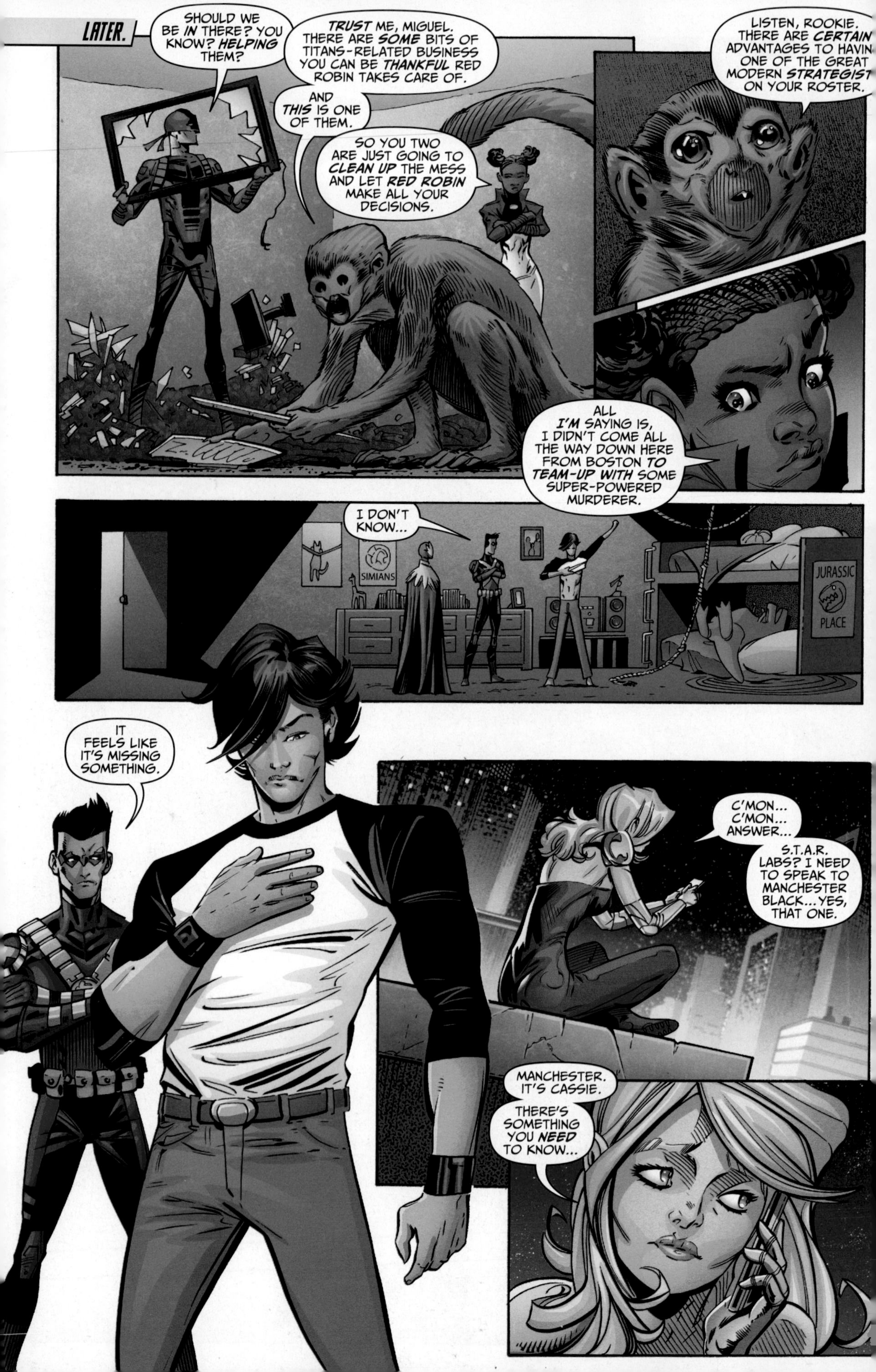
LATER.
SHOULD WE BE IN THERE? YOU KNOW? HELPING THEM?
TRUST ME, MIGUEL. THERE ARE SOME BITS OF TITANS-RELATED BUSINESS YOU CAN BE THANKFUL RED ROBIN TAKES CARE OF.
AND THIS IS ONE OF THEM.
SO YOU TWO ARE JUST GOING TO CLEAN UP THE MESS AND LET RED ROBIN MAKE ALL YOUR DECISIONS.
LISTEN, ROOKIE. THERE ARE CERTAIN ADVANTAGES TO HAVIN ONE OF THE GREAT MODERN STRATEGIST ON YOUR ROSTER.
ALL I'M SAYING IS, I DIDN'T COME ALL THE WAY DOWN HERE FROM BOSTON TO TEAM-UP WITH SOME SUPER-POWERED MURDERER.
I DON'T KNOW...
SIMIANS
JURASSIC PLACE
IT FEELS LIKE IT'S MISSING SOMETHING.
C'MON... C'MON... ANSWER...
S.T.A.R. LABS? I NEED TO SPEAK TO MANCHESTER BLACK... YES, THAT ONE.
MANCHESTER. IT'S CASSIE.
THERE'S SOMETHING YOU NEED TO KNOW...

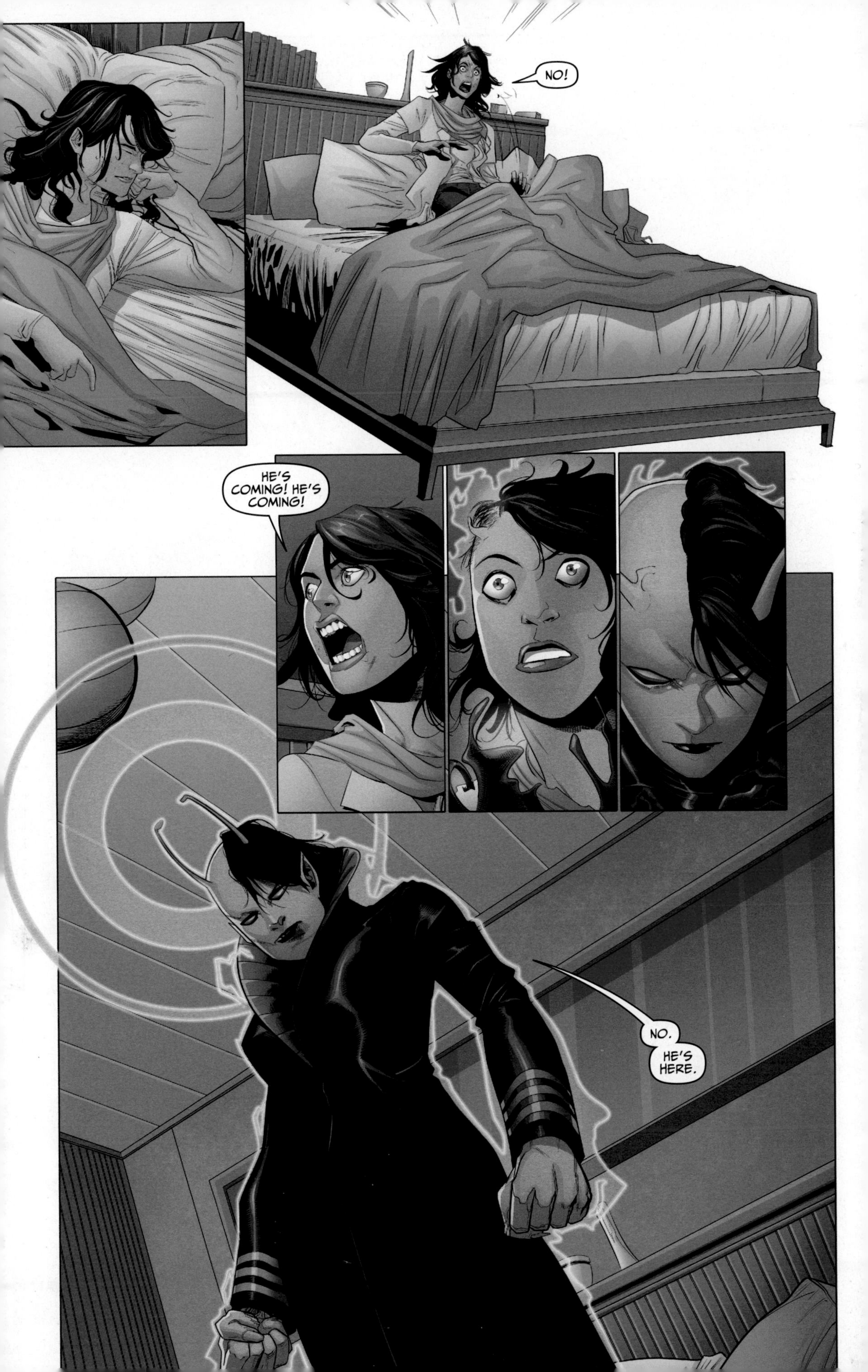
NO!
HE'S COMING! HE'S COMING!
NO. HE'S HERE.

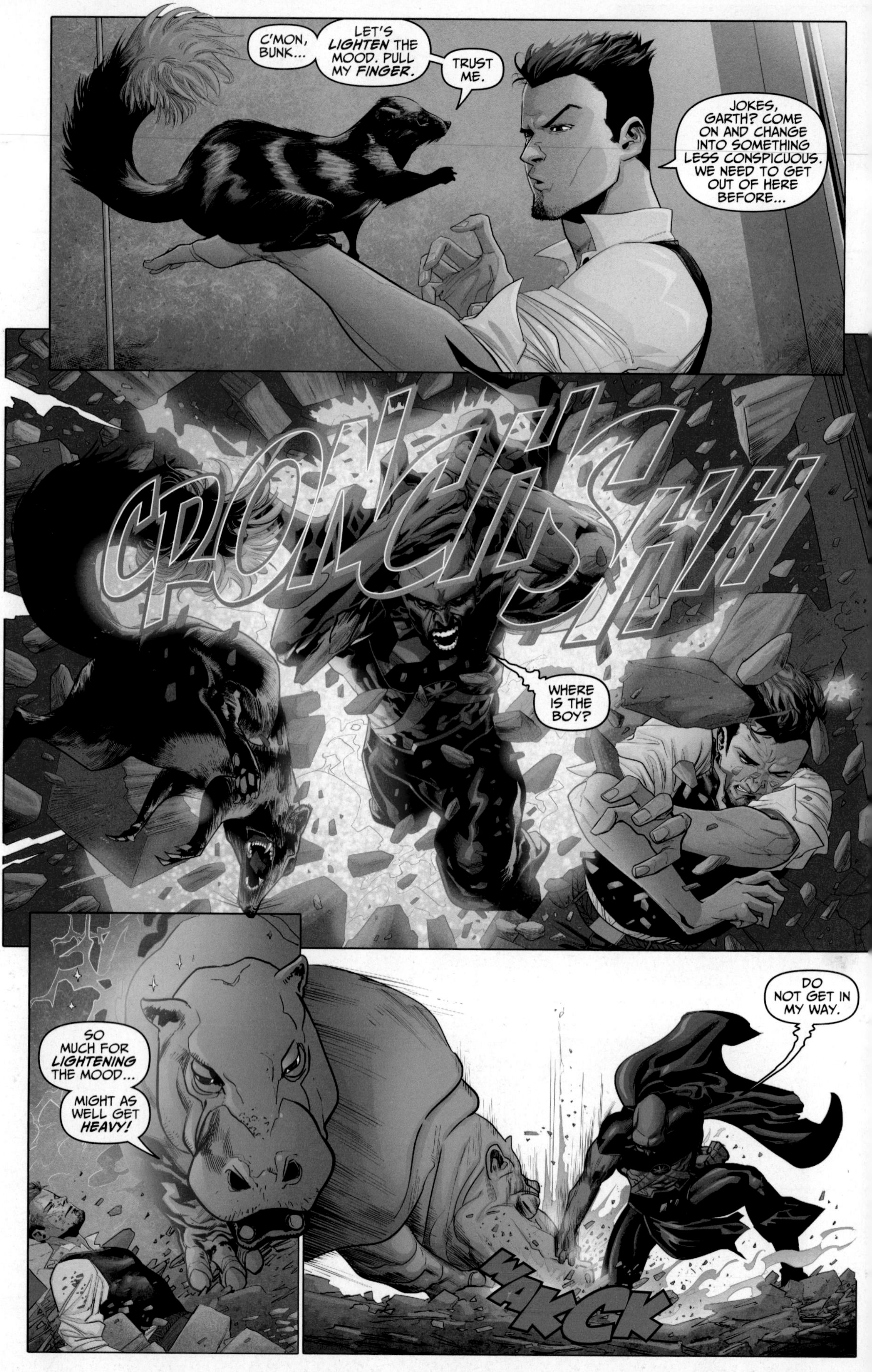
C'MON, BUNK...
LET'S LIGHTEN THE MOOD. PULL MY FINGER.
TRUST ME.
JOKES, GARTH? COME ON AND CHANGE INTO SOMETHING LESS CONSPICUOUS. WE NEED TO GET OUT OF HERE BEFORE...
CRUNCHSHH
WHERE IS THE BOY?
SO MUCH FOR LIGHTENING THE MOOD...
MIGHT AS WELL GET HEAVY!
DO NOT GET IN MY WAY.
WAKCK

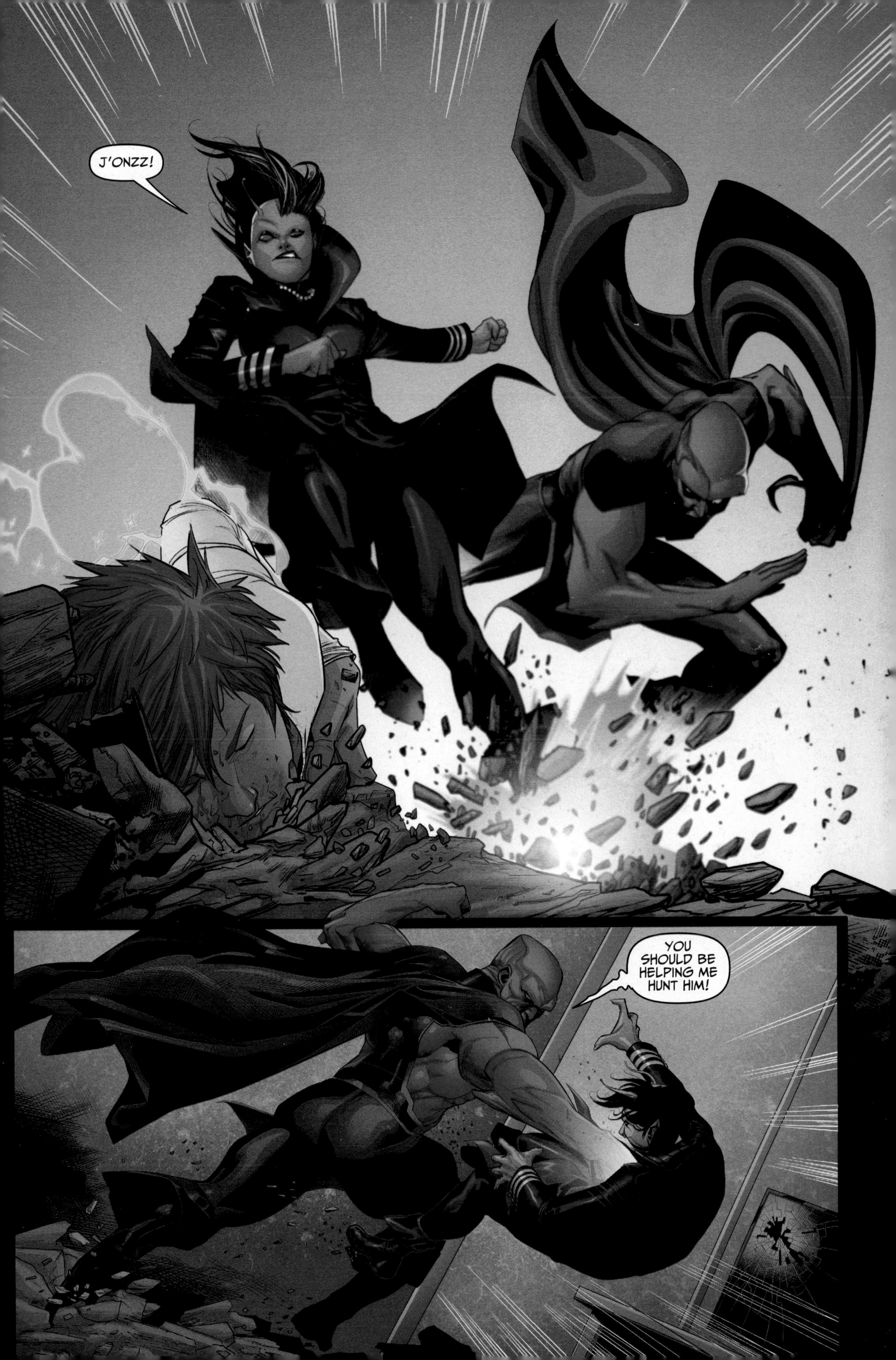
J'ONZZ!
YOU SHOULD BE HELPING ME HUNT HIM!

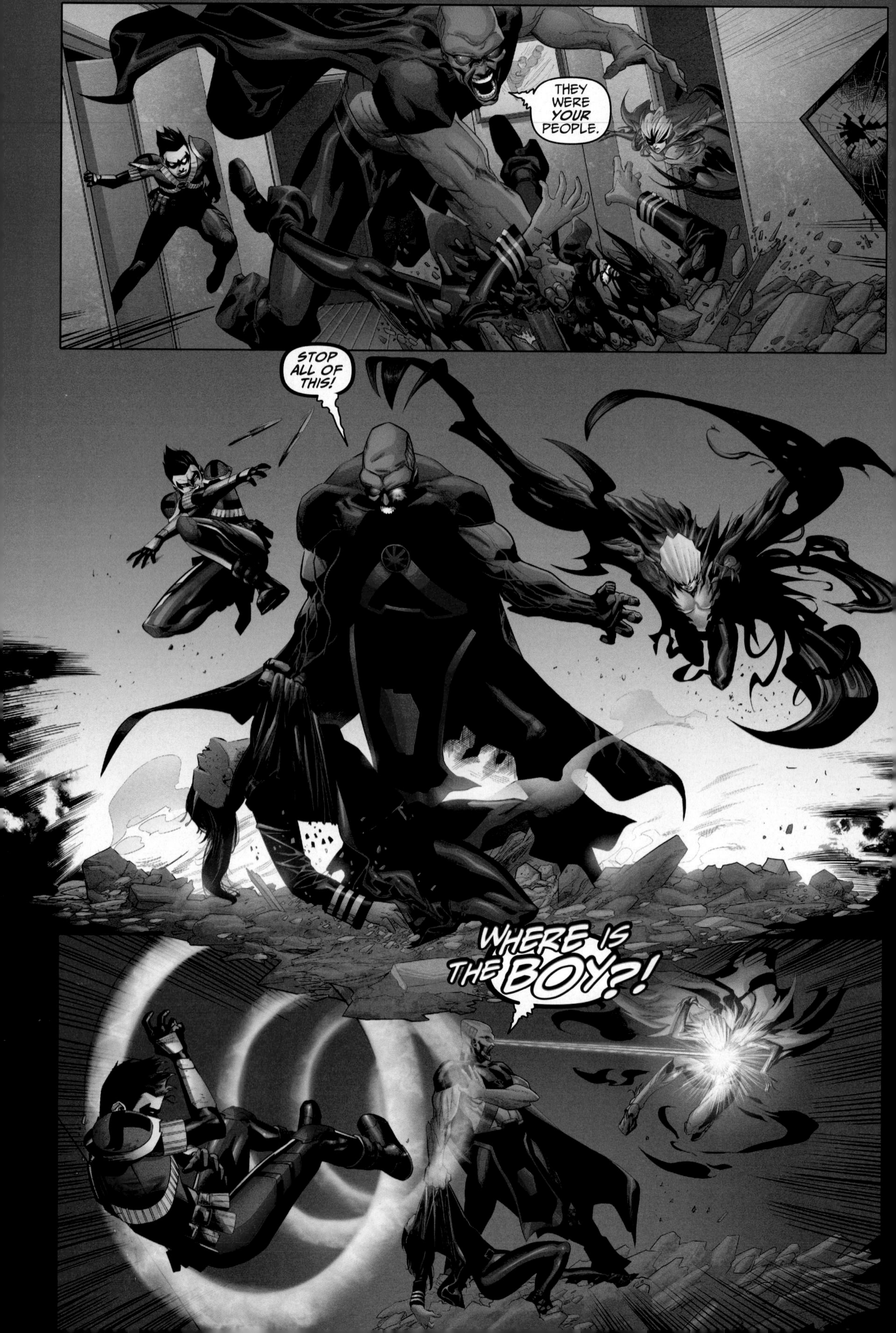
THEY WERE YOUR PEOPLE.
STOP ALL OF THIS!
WHERE IS THE BOY?!

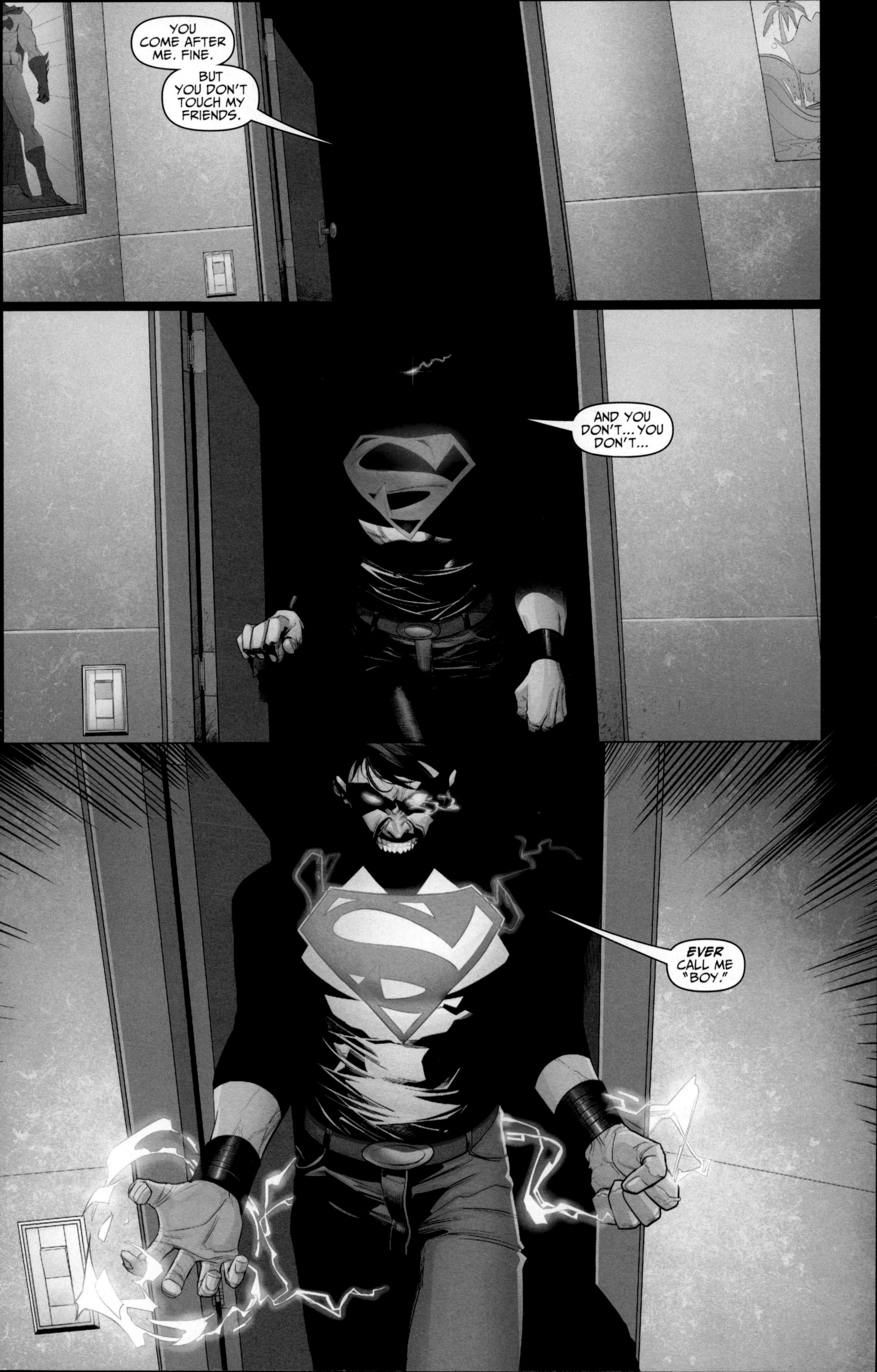
YOU COME AFTER ME. FINE.
BUT YOU DON'T TOUCH MY FRIENDS.
AND YOU DON'T... YOU DON'T...
EVER CALL ME "BOY."

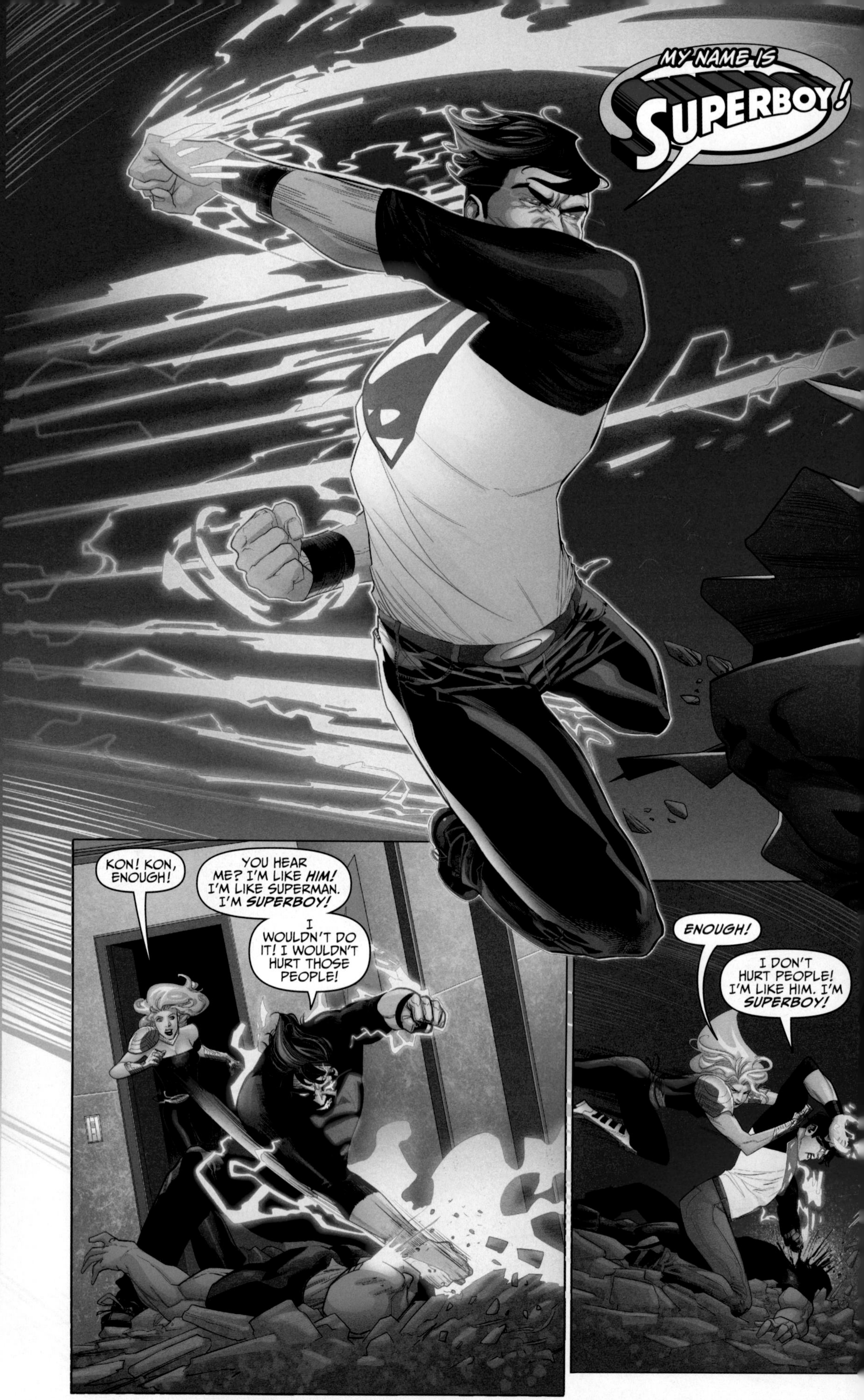
MY NAME IS SUPERBOY!
KON! KON, ENOUGH!
YOU HEAR ME? I'M LIKE HIM! I'M LIKE SUPERMAN. I'M SUPERBOY!
I WOULDN'T DO IT! I WOULDN'T HURT THOSE PEOPLE!
ENOUGH!
I DON'T HURT PEOPLE! I'M LIKE HIM. I'M SUPERBOY!

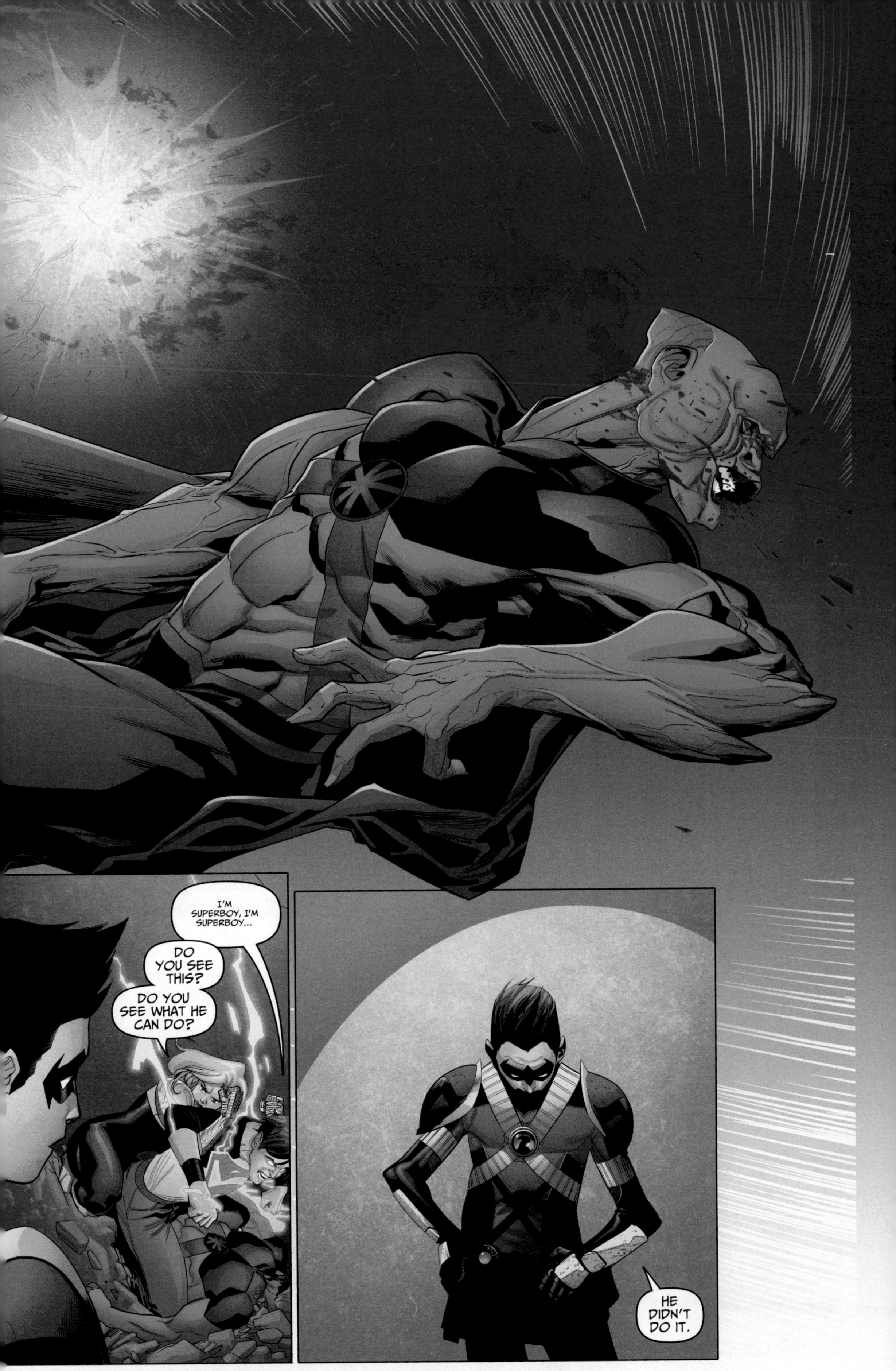
I'M SUPERBOY, I'M SUPERBOY...
DO YOU SEE THIS?
DO YOU SEE WHAT HE CAN DO?
HE DIDN'T DO IT.

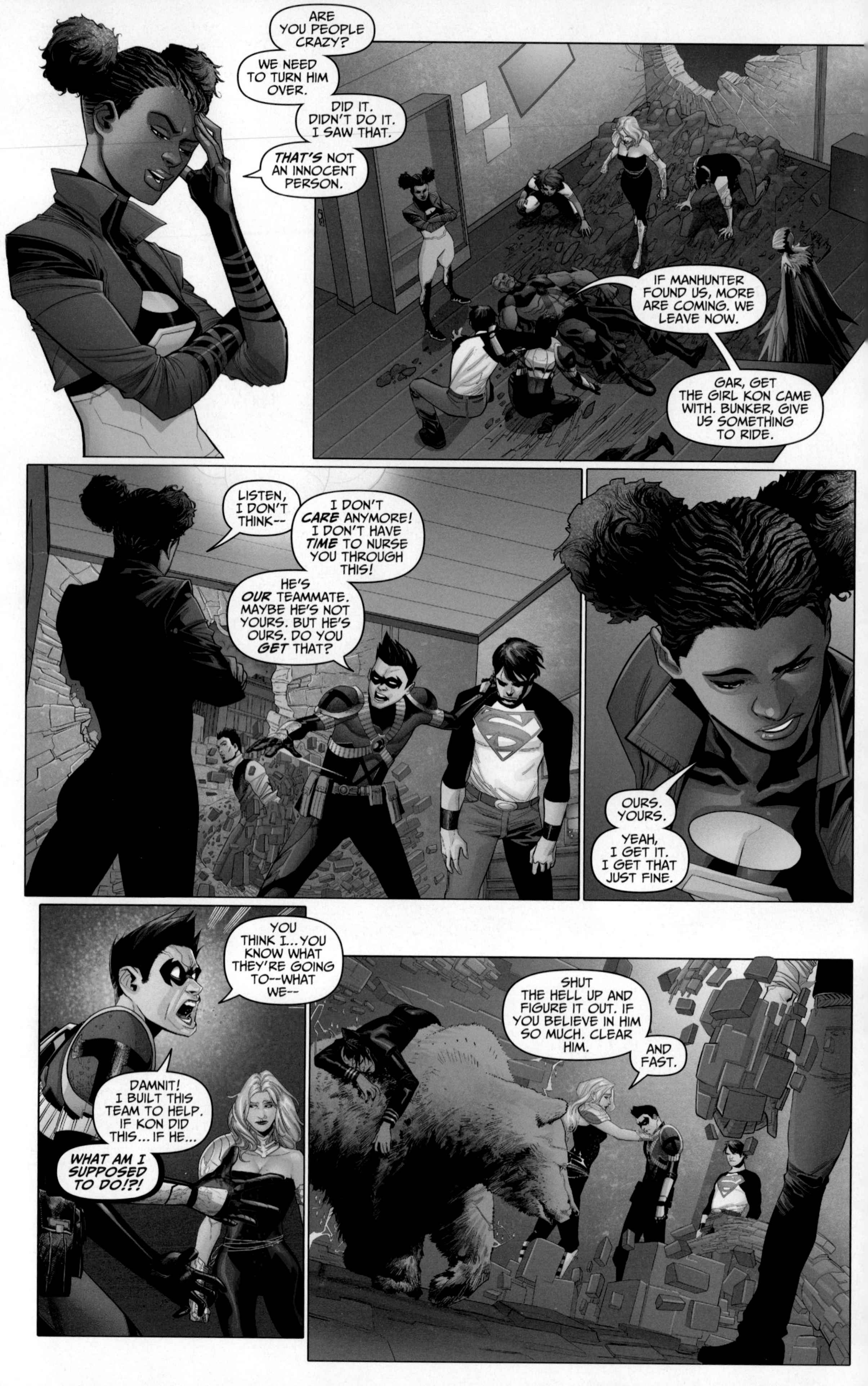
ARE YOU PEOPLE CRAZY?
WE NEED TO TURN HIM OVER.
DID IT. DIDN'T DO IT. I SAW THAT.
THAT'S NOT AN INNOCENT PERSON.
IF MANHUNTER FOUND US, MORE ARE COMING. WE LEAVE NOW.
GAR, GET THE GIRL KON CAME WITH. BUNKER, GIVE US SOMETHING TO RIDE.
LISTEN, I DON'T THINK--
I DON'T CARE ANYMORE! I DON'T HAVE TIME TO NURSE YOU THROUGH THIS!
HE'S OUR TEAMMATE. MAYBE HE'S NOT YOURS. BUT HE'S OURS. DO YOU GET THAT?
OURS. YOURS.
YEAH, I GET IT. I GET THAT JUST FINE.
YOU THINK I... YOU KNOW WHAT THEY'RE GOING TO--WHAT WE--
DAMNIT! I BUILT THIS TEAM TO HELP. IF KON DID THIS... IF HE...
WHAT AM I SUPPOSED TO DO!?!
SHUT THE HELL UP AND FIGURE IT OUT. IF YOU BELIEVE IN HIM SO MUCH. CLEAR HIM.
AND FAST.

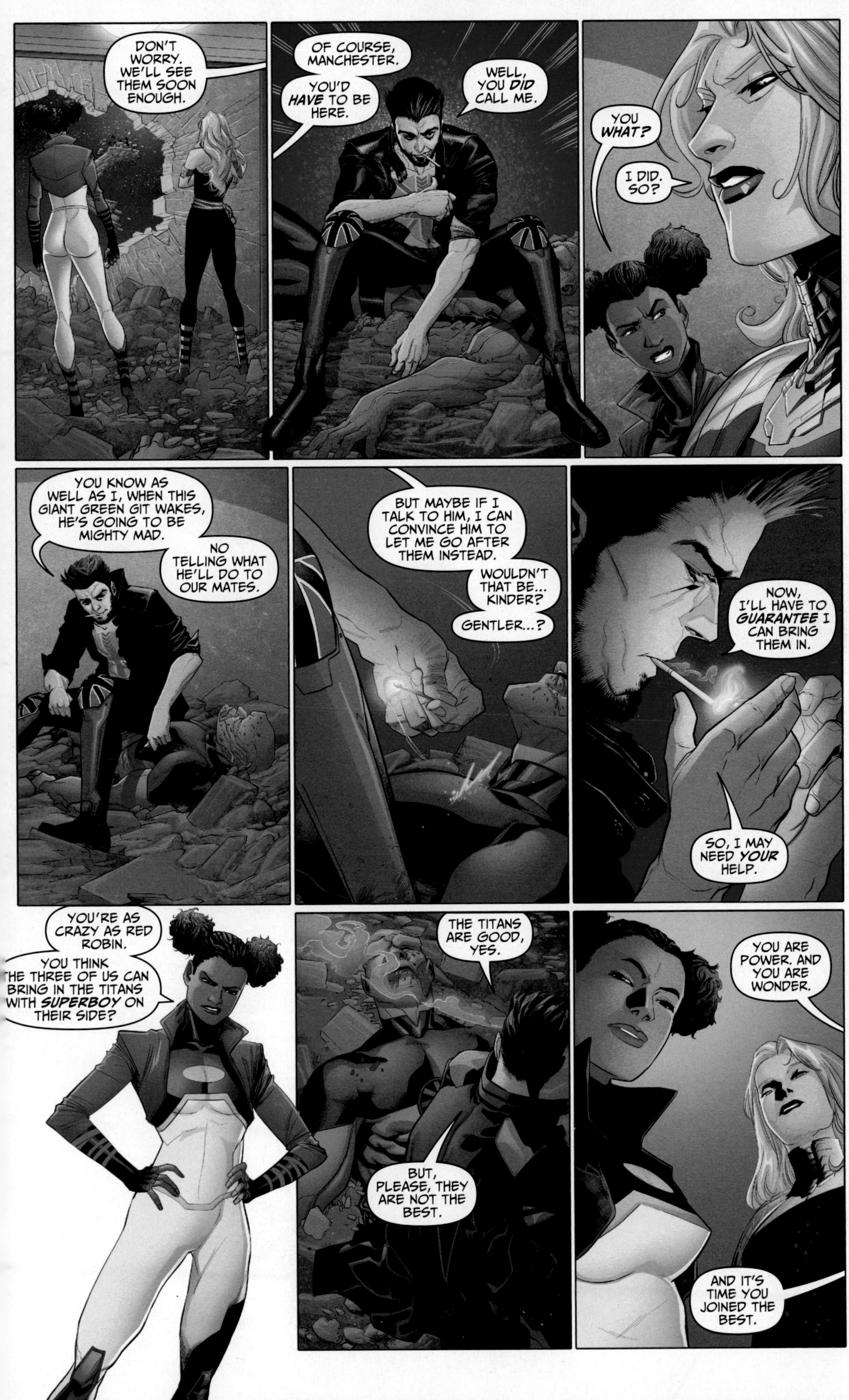

DON'T WORRY. WE'LL SEE THEM SOON ENOUGH.
OF COURSE, MANCHESTER.
YOU'D HAVE TO BE HERE.
WELL, YOU DID CALL ME.
YOU WHAT?
I DID. SO?
YOU KNOW AS WELL AS I, WHEN THIS GIANT GREEN GIT WAKES, HE'S GOING TO BE MIGHTY MAD.
NO TELLING WHAT HE'LL DO TO OUR MATES.
BUT MAYBE IF I TALK TO HIM, I CAN CONVINCE HIM TO LET ME GO AFTER THEM INSTEAD.
WOULDN'T THAT BE... KINDER?
GENTLER...?
NOW, I'LL HAVE TO GUARANTEE I CAN BRING THEM IN.
SO, I MAY NEED YOUR HELP.
YOU'RE AS CRAZY AS RED ROBIN.
YOU THINK THE THREE OF US CAN BRING IN THE TITANS WITH SUPERBOY ON THEIR SIDE?
THE TITANS ARE GOOD, YES.
BUT, PLEASE, THEY ARE NOT THE BEST.
YOU ARE POWER. AND YOU ARE WONDER.
AND IT'S TIME YOU JOINED THE BEST.

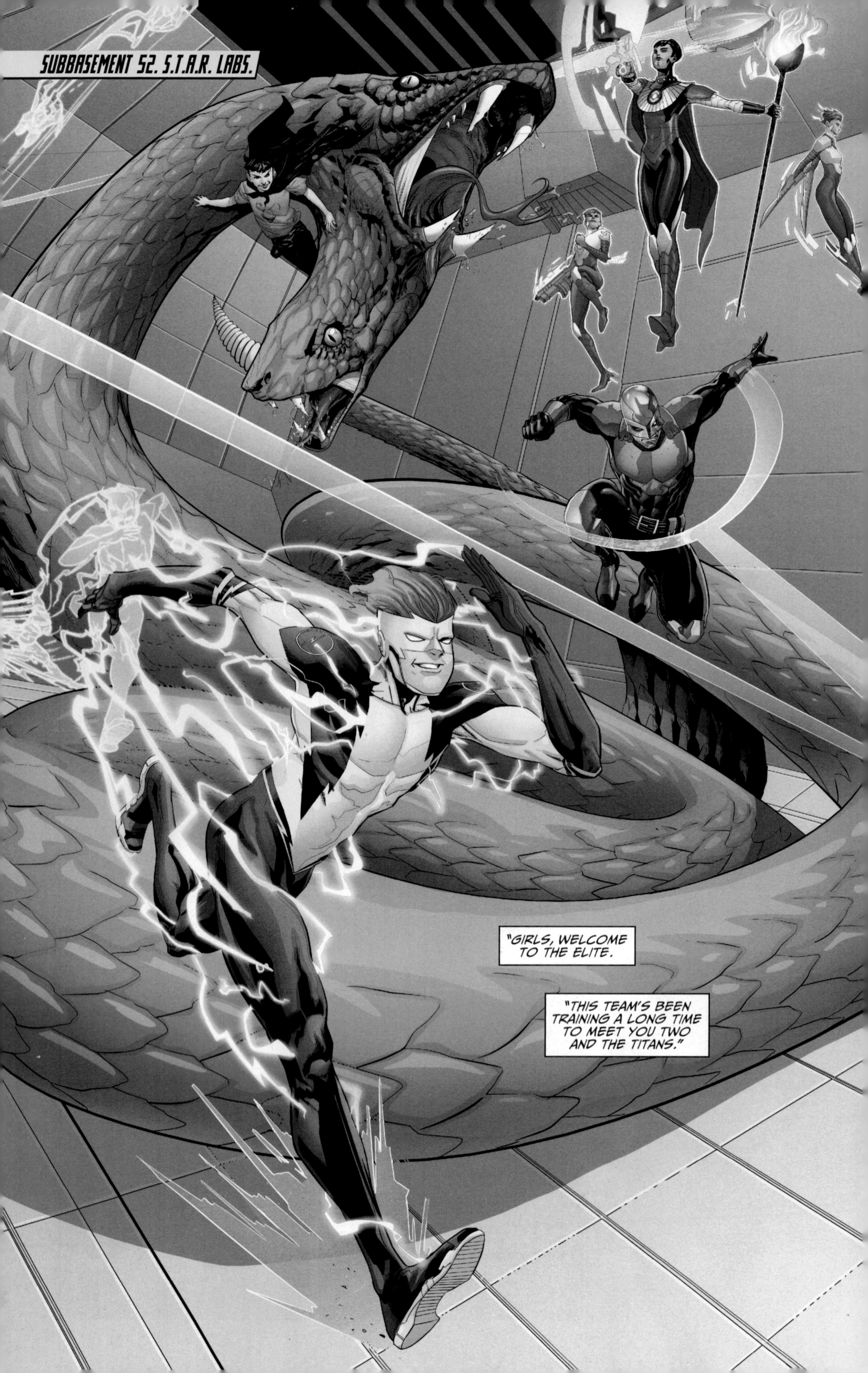
SUBBASEMENT 52. S.T.A.R. LABS.
"GIRLS, WELCOME TO THE ELITE.
"THIS TEAM'S BEEN TRAINING A LONG TIME TO MEET YOU TWO AND THE TITANS."

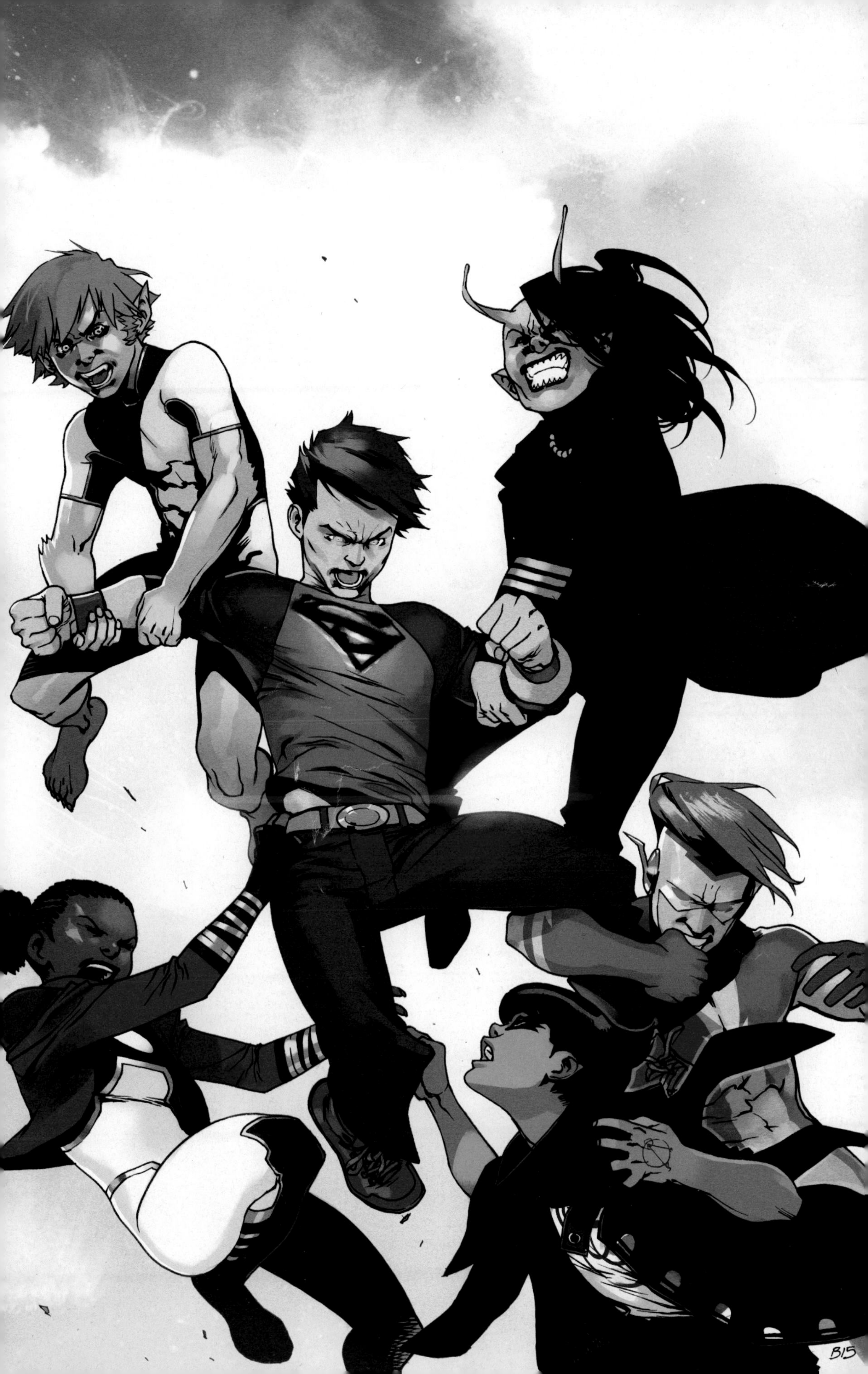

ROGUE TARGETS PART ONE

WILL PFEIFER writer KENNETH ROCAFORT artist DAN BROWN colorist JOHN J. HILL letterer cover art by BENGAL

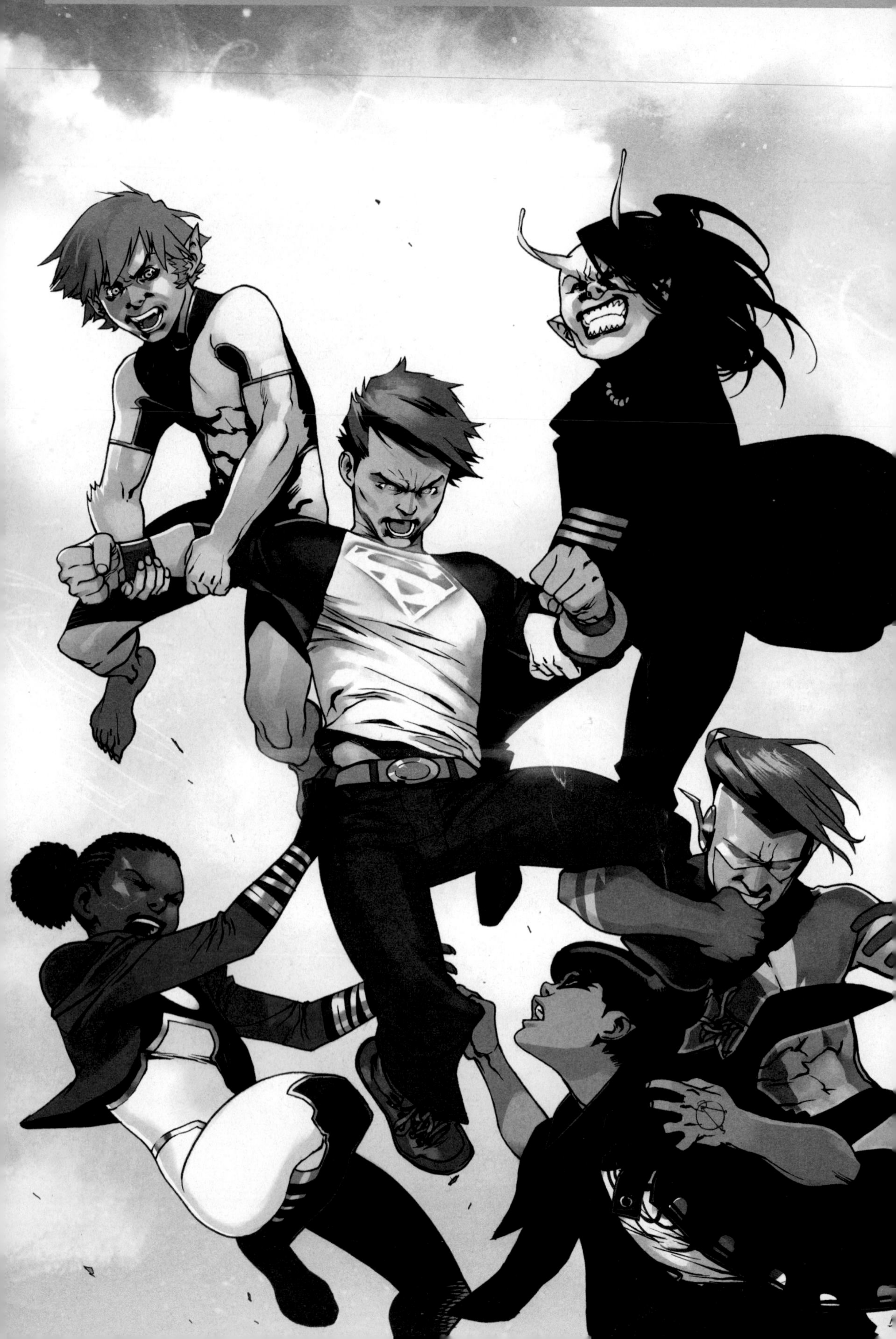

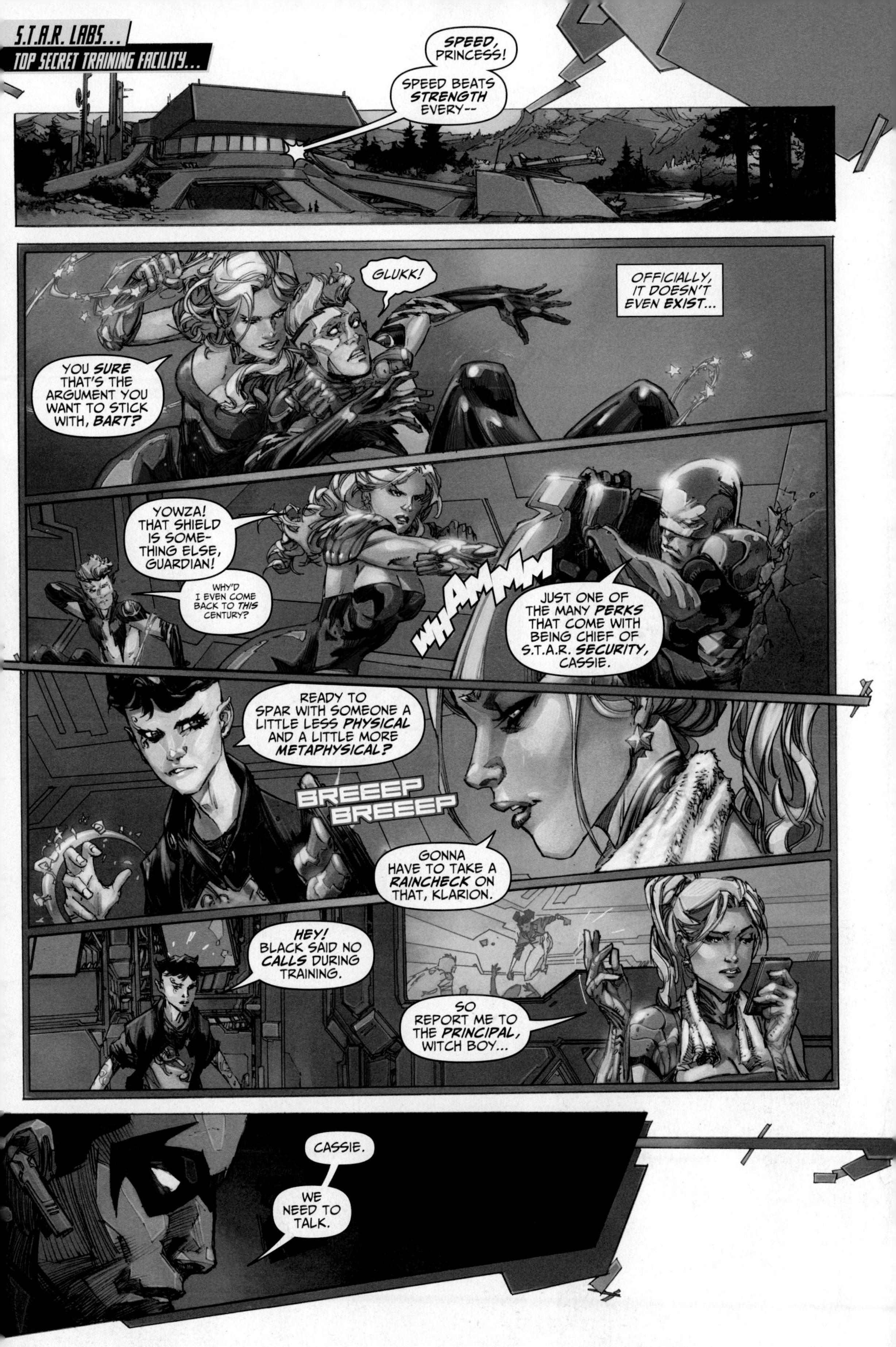
S.T.A.R. LABS...
TOP SECRET TRAINING FACILITY...
SPEED, PRINCESS!
SPEED BEATS STRENGTH EVERY--
GLUKK!
OFFICIALLY, IT DOESN'T EVEN EXIST...
YOU SURE THAT'S THE ARGUMENT YOU WANT TO STICK WITH, BART?
YOWZA! THAT SHIELD IS SOME-THING ELSE, GUARDIAN!
WHY'D I EVEN COME BACK TO THIS CENTURY?
WHAMMM
JUST ONE OF THE MANY PERKS THAT COME WITH BEING CHIEF OF S.T.A.R. SECURITY, CASSIE.
READY TO SPAR WITH SOMEONE A LITTLE LESS PHYSICAL AND A LITTLE MORE METAPHYSICAL?
BREEEP BREEEP
GONNA HAVE TO TAKE A RAINCHECK ON THAT, KLARION.
HEY! BLACK SAID NO CALLS DURING TRAINING.
SO REPORT ME TO THE PRINCIPAL, WITCH BOY...
CASSIE.
WE NEED TO TALK.

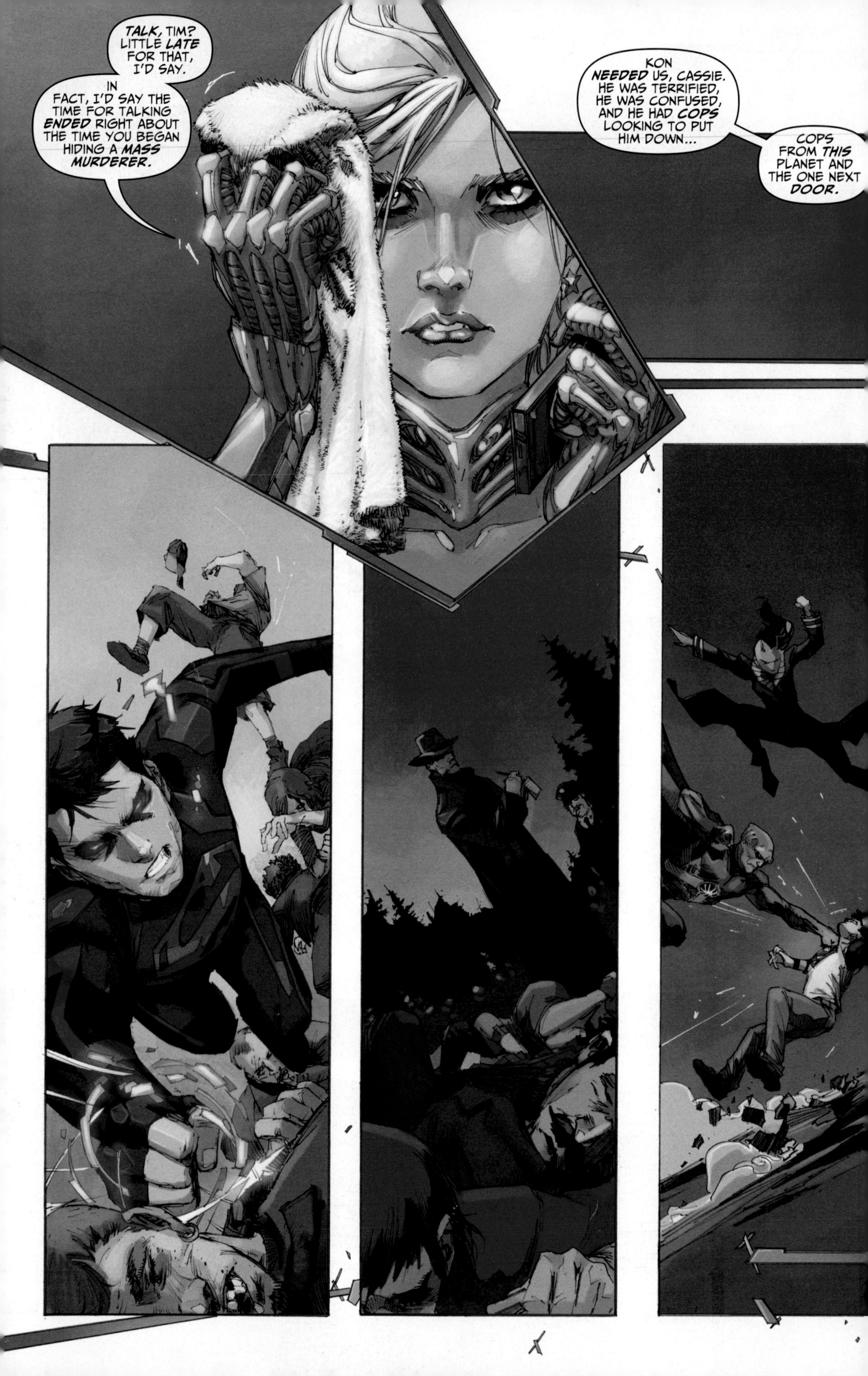
TALK, TIM? LITTLE LATE FOR THAT, I'D SAY.
IN FACT, I'D SAY THE TIME FOR TALKING ENDED RIGHT ABOUT THE TIME YOU BEGAN HIDING A MASS MURDERER.
KON NEEDED US, CASSIE. HE WAS TERRIFIED, HE WAS CONFUSED, AND HE HAD COPS LOOKING TO PUT HIM DOWN...
COPS FROM THIS PLANET AND THE ONE NEXT DOOR.

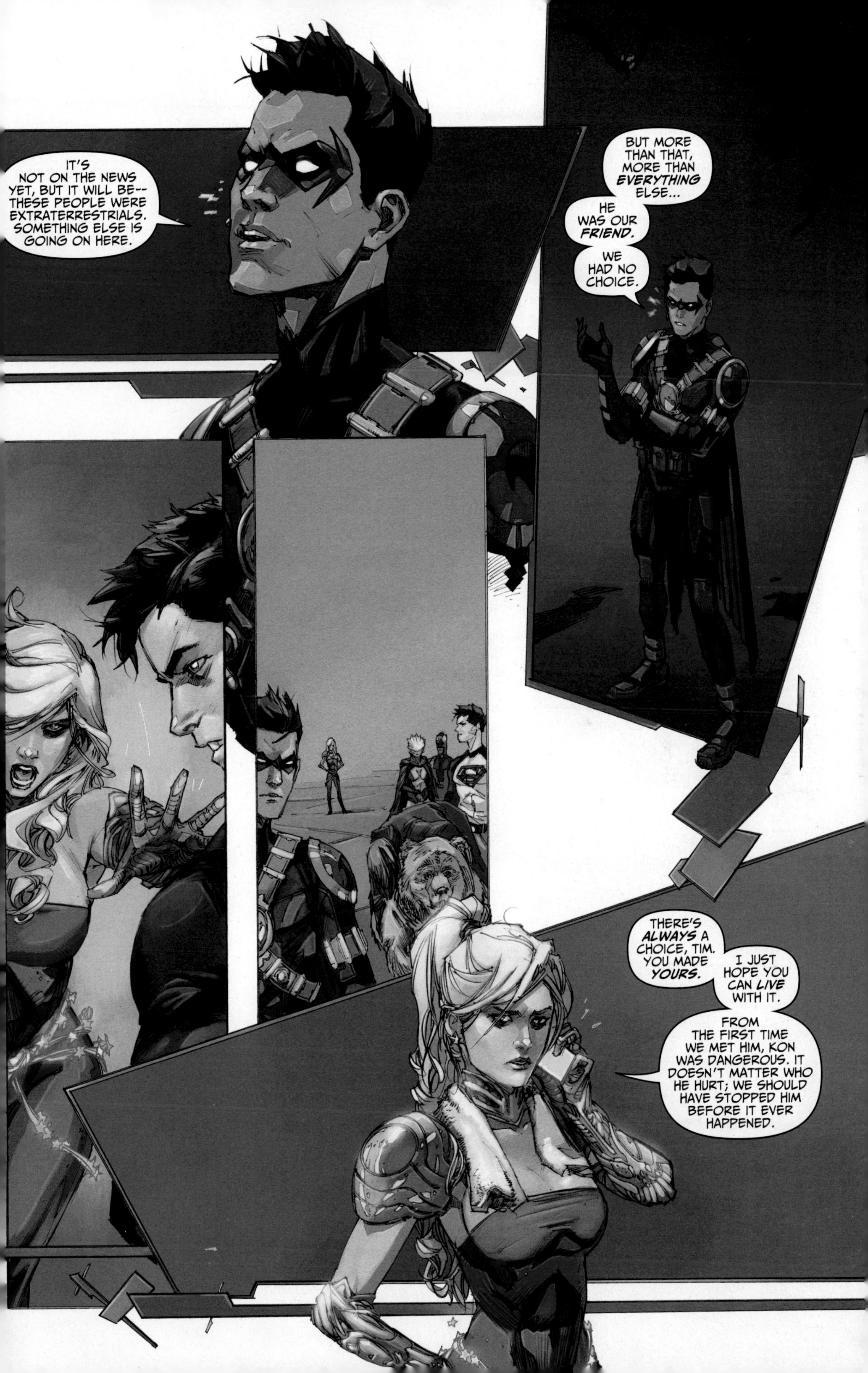

IT'S NOT ON THE NEWS YET, BUT IT WILL BE-- THESE PEOPLE WERE EXTRATERRESTRIALS. SOMETHING ELSE IS GOING ON HERE.
BUT MORE THAN THAT, MORE THAN *EVERYTHING* ELSE...
HE WAS OUR *FRIEND.*
WE HAD NO CHOICE.
THERE'S *ALWAYS* A CHOICE, TIM. YOU MADE *YOURS.*
I JUST HOPE YOU CAN *LIVE* WITH IT.
FROM THE FIRST TIME WE MET HIM, KON WAS DANGEROUS. IT DOESN'T MATTER WHO HE HURT; WE SHOULD HAVE STOPPED HIM BEFORE IT EVER HAPPENED.

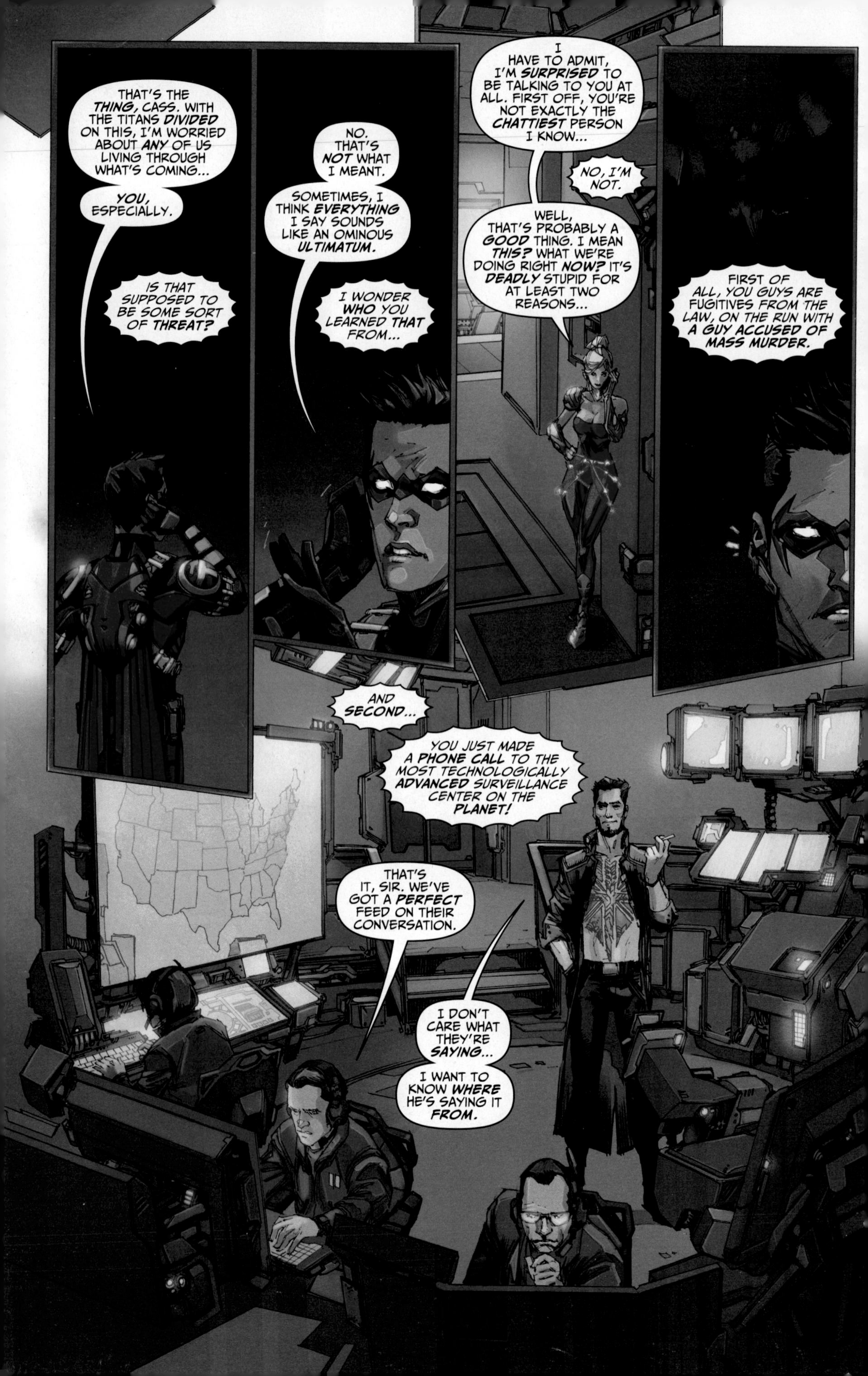

THAT'S THE THING, CASS. WITH THE TITANS DIVIDED ON THIS, I'M WORRIED ABOUT ANY OF US LIVING THROUGH WHAT'S COMING...
YOU, ESPECIALLY.
IS THAT SUPPOSED TO BE SOME SORT OF THREAT?
NO. THAT'S NOT WHAT I MEANT.
SOMETIMES, I THINK EVERYTHING I SAY SOUNDS LIKE AN OMINOUS ULTIMATUM.
I WONDER WHO YOU LEARNED THAT FROM...
I HAVE TO ADMIT, I'M SURPRISED TO BE TALKING TO YOU AT ALL. FIRST OFF, YOU'RE NOT EXACTLY THE CHATTIEST PERSON I KNOW...
NO, I'M NOT.
WELL, THAT'S PROBABLY A GOOD THING. I MEAN THIS? WHAT WE'RE DOING RIGHT NOW? IT'S DEADLY STUPID FOR AT LEAST TWO REASONS...
FIRST OF ALL, YOU GUYS ARE FUGITIVES FROM THE LAW, ON THE RUN WITH A GUY ACCUSED OF MASS MURDER.
AND SECOND...
YOU JUST MADE A PHONE CALL TO THE MOST TECHNOLOGICALLY ADVANCED SURVEILLANCE CENTER ON THE PLANET!
THAT'S IT, SIR. WE'VE GOT A PERFECT FEED ON THEIR CONVERSATION.
I DON'T CARE WHAT THEY'RE SAYING...
I WANT TO KNOW WHERE HE'S SAYING IT FROM.

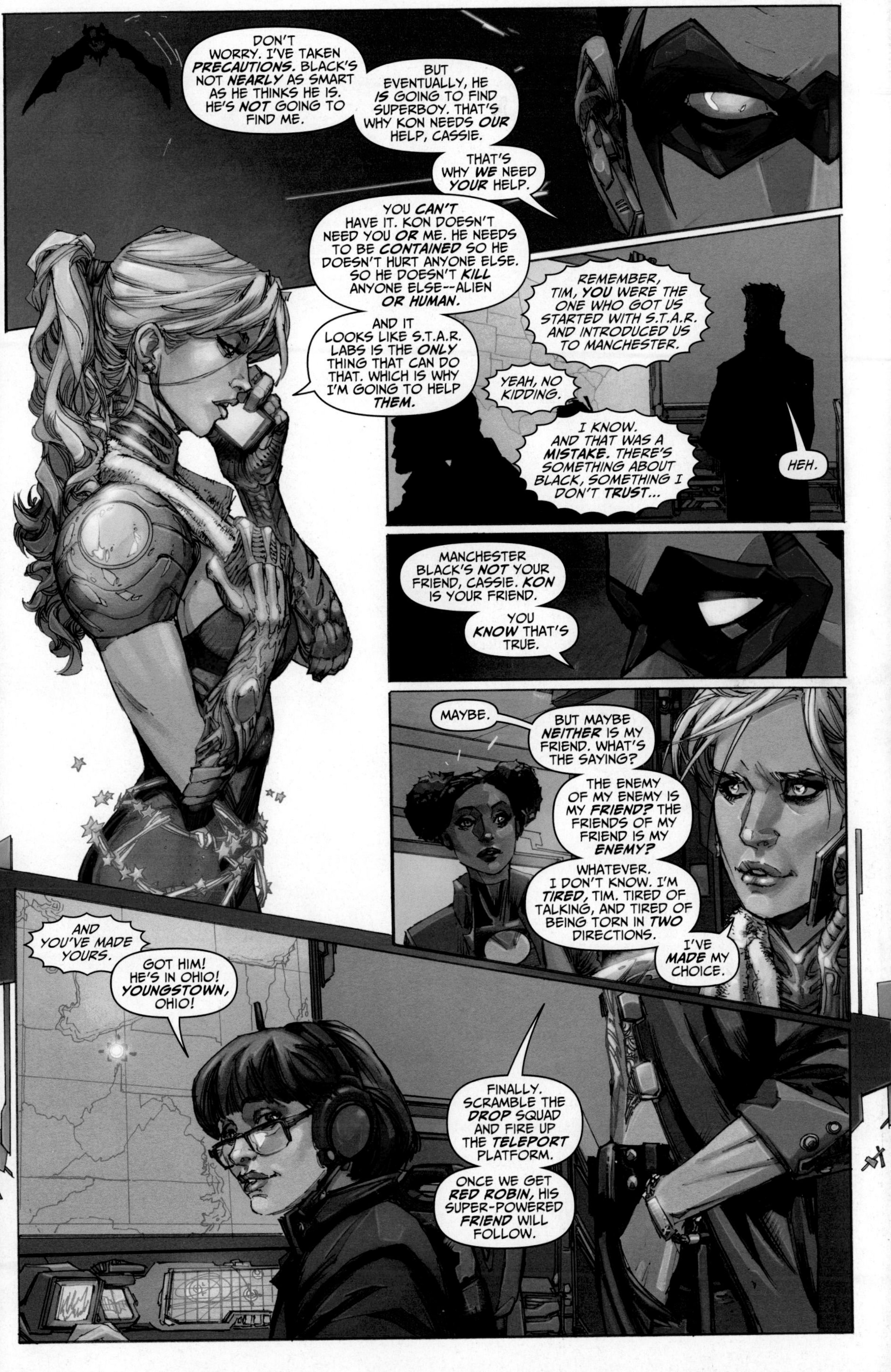
DON'T WORRY. I'VE TAKEN PRECAUTIONS. BLACK'S NOT NEARLY AS SMART AS HE THINKS HE IS. HE'S NOT GOING TO FIND ME.
BUT EVENTUALLY, HE IS GOING TO FIND SUPERBOY. THAT'S WHY KON NEEDS OUR HELP, CASSIE.
THAT'S WHY WE NEED YOUR HELP.
YOU CAN'T HAVE IT. KON DOESN'T NEED YOU OR ME. HE NEEDS TO BE CONTAINED SO HE DOESN'T HURT ANYONE ELSE. SO HE DOESN'T KILL ANYONE ELSE--ALIEN OR HUMAN.
AND IT LOOKS LIKE S.T.A.R. LABS IS THE ONLY THING THAT CAN DO THAT. WHICH IS WHY I'M GOING TO HELP THEM.
REMEMBER, TIM, YOU WERE THE ONE WHO GOT US STARTED WITH S.T.A.R. AND INTRODUCED US TO MANCHESTER.
YEAH, NO KIDDING.
I KNOW. AND THAT WAS A MISTAKE. THERE'S SOMETHING ABOUT BLACK, SOMETHING I DON'T TRUST...
HEH.
MANCHESTER BLACK'S NOT YOUR FRIEND, CASSIE. KON IS YOUR FRIEND.
YOU KNOW THAT'S TRUE.
MAYBE.
BUT MAYBE NEITHER IS MY FRIEND. WHAT'S THE SAYING?
THE ENEMY OF MY ENEMY IS MY FRIEND? THE FRIENDS OF MY FRIEND IS MY ENEMY?
WHATEVER. I DON'T KNOW. I'M TIRED, TIM. TIRED OF TALKING, AND TIRED OF BEING TORN IN TWO DIRECTIONS.
I'VE MADE MY CHOICE.
AND YOU'VE MADE YOURS.
GOT HIM! HE'S IN OHIO! YOUNGSTOWN, OHIO!
FINALLY. SCRAMBLE THE DROP SQUAD AND FIRE UP THE TELEPORT PLATFORM.
ONCE WE GET RED ROBIN, HIS SUPER-POWERED FRIEND WILL FOLLOW.

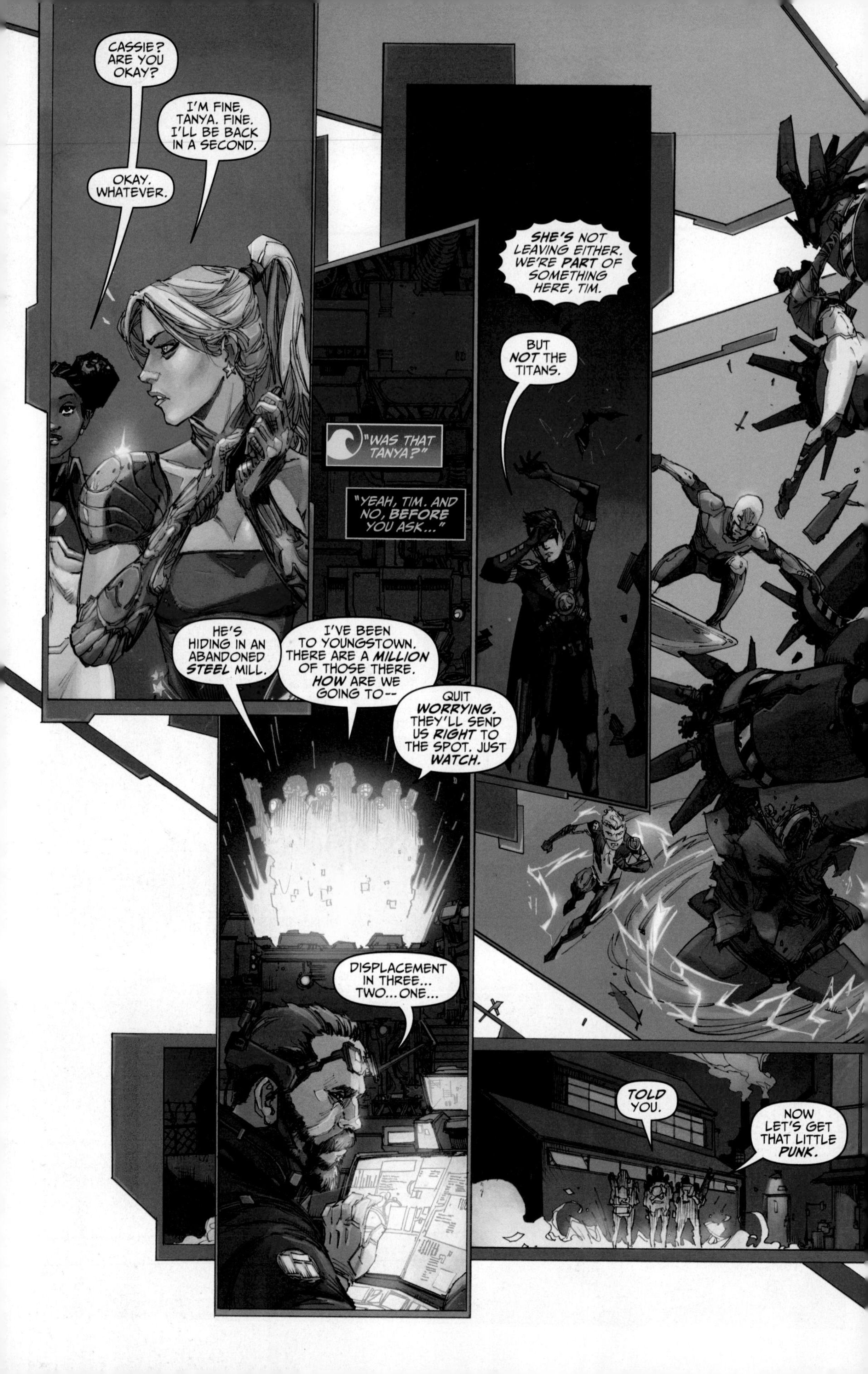
CASSIE? ARE YOU OKAY?
I'M FINE, TANYA. FINE. I'LL BE BACK IN A SECOND.
OKAY. WHATEVER.
"WAS THAT TANYA?"
"YEAH, TIM. AND NO, BEFORE YOU ASK..."
SHE'S NOT LEAVING EITHER. WE'RE PART OF SOMETHING HERE, TIM.
BUT NOT THE TITANS.
HE'S HIDING IN AN ABANDONED STEEL MILL.
I'VE BEEN TO YOUNGSTOWN. THERE ARE A MILLION OF THOSE THERE. HOW ARE WE GOING TO--
QUIT WORRYING. THEY'LL SEND US RIGHT TO THE SPOT. JUST WATCH.
DISPLACEMENT IN THREE... TWO...ONE...
TOLD YOU.
NOW LET'S GET THAT LITTLE PUNK.

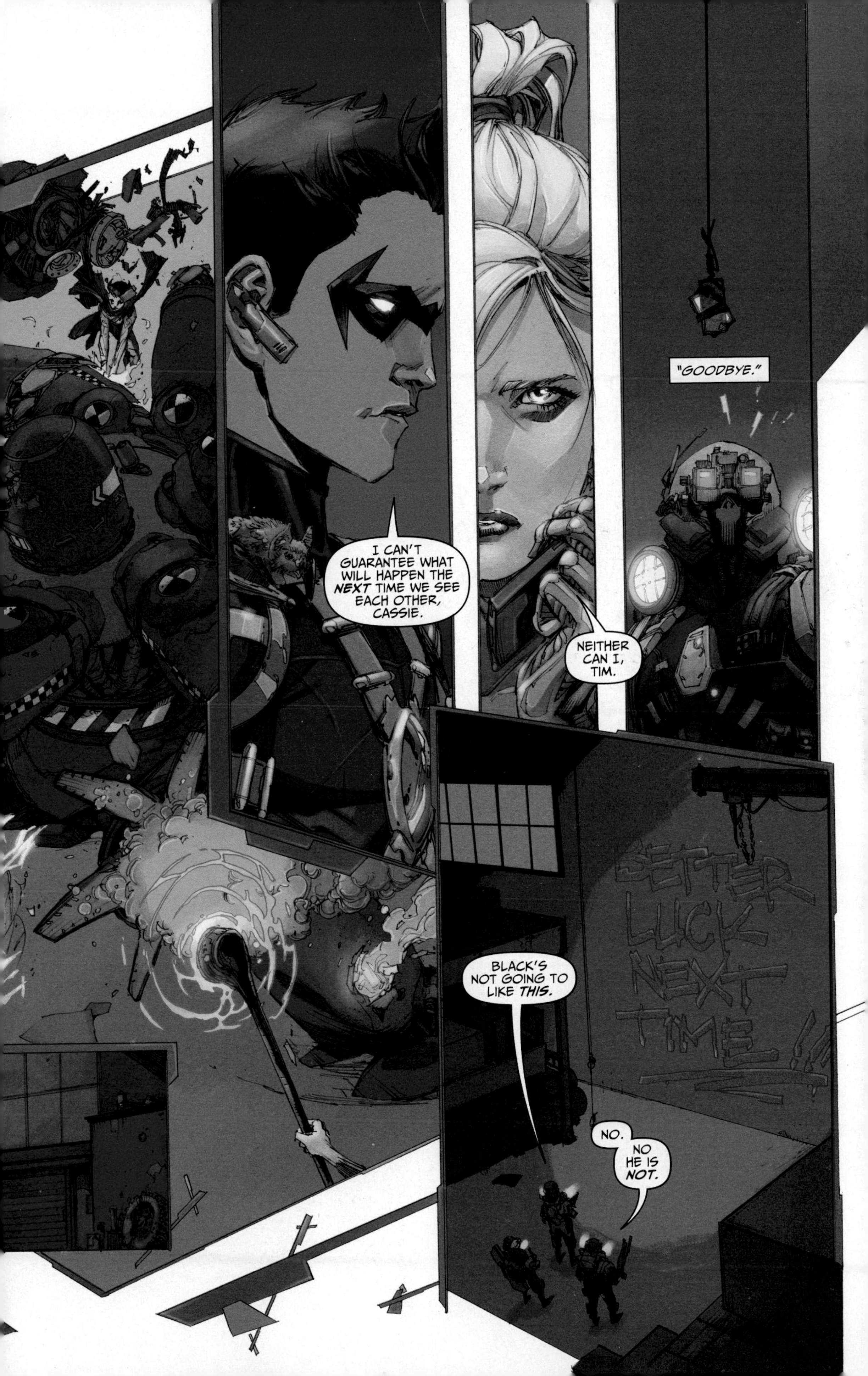
I CAN'T GUARANTEE WHAT WILL HAPPEN THE NEXT TIME WE SEE EACH OTHER, CASSIE.
NEITHER CAN I, TIM.
"GOODBYE."
BETTER LUCK NEXT TIME
BLACK'S NOT GOING TO LIKE THIS.
NO.
NO HE IS NOT.

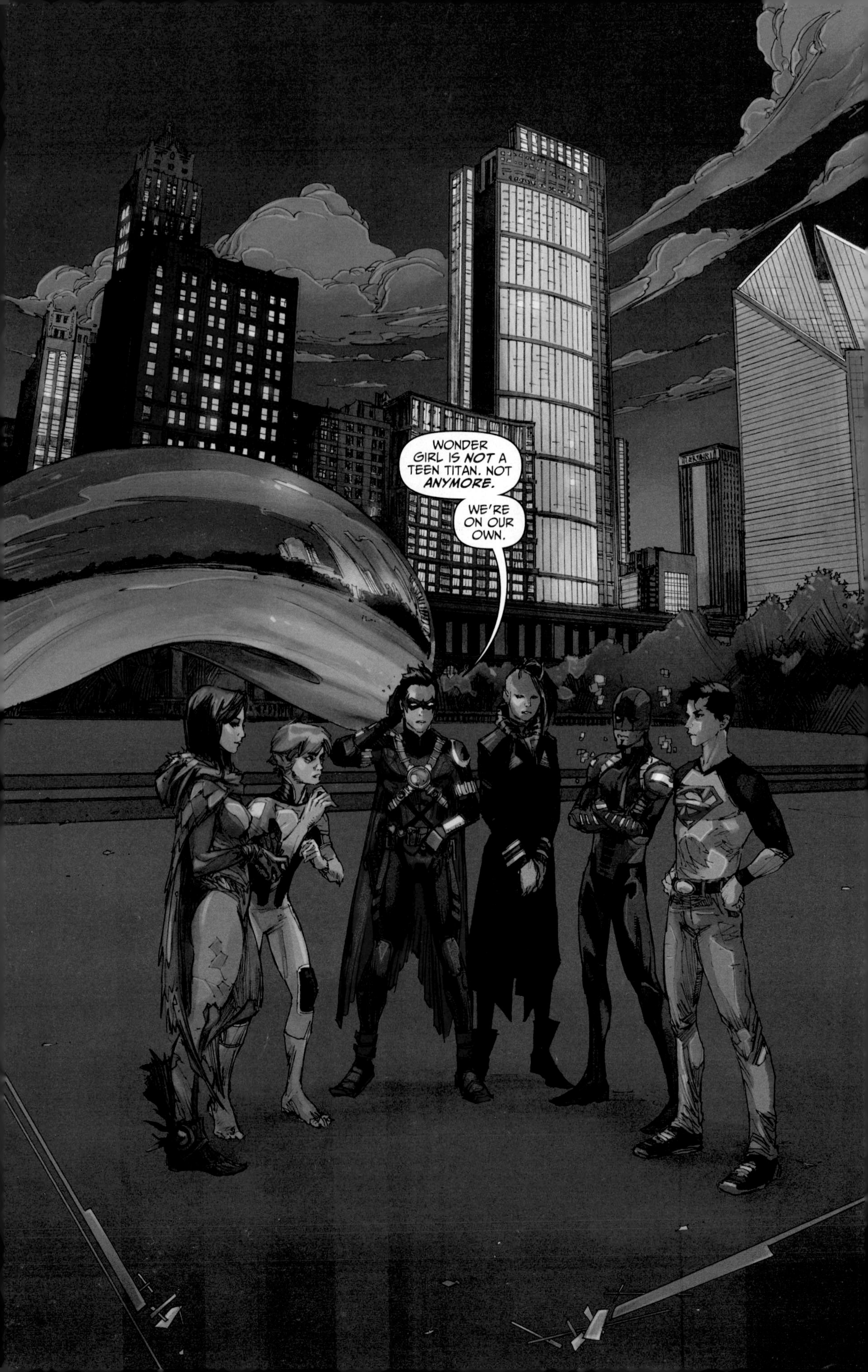
WONDER GIRL IS *NOT* A TEEN TITAN. NOT *ANYMORE.*
WE'RE ON OUR OWN.

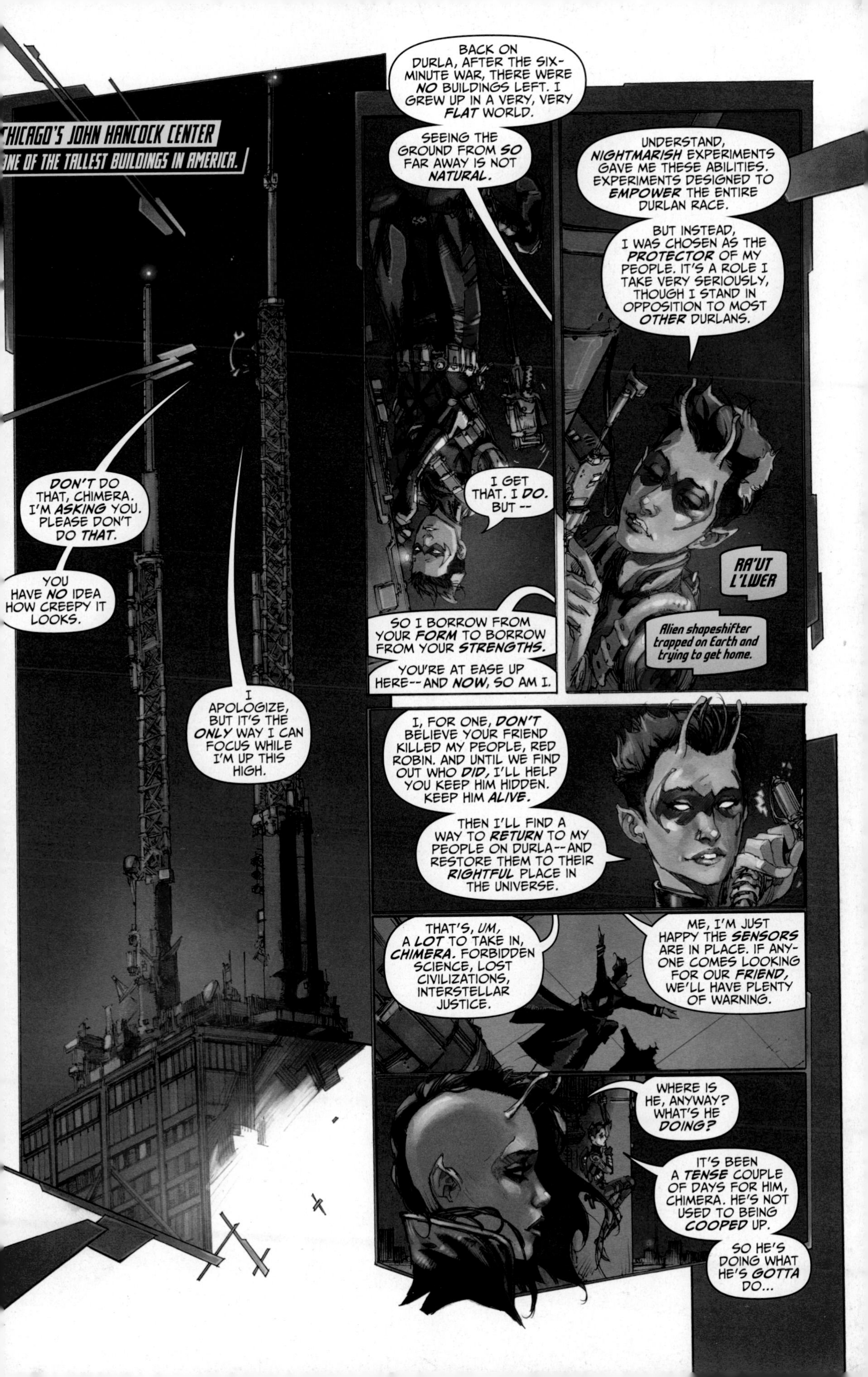
CHICAGO'S JOHN HANCOCK CENTER
ONE OF THE TALLEST BUILDINGS IN AMERICA.
DON'T DO THAT, CHIMERA. I'M ASKING YOU. PLEASE DON'T DO THAT.
YOU HAVE NO IDEA HOW CREEPY IT LOOKS.
I APOLOGIZE, BUT IT'S THE ONLY WAY I CAN FOCUS WHILE I'M UP THIS HIGH.
BACK ON DURLA, AFTER THE SIX-MINUTE WAR, THERE WERE NO BUILDINGS LEFT. I GREW UP IN A VERY, VERY FLAT WORLD.
SEEING THE GROUND FROM SO FAR AWAY IS NOT NATURAL.
I GET THAT. I DO. BUT --
SO I BORROW FROM YOUR FORM TO BORROW FROM YOUR STRENGTHS.
YOU'RE AT EASE UP HERE--AND NOW, SO AM I.
UNDERSTAND, NIGHTMARISH EXPERIMENTS GAVE ME THESE ABILITIES. EXPERIMENTS DESIGNED TO EMPOWER THE ENTIRE DURLAN RACE.
BUT INSTEAD, I WAS CHOSEN AS THE PROTECTOR OF MY PEOPLE. IT'S A ROLE I TAKE VERY SERIOUSLY, THOUGH I STAND IN OPPOSITION TO MOST OTHER DURLANS.
RA'UT L'LWER
Alien shapeshifter trapped on Earth and trying to get home.
I, FOR ONE, DON'T BELIEVE YOUR FRIEND KILLED MY PEOPLE, RED ROBIN. AND UNTIL WE FIND OUT WHO DID, I'LL HELP YOU KEEP HIM HIDDEN. KEEP HIM ALIVE.
THEN I'LL FIND A WAY TO RETURN TO MY PEOPLE ON DURLA--AND RESTORE THEM TO THEIR RIGHTFUL PLACE IN THE UNIVERSE.
THAT'S, UM, A LOT TO TAKE IN, CHIMERA. FORBIDDEN SCIENCE, LOST CIVILIZATIONS, INTERSTELLAR JUSTICE.
ME, I'M JUST HAPPY THE SENSORS ARE IN PLACE. IF ANY-ONE COMES LOOKING FOR OUR FRIEND, WE'LL HAVE PLENTY OF WARNING.
WHERE IS HE, ANYWAY? WHAT'S HE DOING?
IT'S BEEN A TENSE COUPLE OF DAYS FOR HIM, CHIMERA. HE'S NOT USED TO BEING COOPED UP.
SO HE'S DOING WHAT HE'S GOTTA DO...

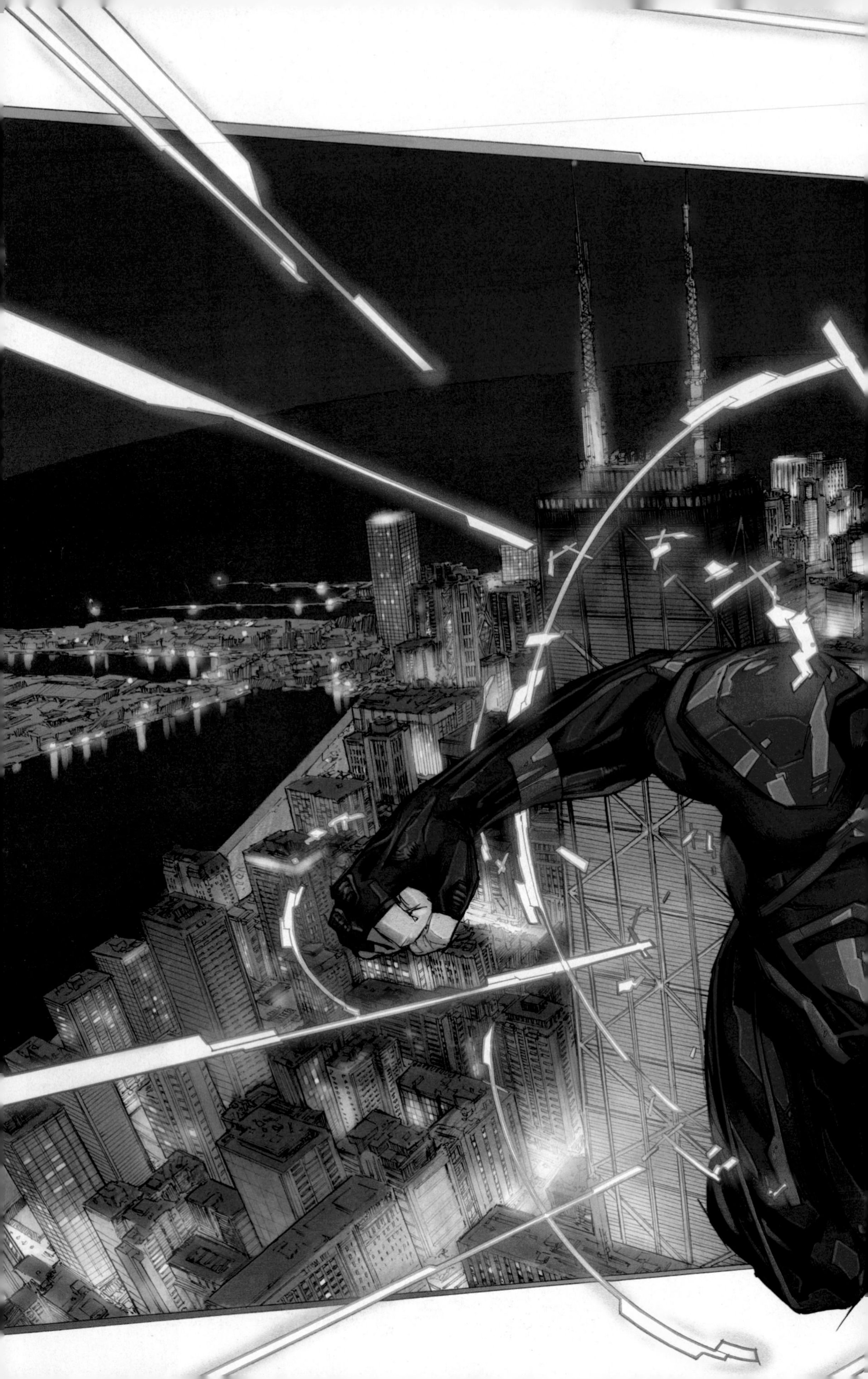

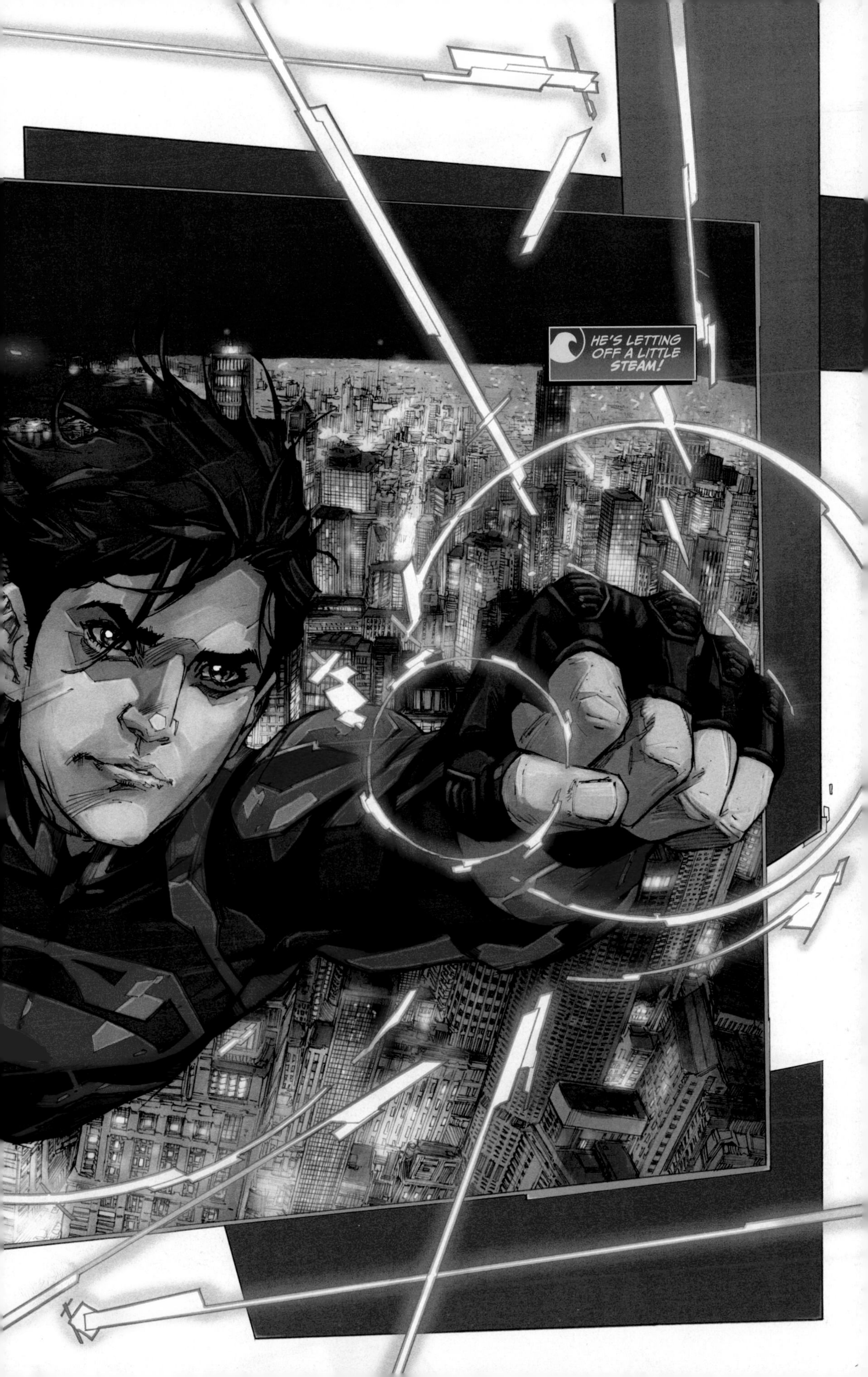
HE'S LETTING
OFF A LITTLE
STEAM!

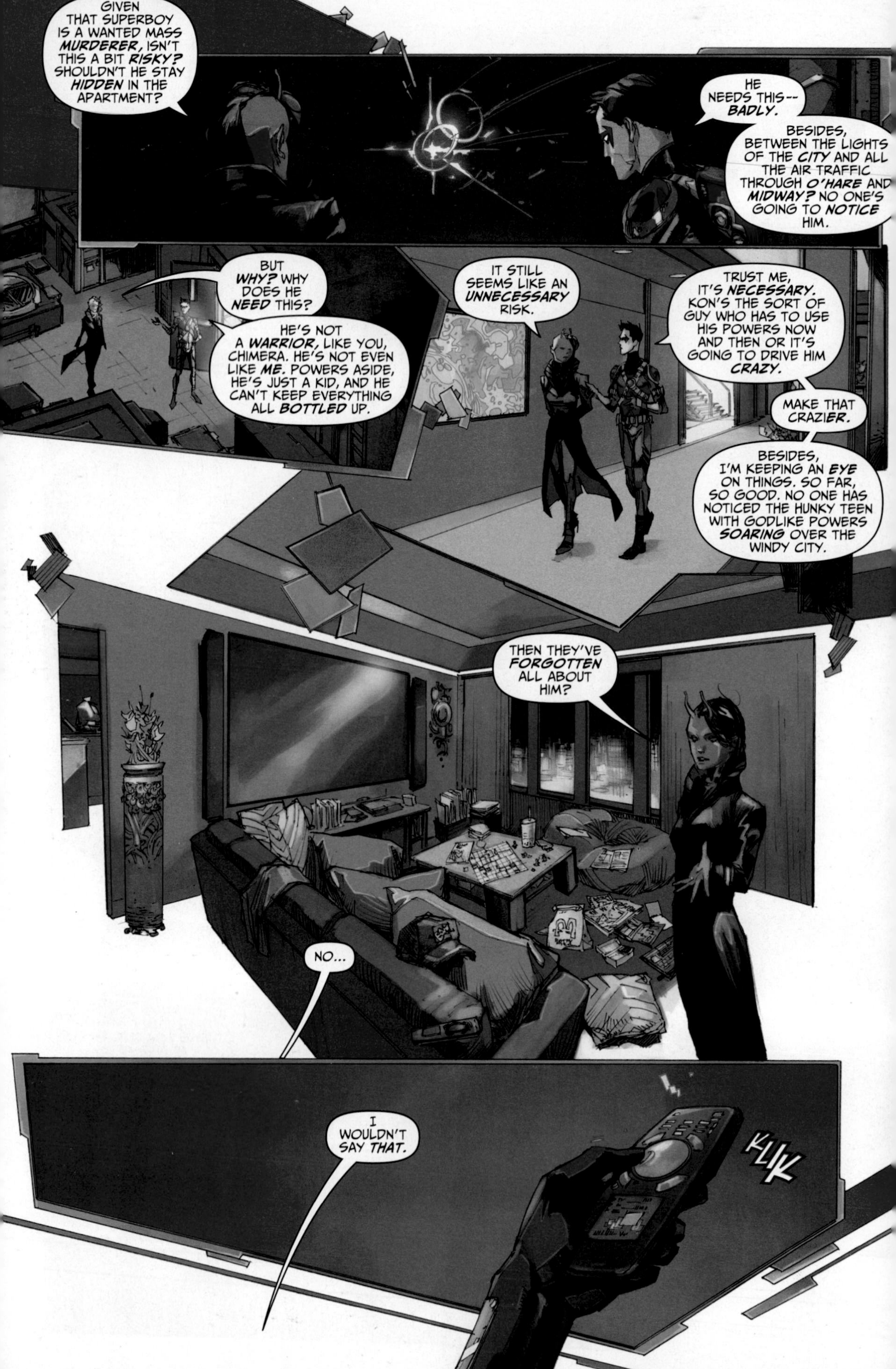
GIVEN THAT SUPERBOY IS A WANTED MASS MURDERER, ISN'T THIS A BIT RISKY? SHOULDN'T HE STAY HIDDEN IN THE APARTMENT?
HE NEEDS THIS-- BADLY.
BESIDES, BETWEEN THE LIGHTS OF THE CITY AND ALL THE AIR TRAFFIC THROUGH O'HARE AND MIDWAY? NO ONE'S GOING TO NOTICE HIM.
BUT WHY? WHY DOES HE NEED THIS?
HE'S NOT A WARRIOR, LIKE YOU, CHIMERA. HE'S NOT EVEN LIKE ME. POWERS ASIDE, HE'S JUST A KID, AND HE CAN'T KEEP EVERYTHING ALL BOTTLED UP.
IT STILL SEEMS LIKE AN UNNECESSARY RISK.
TRUST ME, IT'S NECESSARY. KON'S THE SORT OF GUY WHO HAS TO USE HIS POWERS NOW AND THEN OR IT'S GOING TO DRIVE HIM CRAZY.
MAKE THAT CRAZIER.
BESIDES, I'M KEEPING AN EYE ON THINGS. SO FAR, SO GOOD. NO ONE HAS NOTICED THE HUNKY TEEN WITH GODLIKE POWERS SOARING OVER THE WINDY CITY.
THEN THEY'VE FORGOTTEN ALL ABOUT HIM?
NO...
I WOULDN'T SAY THAT.
KLIK

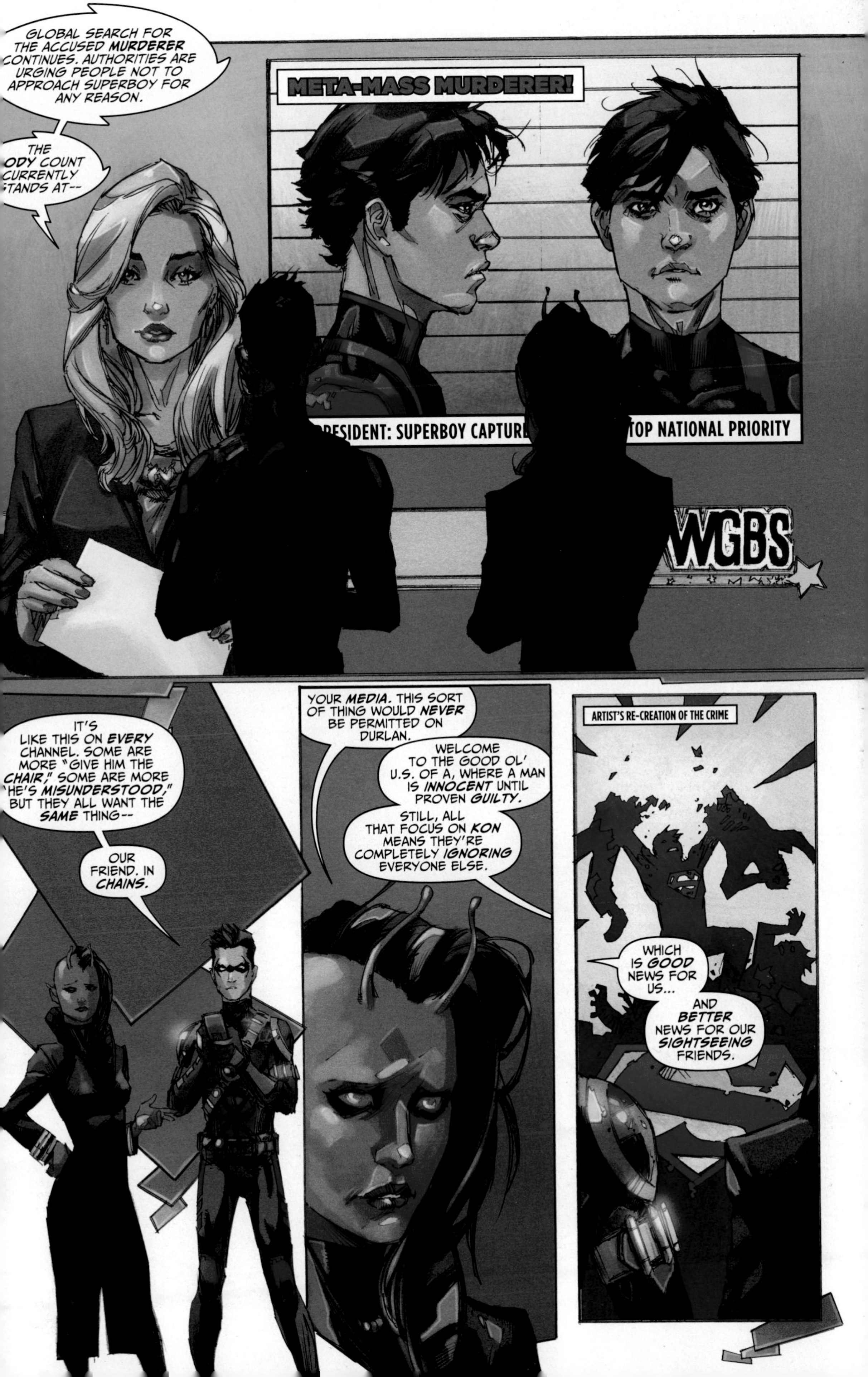
GLOBAL SEARCH FOR THE ACCUSED MURDERER CONTINUES. AUTHORITIES ARE URGING PEOPLE NOT TO APPROACH SUPERBOY FOR ANY REASON.
THE ODY COUNT CURRENTLY TANDS AT--
META-MASS MURDERER!
PRESIDENT: SUPERBOY CAPTUR
TOP NATIONAL PRIORITY
WGBS
IT'S LIKE THIS ON EVERY CHANNEL. SOME ARE MORE "GIVE HIM THE CHAIR," SOME ARE MORE "HE'S MISUNDERSTOOD," BUT THEY ALL WANT THE SAME THING--
OUR FRIEND. IN CHAINS.
YOUR MEDIA. THIS SORT OF THING WOULD NEVER BE PERMITTED ON DURLAN.
WELCOME TO THE GOOD OL' U.S. OF A, WHERE A MAN IS INNOCENT UNTIL PROVEN GUILTY.
STILL, ALL THAT FOCUS ON KON MEANS THEY'RE COMPLETELY IGNORING EVERYONE ELSE.
ARTIST'S RE-CREATION OF THE CRIME
WHICH IS GOOD NEWS FOR US...
AND BETTER NEWS FOR OUR SIGHTSEEING FRIENDS.

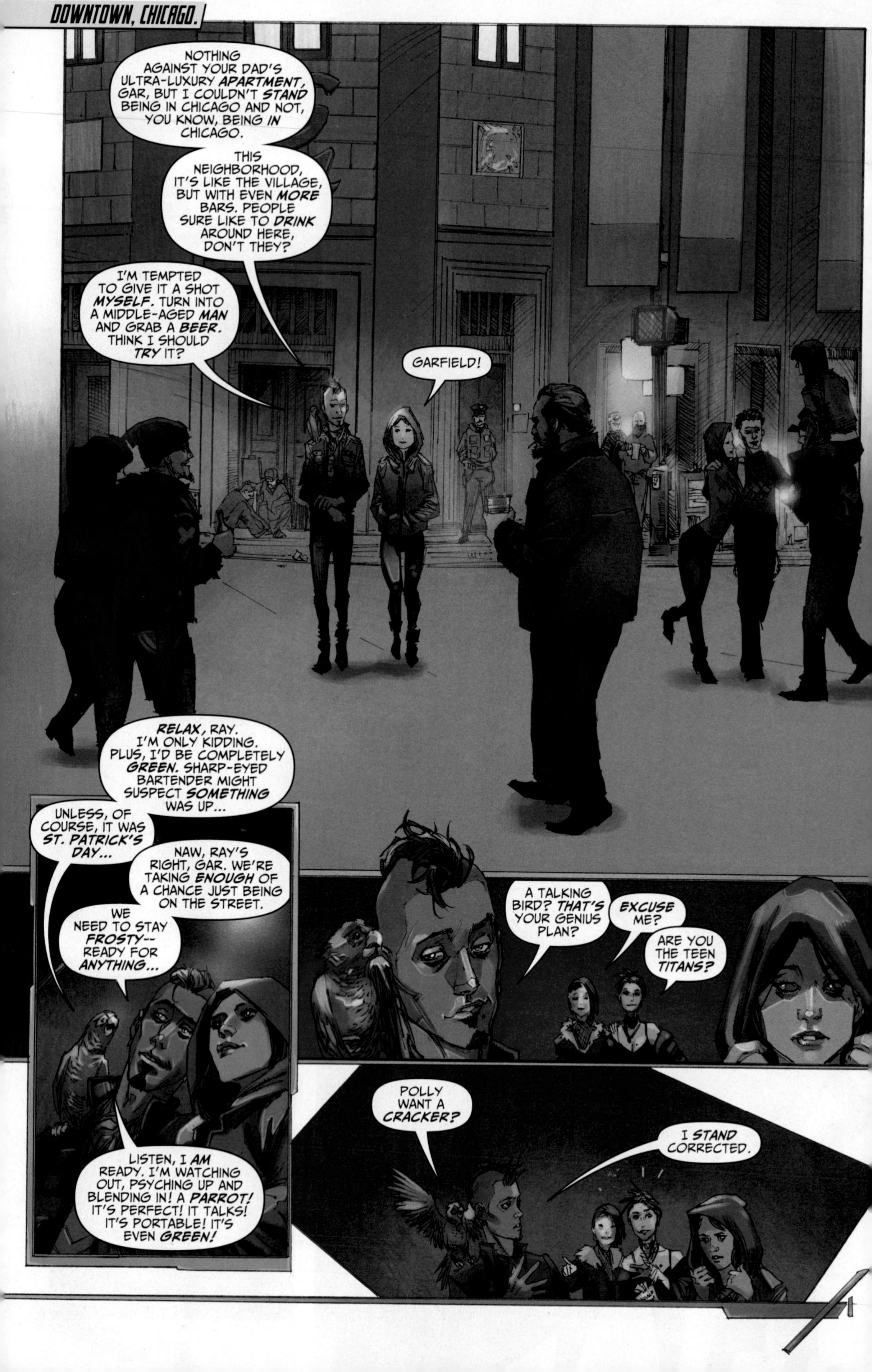
DOWNTOWN, CHICAGO.
NOTHING AGAINST YOUR DAD'S ULTRA-LUXURY APARTMENT, GAR, BUT I COULDN'T STAND BEING IN CHICAGO AND NOT, YOU KNOW, BEING IN CHICAGO.
THIS NEIGHBORHOOD, IT'S LIKE THE VILLAGE, BUT WITH EVEN MORE BARS. PEOPLE SURE LIKE TO DRINK AROUND HERE, DON'T THEY?
I'M TEMPTED TO GIVE IT A SHOT MYSELF. TURN INTO A MIDDLE-AGED MAN AND GRAB A BEER. THINK I SHOULD TRY IT?
GARFIELD!
RELAX, RAY. I'M ONLY KIDDING. PLUS, I'D BE COMPLETELY GREEN. SHARP-EYED BARTENDER MIGHT SUSPECT SOMETHING WAS UP...
UNLESS, OF COURSE, IT WAS ST. PATRICK'S DAY...
NAW, RAY'S RIGHT, GAR. WE'RE TAKING ENOUGH OF A CHANCE JUST BEING ON THE STREET.
WE NEED TO STAY FROSTY--READY FOR ANYTHING...
LISTEN, I AM READY. I'M WATCHING OUT, PSYCHING UP AND BLENDING IN! A PARROT! IT'S PERFECT! IT TALKS! IT'S PORTABLE! IT'S EVEN GREEN!
A TALKING BIRD? THAT'S YOUR GENIUS PLAN?
EXCUSE ME?
ARE YOU THE TEEN TITANS?
POLLY WANT A CRACKER?
I STAND CORRECTED.

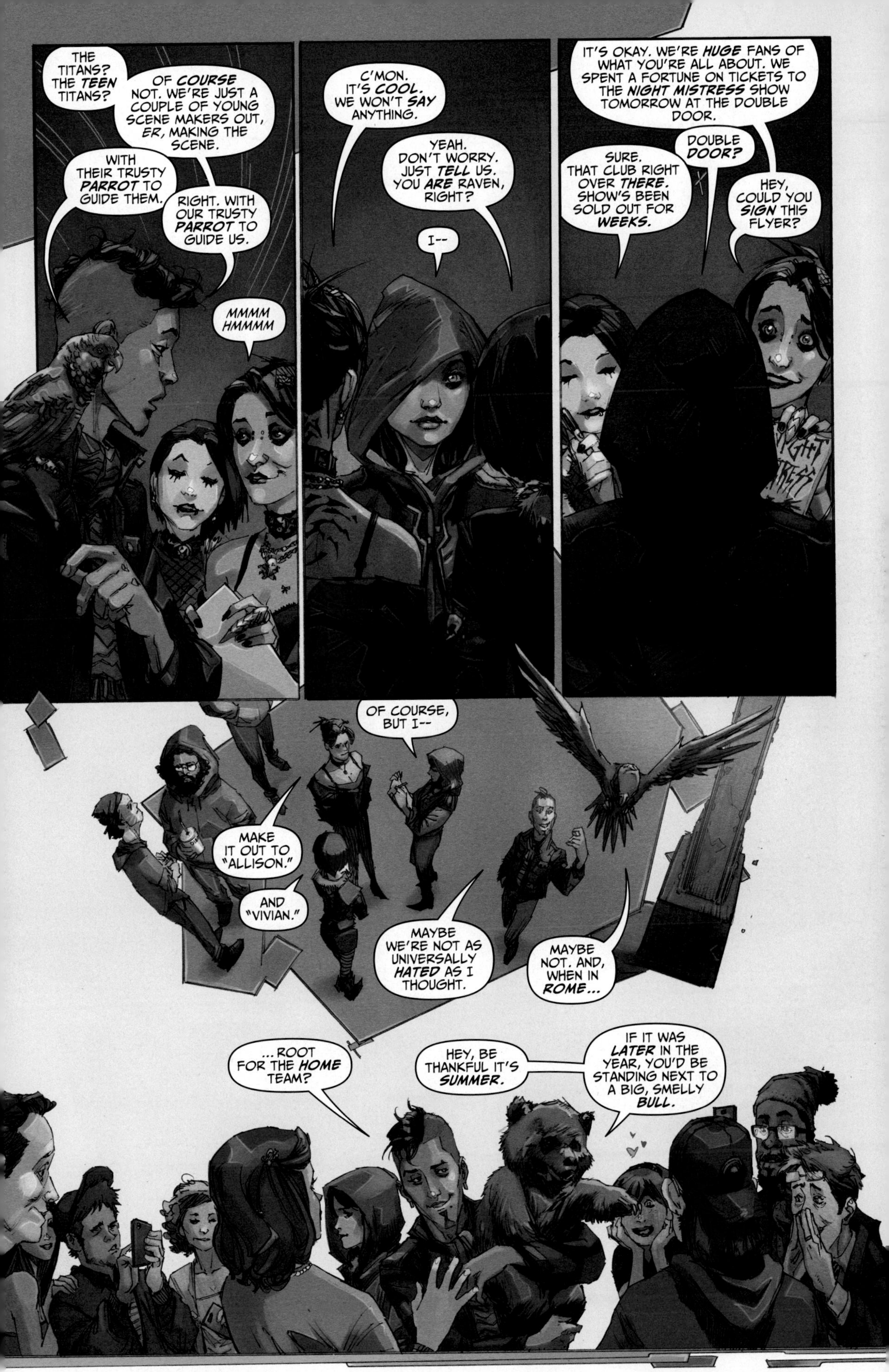
THE TITANS? THE TEEN TITANS?
OF COURSE NOT. WE'RE JUST A COUPLE OF YOUNG SCENE MAKERS OUT, ER, MAKING THE SCENE.
WITH THEIR TRUSTY PARROT TO GUIDE THEM.
RIGHT. WITH OUR TRUSTY PARROT TO GUIDE US.
MMMM HMMMM
C'MON. IT'S COOL. WE WON'T SAY ANYTHING.
YEAH. DON'T WORRY. JUST TELL US. YOU ARE RAVEN, RIGHT?
I--
IT'S OKAY. WE'RE HUGE FANS OF WHAT YOU'RE ALL ABOUT. WE SPENT A FORTUNE ON TICKETS TO THE NIGHT MISTRESS SHOW TOMORROW AT THE DOUBLE DOOR.
DOUBLE DOOR?
SURE. THAT CLUB RIGHT OVER THERE. SHOW'S BEEN SOLD OUT FOR WEEKS.
HEY, COULD YOU SIGN THIS FLYER?
OF COURSE, BUT I--
MAKE IT OUT TO "ALLISON."
AND "VIVIAN."
MAYBE WE'RE NOT AS UNIVERSALLY HATED AS I THOUGHT.
MAYBE NOT. AND, WHEN IN ROME...
...ROOT FOR THE HOME TEAM?
HEY, BE THANKFUL IT'S SUMMER.
IF IT WAS LATER IN THE YEAR, YOU'D BE STANDING NEXT TO A BIG, SMELLY BULL.

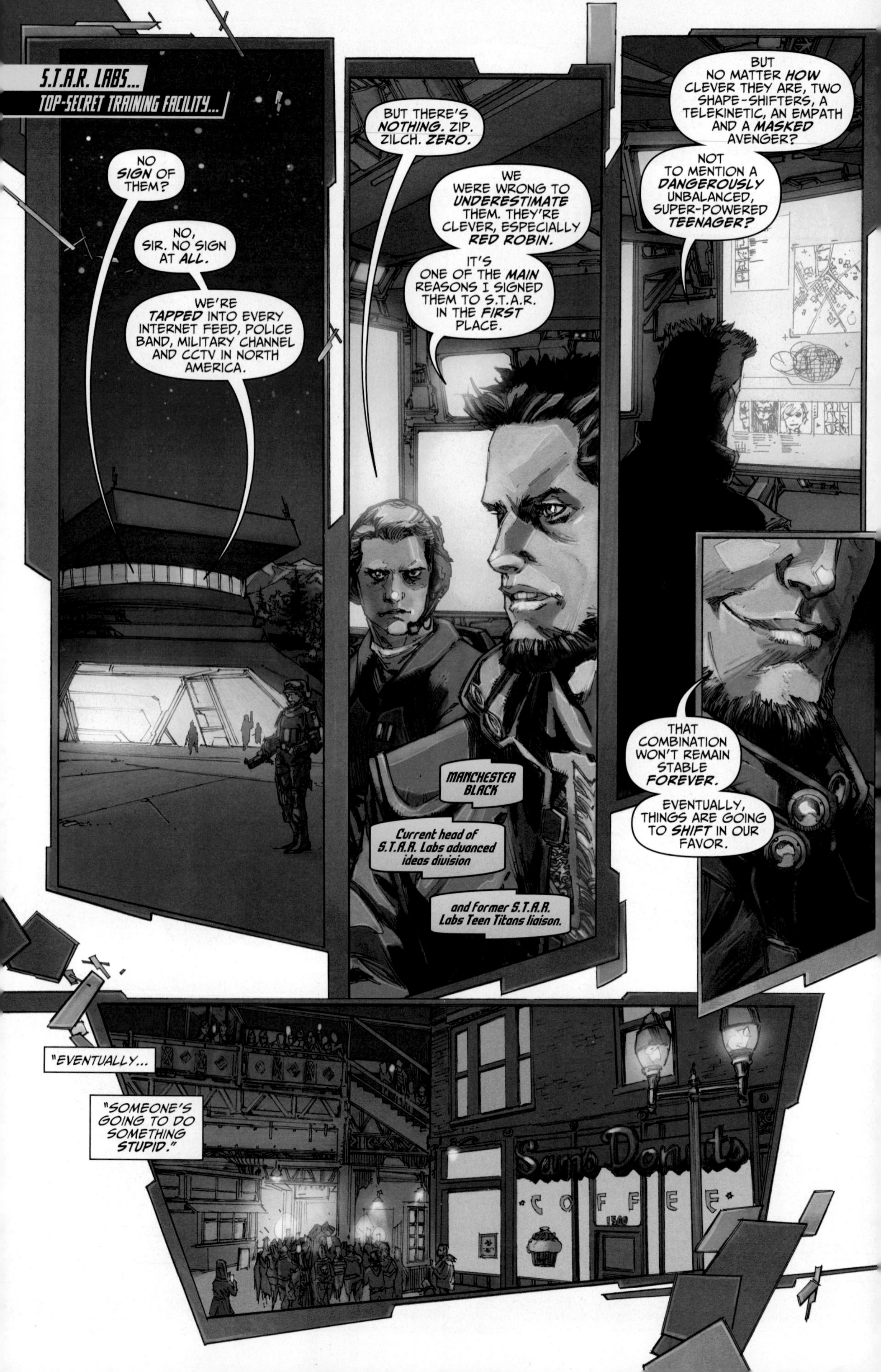
S.T.A.R. LABS...
TOP-SECRET TRAINING FACILITY...
NO SIGN OF THEM?
NO, SIR. NO SIGN AT ALL.
WE'RE TAPPED INTO EVERY INTERNET FEED, POLICE BAND, MILITARY CHANNEL AND CCTV IN NORTH AMERICA.
BUT THERE'S NOTHING. ZIP. ZILCH. ZERO.
WE WERE WRONG TO UNDERESTIMATE THEM. THEY'RE CLEVER, ESPECIALLY RED ROBIN.
IT'S ONE OF THE MAIN REASONS I SIGNED THEM TO S.T.A.R. IN THE FIRST PLACE.
MANCHESTER BLACK
Current head of S.T.A.R. Labs advanced ideas division
and former S.T.A.R. Labs Teen Titans liaison.
BUT NO MATTER HOW CLEVER THEY ARE, TWO SHAPE-SHIFTERS, A TELEKINETIC, AN EMPATH AND A MASKED AVENGER?
NOT TO MENTION A DANGEROUSLY UNBALANCED, SUPER-POWERED TEENAGER?
THAT COMBINATION WON'T REMAIN STABLE FOREVER.
EVENTUALLY, THINGS ARE GOING TO SHIFT IN OUR FAVOR.
"EVENTUALLY...
"SOMEONE'S GOING TO DO SOMETHING STUPID."
Sam's Donuts
COFFEE
1560

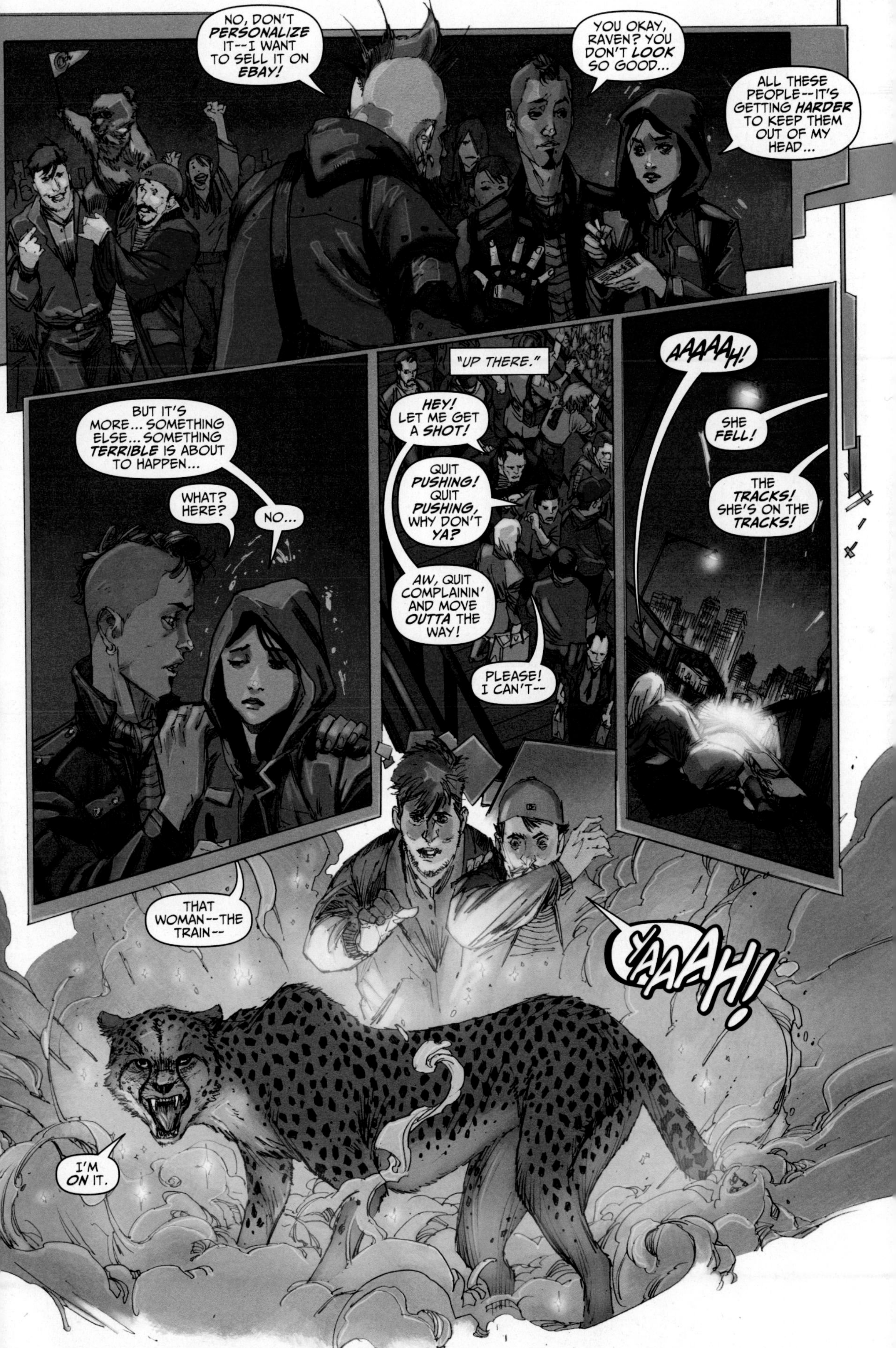
NO, DON'T PERSONALIZE IT--I WANT TO SELL IT ON EBAY!
YOU OKAY, RAVEN? YOU DON'T LOOK SO GOOD...
ALL THESE PEOPLE--IT'S GETTING HARDER TO KEEP THEM OUT OF MY HEAD...
BUT IT'S MORE... SOMETHING ELSE... SOMETHING TERRIBLE IS ABOUT TO HAPPEN...
WHAT? HERE?
NO...
"UP THERE."
HEY! LET ME GET A SHOT!
QUIT PUSHING! QUIT PUSHING, WHY DON'T YA?
AW, QUIT COMPLAININ' AND MOVE OUTTA THE WAY!
PLEASE! I CAN'T--
AAAAAH!
SHE FELL!
THE TRACKS! SHE'S ON THE TRACKS!
THAT WOMAN--THE TRAIN--
YAAAH!
I'M ON IT.

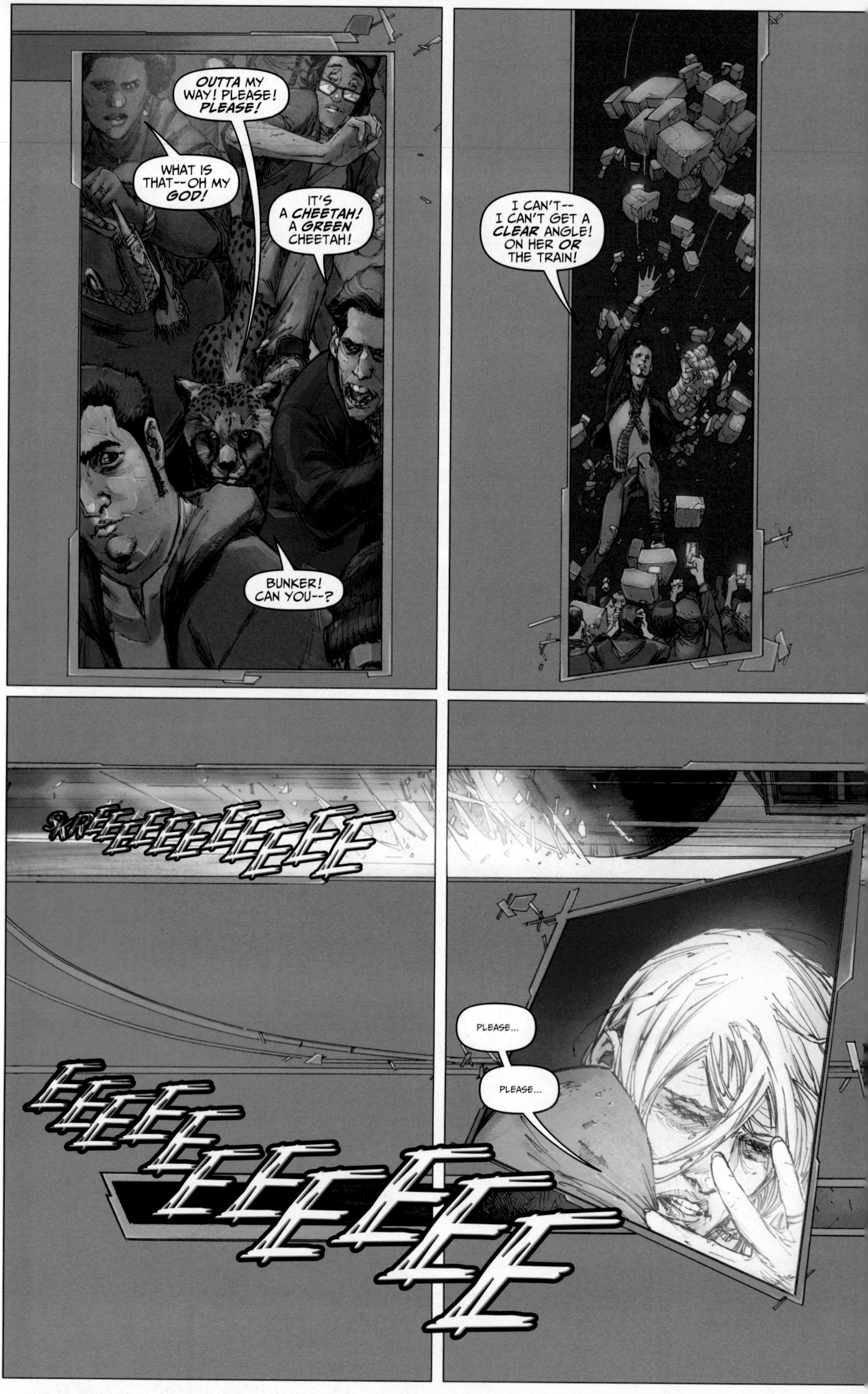

OUTTA MY WAY! PLEASE! PLEASE!
WHAT IS THAT--OH MY GOD!
IT'S A CHEETAH! A GREEN CHEETAH!
BUNKER! CAN YOU--?
I CAN'T-- I CAN'T GET A CLEAR ANGLE! ON HER OR THE TRAIN!
SKREEEEEEEEEEEEEE
EEEEEEEEEEEEEE
PLEASE...
PLEASE...

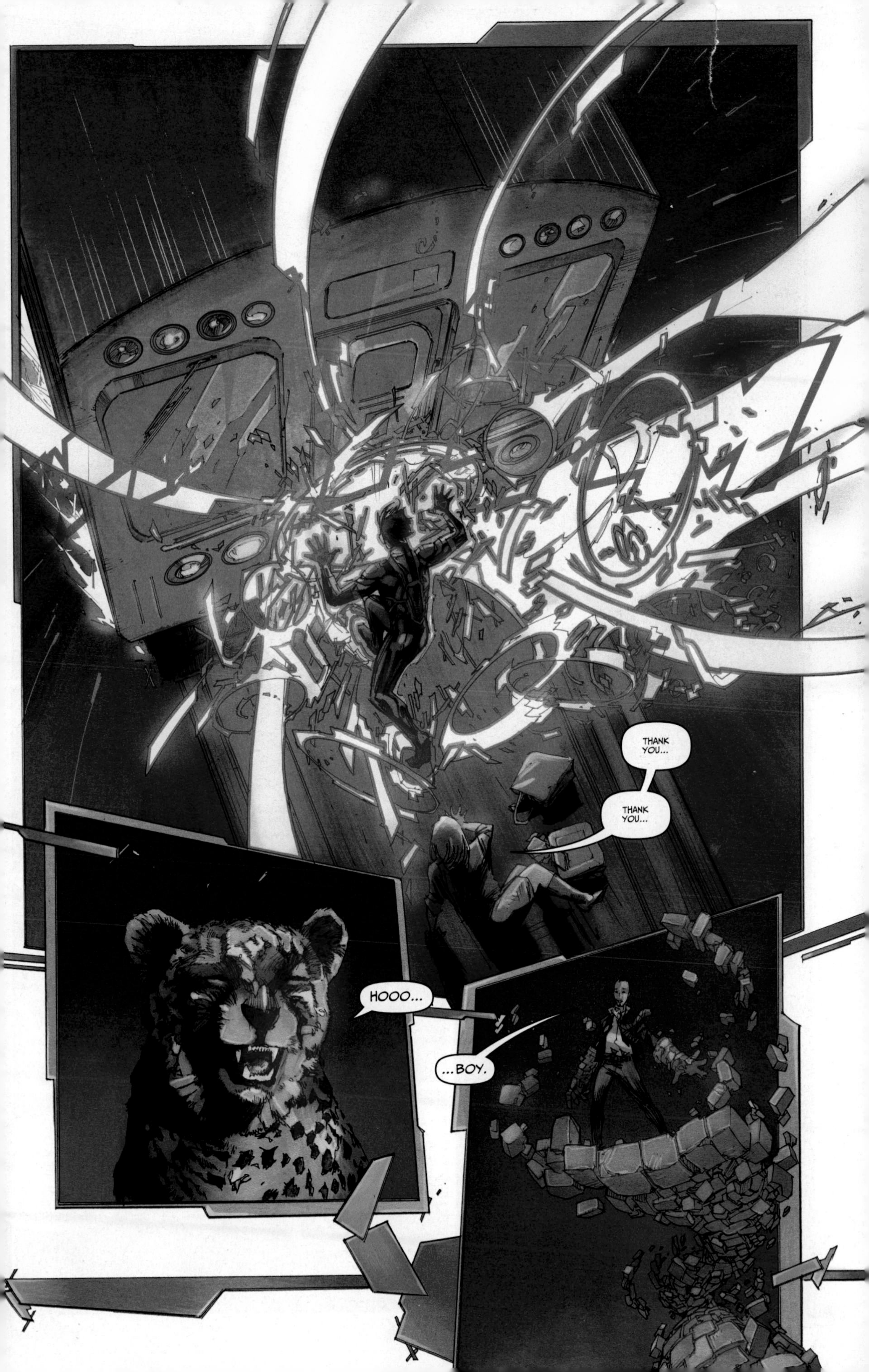
THANK YOU...
THANK YOU...
HOOO...
...BOY.

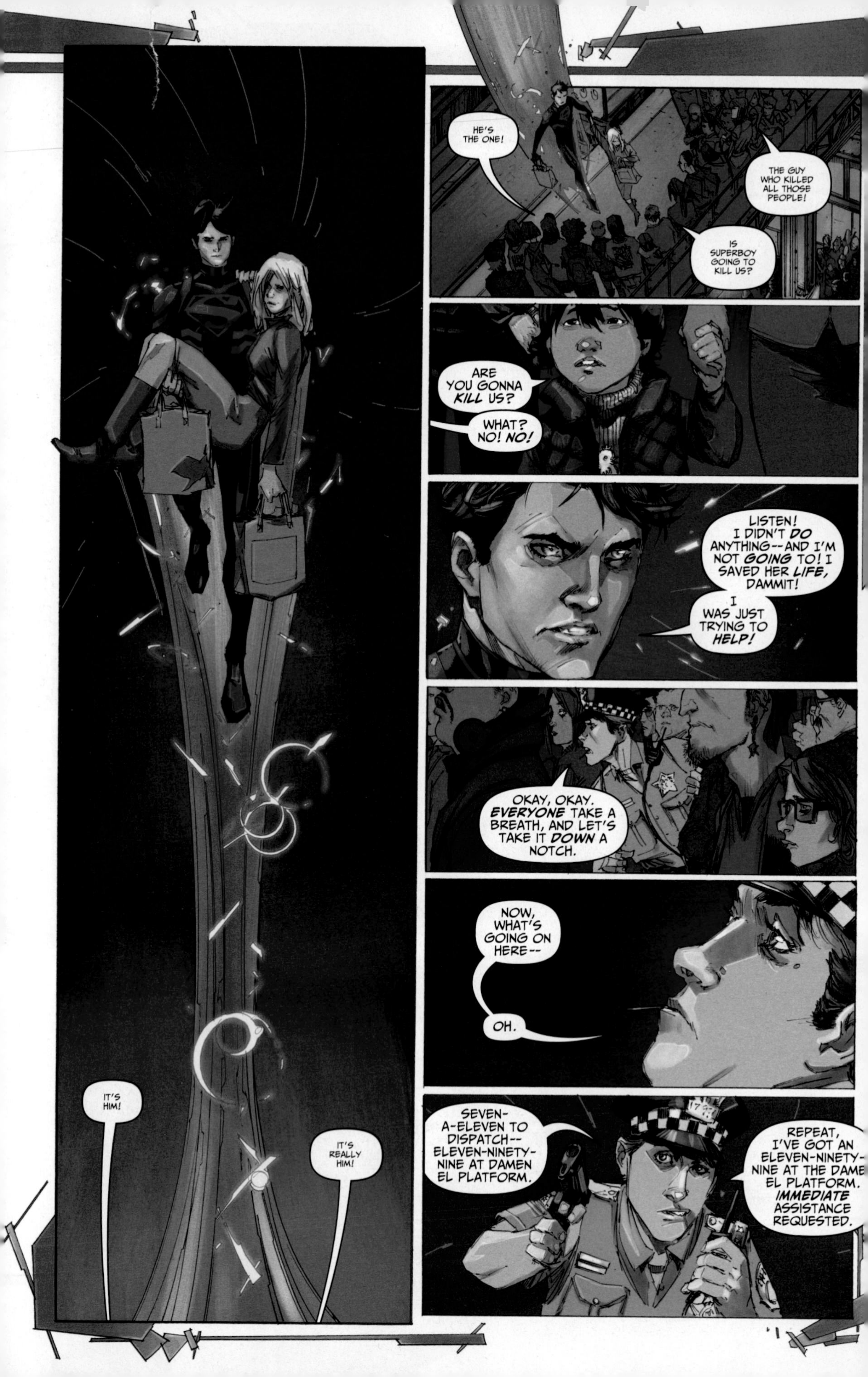
HE'S THE ONE!
THE GUY WHO KILLED ALL THOSE PEOPLE!
IS SUPERBOY GOING TO KILL US?
ARE YOU GONNA KILL US?
WHAT? NO! NO!
LISTEN! I DIDN'T DO ANYTHING--AND I'M NOT GOING TO! I SAVED HER LIFE, DAMMIT!
I WAS JUST TRYING TO HELP!
OKAY, OKAY. EVERYONE TAKE A BREATH, AND LET'S TAKE IT DOWN A NOTCH.
NOW, WHAT'S GOING ON HERE--
OH.
IT'S HIM!
IT'S REALLY HIM!
SEVEN-A-ELEVEN TO DISPATCH--ELEVEN-NINETY-NINE AT DAMEN EL PLATFORM.
REPEAT, I'VE GOT AN ELEVEN-NINETY-NINE AT THE DAME EL PLATFORM. IMMEDIATE ASSISTANCE REQUESTED.

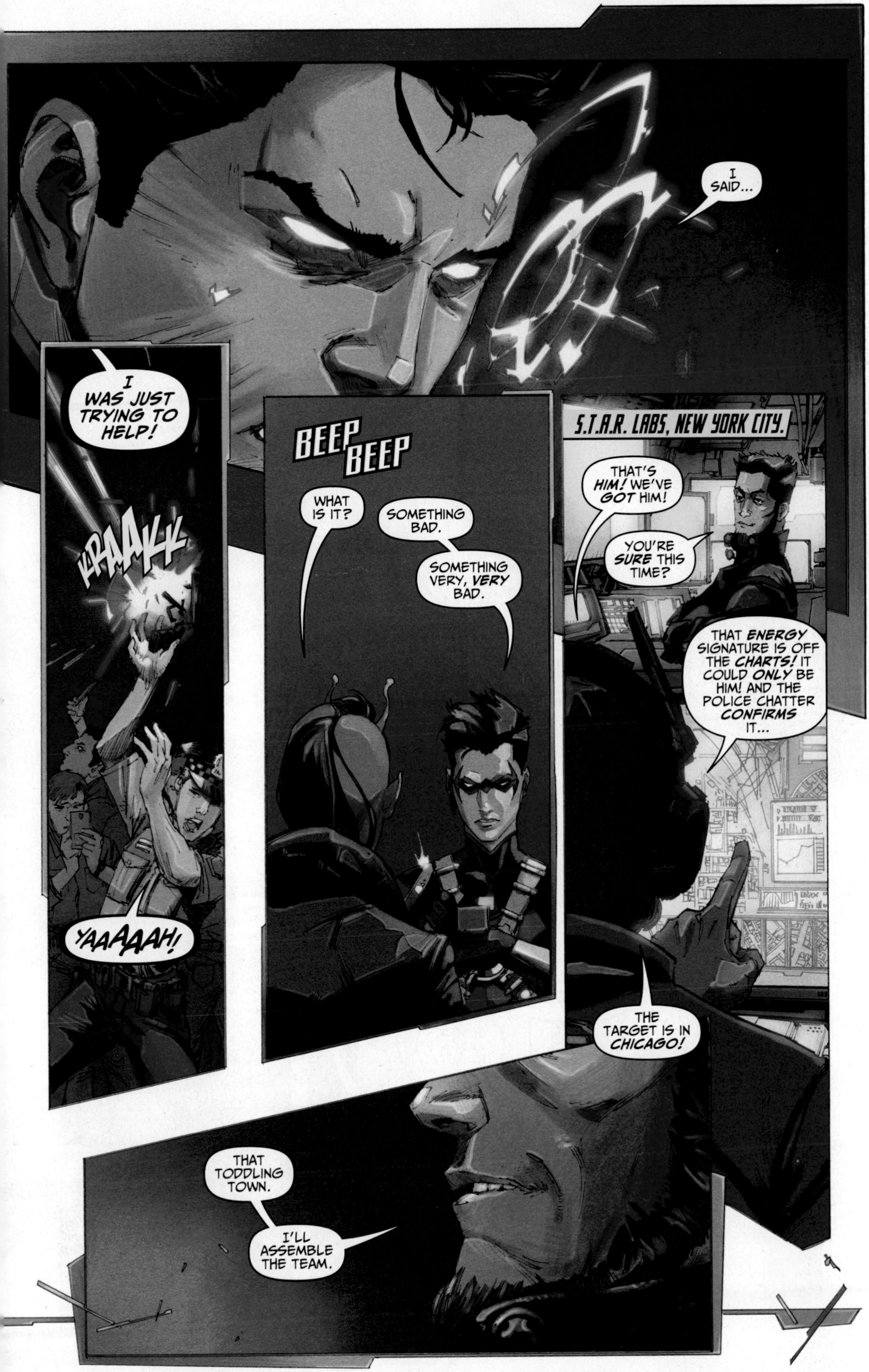
I SAID...
I WAS JUST TRYING TO HELP!
KRAAKK
YAAAAAH!
BEEP BEEP
WHAT IS IT?
SOMETHING BAD.
SOMETHING VERY, VERY BAD.
S.T.A.R. LABS, NEW YORK CITY.
THAT'S HIM! WE'VE GOT HIM!
YOU'RE SURE THIS TIME?
THAT ENERGY SIGNATURE IS OFF THE CHARTS! IT COULD ONLY BE HIM! AND THE POLICE CHATTER CONFIRMS IT...
THE TARGET IS IN CHICAGO!
THAT TODDLING TOWN.
I'LL ASSEMBLE THE TEAM.

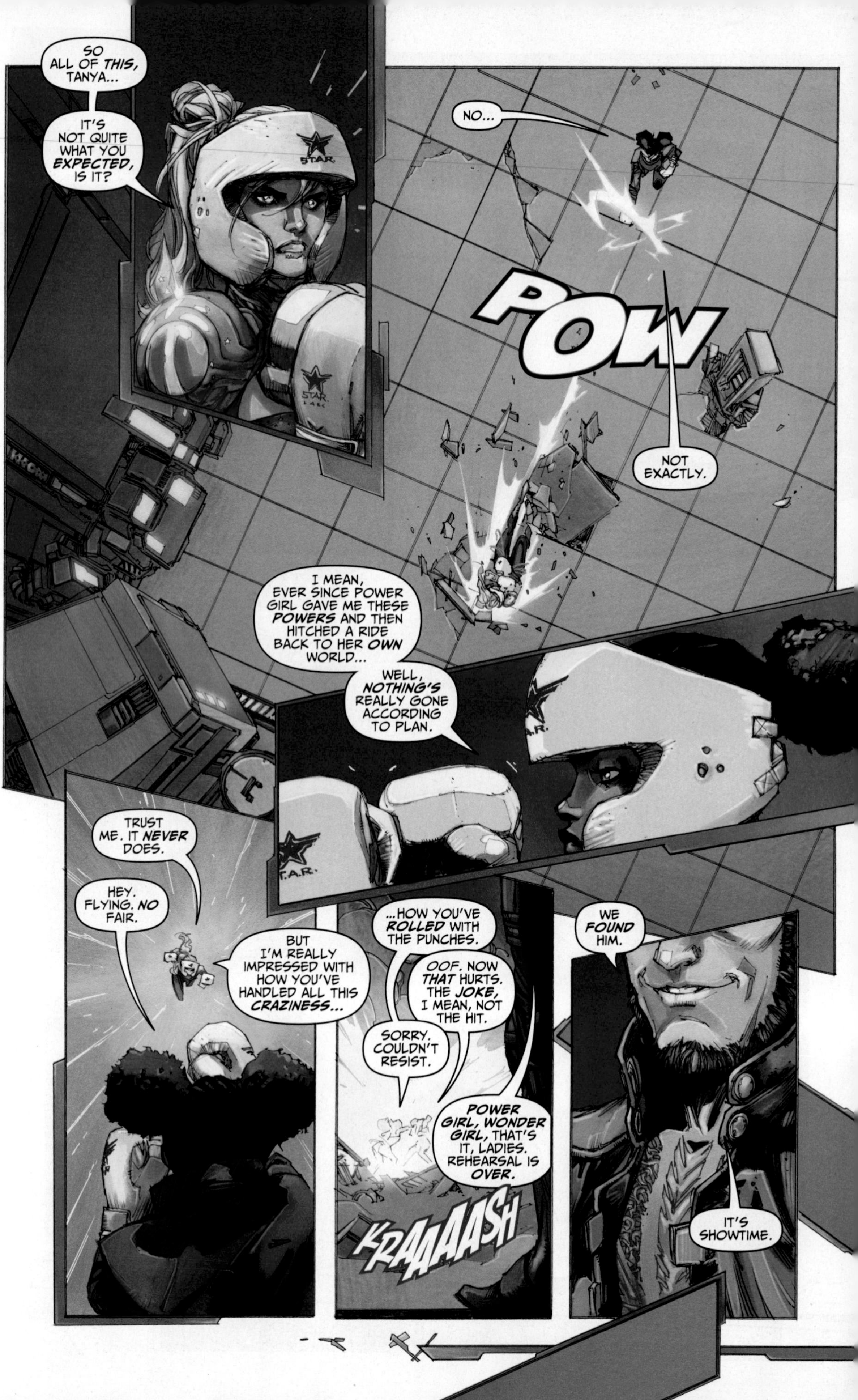
SO ALL OF THIS, TANYA...
IT'S NOT QUITE WHAT YOU EXPECTED, IS IT?
NO...
POW
NOT EXACTLY.
I MEAN, EVER SINCE POWER GIRL GAVE ME THESE POWERS AND THEN HITCHED A RIDE BACK TO HER OWN WORLD...
WELL, NOTHING'S REALLY GONE ACCORDING TO PLAN.
TRUST ME. IT NEVER DOES.
HEY. FLYING. NO FAIR.
BUT I'M REALLY IMPRESSED WITH HOW YOU'VE HANDLED ALL THIS CRAZINESS...
...HOW YOU'VE ROLLED WITH THE PUNCHES.
OOF. NOW THAT HURTS. THE JOKE, I MEAN, NOT THE HIT.
SORRY. COULDN'T RESIST.
POWER GIRL, WONDER GIRL, THAT'S IT, LADIES. REHEARSAL IS OVER.
KRAAAASH
WE FOUND HIM.
IT'S SHOWTIME.

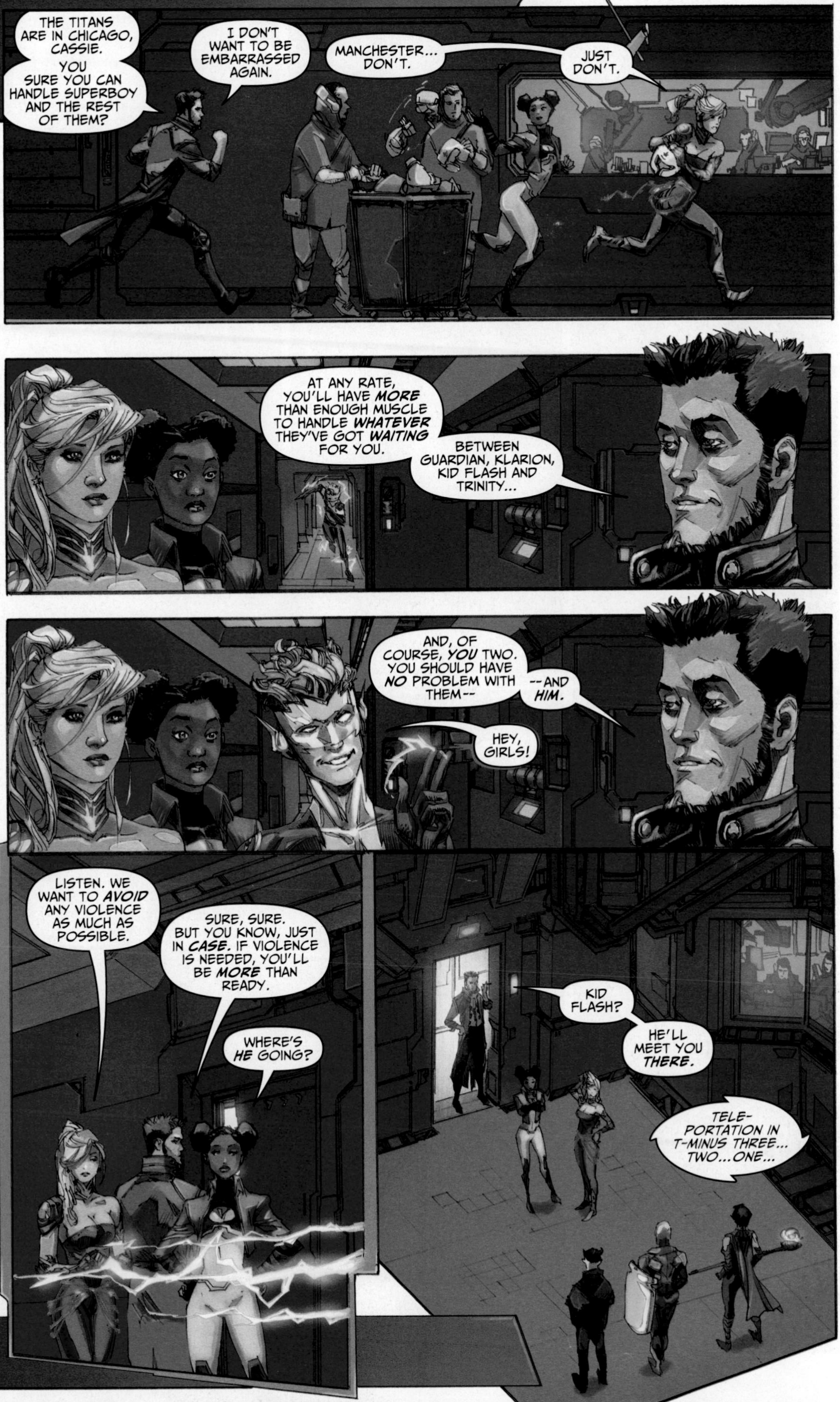
THE TITANS ARE IN CHICAGO, CASSIE.
YOU SURE YOU CAN HANDLE SUPERBOY AND THE REST OF THEM?
I DON'T WANT TO BE EMBARRASSED AGAIN.
MANCHESTER... DON'T.
JUST DON'T.
AT ANY RATE, YOU'LL HAVE MORE THAN ENOUGH MUSCLE TO HANDLE WHATEVER THEY'VE GOT WAITING FOR YOU.
BETWEEN GUARDIAN, KLARION, KID FLASH AND TRINITY...
AND, OF COURSE, YOU TWO. YOU SHOULD HAVE NO PROBLEM WITH THEM--
--AND HIM.
HEY, GIRLS!
LISTEN. WE WANT TO AVOID ANY VIOLENCE AS MUCH AS POSSIBLE.
SURE, SURE. BUT YOU KNOW, JUST IN CASE. IF VIOLENCE IS NEEDED, YOU'LL BE MORE THAN READY.
WHERE'S HE GOING?
KID FLASH?
HE'LL MEET YOU THERE.
TELE-PORTATION IN T-MINUS THREE... TWO...ONE...

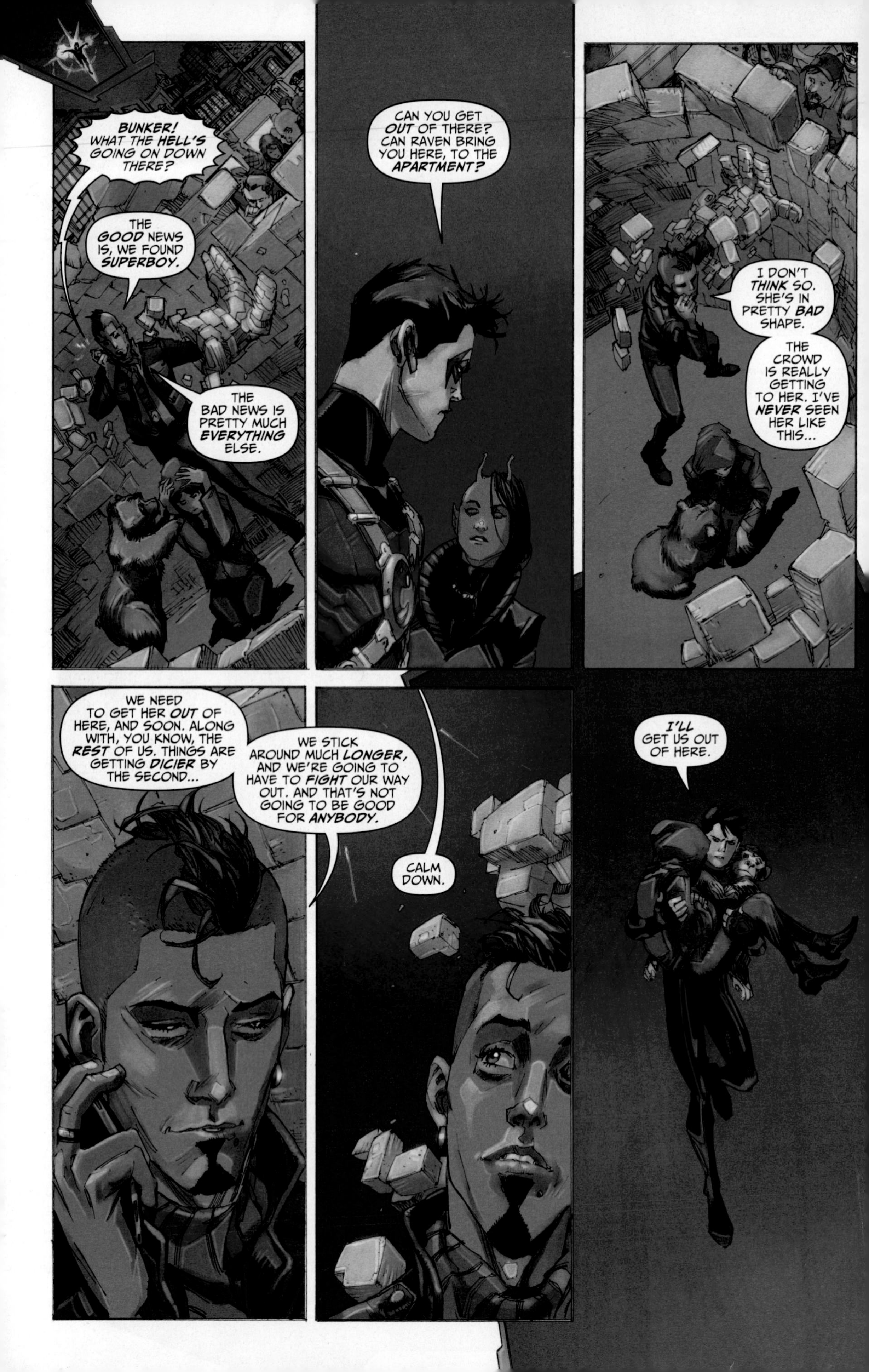
BUNKER! WHAT THE HELL'S GOING ON DOWN THERE?
THE GOOD NEWS IS, WE FOUND SUPERBOY.
THE BAD NEWS IS PRETTY MUCH EVERYTHING ELSE.
CAN YOU GET OUT OF THERE? CAN RAVEN BRING YOU HERE, TO THE APARTMENT?
I DON'T THINK SO. SHE'S IN PRETTY BAD SHAPE.
THE CROWD IS REALLY GETTING TO HER. I'VE NEVER SEEN HER LIKE THIS...
WE NEED TO GET HER OUT OF HERE, AND SOON. ALONG WITH, YOU KNOW, THE REST OF US. THINGS ARE GETTING DICIER BY THE SECOND...
WE STICK AROUND MUCH LONGER, AND WE'RE GOING TO HAVE TO FIGHT OUR WAY OUT. AND THAT'S NOT GOING TO BE GOOD FOR ANYBODY.
CALM DOWN.
I'LL GET US OUT OF HERE.

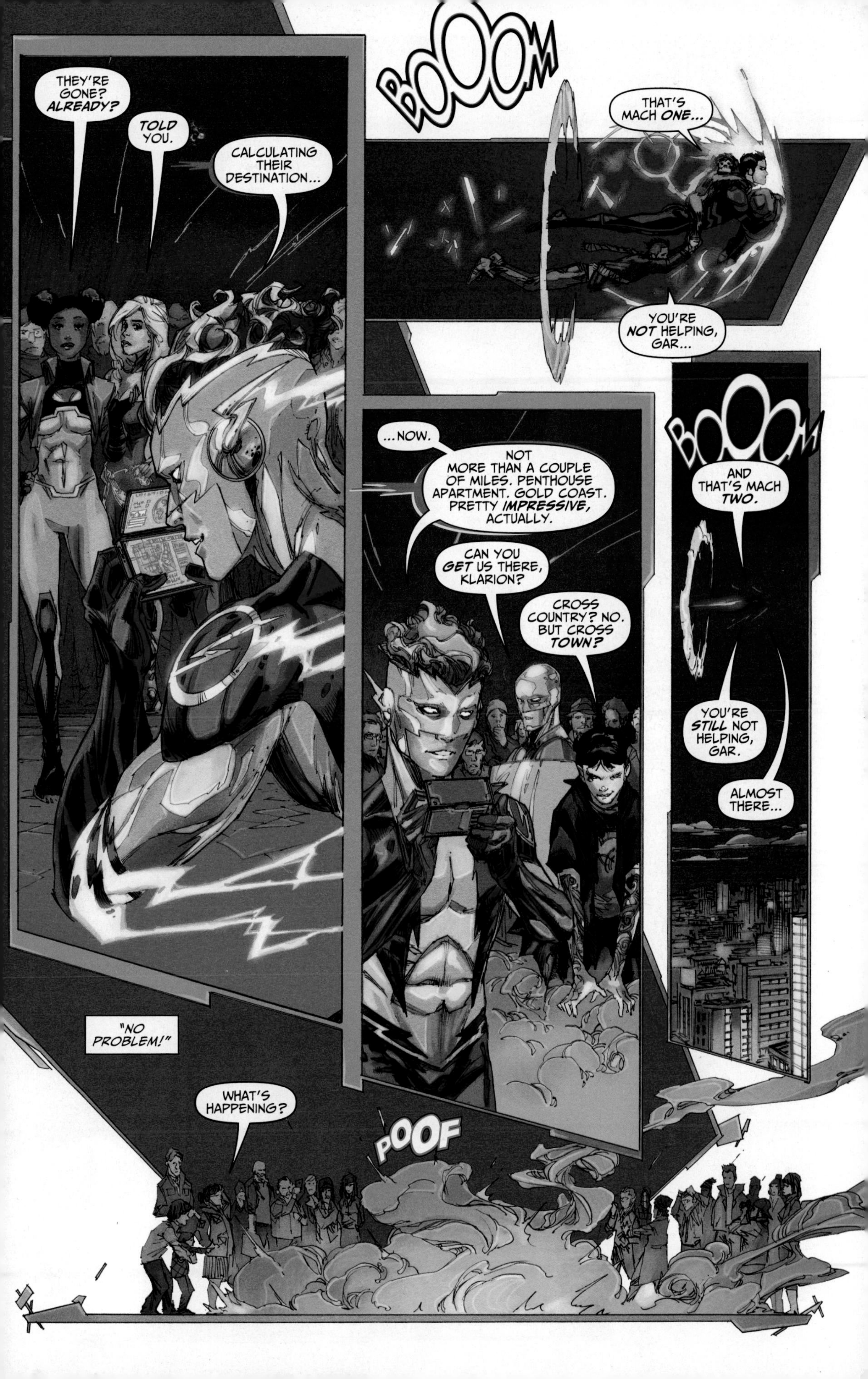

THEY'RE GONE? ALREADY?
TOLD YOU.
CALCULATING THEIR DESTINATION...
BOOOOM
THAT'S MACH ONE...
YOU'RE NOT HELPING, GAR...
...NOW.
NOT MORE THAN A COUPLE OF MILES. PENTHOUSE APARTMENT. GOLD COAST. PRETTY IMPRESSIVE, ACTUALLY.
CAN YOU GET US THERE, KLARION?
CROSS COUNTRY? NO. BUT CROSS TOWN?
BOOOOM
AND THAT'S MACH TWO.
YOU'RE STILL NOT HELPING, GAR.
ALMOST THERE...
"NO PROBLEM!"
WHAT'S HAPPENING?
POOF

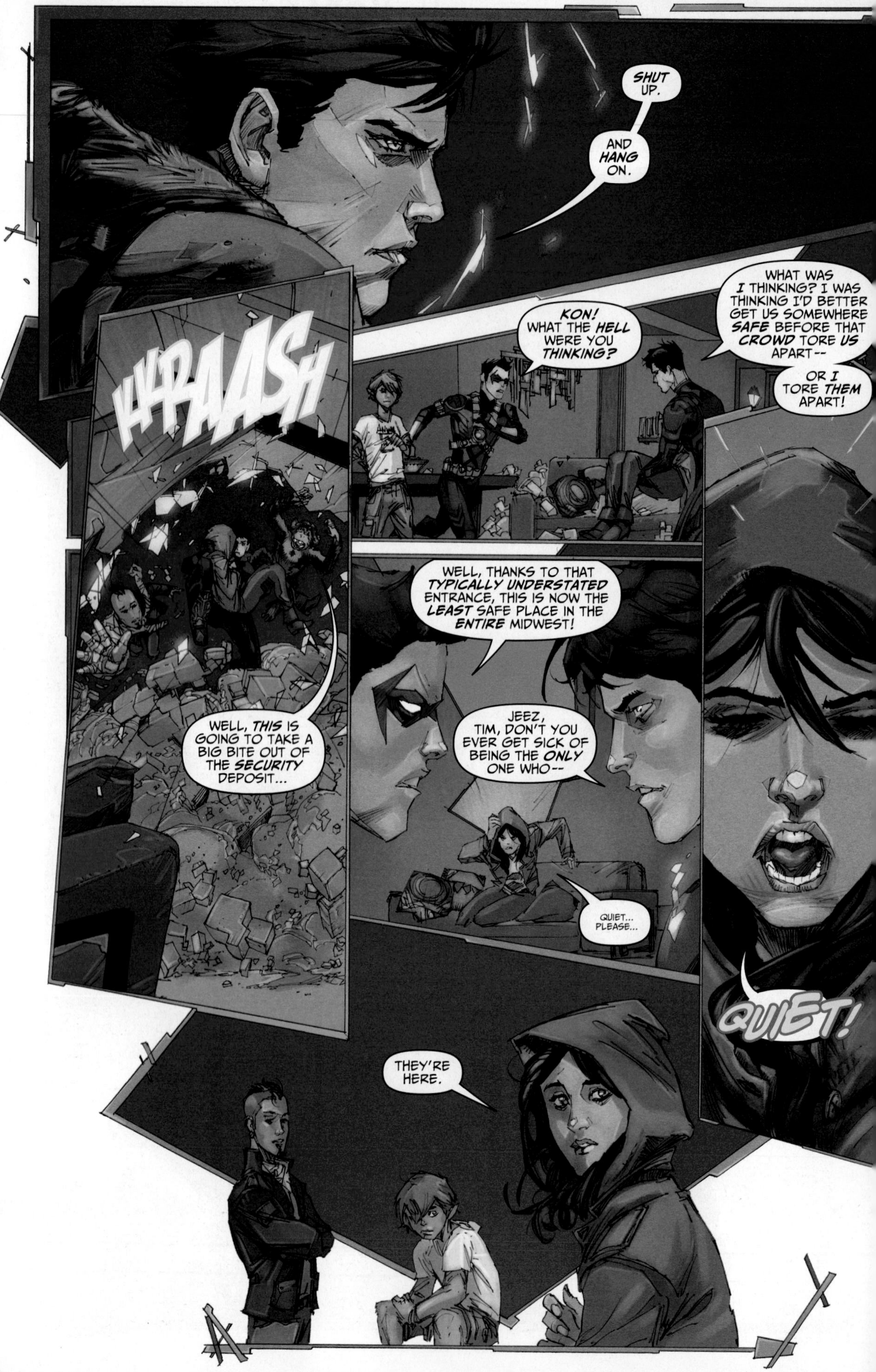

SHUT UP.
AND HANG ON.
K-KRAASH
WELL, THIS IS GOING TO TAKE A BIG BITE OUT OF THE SECURITY DEPOSIT...
KON! WHAT THE HELL WERE YOU THINKING?
WHAT WAS I THINKING? I WAS THINKING I'D BETTER GET US SOMEWHERE SAFE BEFORE THAT CROWD TORE US APART--
OR I TORE THEM APART!
WELL, THANKS TO THAT TYPICALLY UNDERSTATED ENTRANCE, THIS IS NOW THE LEAST SAFE PLACE IN THE ENTIRE MIDWEST!
JEEZ, TIM, DON'T YOU EVER GET SICK OF BEING THE ONLY ONE WHO--
QUIET... PLEASE...
QUIET!
THEY'RE HERE.

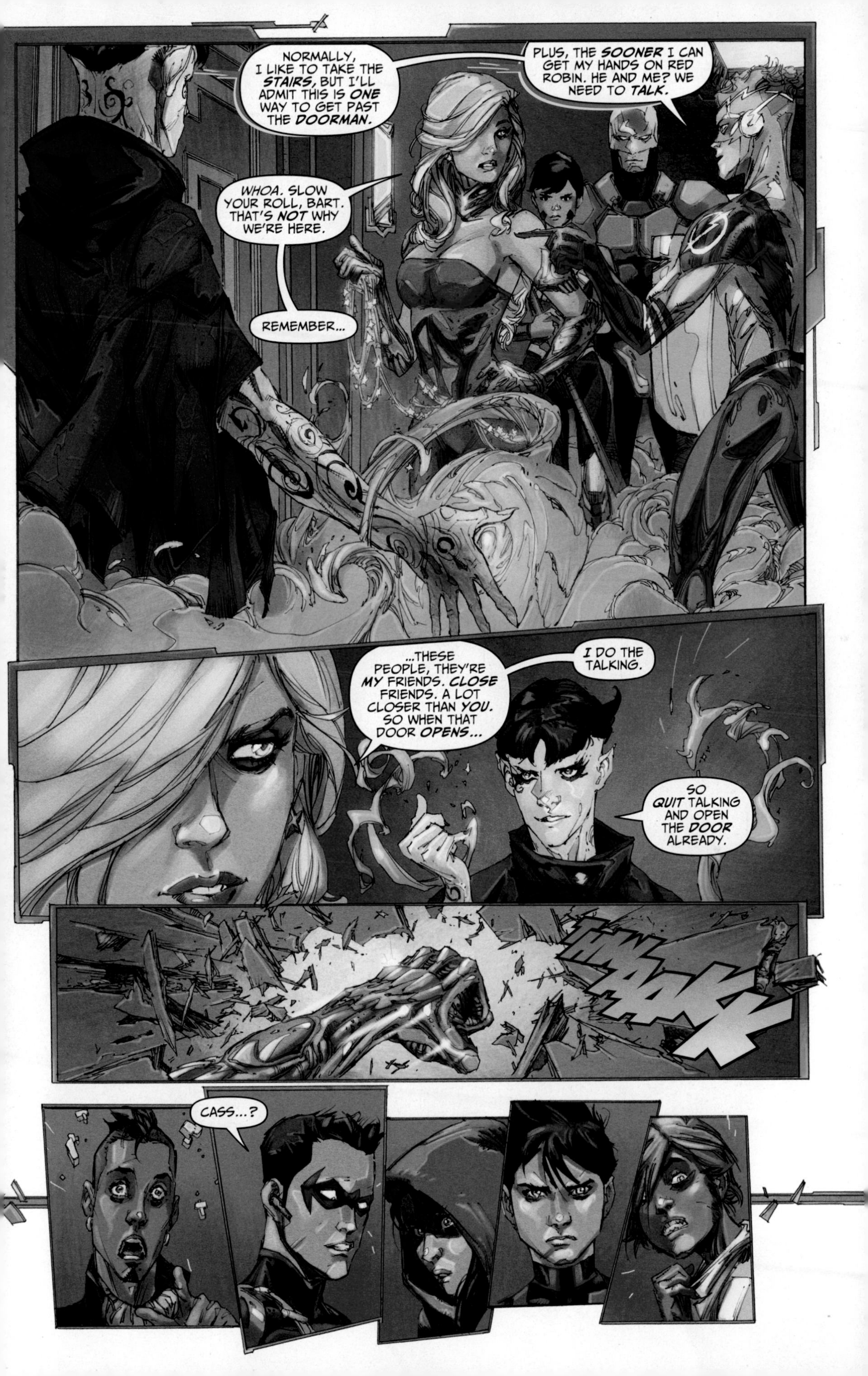
NORMALLY, I LIKE TO TAKE THE STAIRS, BUT I'LL ADMIT THIS IS ONE WAY TO GET PAST THE DOORMAN.
PLUS, THE SOONER I CAN GET MY HANDS ON RED ROBIN. HE AND ME? WE NEED TO TALK.
WHOA. SLOW YOUR ROLL, BART. THAT'S NOT WHY WE'RE HERE.
REMEMBER...
...THESE PEOPLE, THEY'RE MY FRIENDS. CLOSE FRIENDS. A LOT CLOSER THAN YOU. SO WHEN THAT DOOR OPENS...
I DO THE TALKING.
SO QUIT TALKING AND OPEN THE DOOR ALREADY.
CASS...?

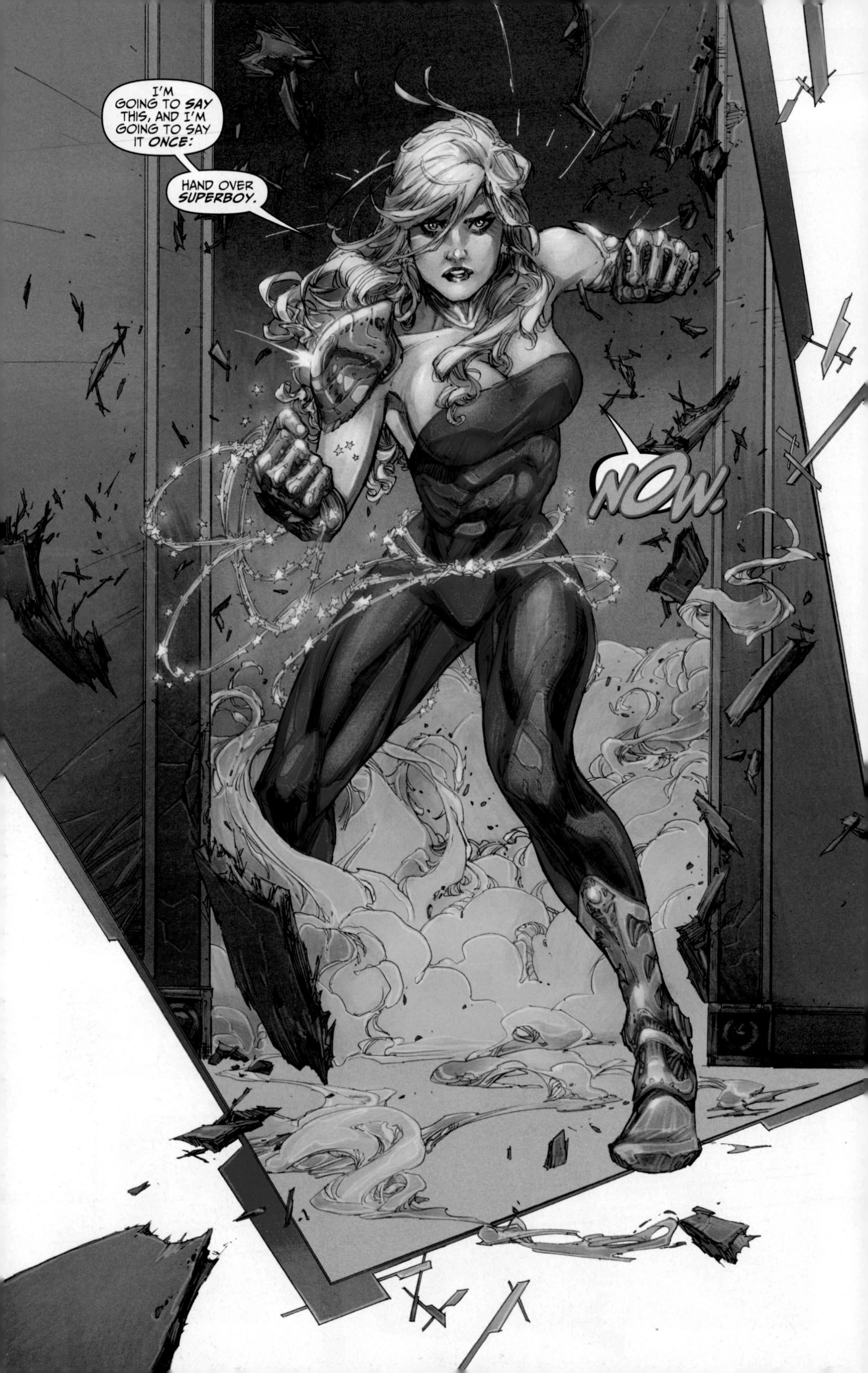
I'M GOING TO SAY THIS, AND I'M GOING TO SAY IT ONCE:
HAND OVER SUPERBOY.
NOW.

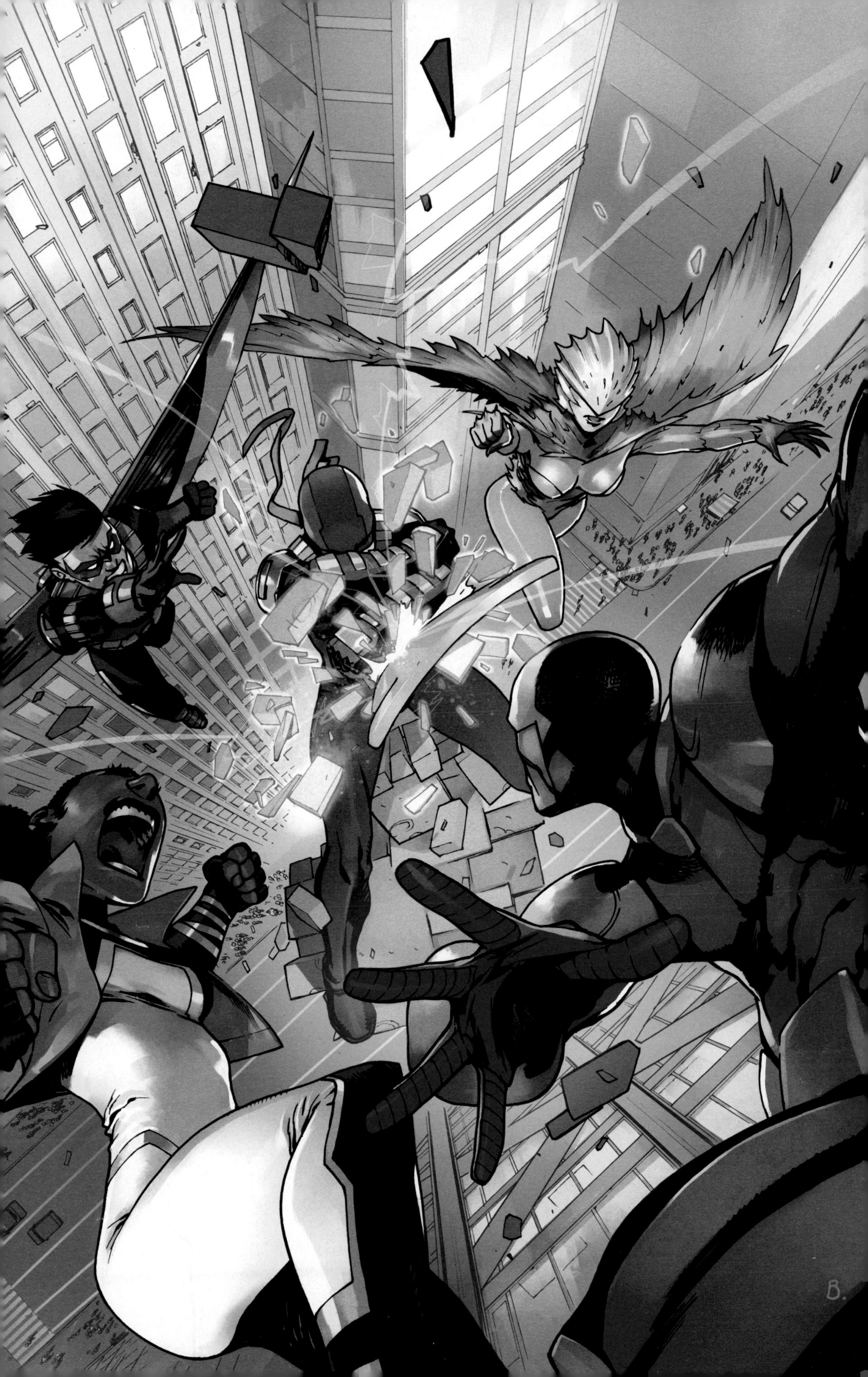
B.

ROGUE TARGETS PART TWO

WILL PFEIFER writer FELIPE WATANABE penciller TREVOR SCOTT inker DAN BROWN colorist JOHN J. HILL letterer cover art by BENGAL

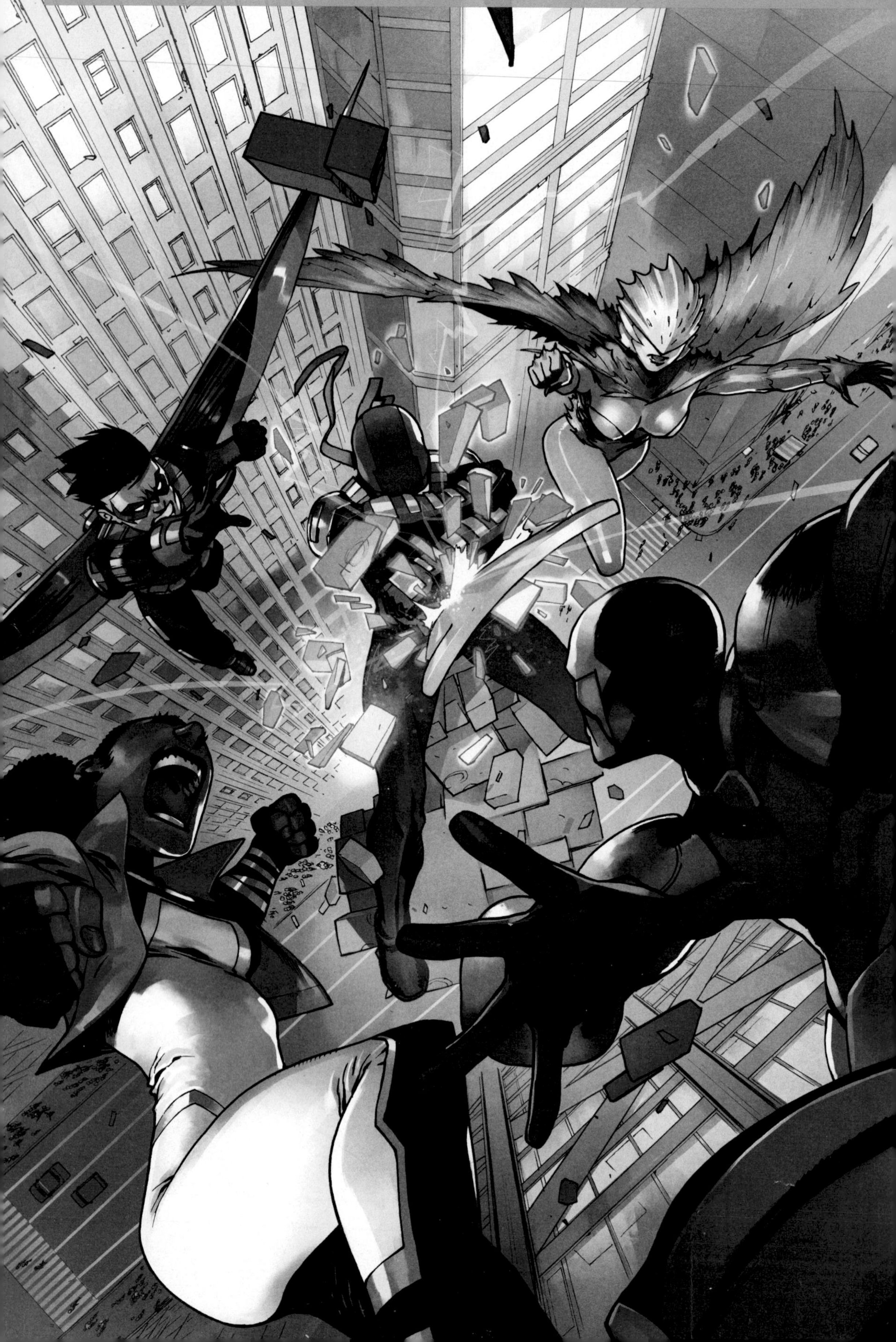

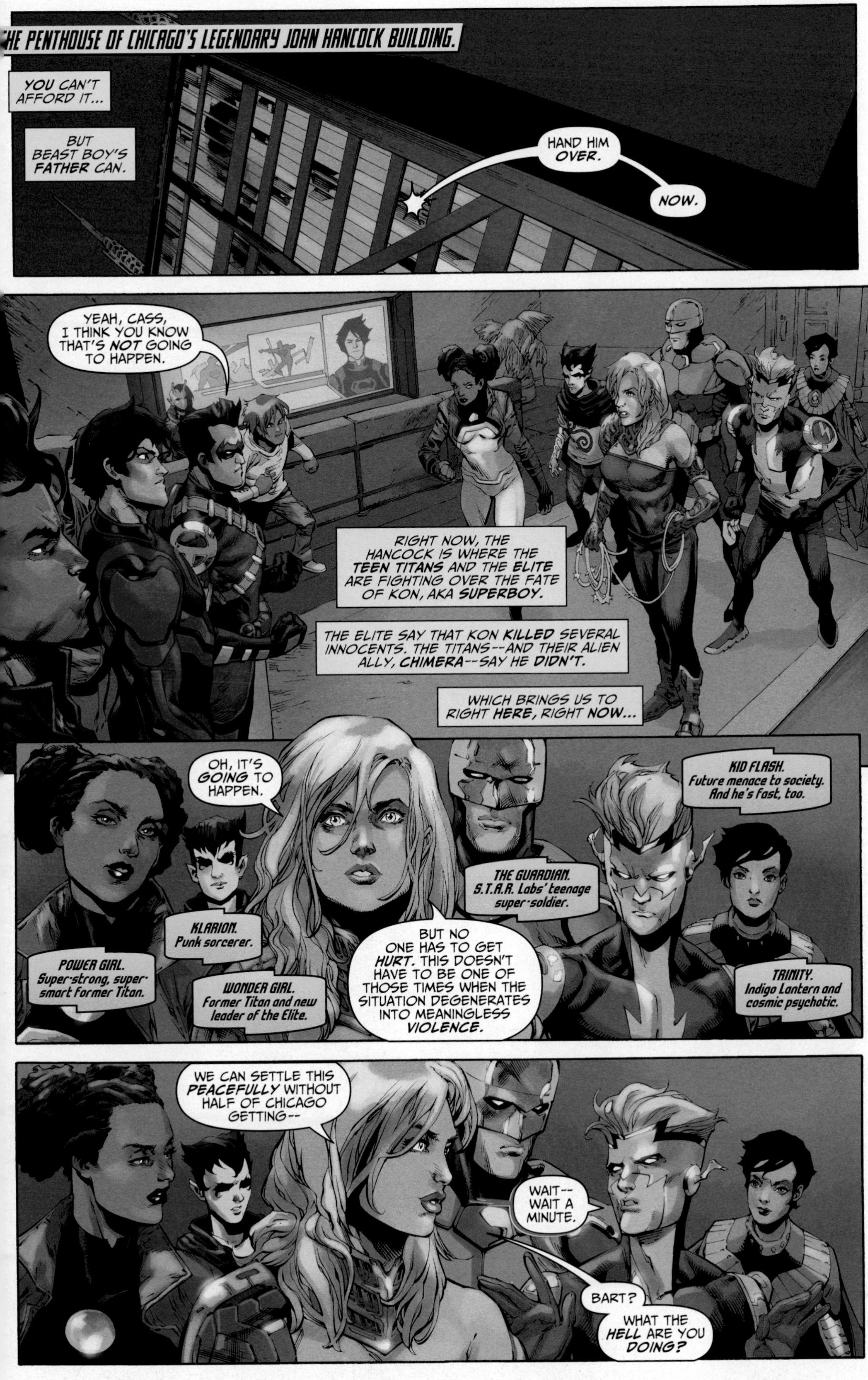

THE PENTHOUSE OF CHICAGO'S LEGENDARY JOHN HANCOCK BUILDING.
YOU CAN'T AFFORD IT...
BUT BEAST BOY'S FATHER CAN.
HAND HIM OVER.
NOW.
YEAH, CASS, I THINK YOU KNOW THAT'S NOT GOING TO HAPPEN.
RIGHT NOW, THE HANCOCK IS WHERE THE TEEN TITANS AND THE ELITE ARE FIGHTING OVER THE FATE OF KON, AKA SUPERBOY.
THE ELITE SAY THAT KON KILLED SEVERAL INNOCENTS. THE TITANS--AND THEIR ALIEN ALLY, CHIMERA--SAY HE DIDN'T.
WHICH BRINGS US TO RIGHT HERE, RIGHT NOW...
OH, IT'S GOING TO HAPPEN.
KID FLASH. Future menace to society. And he's fast, too.
THE GUARDIAN. S.T.A.R. Labs' teenage super-soldier.
KLARION. Punk sorcerer.
POWER GIRL. Super-strong, super-smart former Titan.
WONDER GIRL. Former Titan and new leader of the Elite.
BUT NO ONE HAS TO GET HURT. THIS DOESN'T HAVE TO BE ONE OF THOSE TIMES WHEN THE SITUATION DEGENERATES INTO MEANINGLESS VIOLENCE.
TRINITY. Indigo Lantern and cosmic psychotic.
WE CAN SETTLE THIS PEACEFULLY WITHOUT HALF OF CHICAGO GETTING--
WAIT-- WAIT A MINUTE.
BART?
WHAT THE HELL ARE YOU DOING?

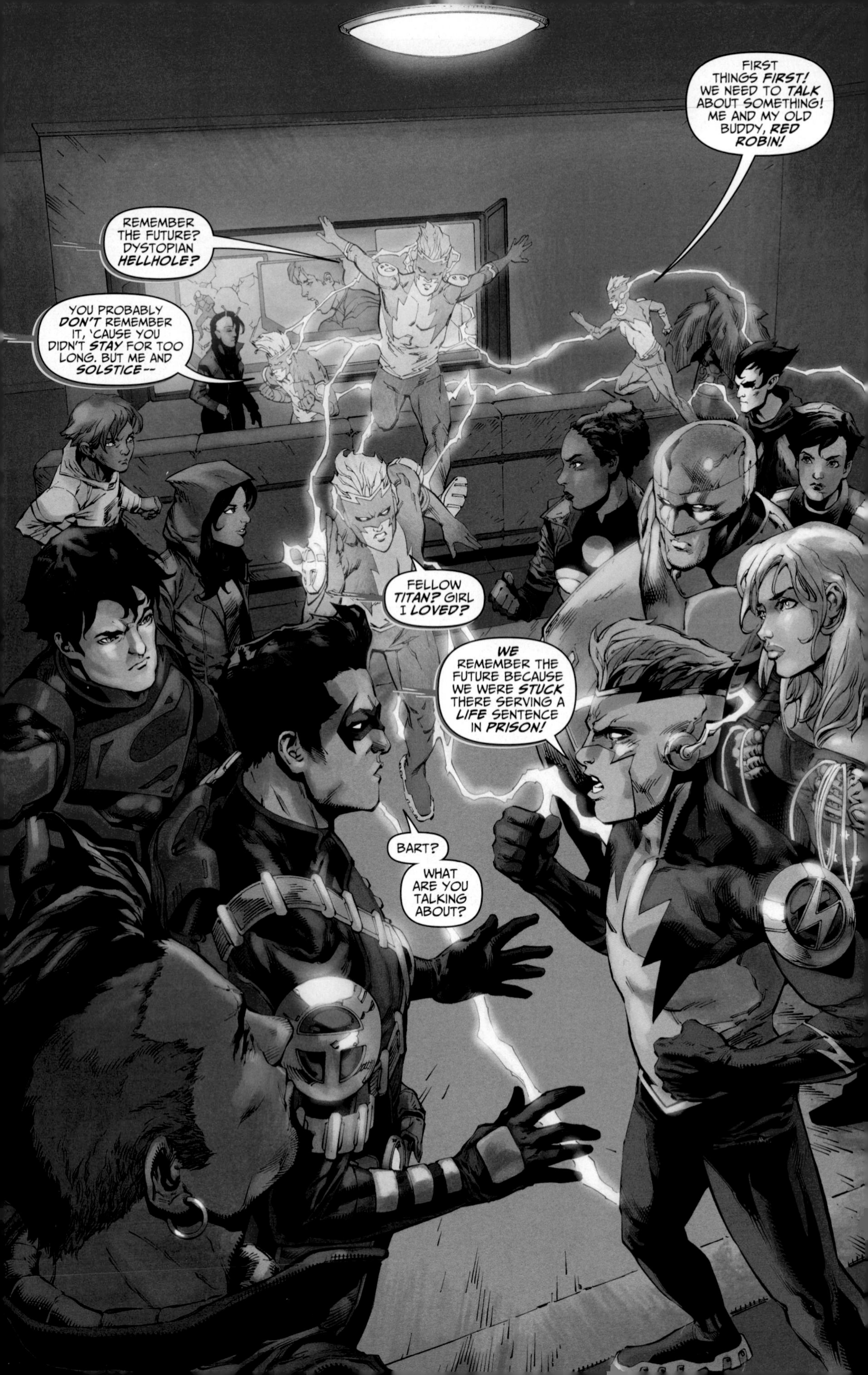
FIRST THINGS FIRST! WE NEED TO TALK ABOUT SOMETHING! ME AND MY OLD BUDDY, RED ROBIN!
REMEMBER THE FUTURE? DYSTOPIAN HELLHOLE?
YOU PROBABLY DON'T REMEMBER IT, 'CAUSE YOU DIDN'T STAY FOR TOO LONG. BUT ME AND SOLSTICE--
FELLOW TITAN? GIRL I LOVED?
WE REMEMBER THE FUTURE BECAUSE WE WERE STUCK THERE SERVING A LIFE SENTENCE IN PRISON!
BART?
WHAT ARE YOU TALKING ABOUT?

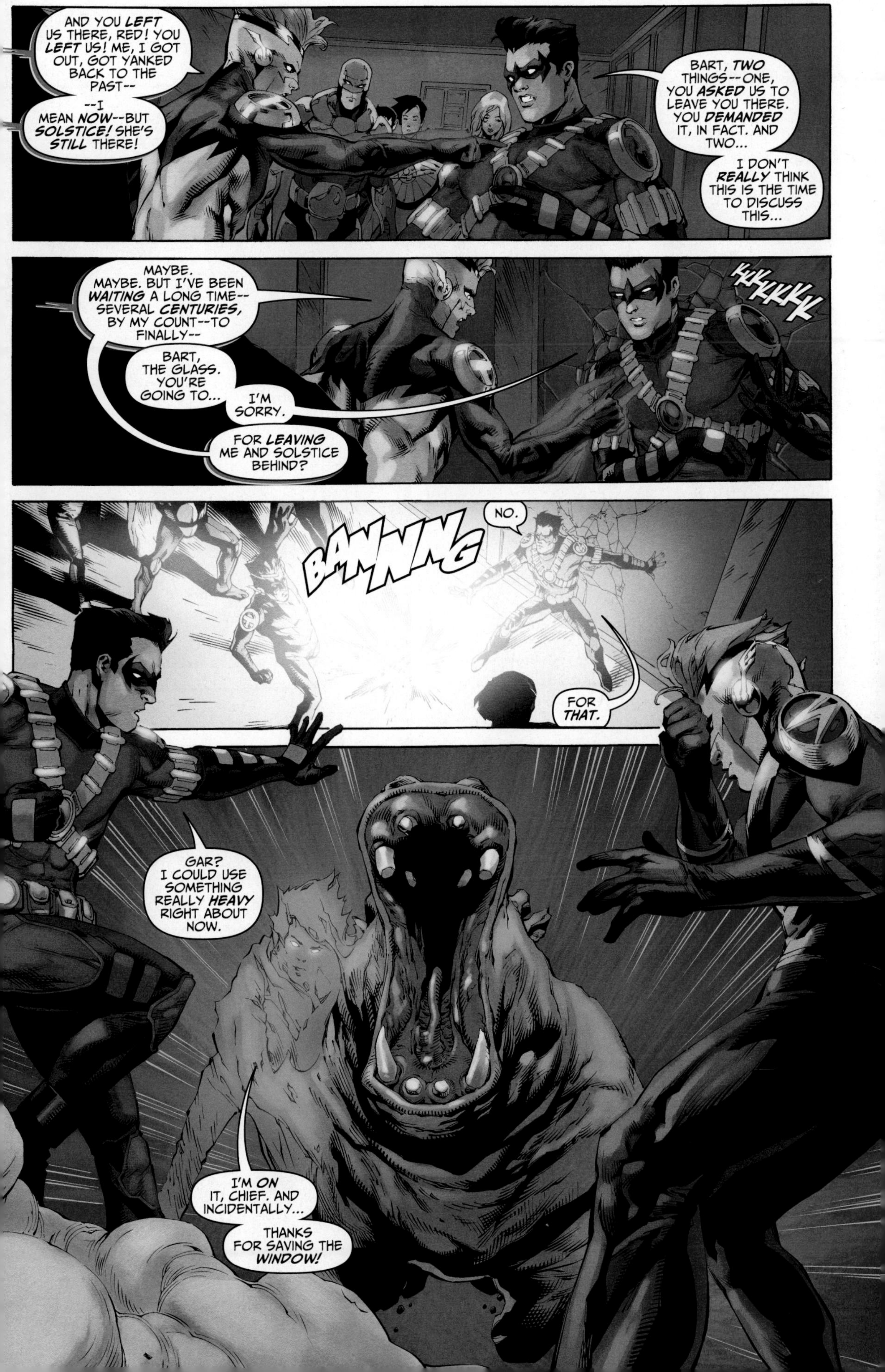
AND YOU LEFT US THERE, RED! YOU LEFT US! ME, I GOT OUT, GOT YANKED BACK TO THE PAST--
--I MEAN NOW--BUT SOLSTICE! SHE'S STILL THERE!
BART, TWO THINGS--ONE, YOU ASKED US TO LEAVE YOU THERE. YOU DEMANDED IT, IN FACT. AND TWO...
I DON'T REALLY THINK THIS IS THE TIME TO DISCUSS THIS...
MAYBE. MAYBE. BUT I'VE BEEN WAITING A LONG TIME--SEVERAL CENTURIES, BY MY COUNT--TO FINALLY--
KKKKKKK
BART, THE GLASS. YOU'RE GOING TO...
I'M SORRY.
FOR LEAVING ME AND SOLSTICE BEHIND?
NO.
BANNNG
FOR THAT.
GAR? I COULD USE SOMETHING REALLY HEAVY RIGHT ABOUT NOW.
I'M ON IT, CHIEF. AND INCIDENTALLY...
THANKS FOR SAVING THE WINDOW!

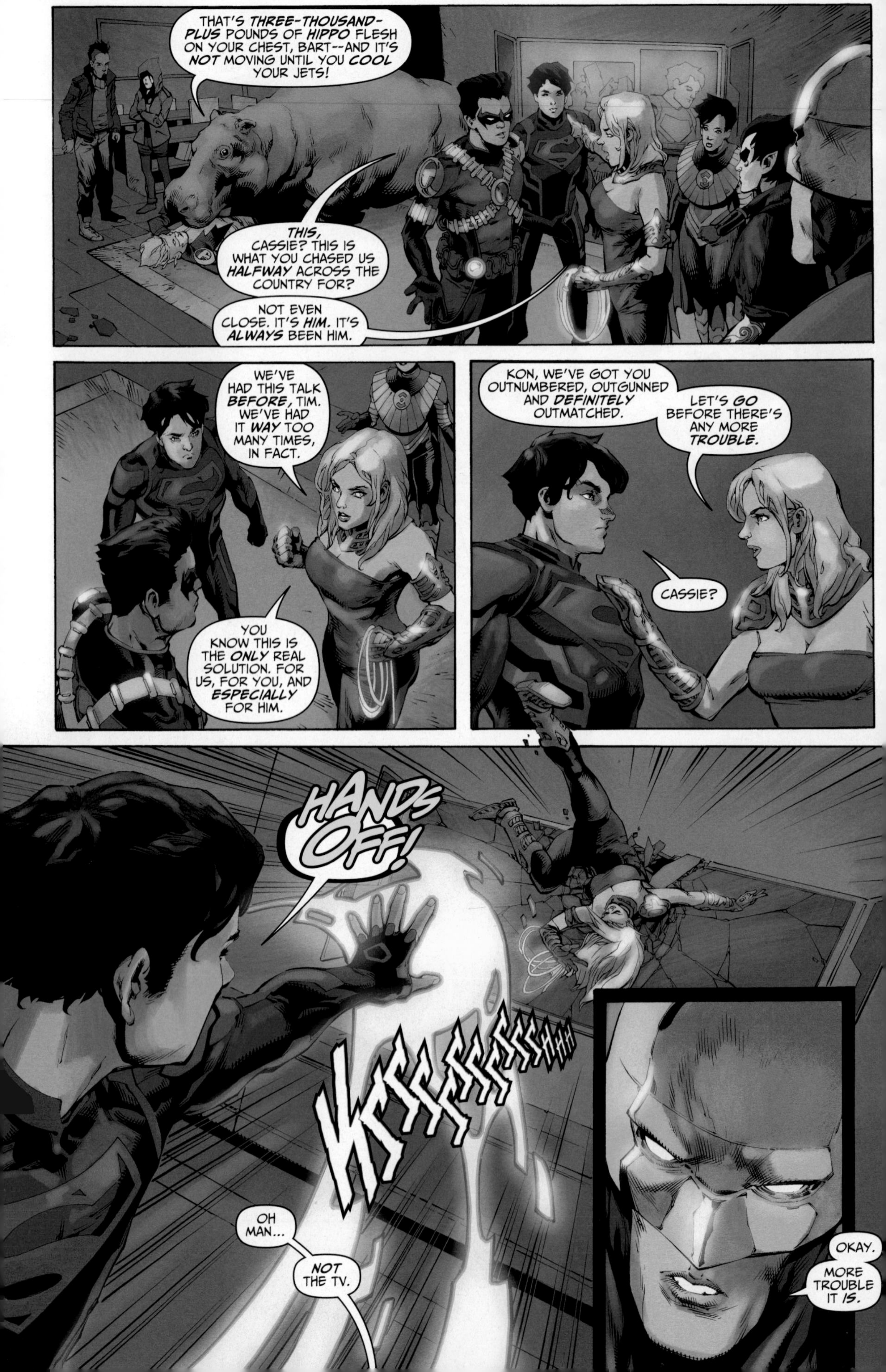
THAT'S THREE-THOUSAND-PLUS POUNDS OF HIPPO FLESH ON YOUR CHEST, BART--AND IT'S NOT MOVING UNTIL YOU COOL YOUR JETS!
THIS, CASSIE? THIS IS WHAT YOU CHASED US HALFWAY ACROSS THE COUNTRY FOR?
NOT EVEN CLOSE. IT'S HIM. IT'S ALWAYS BEEN HIM.
WE'VE HAD THIS TALK BEFORE, TIM. WE'VE HAD IT WAY TOO MANY TIMES, IN FACT.
YOU KNOW THIS IS THE ONLY REAL SOLUTION. FOR US, FOR YOU, AND ESPECIALLY FOR HIM.
KON, WE'VE GOT YOU OUTNUMBERED, OUTGUNNED AND DEFINITELY OUTMATCHED.
LET'S GO BEFORE THERE'S ANY MORE TROUBLE.
CASSIE?
HANDS OFF!
KSSSSSSSHHH
OH MAN...
NOT THE TV.
OKAY.
MORE TROUBLE IT IS.

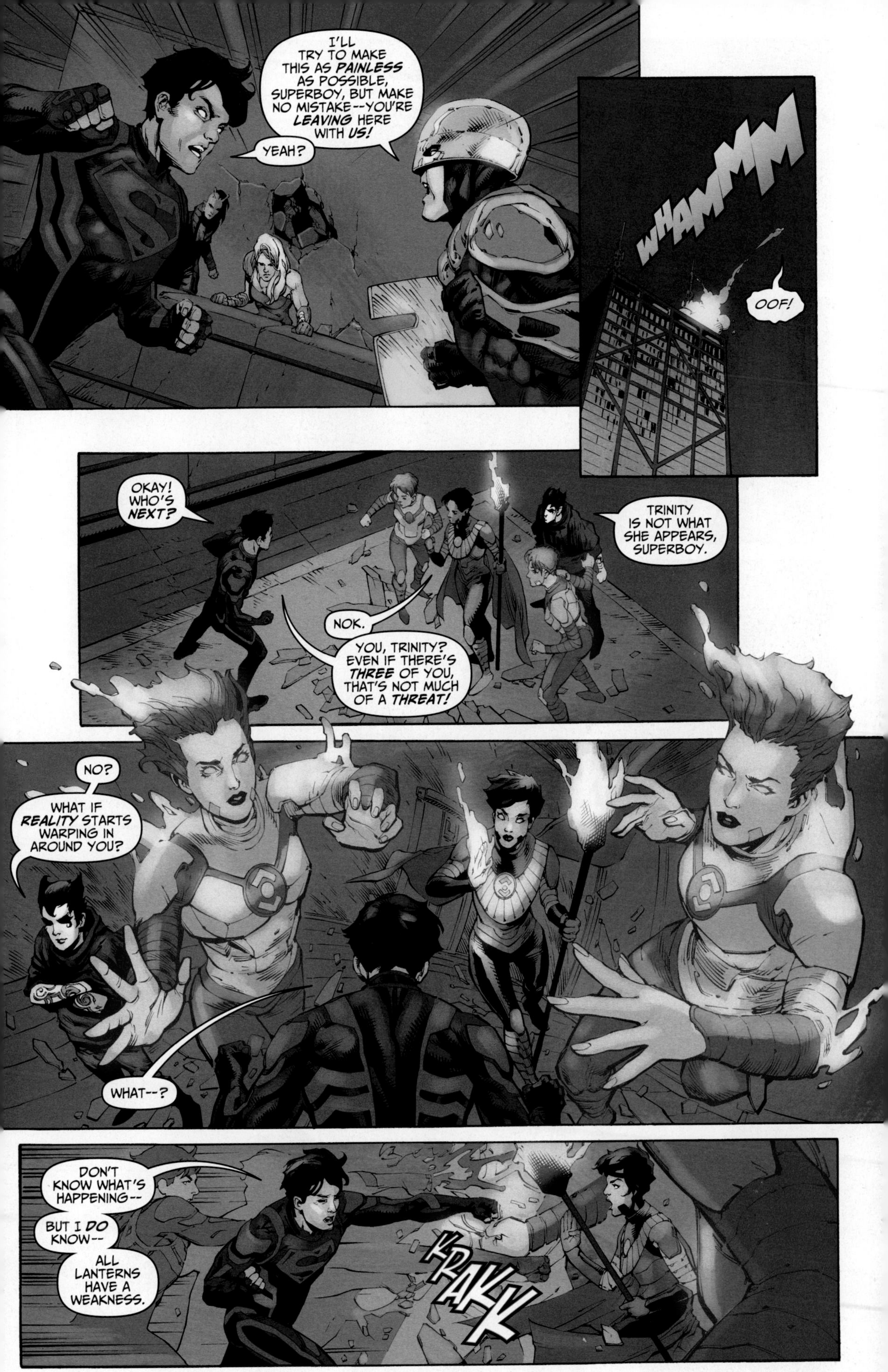
I'LL TRY TO MAKE THIS AS *PAINLESS* AS POSSIBLE, SUPERBOY, BUT MAKE NO MISTAKE--YOU'RE *LEAVING* HERE WITH *US!*
YEAH?
WHAMMM
OOF!
OKAY! WHO'S *NEXT?*
TRINITY IS NOT WHAT SHE APPEARS, SUPERBOY.
NOK.
YOU, TRINITY? EVEN IF THERE'S *THREE* OF YOU, THAT'S NOT MUCH OF A *THREAT!*
NO?
WHAT IF *REALITY* STARTS WARPING IN AROUND YOU?
WHAT--?
DON'T KNOW WHAT'S HAPPENING--
BUT I *DO* KNOW--
ALL LANTERNS HAVE A WEAKNESS.
KRAKK

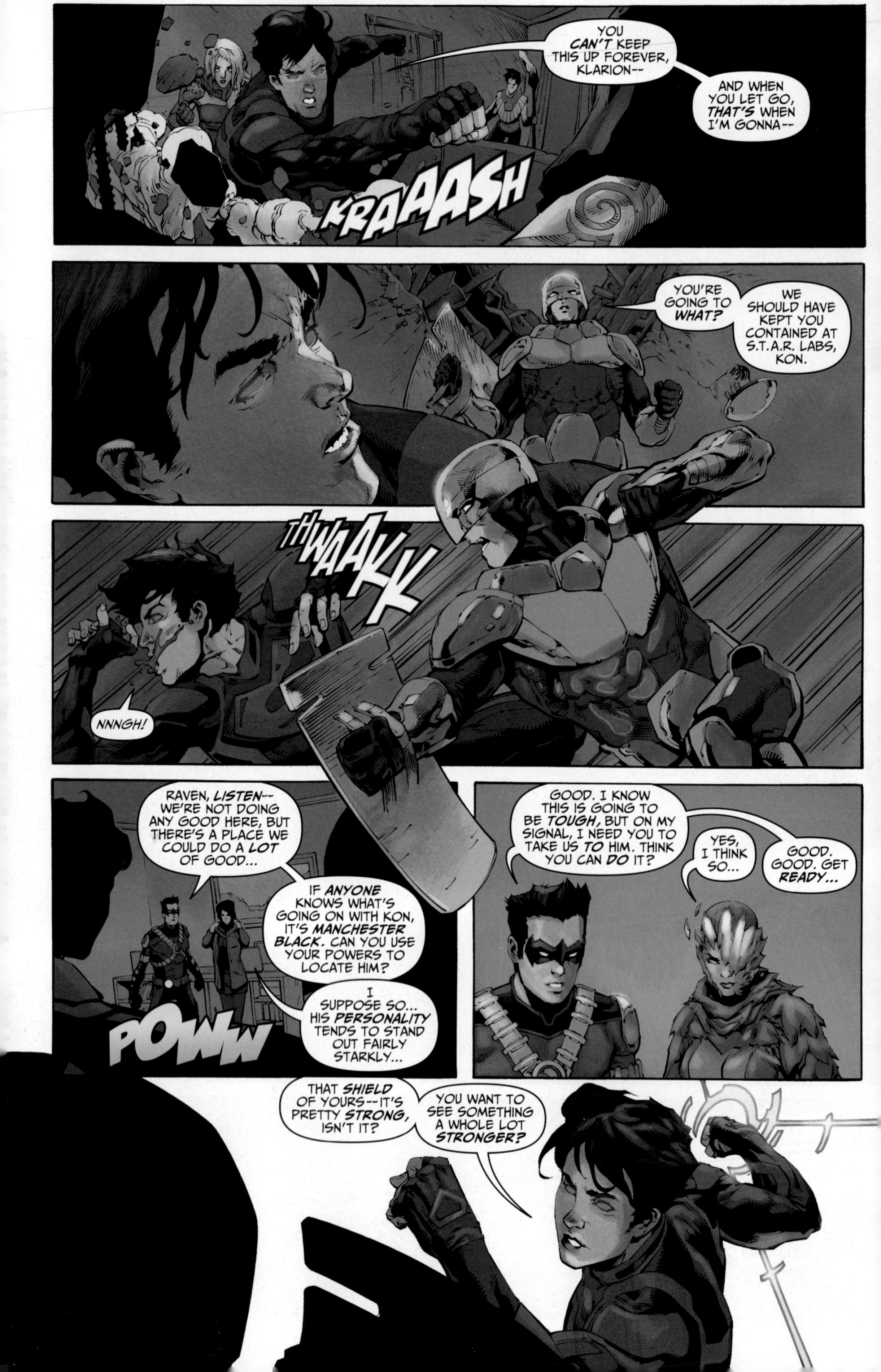
YOU CAN'T KEEP THIS UP FOREVER, KLARION--
AND WHEN YOU LET GO, THAT'S WHEN I'M GONNA--
KRAAASH
YOU'RE GOING TO WHAT?
WE SHOULD HAVE KEPT YOU CONTAINED AT S.T.A.R. LABS, KON.
THWAAKK
NNNGH!
RAVEN, LISTEN-- WE'RE NOT DOING ANY GOOD HERE, BUT THERE'S A PLACE WE COULD DO A LOT OF GOOD...
IF ANYONE KNOWS WHAT'S GOING ON WITH KON, IT'S MANCHESTER BLACK. CAN YOU USE YOUR POWERS TO LOCATE HIM?
I SUPPOSE SO... HIS PERSONALITY TENDS TO STAND OUT FAIRLY STARKLY...
POWW
GOOD. I KNOW THIS IS GOING TO BE TOUGH, BUT ON MY SIGNAL, I NEED YOU TO TAKE US TO HIM. THINK YOU CAN DO IT?
YES, I THINK SO...
GOOD. GOOD. GET READY...
THAT SHIELD OF YOURS--IT'S PRETTY STRONG, ISN'T IT?
YOU WANT TO SEE SOMETHING A WHOLE LOT STRONGER?

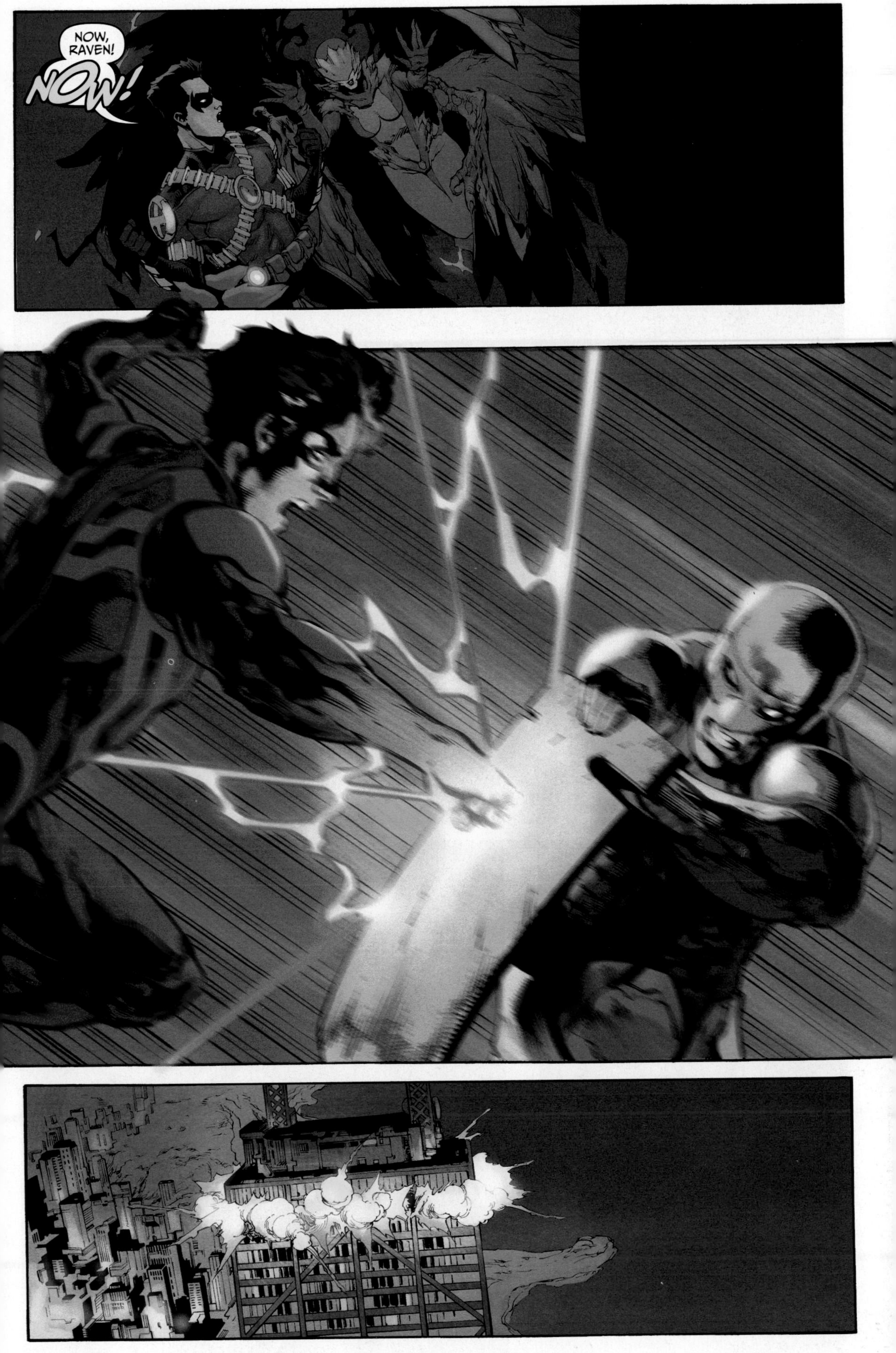
NOW, RAVEN!
NOW!

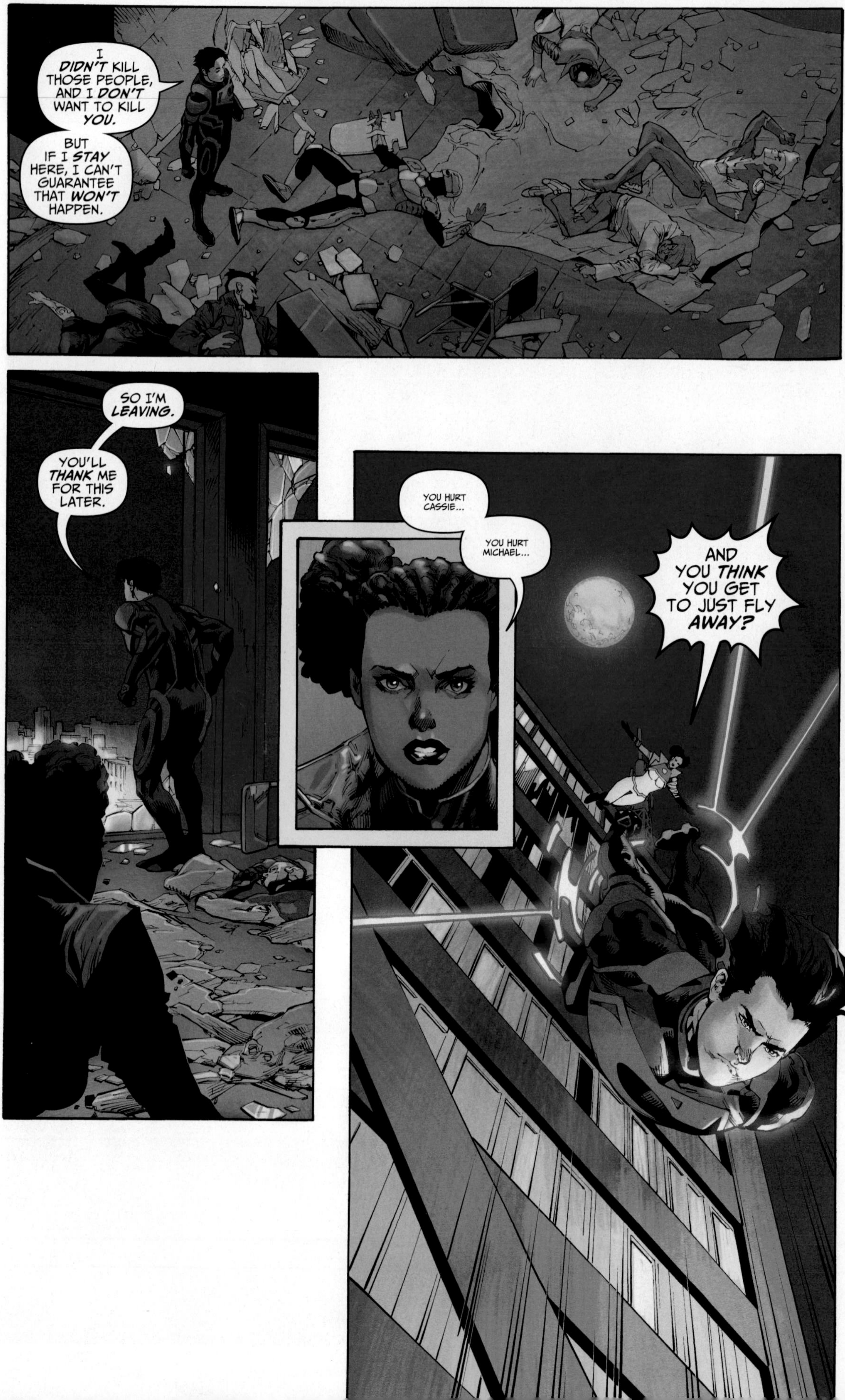
I DIDN'T KILL THOSE PEOPLE, AND I DON'T WANT TO KILL YOU.
BUT IF I STAY HERE, I CAN'T GUARANTEE THAT WON'T HAPPEN.
SO I'M LEAVING.
YOU'LL THANK ME FOR THIS LATER.
YOU HURT CASSIE...
YOU HURT MICHAEL...
AND YOU THINK YOU GET TO JUST FLY AWAY?

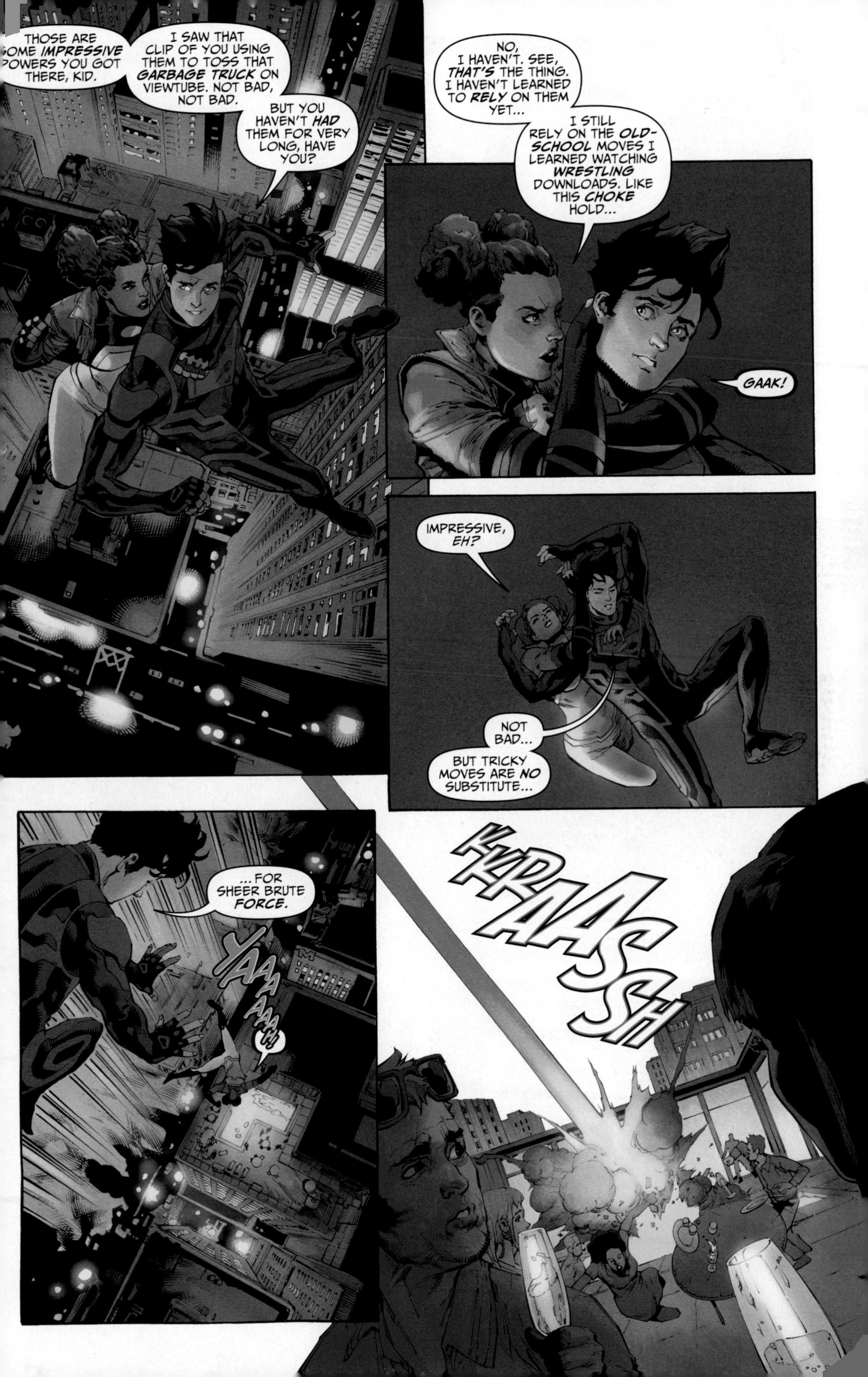
THOSE ARE SOME IMPRESSIVE POWERS YOU GOT THERE, KID.
I SAW THAT CLIP OF YOU USING THEM TO TOSS THAT GARBAGE TRUCK ON VIEWTUBE. NOT BAD, NOT BAD.
BUT YOU HAVEN'T HAD THEM FOR VERY LONG, HAVE YOU?
NO, I HAVEN'T. SEE, THAT'S THE THING. I HAVEN'T LEARNED TO RELY ON THEM YET...
I STILL RELY ON THE OLD-SCHOOL MOVES I LEARNED WATCHING WRESTLING DOWNLOADS. LIKE THIS CHOKE HOLD...
GAAK!
IMPRESSIVE, EH?
NOT BAD...
BUT TRICKY MOVES ARE NO SUBSTITUTE...
...FOR SHEER BRUTE FORCE.
YAAAAAAH!
KRAAASH

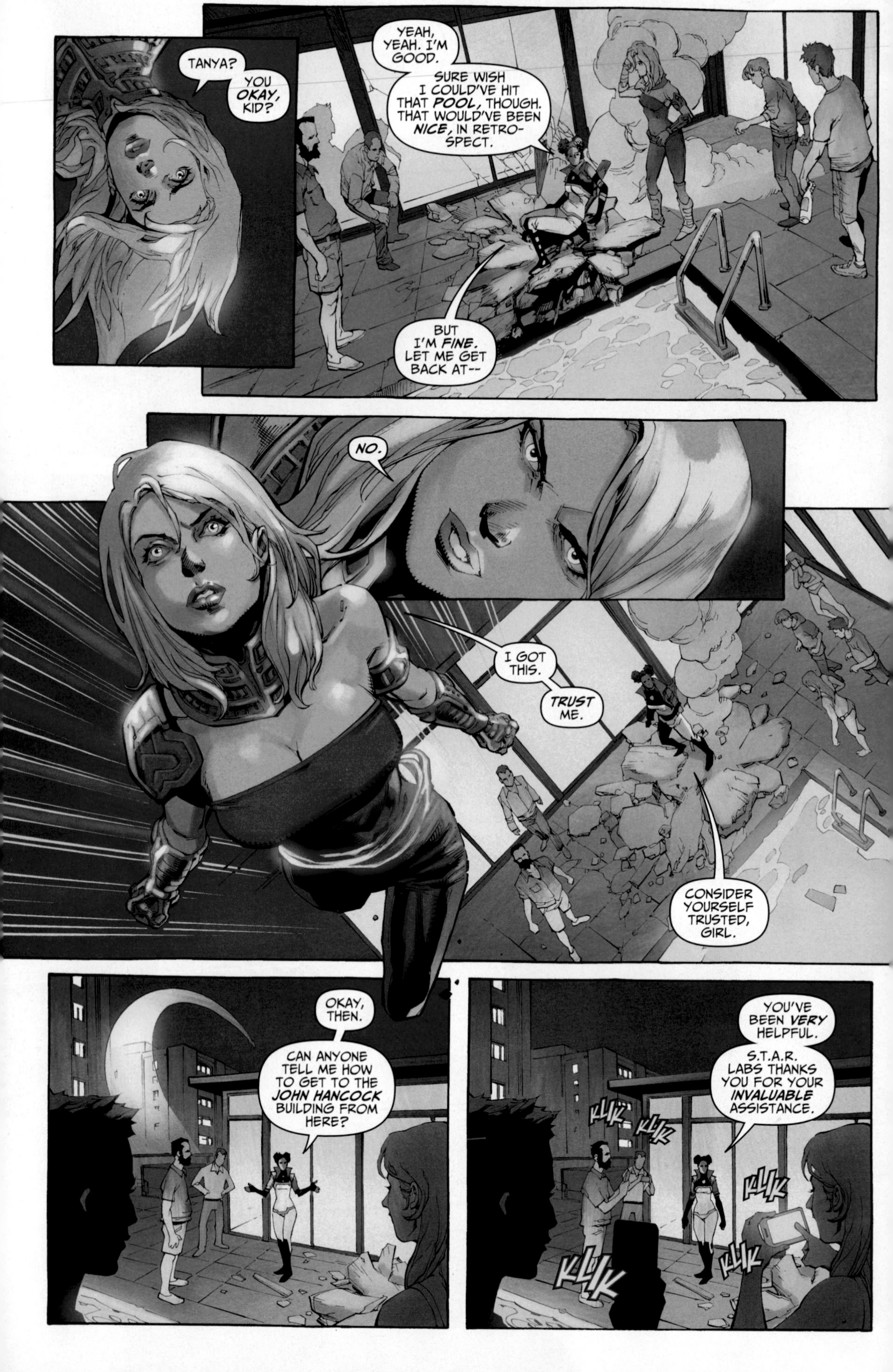
TANYA?
YOU OKAY, KID?
YEAH, YEAH. I'M GOOD.
SURE WISH I COULD'VE HIT THAT POOL, THOUGH. THAT WOULD'VE BEEN NICE, IN RETRO-SPECT.
BUT I'M FINE. LET ME GET BACK AT--
NO.
I GOT THIS.
TRUST ME.
CONSIDER YOURSELF TRUSTED, GIRL.
OKAY, THEN.
CAN ANYONE TELL ME HOW TO GET TO THE JOHN HANCOCK BUILDING FROM HERE?
YOU'VE BEEN VERY HELPFUL.
S.T.A.R. LABS THANKS YOU FOR YOUR INVALUABLE ASSISTANCE.
KLIK
KLIK
KLIK
KLIK
KLIK

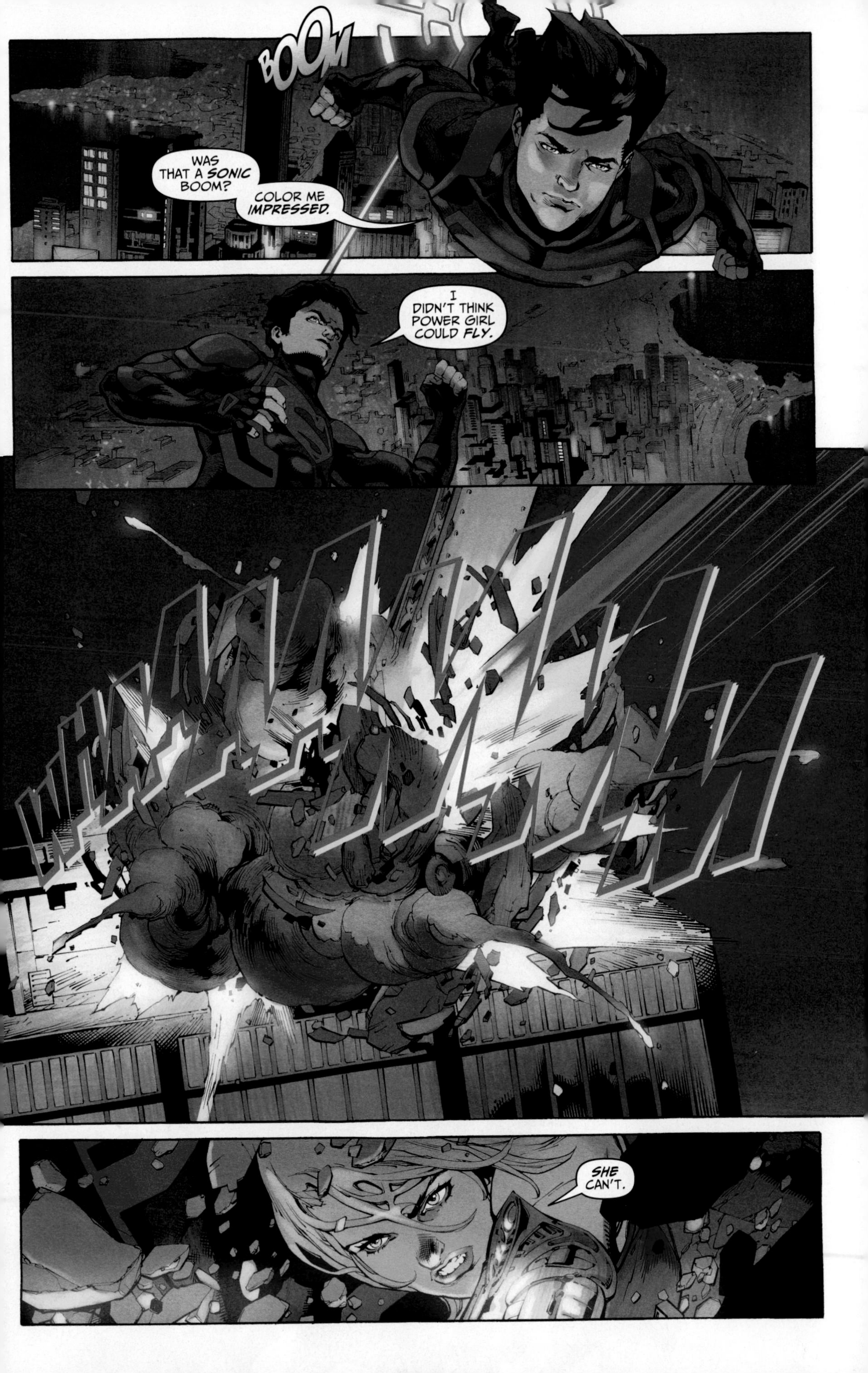
BOOM
WAS THAT A SONIC BOOM?
COLOR ME IMPRESSED.
I DIDN'T THINK POWER GIRL COULD FLY.
SHE CAN'T.

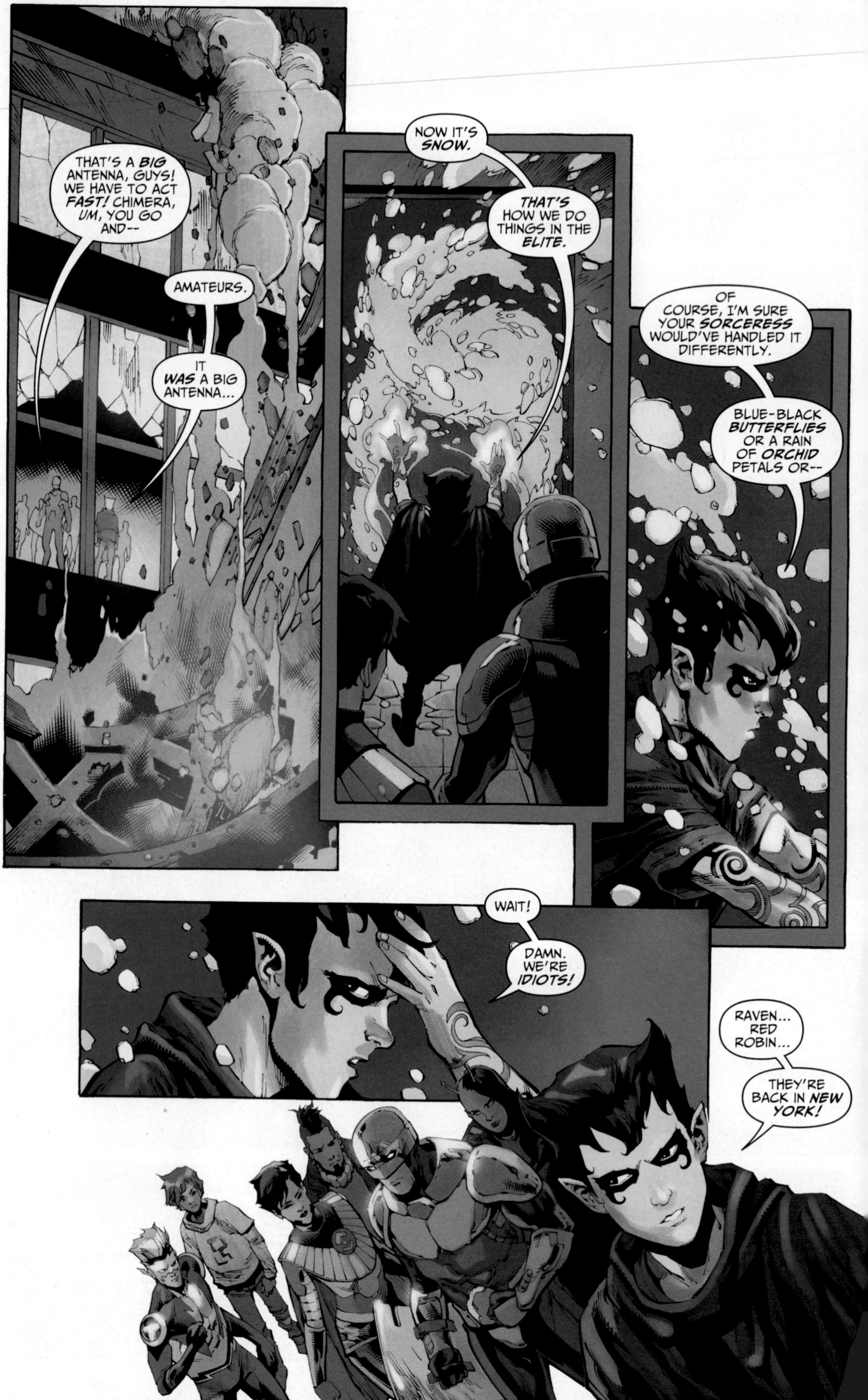
THAT'S A BIG ANTENNA, GUYS! WE HAVE TO ACT FAST! CHIMERA, UM, YOU GO AND--
AMATEURS.
IT WAS A BIG ANTENNA...
NOW IT'S SNOW.
THAT'S HOW WE DO THINGS IN THE ELITE.
OF COURSE, I'M SURE YOUR SORCERESS WOULD'VE HANDLED IT DIFFERENTLY.
BLUE-BLACK BUTTERFLIES OR A RAIN OF ORCHID PETALS OR--
WAIT!
DAMN. WE'RE IDIOTS!
RAVEN... RED ROBIN...
THEY'RE BACK IN NEW YORK!

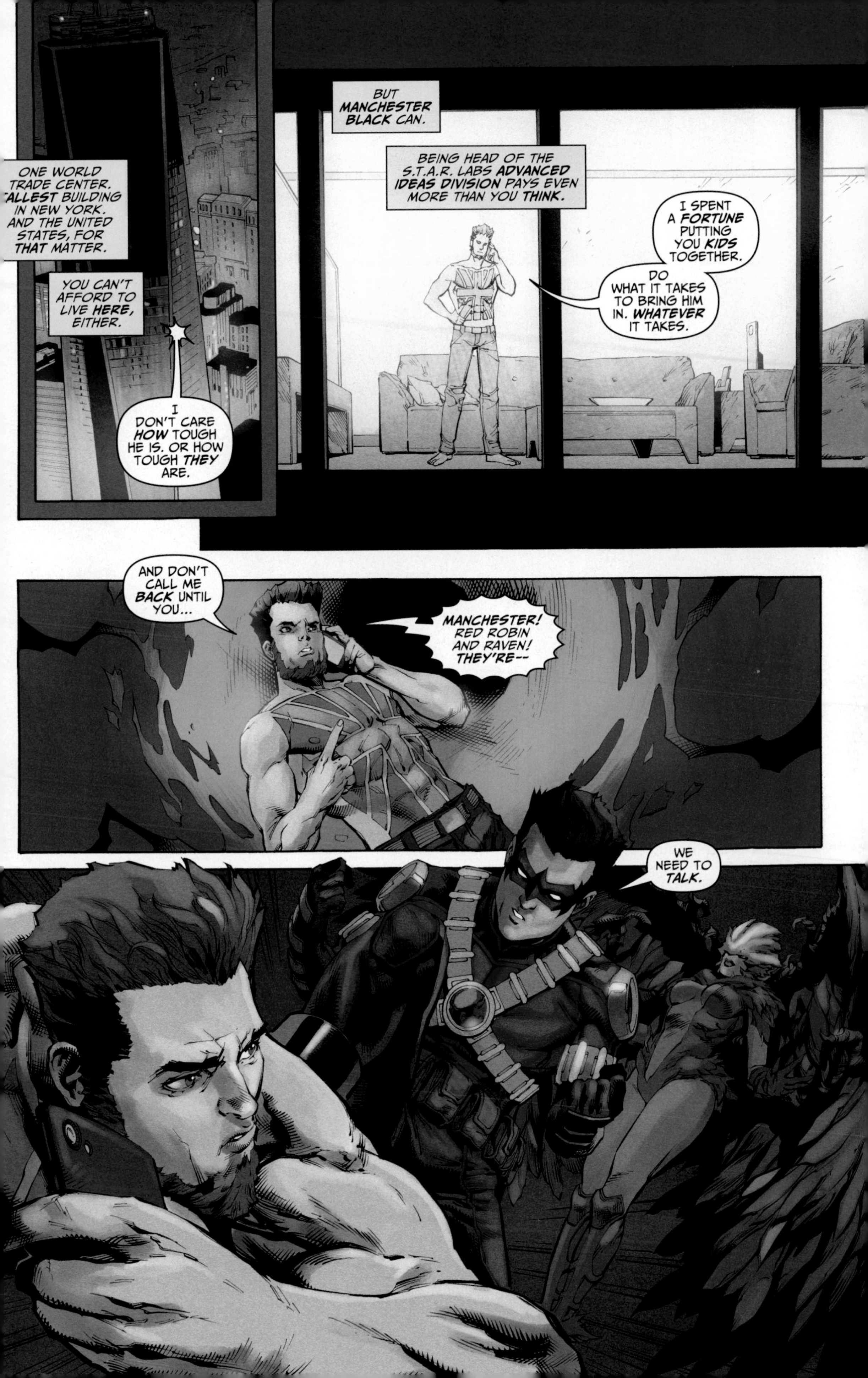
ONE WORLD TRADE CENTER. TALLEST BUILDING IN NEW YORK. AND THE UNITED STATES, FOR THAT MATTER.
YOU CAN'T AFFORD TO LIVE HERE, EITHER.
I DON'T CARE HOW TOUGH HE IS. OR HOW TOUGH THEY ARE.
BUT MANCHESTER BLACK CAN.
BEING HEAD OF THE S.T.A.R. LABS ADVANCED IDEAS DIVISION PAYS EVEN MORE THAN YOU THINK.
I SPENT A FORTUNE PUTTING YOU KIDS TOGETHER.
DO WHAT IT TAKES TO BRING HIM IN. WHATEVER IT TAKES.
AND DON'T CALL ME BACK UNTIL YOU...
MANCHESTER! RED ROBIN AND RAVEN! THEY'RE--
WE NEED TO TALK.

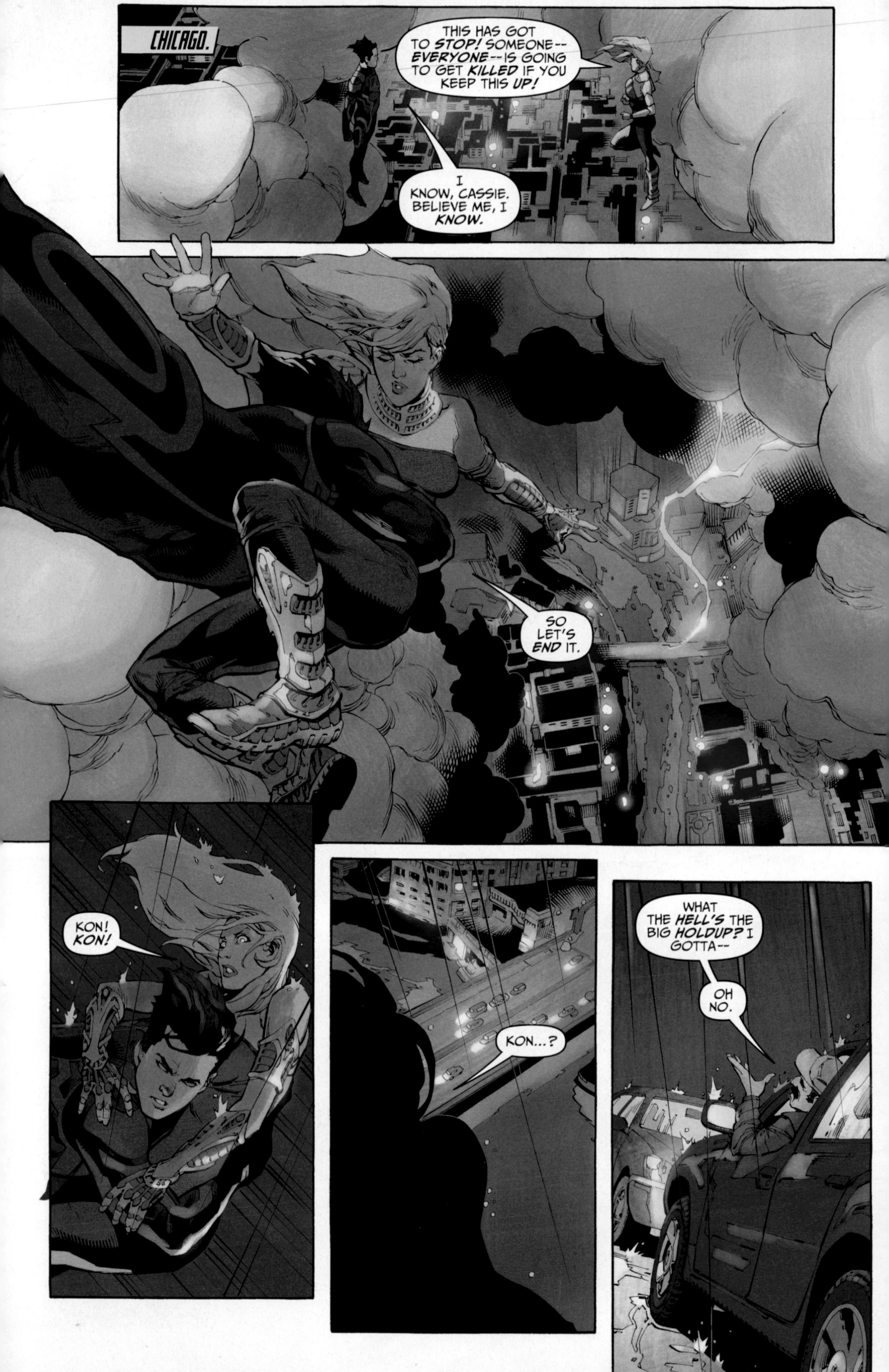
CHICAGO.
THIS HAS GOT TO STOP! SOMEONE--EVERYONE--IS GOING TO GET KILLED IF YOU KEEP THIS UP!
I KNOW, CASSIE. BELIEVE ME, I KNOW.
SO LET'S END IT.
KON! KON!
KON...?
WHAT THE HELL'S THE BIG HOLDUP? I GOTTA--
OH NO.

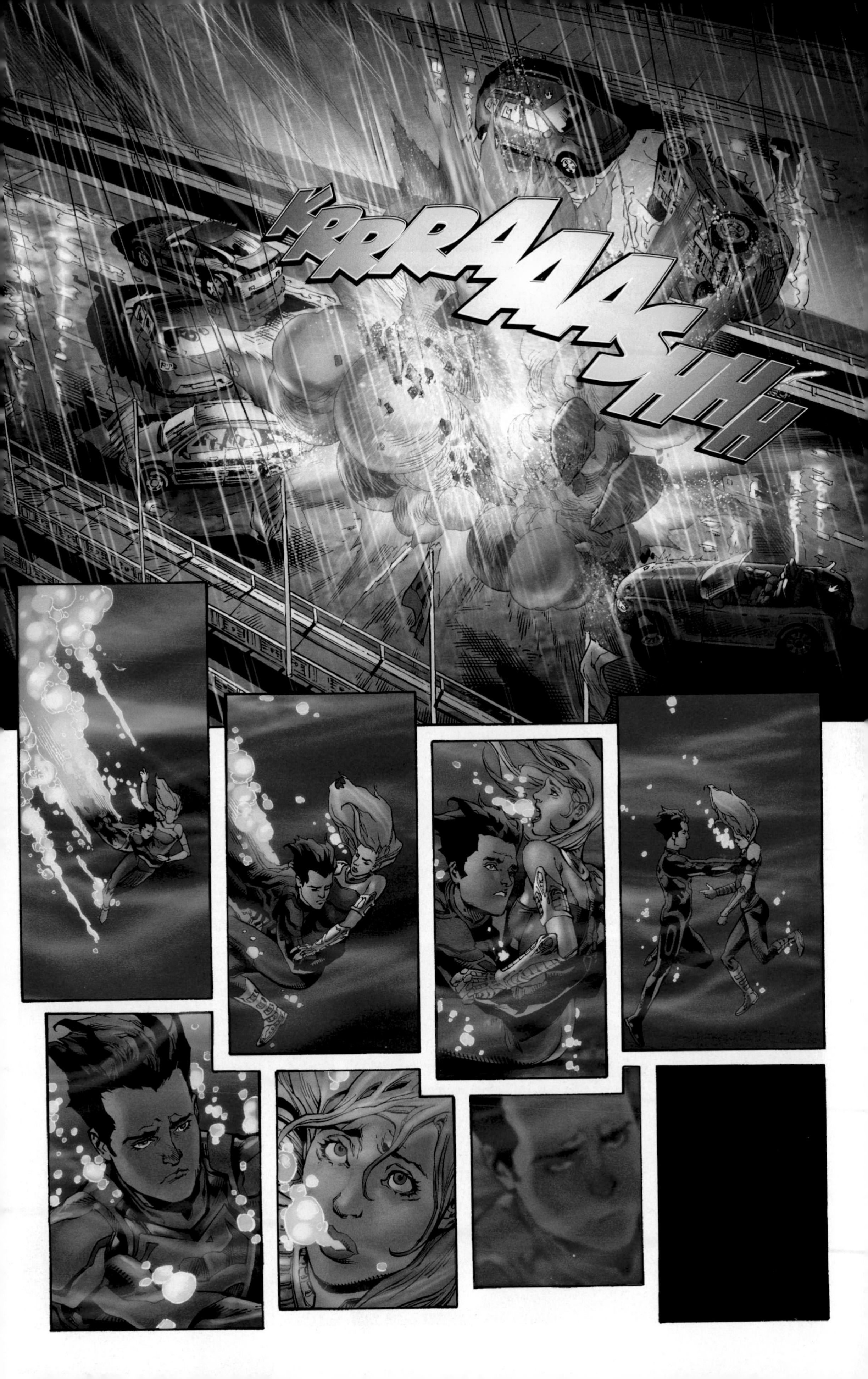
KRRRAAASHHH

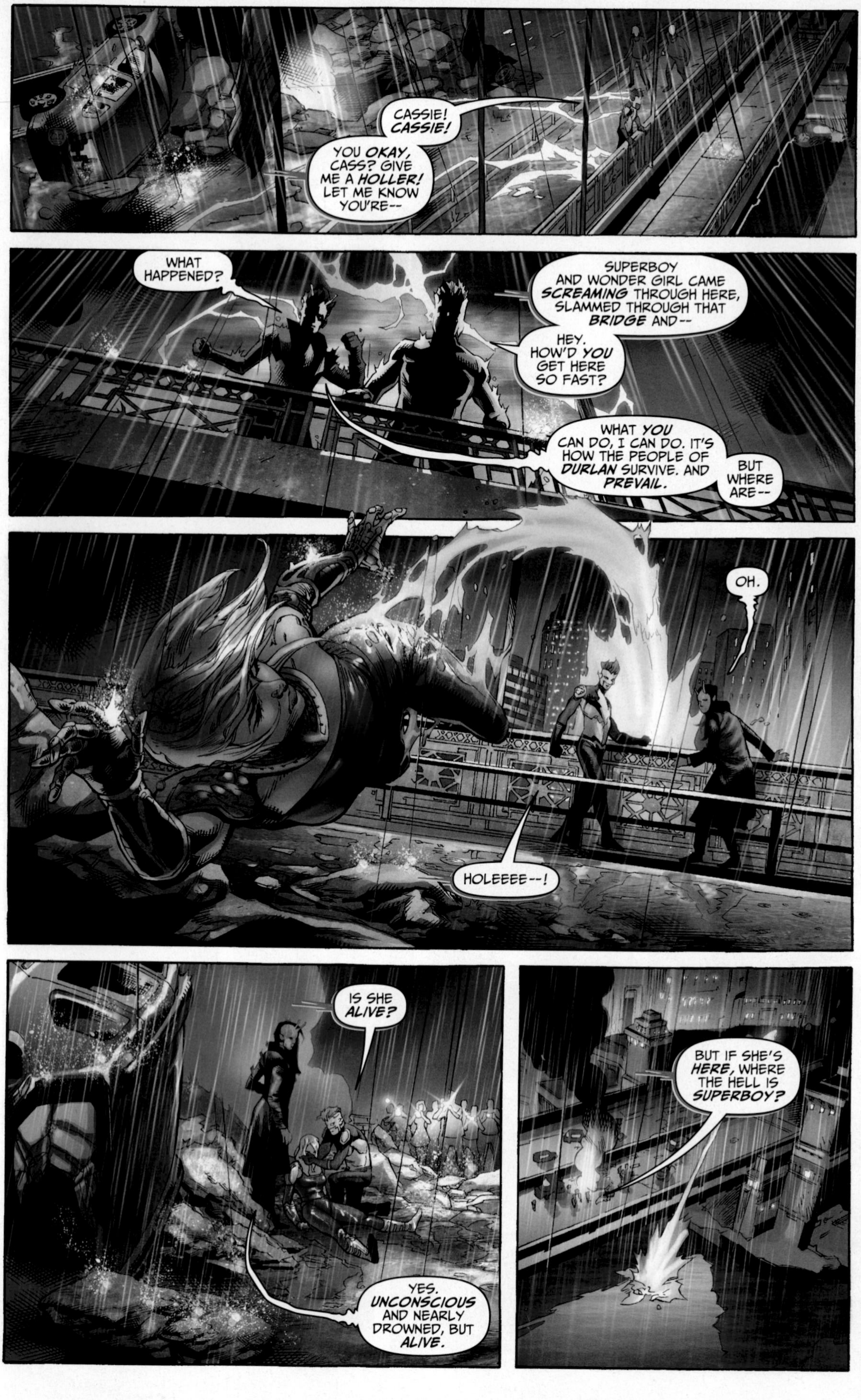
CASSIE! CASSIE!
YOU OKAY, CASS? GIVE ME A HOLLER! LET ME KNOW YOU'RE--
WHAT HAPPENED?
SUPERBOY AND WONDER GIRL CAME SCREAMING THROUGH HERE, SLAMMED THROUGH THAT BRIDGE AND--
HEY. HOW'D YOU GET HERE SO FAST?
WHAT YOU CAN DO, I CAN DO. IT'S HOW THE PEOPLE OF DURLAN SURVIVE. AND PREVAIL.
BUT WHERE ARE--
OH.
HOLEEEE--!
IS SHE ALIVE?
YES. UNCONSCIOUS AND NEARLY DROWNED, BUT ALIVE.
BUT IF SHE'S HERE, WHERE THE HELL IS SUPERBOY?

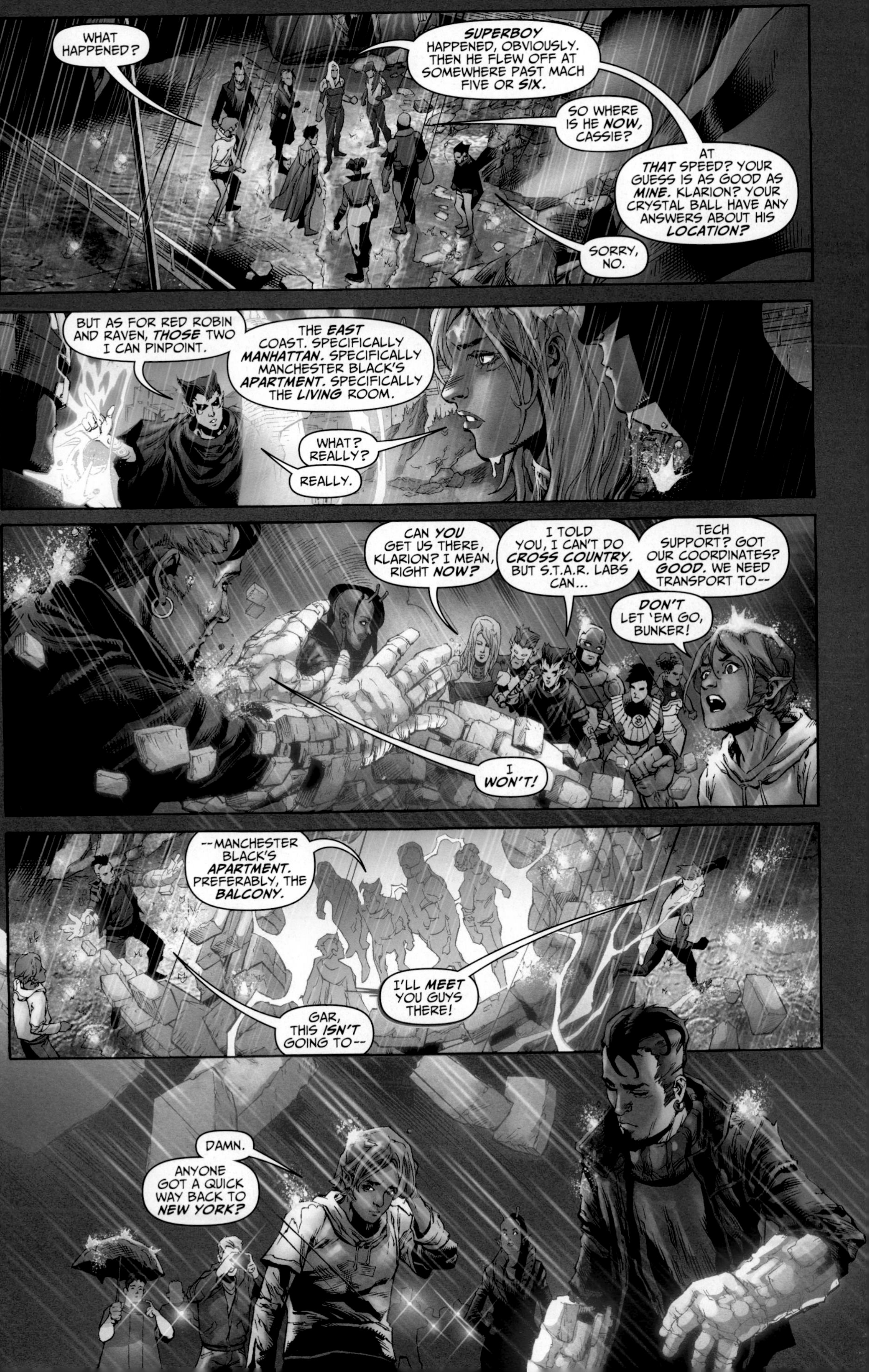
WHAT HAPPENED?
SUPERBOY HAPPENED, OBVIOUSLY. THEN HE FLEW OFF AT SOMEWHERE PAST MACH FIVE OR SIX.
SO WHERE IS HE NOW, CASSIE?
AT THAT SPEED? YOUR GUESS IS AS GOOD AS MINE. KLARION? YOUR CRYSTAL BALL HAVE ANY ANSWERS ABOUT HIS LOCATION?
SORRY, NO.
BUT AS FOR RED ROBIN AND RAVEN, THOSE TWO I CAN PINPOINT.
THE EAST COAST. SPECIFICALLY MANHATTAN. SPECIFICALLY MANCHESTER BLACK'S APARTMENT. SPECIFICALLY THE LIVING ROOM.
WHAT? REALLY?
REALLY.
CAN YOU GET US THERE, KLARION? I MEAN, RIGHT NOW?
I TOLD YOU, I CAN'T DO CROSS COUNTRY. BUT S.T.A.R. LABS CAN...
TECH SUPPORT? GOT OUR COORDINATES? GOOD. WE NEED TRANSPORT TO--
DON'T LET 'EM GO, BUNKER!
I WON'T!
--MANCHESTER BLACK'S APARTMENT. PREFERABLY, THE BALCONY.
I'LL MEET YOU GUYS THERE!
GAR, THIS ISN'T GOING TO--
DAMN.
ANYONE GOT A QUICK WAY BACK TO NEW YORK?

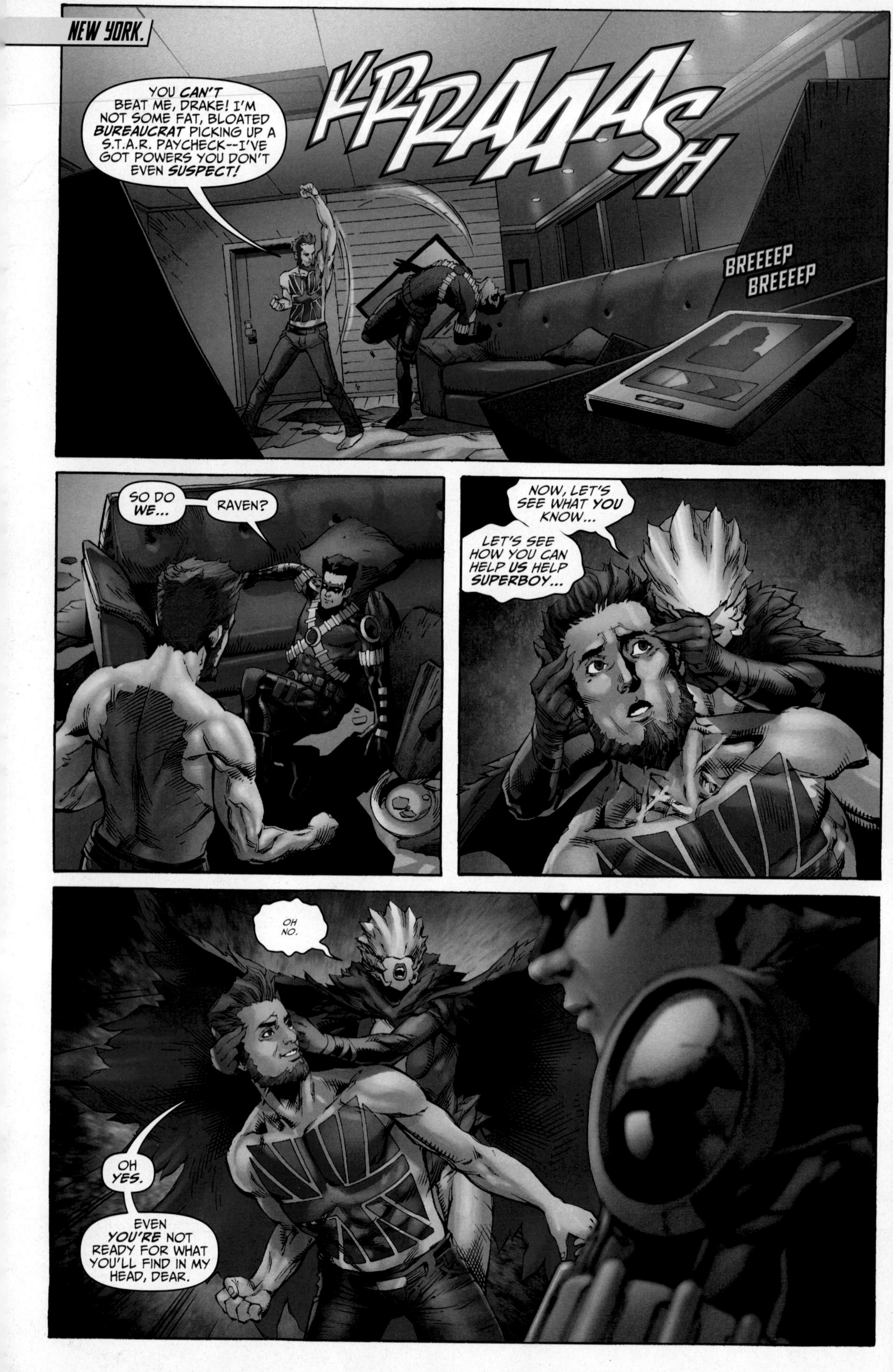
NEW YORK.
YOU CAN'T BEAT ME, DRAKE! I'M NOT SOME FAT, BLOATED BUREAUCRAT PICKING UP A S.T.A.R. PAYCHECK--I'VE GOT POWERS YOU DON'T EVEN SUSPECT!
K'RRAAAASH
BREEEEP BREEEEP
SO DO WE...
RAVEN?
NOW, LET'S SEE WHAT YOU KNOW...
LET'S SEE HOW YOU CAN HELP US HELP SUPERBOY...
OH NO.
OH YES.
EVEN YOU'RE NOT READY FOR WHAT YOU'LL FIND IN MY HEAD, DEAR.

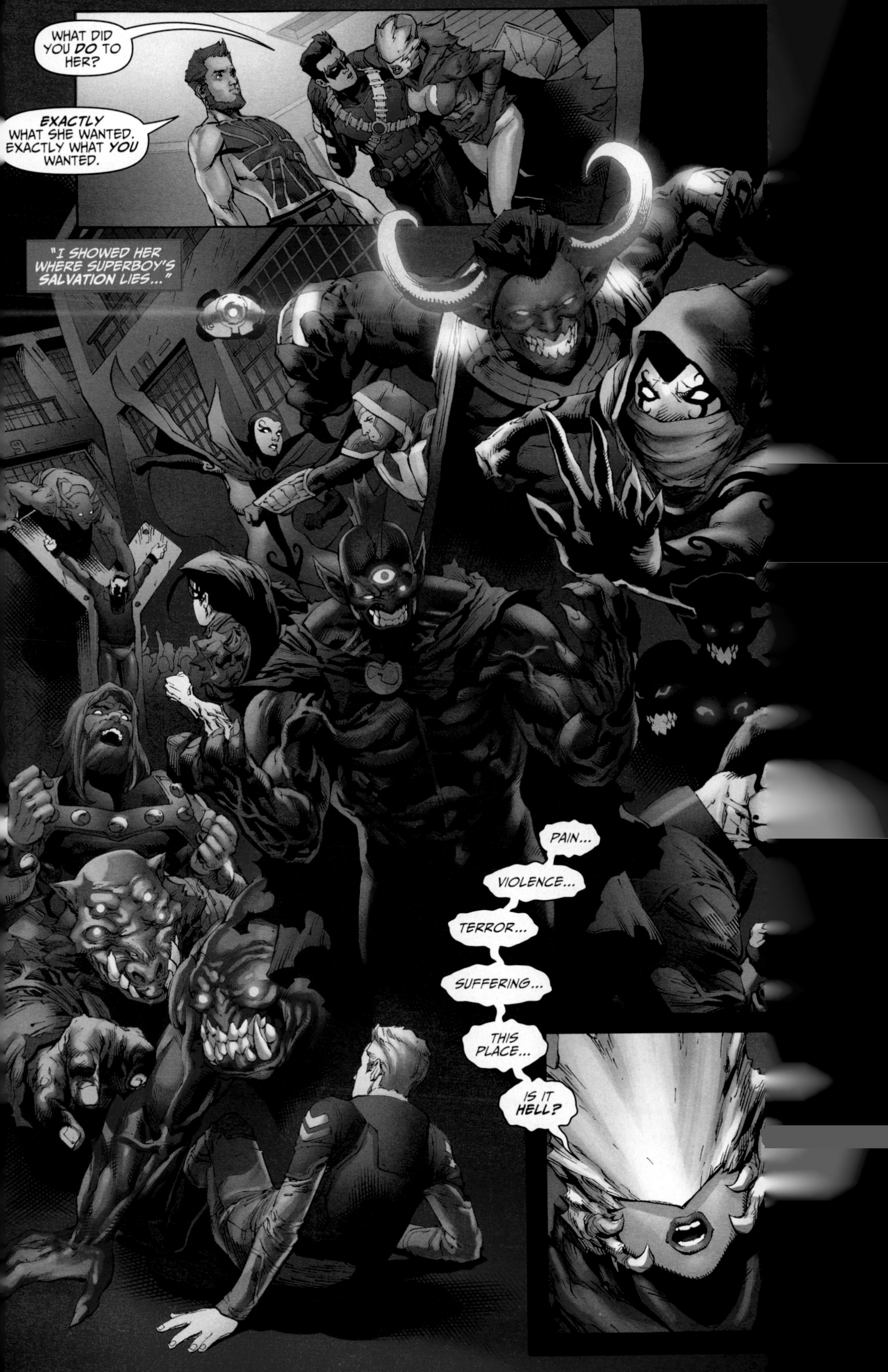

WHAT DID YOU DO TO HER?
EXACTLY WHAT SHE WANTED. EXACTLY WHAT YOU WANTED.
"I SHOWED HER WHERE SUPERBOY'S SALVATION LIES..."
PAIN...
VIOLENCE...
TERROR...
SUFFERING...
THIS PLACE...
IS IT HELL?

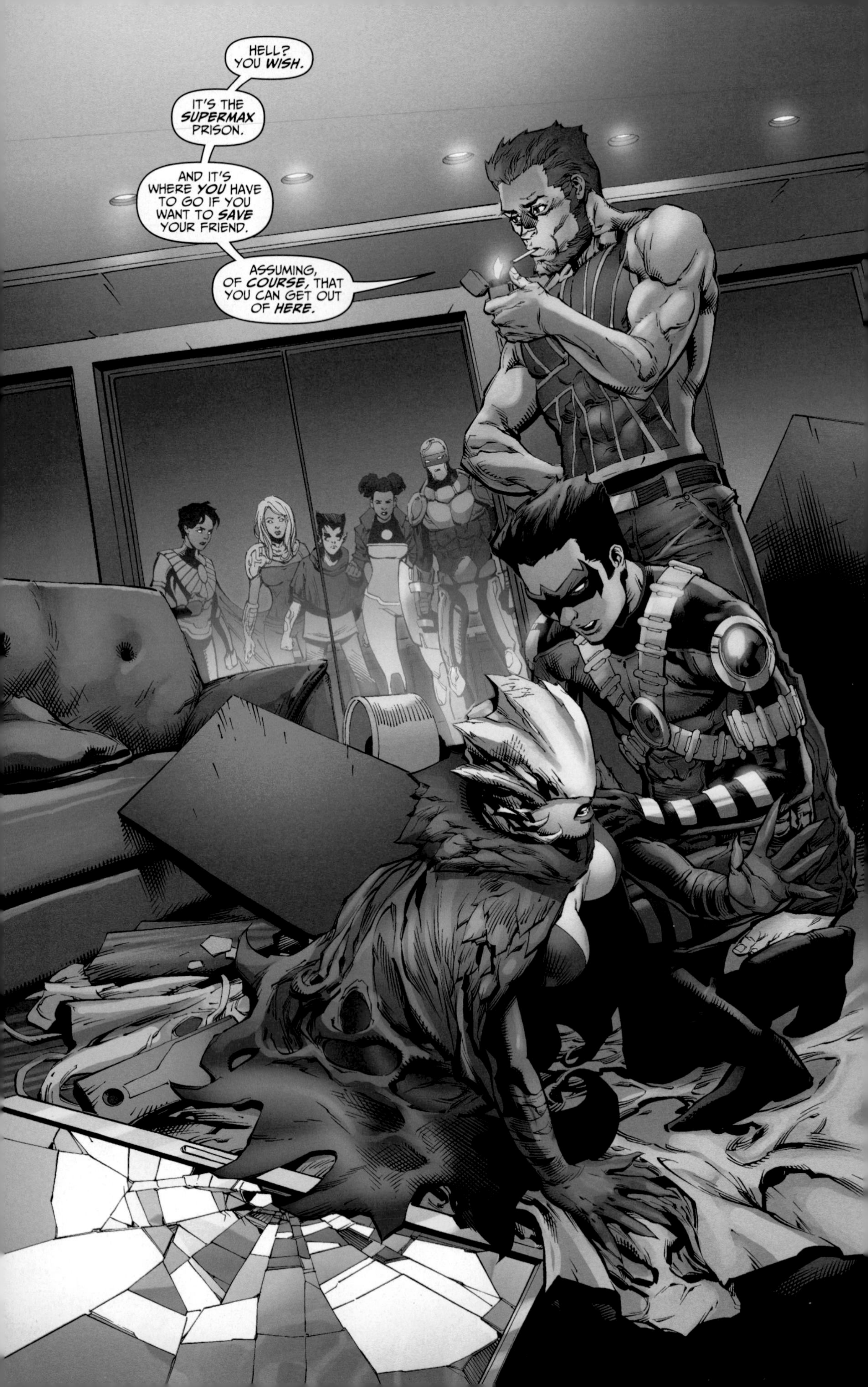
HELL? YOU WISH.
IT'S THE SUPERMAX PRISON.
AND IT'S WHERE YOU HAVE TO GO IF YOU WANT TO SAVE YOUR FRIEND.
ASSUMING, OF COURSE, THAT YOU CAN GET OUT OF HERE.

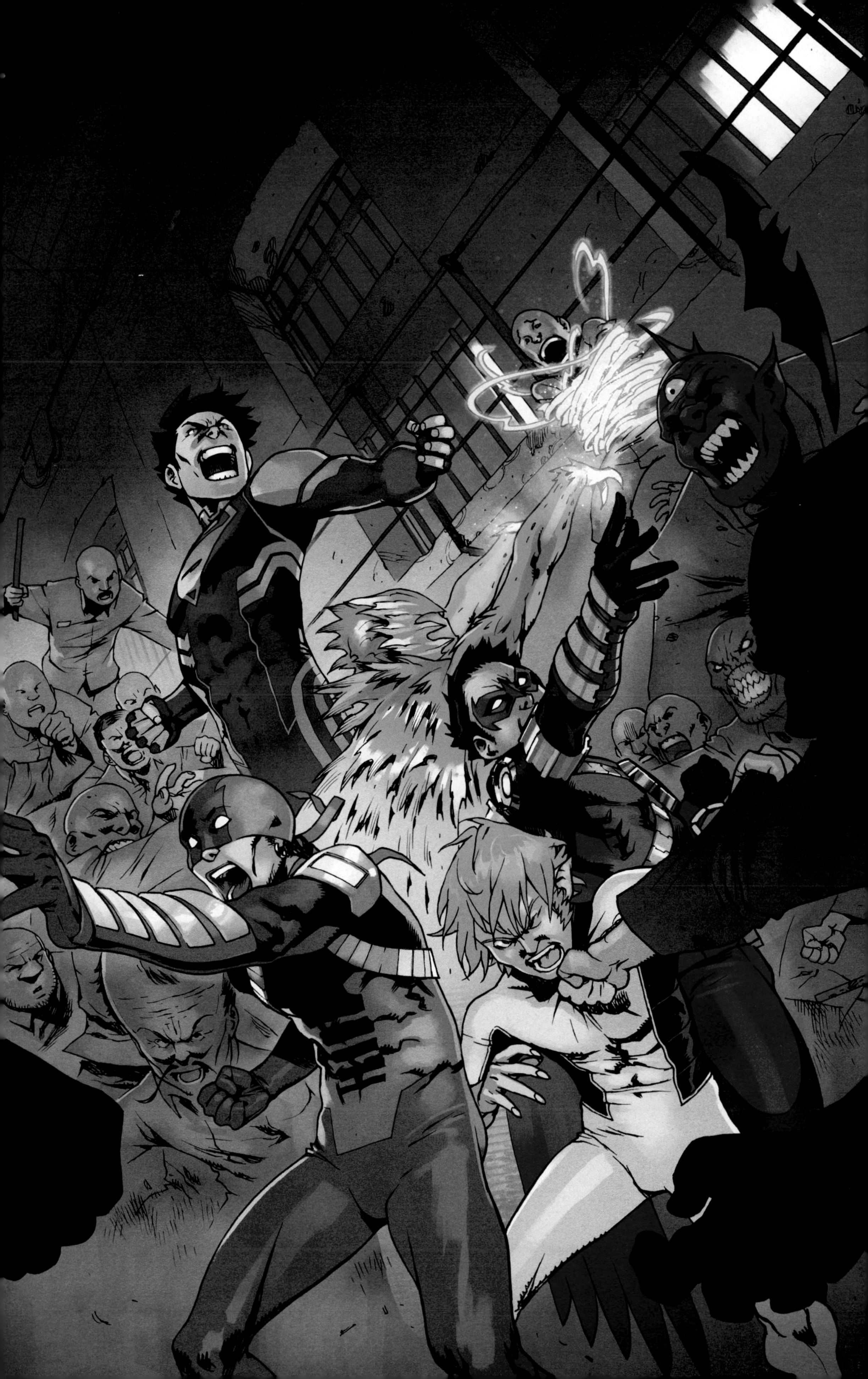

ROGUE TARGETS PART THREE

WILL PFEIFER writer RICKEN artist DAN BROWN colorist JOHN J. HILL letterer cover art by BENGAL

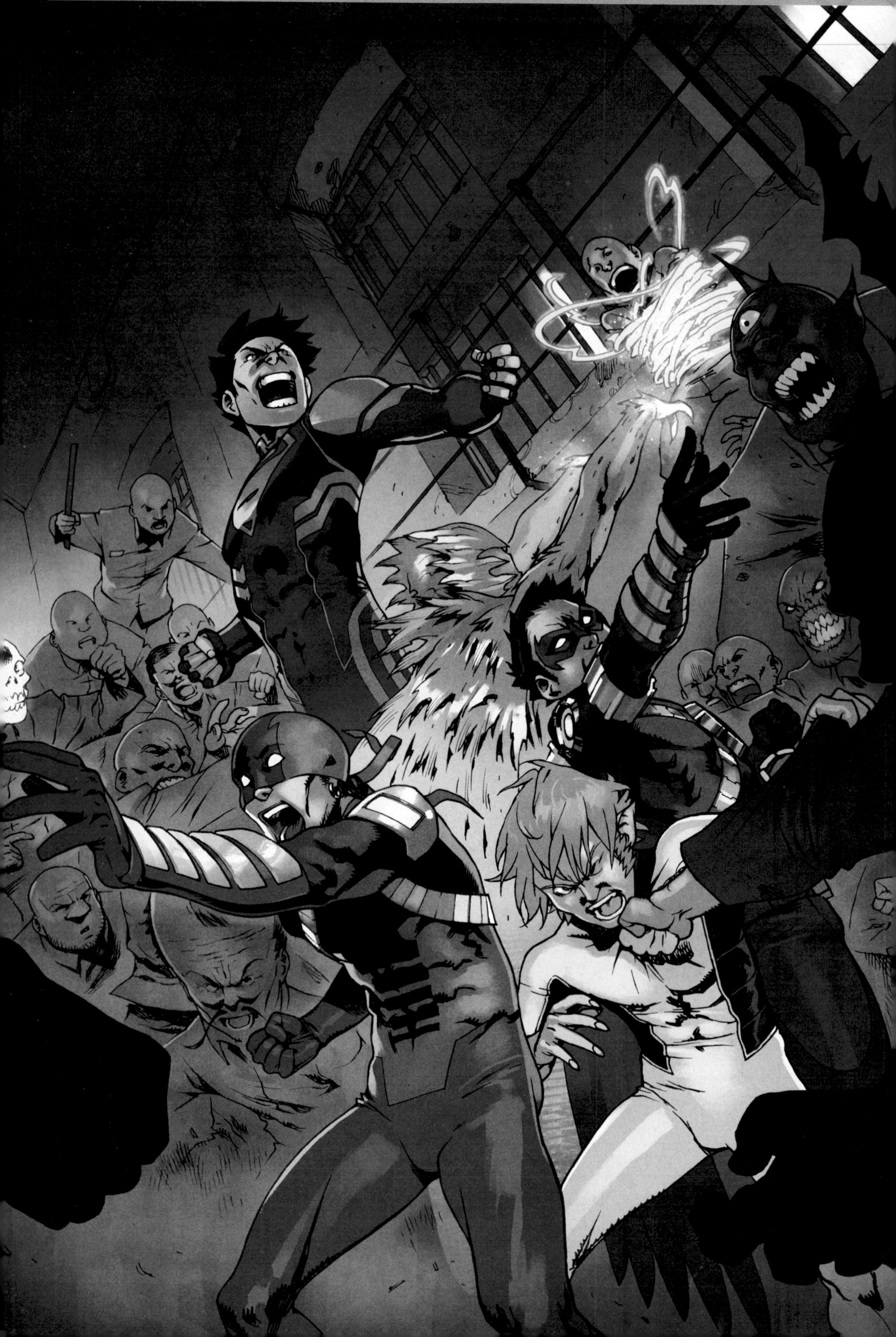

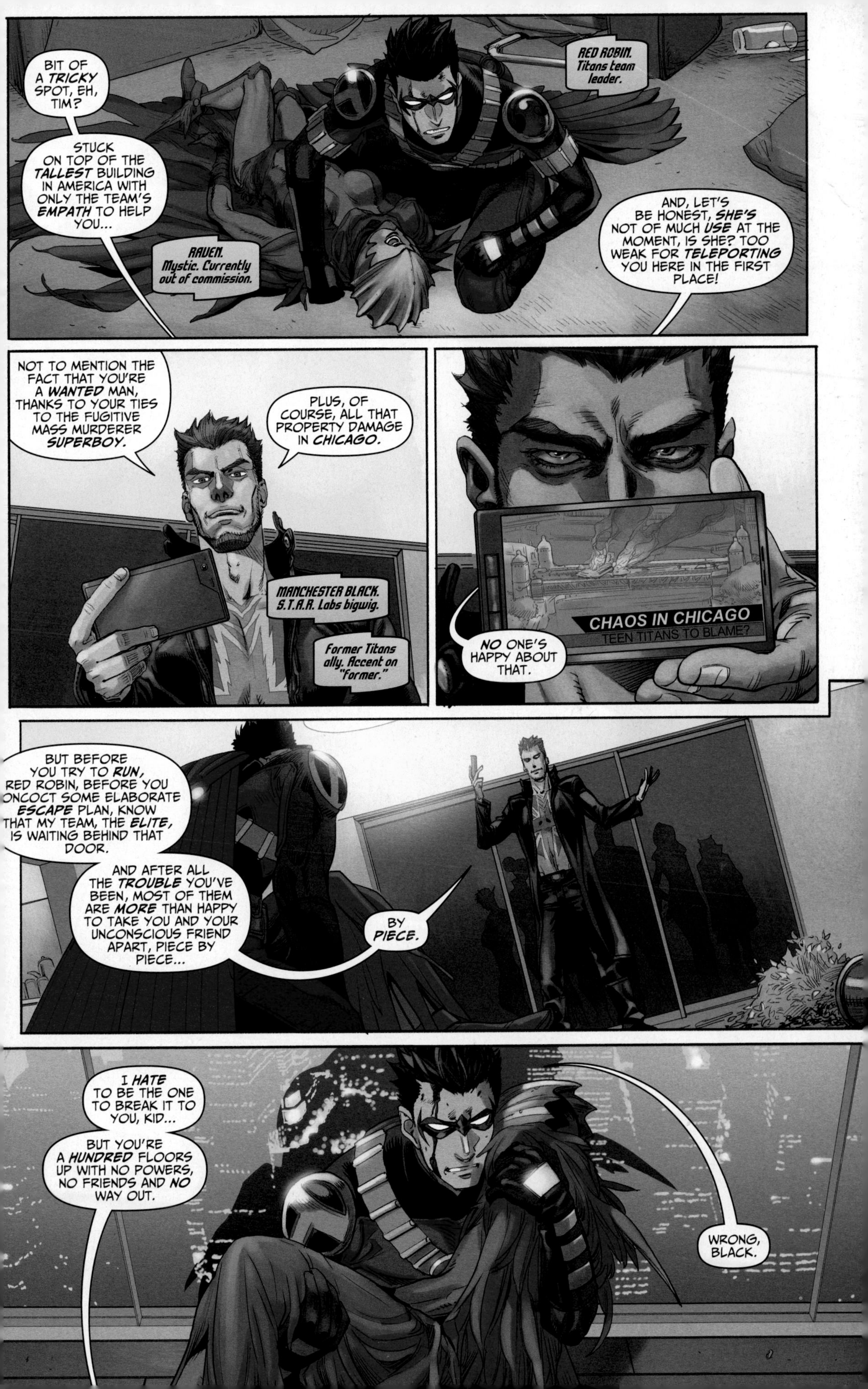
BIT OF A TRICKY SPOT, EH, TIM?
RED ROBIN. Titans team leader.
STUCK ON TOP OF THE TALLEST BUILDING IN AMERICA WITH ONLY THE TEAM'S EMPATH TO HELP YOU...
RAVEN. Mystic. Currently out of commission.
AND, LET'S BE HONEST, SHE'S NOT OF MUCH USE AT THE MOMENT, IS SHE? TOO WEAK FOR TELEPORTING YOU HERE IN THE FIRST PLACE!
NOT TO MENTION THE FACT THAT YOU'RE A WANTED MAN, THANKS TO YOUR TIES TO THE FUGITIVE MASS MURDERER SUPERBOY.
PLUS, OF COURSE, ALL THAT PROPERTY DAMAGE IN CHICAGO.
MANCHESTER BLACK. S.T.A.R. Labs bigwig.
Former Titans ally. Accent on "former."
CHAOS IN CHICAGO
TEEN TITANS TO BLAME?
NO ONE'S HAPPY ABOUT THAT.
BUT BEFORE YOU TRY TO RUN, RED ROBIN, BEFORE YOU CONCOCT SOME ELABORATE ESCAPE PLAN, KNOW THAT MY TEAM, THE ELITE, IS WAITING BEHIND THAT DOOR.
AND AFTER ALL THE TROUBLE YOU'VE BEEN, MOST OF THEM ARE MORE THAN HAPPY TO TAKE YOU AND YOUR UNCONSCIOUS FRIEND APART, PIECE BY PIECE...
BY PIECE.
I HATE TO BE THE ONE TO BREAK IT TO YOU, KID...
BUT YOU'RE A HUNDRED FLOORS UP WITH NO POWERS, NO FRIENDS AND NO WAY OUT.
WRONG, BLACK.

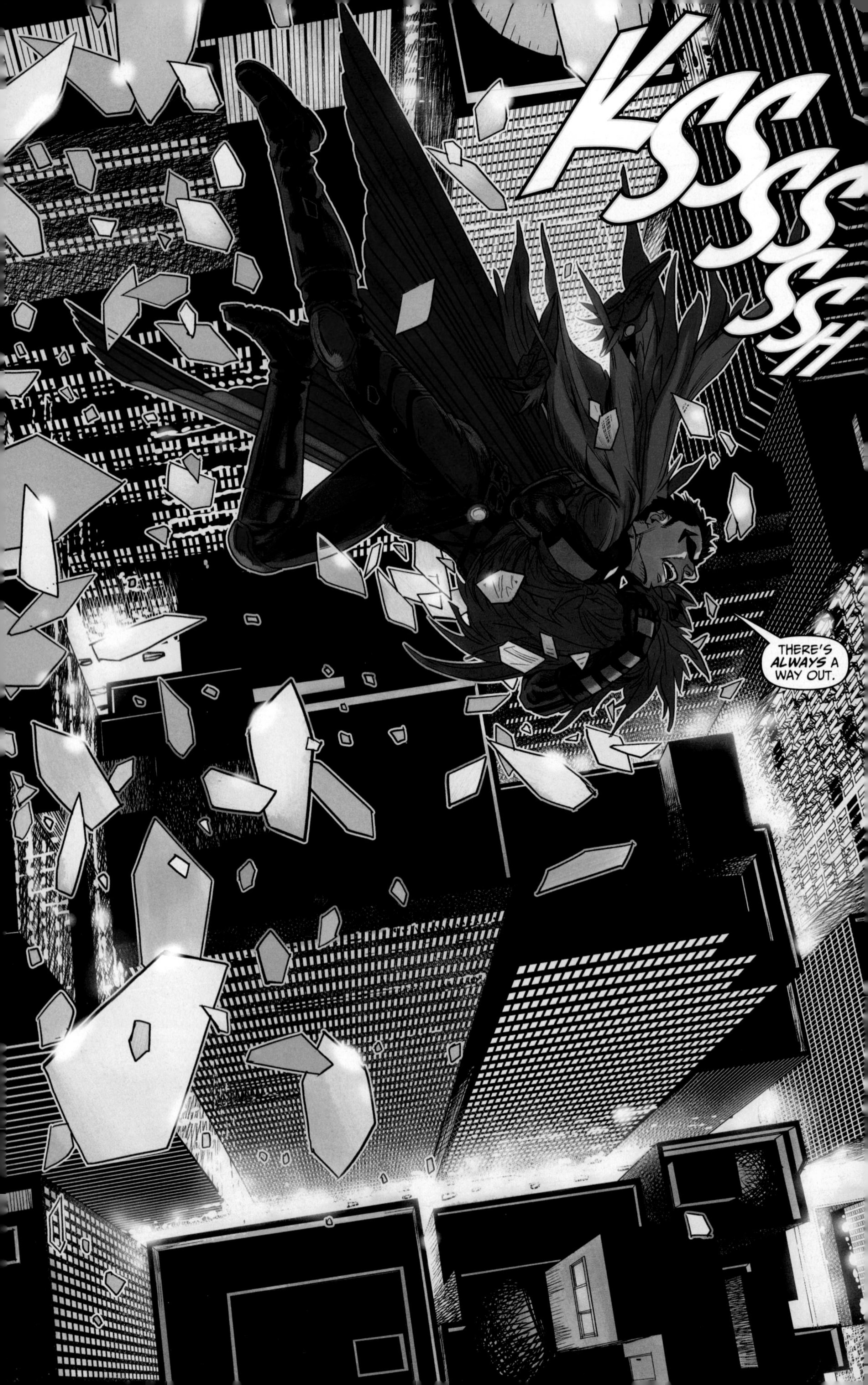
KSSSSSH
THERE'S ALWAYS A WAY OUT.

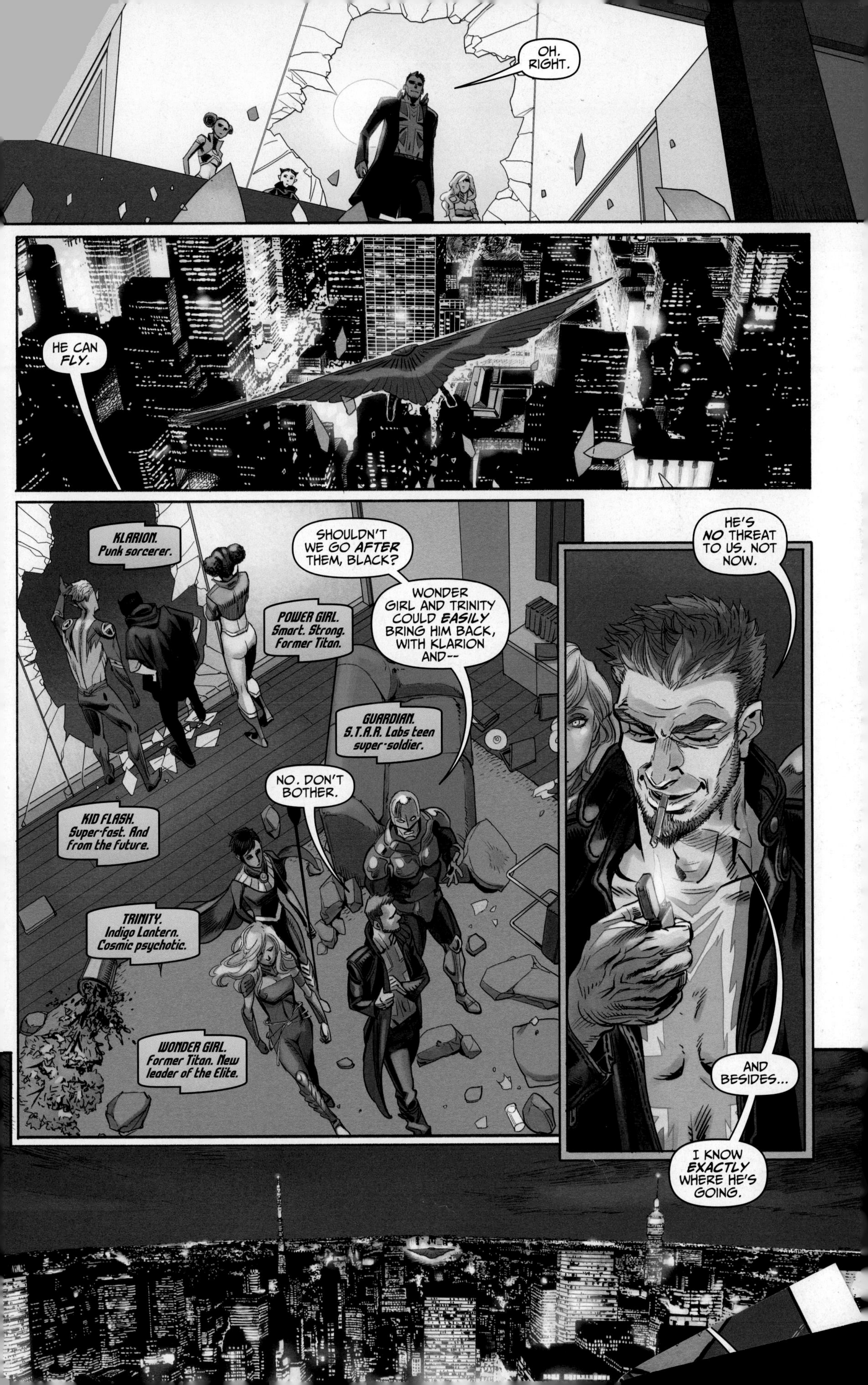
OH. RIGHT.
HE CAN FLY.
KLARION. Punk sorcerer.
POWER GIRL. Smart. Strong. Former Titan.
KID FLASH. Super-fast. And from the future.
TRINITY. Indigo Lantern. Cosmic psychotic.
WONDER GIRL. Former Titan. New leader of the Elite.
GUARDIAN. S.T.A.R. Labs teen super-soldier.
SHOULDN'T WE GO AFTER THEM, BLACK?
WONDER GIRL AND TRINITY COULD EASILY BRING HIM BACK, WITH KLARION AND--
NO. DON'T BOTHER.
HE'S NO THREAT TO US. NOT NOW.
AND BESIDES...
I KNOW EXACTLY WHERE HE'S GOING.

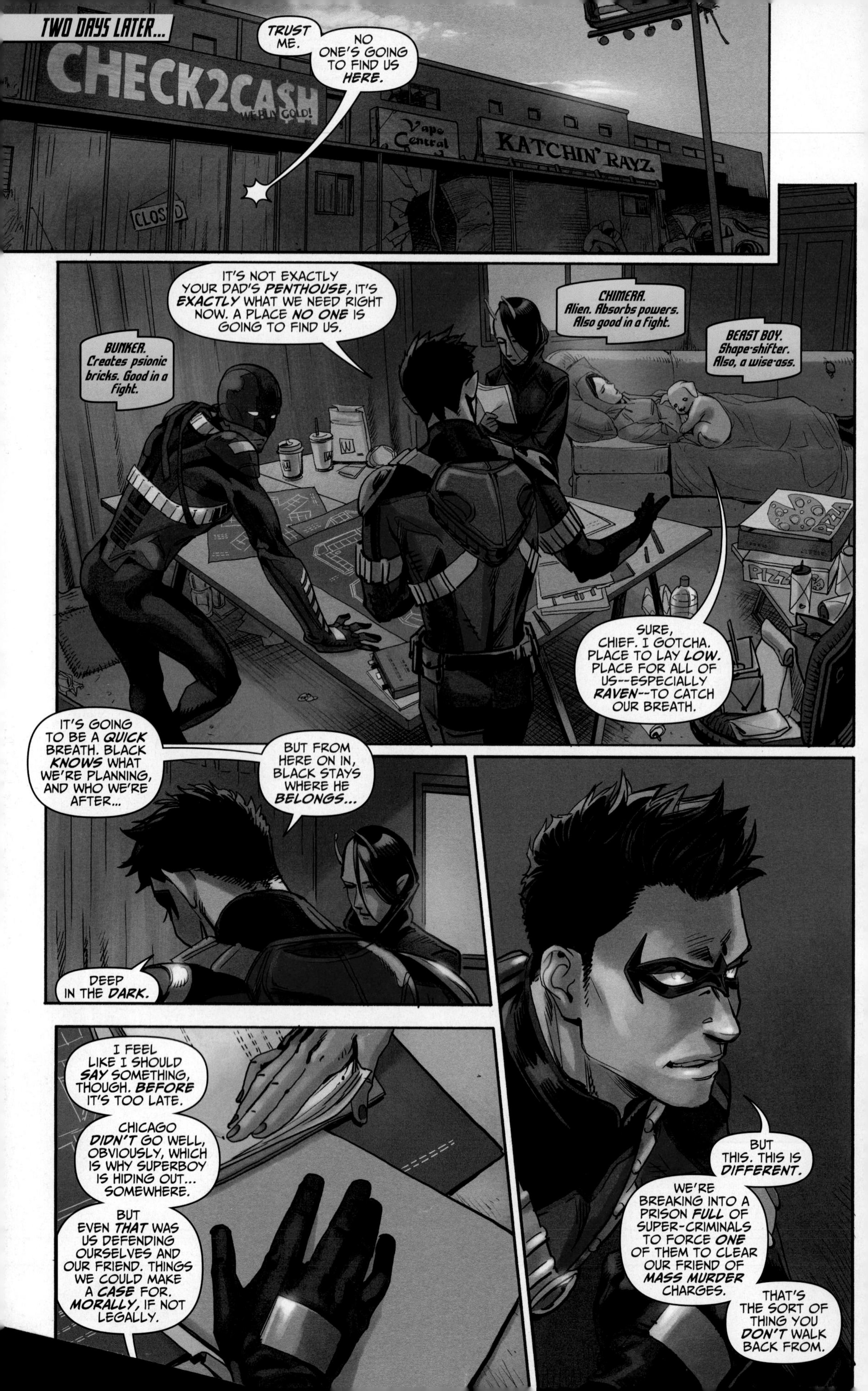
TWO DAYS LATER...
TRUST ME.
NO ONE'S GOING TO FIND US HERE.
CHECK2CASH
WE BUY GOLD!
Vape Central
KATCHIN' RAYZ
CLOSED
IT'S NOT EXACTLY YOUR DAD'S PENTHOUSE, IT'S EXACTLY WHAT WE NEED RIGHT NOW. A PLACE NO ONE IS GOING TO FIND US.
BUNKER. Creates psionic bricks. Good in a fight.
CHIMERA. Alien. Absorbs powers. Also good in a fight.
BEAST BOY. Shape-shifter. Also, a wise-ass.
PIZZA
SURE, CHIEF. I GOTCHA. PLACE TO LAY LOW. PLACE FOR ALL OF US--ESPECIALLY RAVEN--TO CATCH OUR BREATH.
IT'S GOING TO BE A QUICK BREATH. BLACK KNOWS WHAT WE'RE PLANNING, AND WHO WE'RE AFTER...
BUT FROM HERE ON IN, BLACK STAYS WHERE HE BELONGS...
DEEP IN THE DARK.
I FEEL LIKE I SHOULD SAY SOMETHING, THOUGH. BEFORE IT'S TOO LATE.
CHICAGO DIDN'T GO WELL, OBVIOUSLY, WHICH IS WHY SUPERBOY IS HIDING OUT... SOMEWHERE.
BUT EVEN THAT WAS US DEFENDING OURSELVES AND OUR FRIEND. THINGS WE COULD MAKE A CASE FOR. MORALLY, IF NOT LEGALLY.
BUT THIS. THIS IS DIFFERENT.
WE'RE BREAKING INTO A PRISON FULL OF SUPER-CRIMINALS TO FORCE ONE OF THEM TO CLEAR OUR FRIEND OF MASS MURDER CHARGES.
THAT'S THE SORT OF THING YOU DON'T WALK BACK FROM.

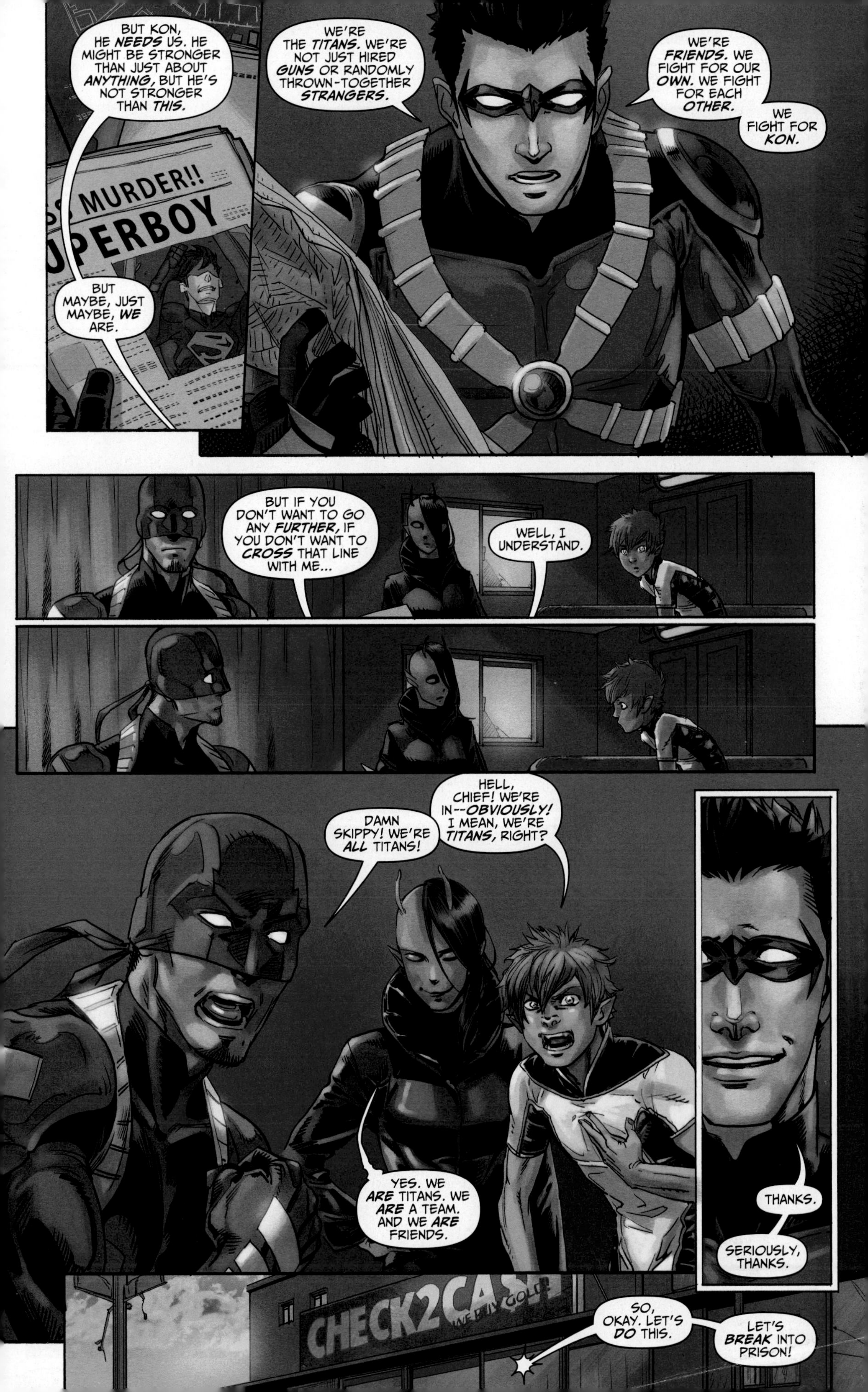
BUT KON, HE NEEDS US. HE MIGHT BE STRONGER THAN JUST ABOUT ANYTHING, BUT HE'S NOT STRONGER THAN THIS.
BUT MAYBE, JUST MAYBE, WE ARE.
MURDER!!
UPERBOY
WE'RE THE TITANS. WE'RE NOT JUST HIRED GUNS OR RANDOMLY THROWN-TOGETHER STRANGERS.
WE'RE FRIENDS. WE FIGHT FOR OUR OWN. WE FIGHT FOR EACH OTHER.
WE FIGHT FOR KON.
BUT IF YOU DON'T WANT TO GO ANY FURTHER, IF YOU DON'T WANT TO CROSS THAT LINE WITH ME...
WELL, I UNDERSTAND.
DAMN SKIPPY! WE'RE ALL TITANS!
HELL, CHIEF! WE'RE IN--OBVIOUSLY! I MEAN, WE'RE TITANS, RIGHT?
YES. WE ARE TITANS. WE ARE A TEAM. AND WE ARE FRIENDS.
THANKS.
SERIOUSLY, THANKS.
CHECK2CASH
SO, OKAY. LET'S DO THIS.
LET'S BREAK INTO PRISON!

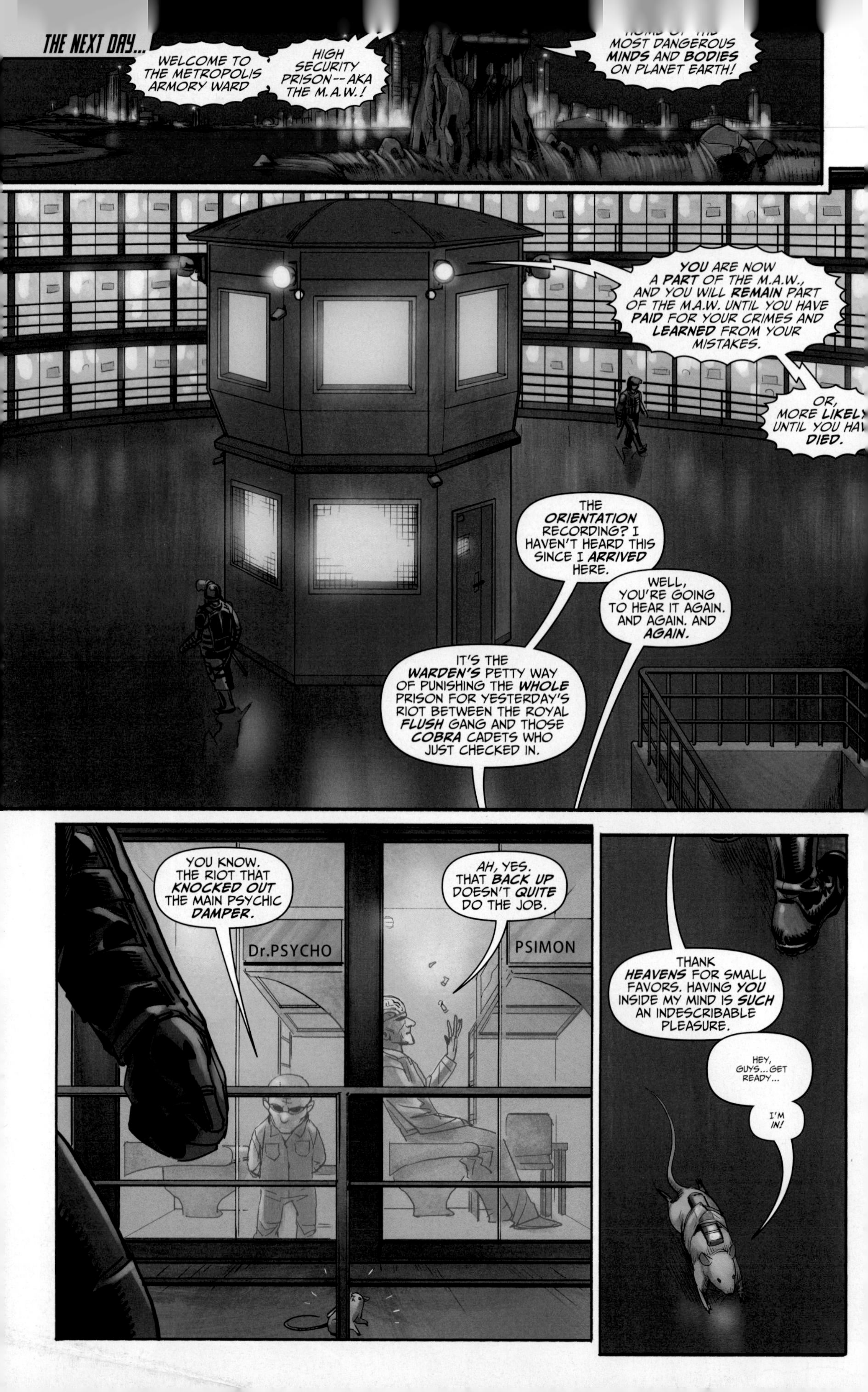
THE NEXT DAY...
WELCOME TO THE METROPOLIS ARMORY WARD
HIGH SECURITY PRISON--AKA THE M.A.W.!
MOST DANGEROUS MINDS AND BODIES ON PLANET EARTH!
YOU ARE NOW A PART OF THE M.A.W., AND YOU WILL REMAIN PART OF THE M.A.W. UNTIL YOU HAVE PAID FOR YOUR CRIMES AND LEARNED FROM YOUR MISTAKES.
OR, MORE LIKEL UNTIL YOU HA DIED.
THE ORIENTATION RECORDING? I HAVEN'T HEARD THIS SINCE I ARRIVED HERE.
WELL, YOU'RE GOING TO HEAR IT AGAIN. AND AGAIN. AND AGAIN.
IT'S THE WARDEN'S PETTY WAY OF PUNISHING THE WHOLE PRISON FOR YESTERDAY'S RIOT BETWEEN THE ROYAL FLUSH GANG AND THOSE COBRA CADETS WHO JUST CHECKED IN.
YOU KNOW. THE RIOT THAT KNOCKED OUT THE MAIN PSYCHIC DAMPER.
AH, YES. THAT BACK UP DOESN'T QUITE DO THE JOB.
Dr.PSYCHO
PSIMON
THANK HEAVENS FOR SMALL FAVORS. HAVING YOU INSIDE MY MIND IS SUCH AN INDESCRIBABLE PLEASURE.
HEY, GUYS...GET READY...
I'M IN!

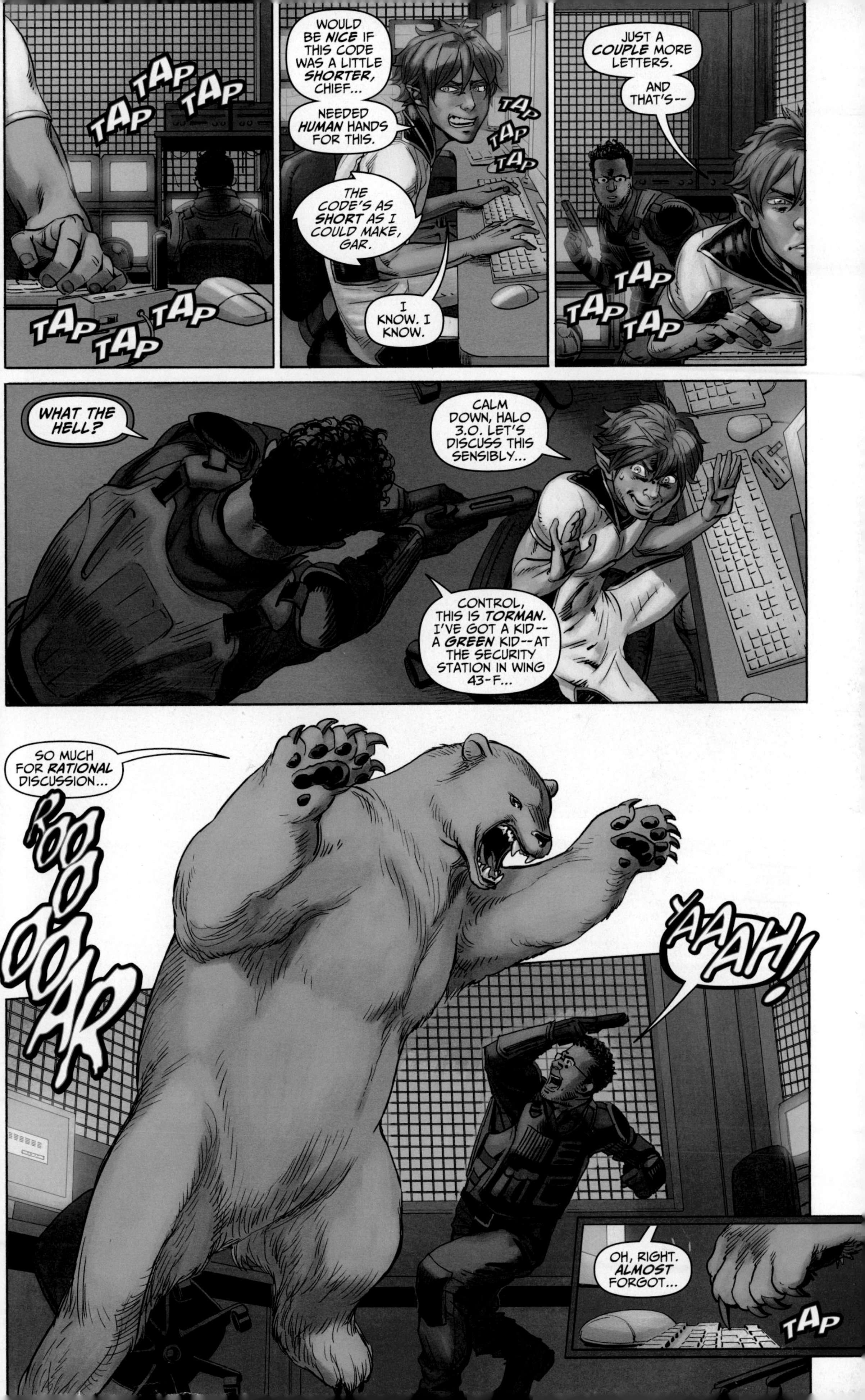
TAP TAP TAP
TAP TAP TAP
WOULD BE NICE IF THIS CODE WAS A LITTLE SHORTER, CHIEF...
NEEDED HUMAN HANDS FOR THIS.
TAP TAP TAP
THE CODE'S AS SHORT AS I COULD MAKE, GAR.
I KNOW. I KNOW.
JUST A COUPLE MORE LETTERS.
AND THAT'S--
TAP TAP TAP
WHAT THE HELL?
CALM DOWN, HALO 3.0. LET'S DISCUSS THIS SENSIBLY...
CONTROL, THIS IS TORMAN. I'VE GOT A KID-- A GREEN KID--AT THE SECURITY STATION IN WING 43-F...
SO MUCH FOR RATIONAL DISCUSSION...
ROOOOOAR
YAAAH!
OH, RIGHT. ALMOST FORGOT...
TAP

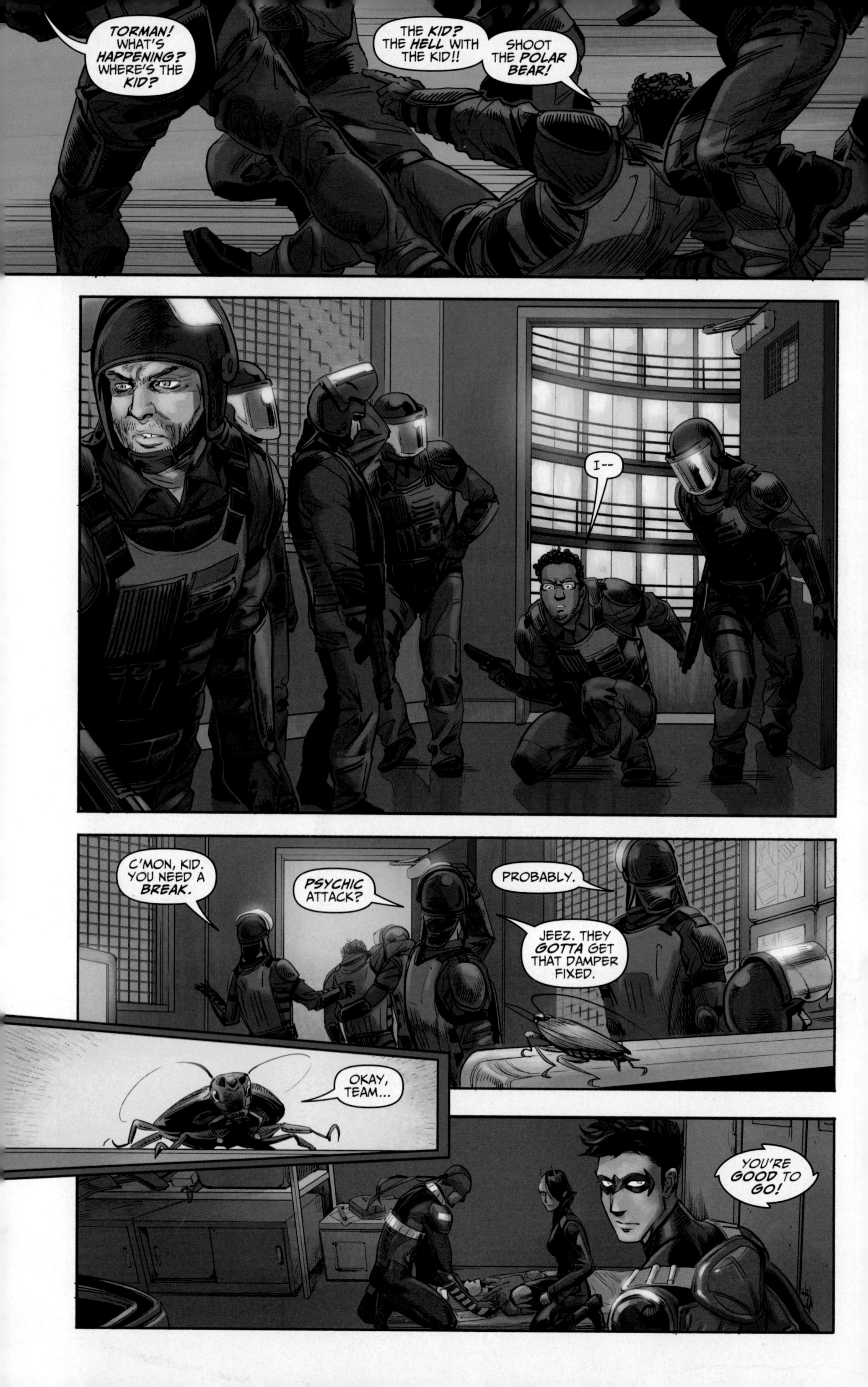
TORMAN! WHAT'S HAPPENING? WHERE'S THE KID?
THE KID? THE HELL WITH THE KID!!
SHOOT THE POLAR BEAR!
I--
C'MON, KID. YOU NEED A BREAK.
PSYCHIC ATTACK?
PROBABLY.
JEEZ. THEY GOTTA GET THAT DAMPER FIXED.
OKAY, TEAM...
YOU'RE GOOD TO GO!

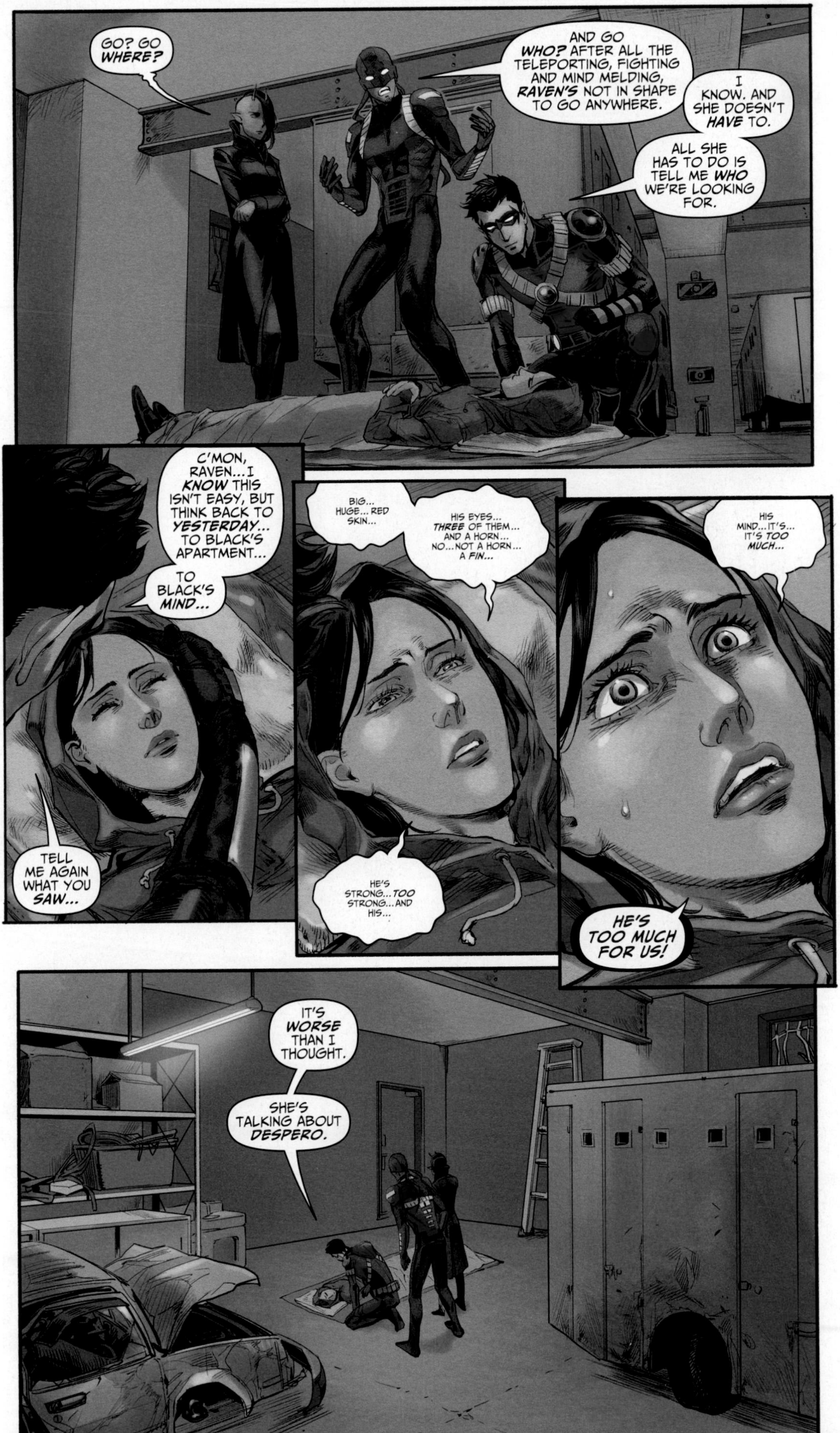
GO? GO WHERE?
AND GO WHO? AFTER ALL THE TELEPORTING, FIGHTING AND MIND MELDING, RAVEN'S NOT IN SHAPE TO GO ANYWHERE.
I KNOW. AND SHE DOESN'T HAVE TO.
ALL SHE HAS TO DO IS TELL ME WHO WE'RE LOOKING FOR.
C'MON, RAVEN... I KNOW THIS ISN'T EASY, BUT THINK BACK TO YESTERDAY... TO BLACK'S APARTMENT...
TO BLACK'S MIND...
TELL ME AGAIN WHAT YOU SAW...
BIG... HUGE... RED SKIN...
HIS EYES... THREE OF THEM... AND A HORN... NO... NOT A HORN... A FIN...
HE'S STRONG... TOO STRONG... AND HIS...
HIS MIND... IT'S... IT'S TOO MUCH...
HE'S TOO MUCH FOR US!
IT'S WORSE THAN I THOUGHT.
SHE'S TALKING ABOUT DESPERO.

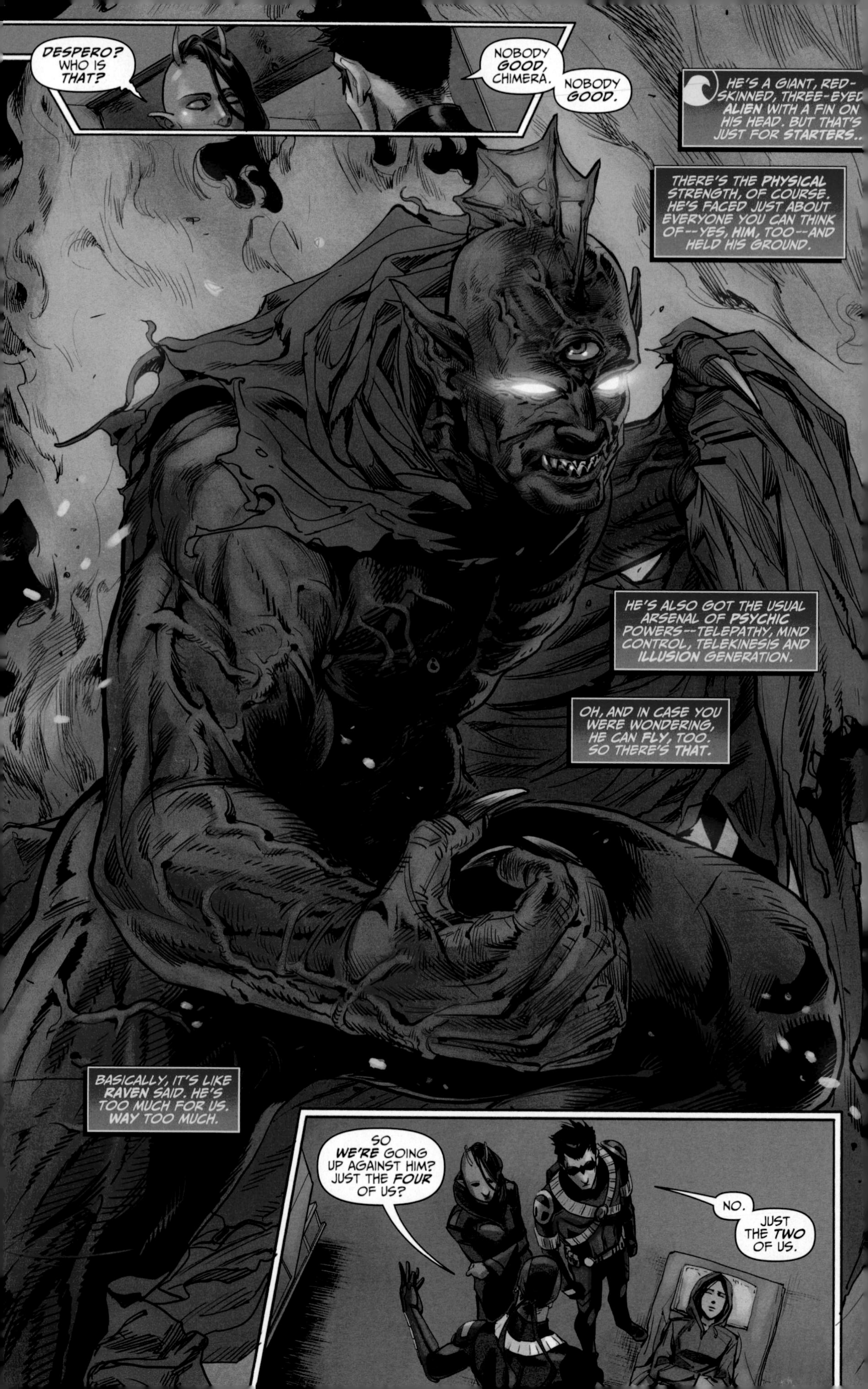
DESPERO? WHO IS THAT?
NOBODY GOOD, CHIMERA.
NOBODY GOOD.
HE'S A GIANT, RED-SKINNED, THREE-EYED ALIEN WITH A FIN ON HIS HEAD. BUT THAT'S JUST FOR STARTERS...
THERE'S THE PHYSICAL STRENGTH, OF COURSE. HE'S FACED JUST ABOUT EVERYONE YOU CAN THINK OF--YES, HIM, TOO--AND HELD HIS GROUND.
HE'S ALSO GOT THE USUAL ARSENAL OF PSYCHIC POWERS--TELEPATHY, MIND CONTROL, TELEKINESIS AND ILLUSION GENERATION.
OH, AND IN CASE YOU WERE WONDERING, HE CAN FLY, TOO. SO THERE'S THAT.
BASICALLY, IT'S LIKE RAVEN SAID. HE'S TOO MUCH FOR US. WAY TOO MUCH.
SO WE'RE GOING UP AGAINST HIM? JUST THE FOUR OF US?
NO.
JUST THE TWO OF US.

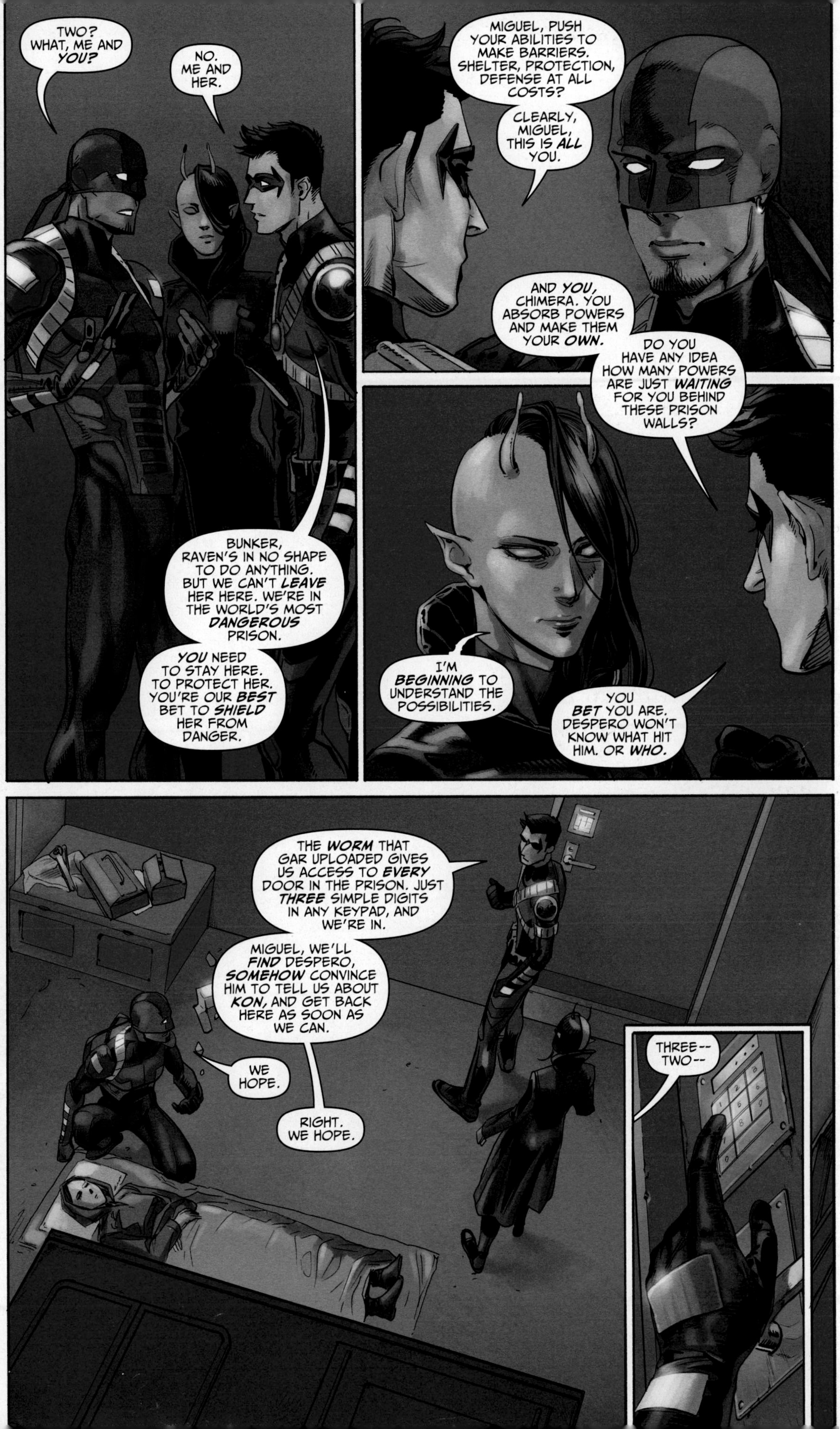
TWO? WHAT, ME AND YOU?
NO. ME AND HER.
BUNKER, RAVEN'S IN NO SHAPE TO DO ANYTHING. BUT WE CAN'T LEAVE HER HERE. WE'RE IN THE WORLD'S MOST DANGEROUS PRISON.
YOU NEED TO STAY HERE. TO PROTECT HER. YOU'RE OUR BEST BET TO SHIELD HER FROM DANGER.
MIGUEL, PUSH YOUR ABILITIES TO MAKE BARRIERS. SHELTER, PROTECTION, DEFENSE AT ALL COSTS?
CLEARLY, MIGUEL, THIS IS ALL YOU.
AND YOU, CHIMERA. YOU ABSORB POWERS AND MAKE THEM YOUR OWN.
DO YOU HAVE ANY IDEA HOW MANY POWERS ARE JUST WAITING FOR YOU BEHIND THESE PRISON WALLS?
I'M BEGINNING TO UNDERSTAND THE POSSIBILITIES.
YOU BET YOU ARE. DESPERO WON'T KNOW WHAT HIT HIM. OR WHO.
THE WORM THAT GAR UPLOADED GIVES US ACCESS TO EVERY DOOR IN THE PRISON. JUST THREE SIMPLE DIGITS IN ANY KEYPAD, AND WE'RE IN.
MIGUEL, WE'LL FIND DESPERO, SOMEHOW CONVINCE HIM TO TELL US ABOUT KON, AND GET BACK HERE AS SOON AS WE CAN.
WE HOPE.
RIGHT. WE HOPE.
THREE-- TWO--

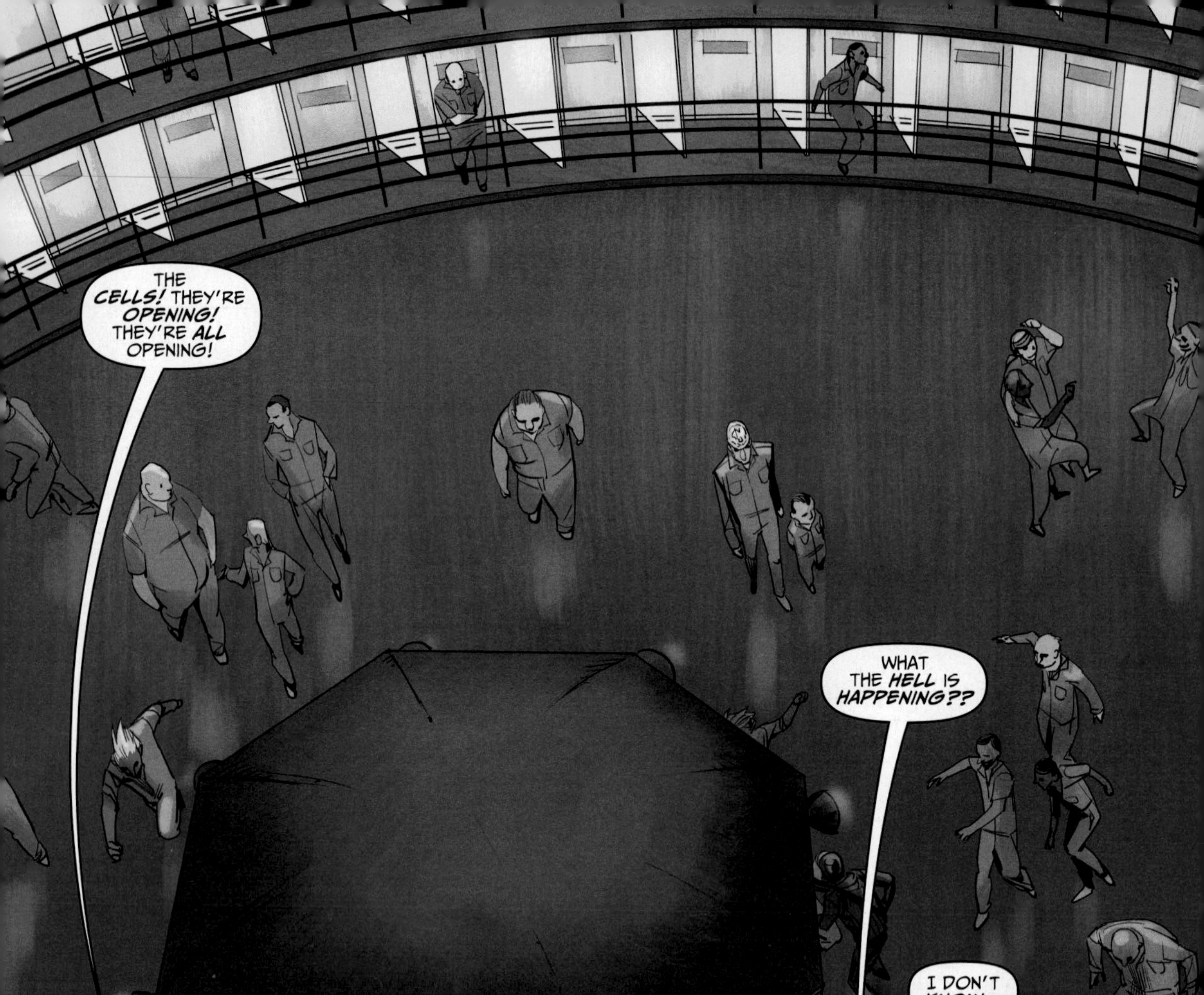
THE CELLS! THEY'RE OPENING! THEY'RE ALL OPENING!
WHAT THE HELL IS HAPPENING??
I DON'T KNOW--
BUT IT'S HAPPENING IN EVERY PART OF THE PRISON!

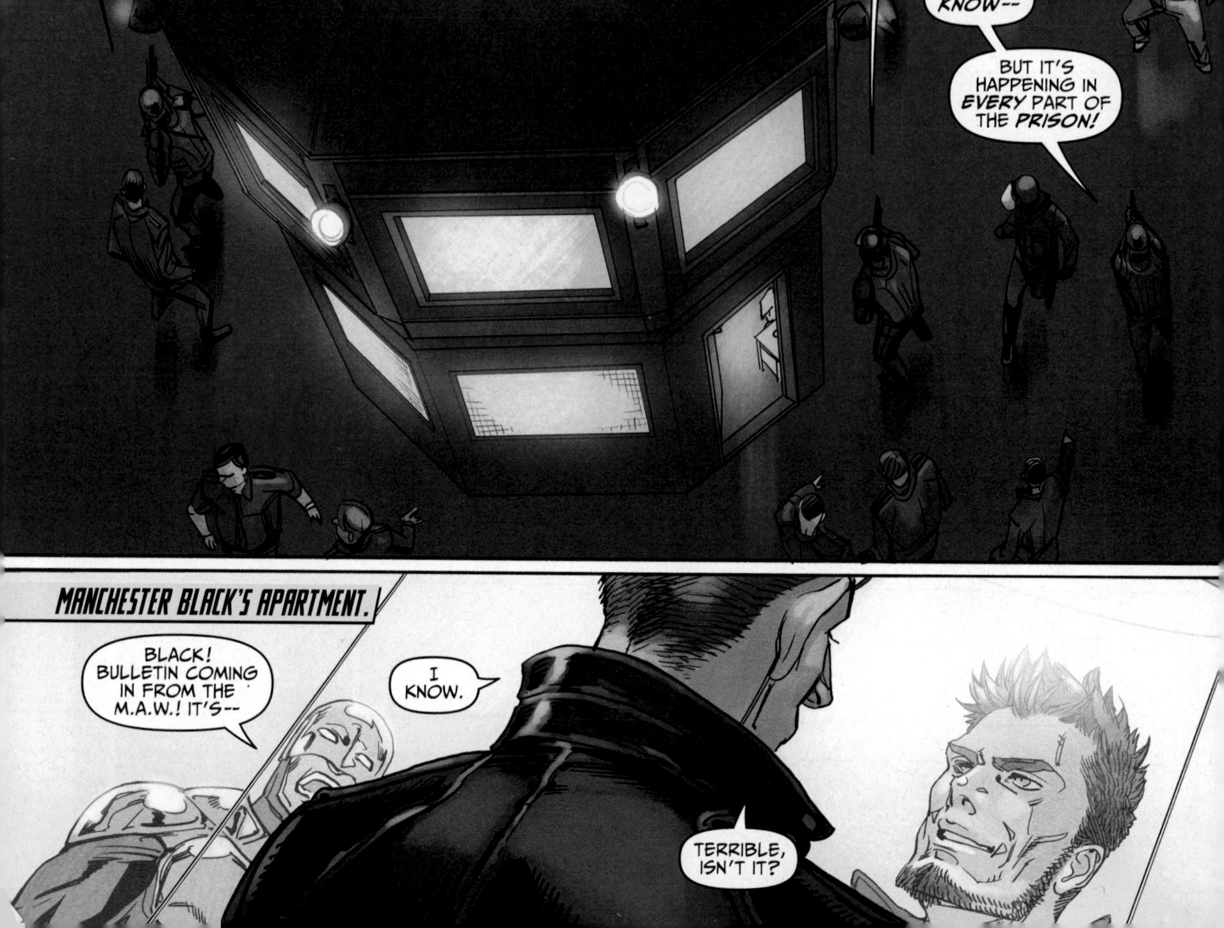
MANCHESTER BLACK'S APARTMENT.
BLACK! BULLETIN COMING IN FROM THE M.A.W.! IT'S--
I KNOW.
TERRIBLE, ISN'T IT?

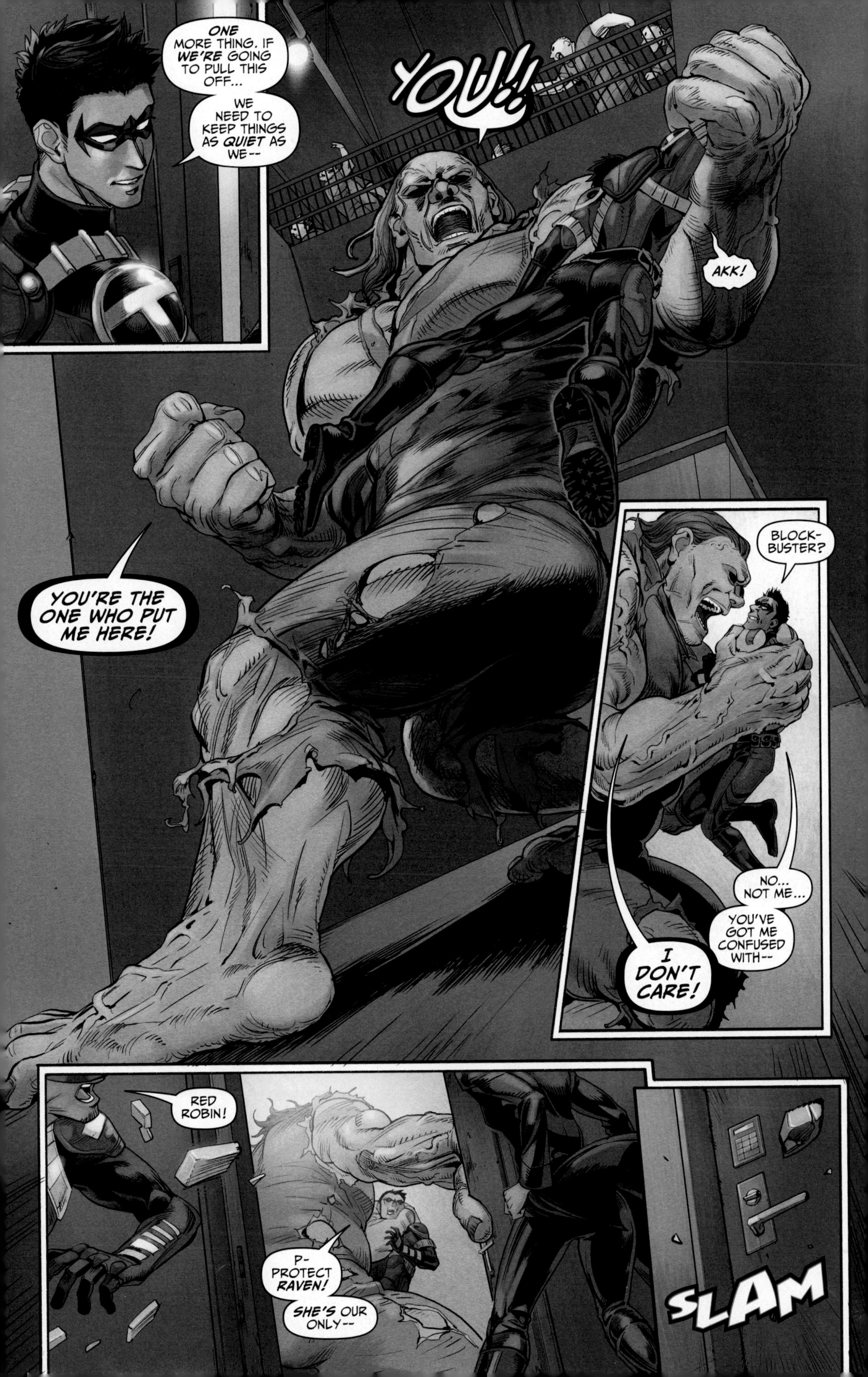

ONE MORE THING. IF WE'RE GOING TO PULL THIS OFF...
WE NEED TO KEEP THINGS AS QUIET AS WE--
YOU!!
AKK!
YOU'RE THE ONE WHO PUT ME HERE!
BLOCK-BUSTER?
NO... NOT ME...
YOU'VE GOT ME CONFUSED WITH--
I DON'T CARE!
RED ROBIN!
P-PROTECT RAVEN!
SHE'S OUR ONLY--
SLAM

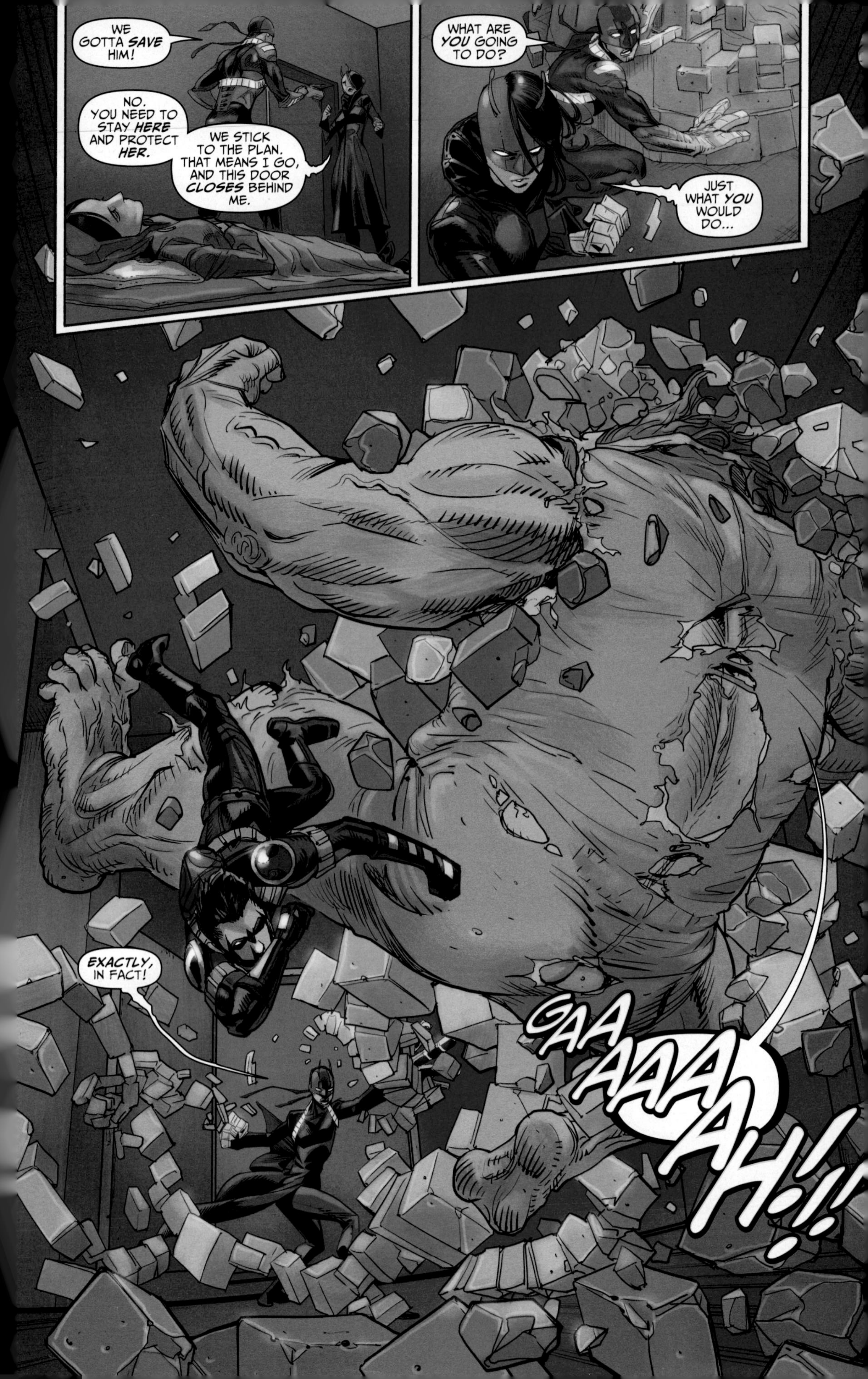
WE GOTTA SAVE HIM!
NO. YOU NEED TO STAY HERE AND PROTECT HER.
WE STICK TO THE PLAN. THAT MEANS I GO, AND THIS DOOR CLOSES BEHIND ME.
WHAT ARE YOU GOING TO DO?
JUST WHAT YOU WOULD DO...
EXACTLY, IN FACT!
GAAAAAAH!!!

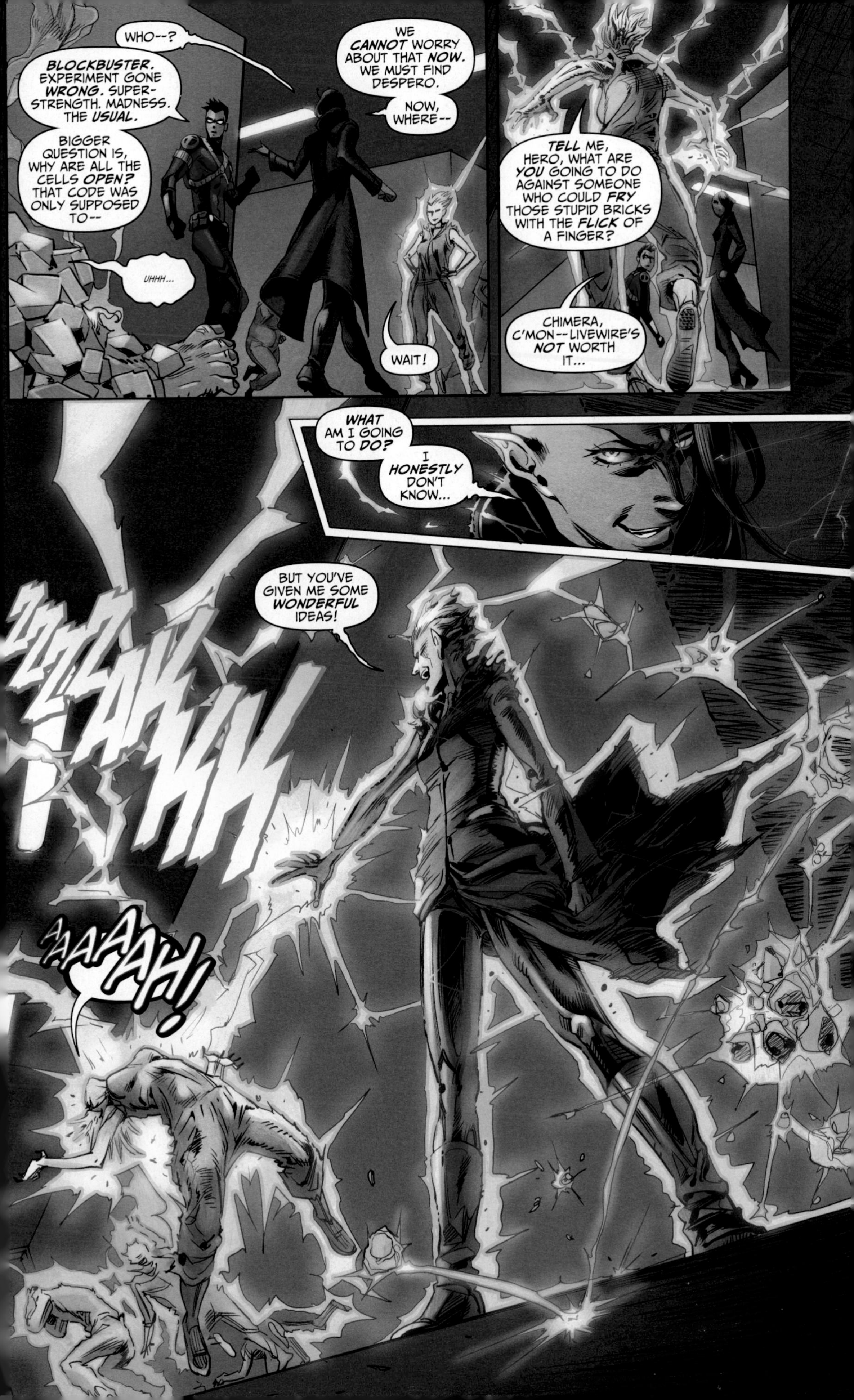
WHO--?
BLOCKBUSTER. EXPERIMENT GONE WRONG. SUPER-STRENGTH. MADNESS. THE USUAL.
BIGGER QUESTION IS, WHY ARE ALL THE CELLS OPEN? THAT CODE WAS ONLY SUPPOSED TO--
UHHH...
WE CANNOT WORRY ABOUT THAT NOW. WE MUST FIND DESPERO.
NOW, WHERE--
WAIT!
TELL ME, HERO, WHAT ARE YOU GOING TO DO AGAINST SOMEONE WHO COULD FRY THOSE STUPID BRICKS WITH THE FLICK OF A FINGER?
CHIMERA, C'MON--LIVEWIRE'S NOT WORTH IT...
WHAT AM I GOING TO DO?
I HONESTLY DON'T KNOW...
BUT YOU'VE GIVEN ME SOME WONDERFUL IDEAS!
ZZZZAKKK
AAAAAH!

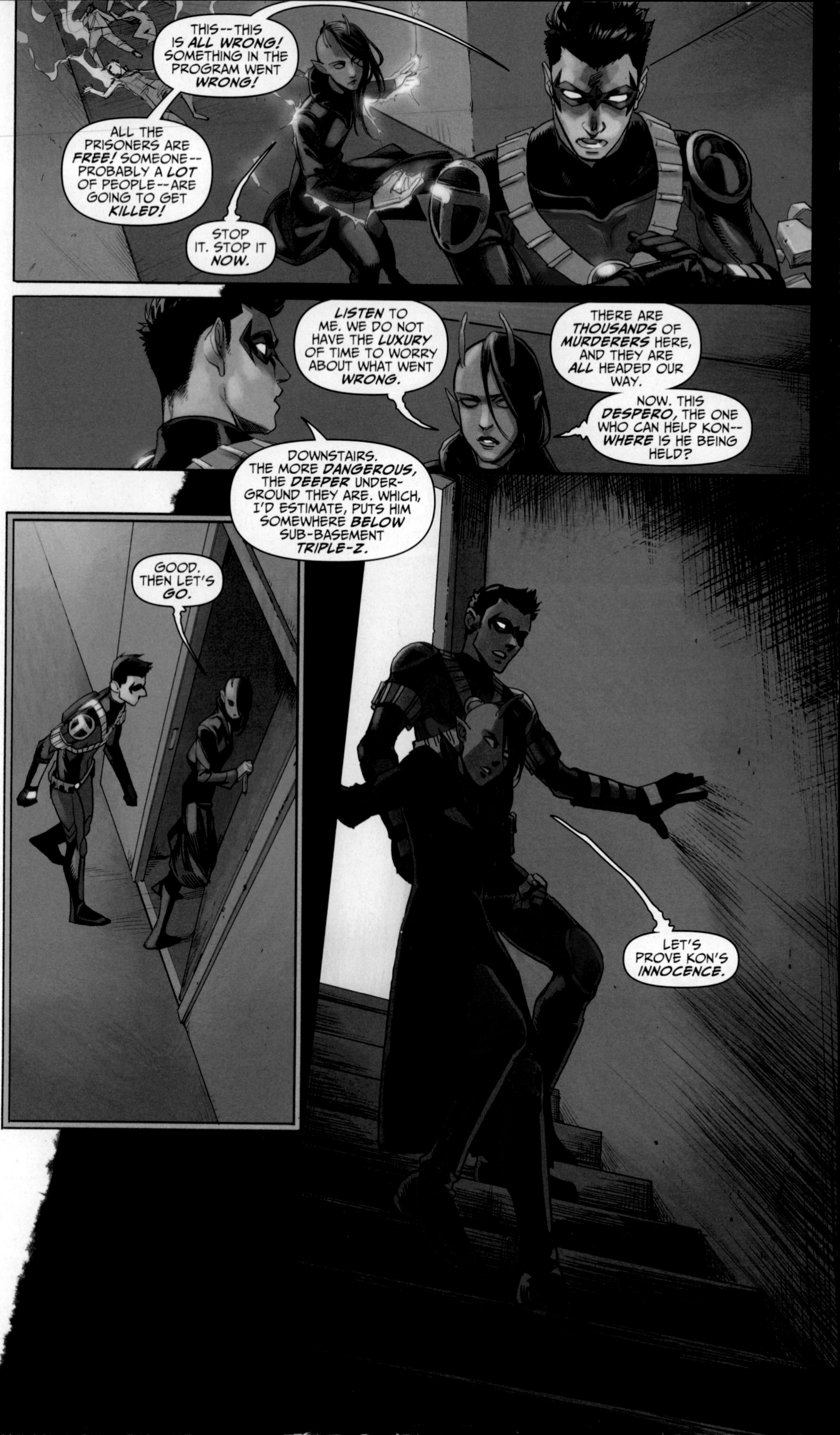
THIS--THIS IS ALL WRONG! SOMETHING IN THE PROGRAM WENT WRONG!
ALL THE PRISONERS ARE FREE! SOMEONE--PROBABLY A LOT OF PEOPLE--ARE GOING TO GET KILLED!
STOP IT. STOP IT NOW.
LISTEN TO ME. WE DO NOT HAVE THE LUXURY OF TIME TO WORRY ABOUT WHAT WENT WRONG.
THERE ARE THOUSANDS OF MURDERERS HERE, AND THEY ARE ALL HEADED OUR WAY.
NOW. THIS DESPERO, THE ONE WHO CAN HELP KON--WHERE IS HE BEING HELD?
DOWNSTAIRS. THE MORE DANGEROUS, THE DEEPER UNDER-GROUND THEY ARE. WHICH, I'D ESTIMATE, PUTS HIM SOMEWHERE BELOW SUB-BASEMENT TRIPLE-Z.
GOOD. THEN LET'S GO.
LET'S PROVE KON'S INNOCENCE.

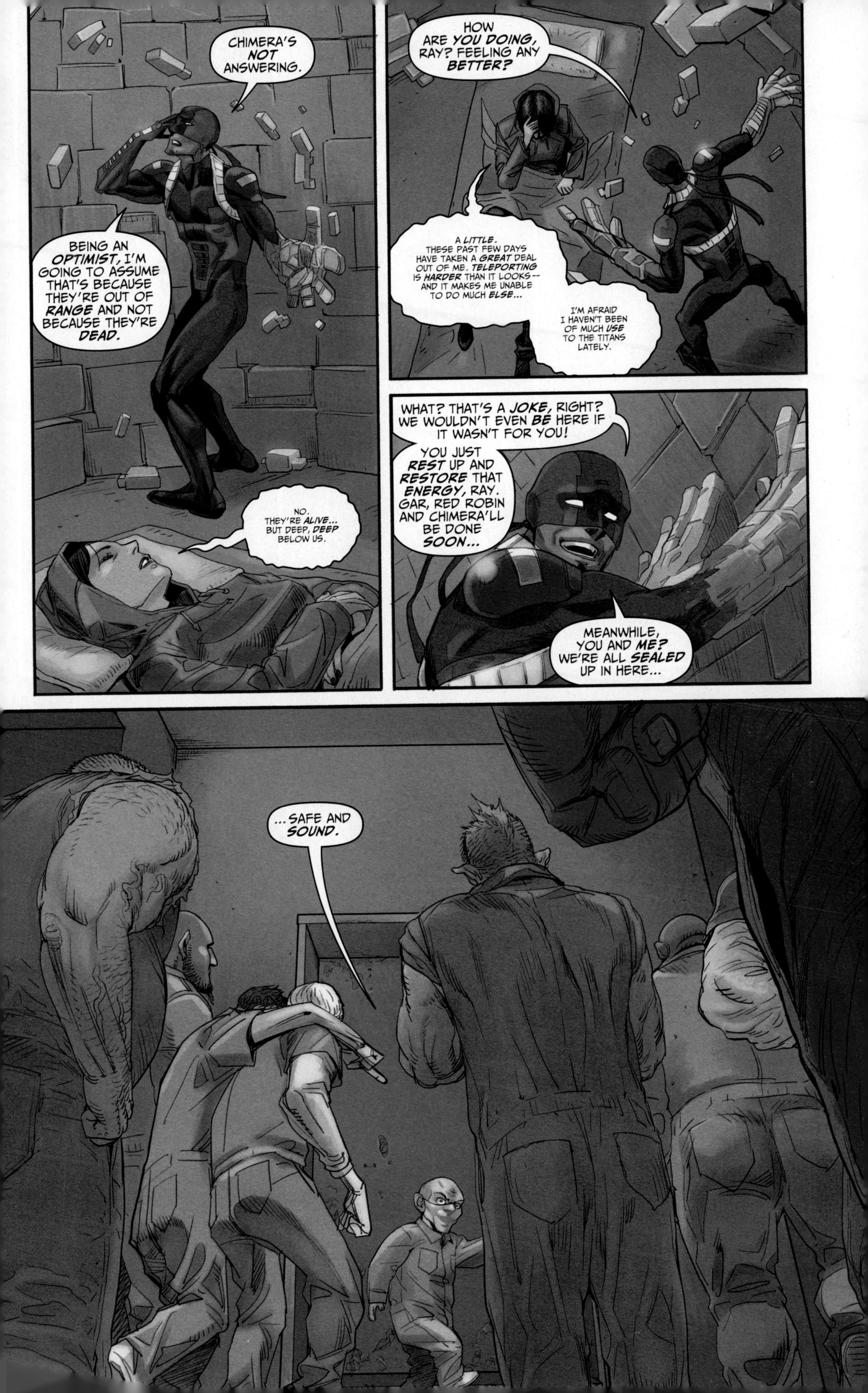
CHIMERA'S NOT ANSWERING.
BEING AN OPTIMIST, I'M GOING TO ASSUME THAT'S BECAUSE THEY'RE OUT OF RANGE AND NOT BECAUSE THEY'RE DEAD.
NO. THEY'RE ALIVE... BUT DEEP, DEEP BELOW US.
HOW ARE YOU DOING, RAY? FEELING ANY BETTER?
A LITTLE. THESE PAST FEW DAYS HAVE TAKEN A GREAT DEAL OUT OF ME. TELEPORTING IS HARDER THAN IT LOOKS-- AND IT MAKES ME UNABLE TO DO MUCH ELSE...
I'M AFRAID I HAVEN'T BEEN OF MUCH USE TO THE TITANS LATELY.
WHAT? THAT'S A JOKE, RIGHT? WE WOULDN'T EVEN BE HERE IF IT WASN'T FOR YOU!
YOU JUST REST UP AND RESTORE THAT ENERGY, RAY. GAR, RED ROBIN AND CHIMERA'LL BE DONE SOON...
MEANWHILE, YOU AND ME? WE'RE ALL SEALED UP IN HERE...
...SAFE AND SOUND.

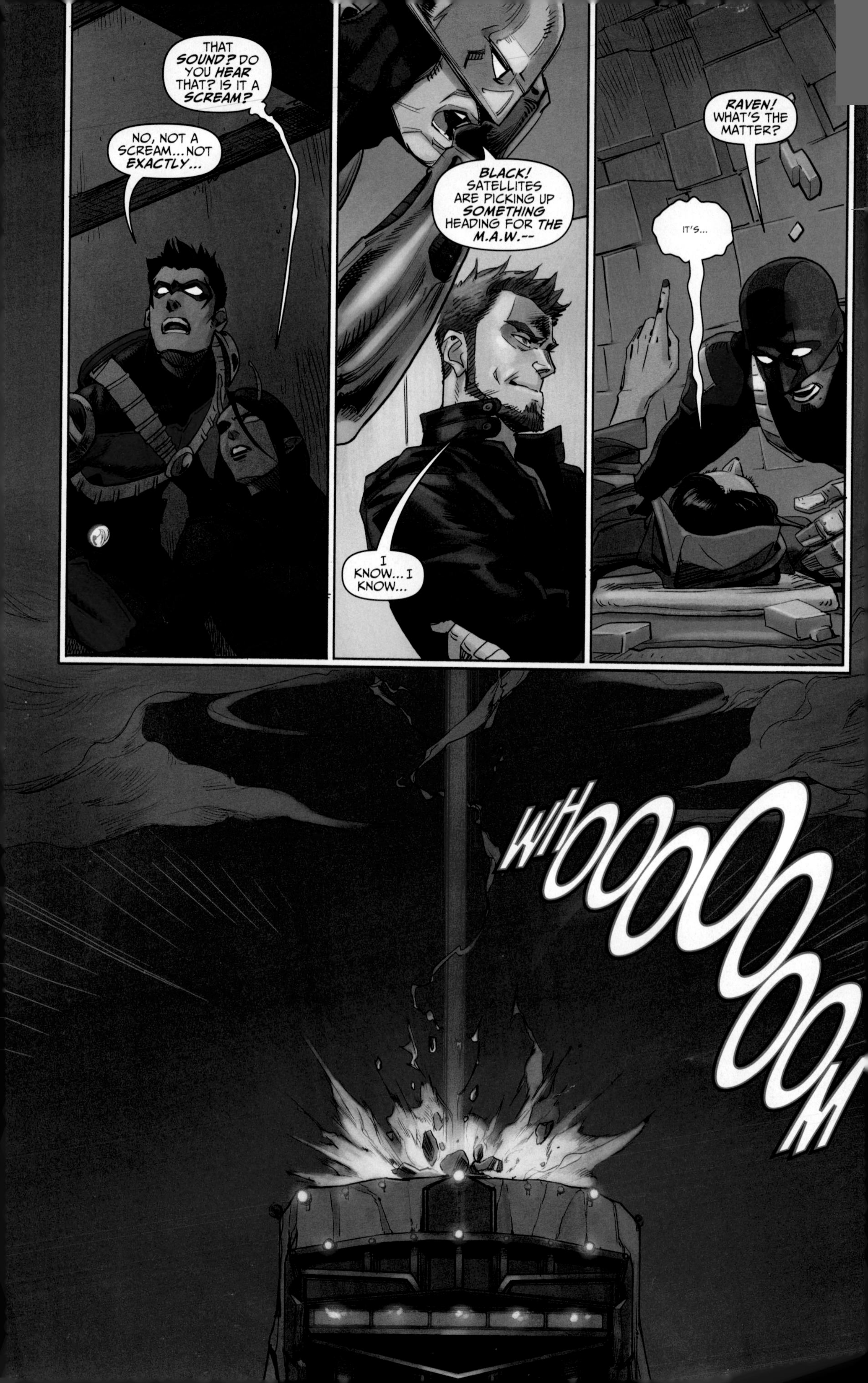
THAT SOUND? DO YOU HEAR THAT? IS IT A SCREAM?
NO, NOT A SCREAM...NOT EXACTLY...
BLACK! SATELLITES ARE PICKING UP SOMETHING HEADING FOR THE M.A.W.--
I KNOW...I KNOW...
RAVEN! WHAT'S THE MATTER?
IT'S...
WHOOOOOOOM

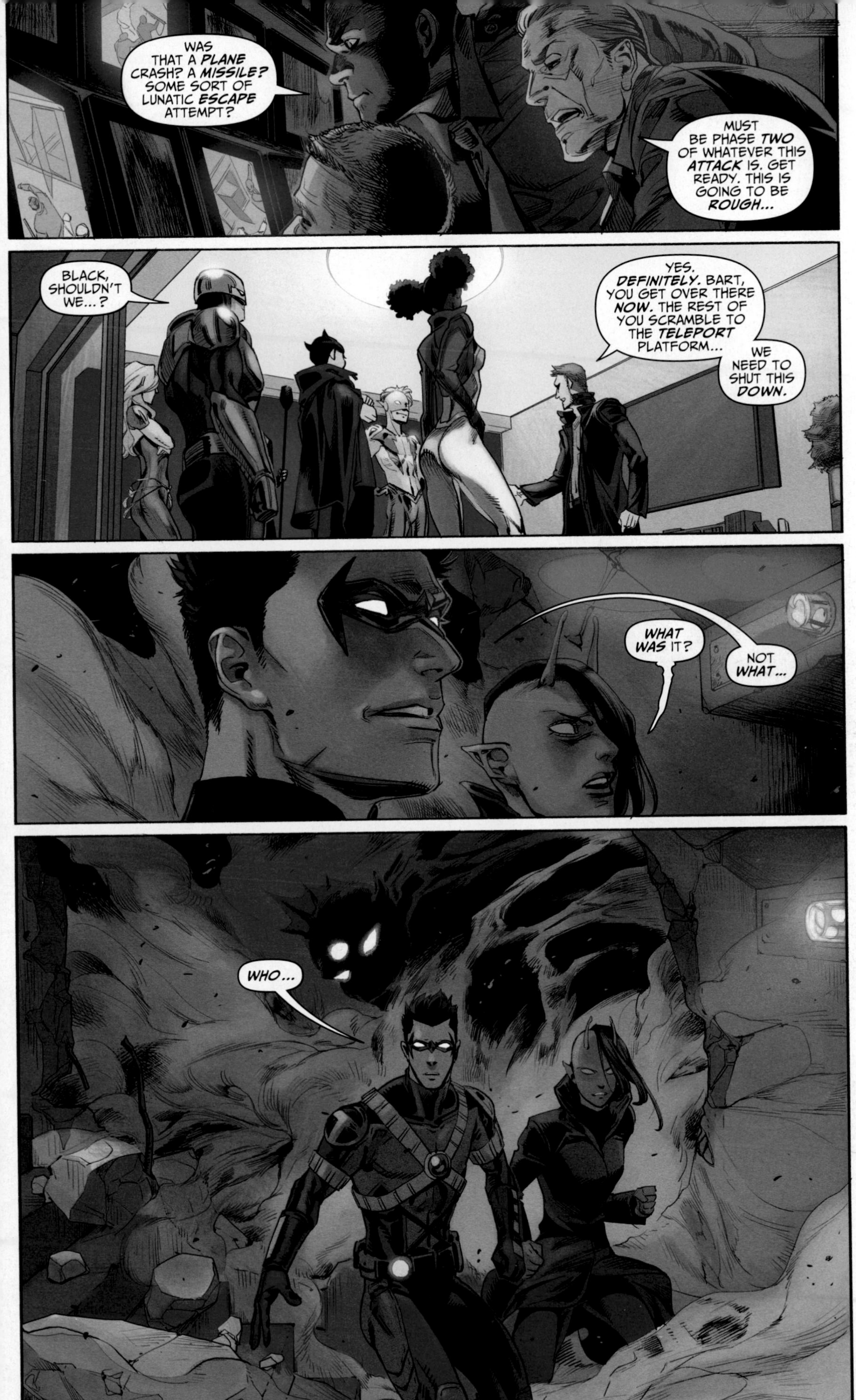
WAS THAT A *PLANE* CRASH? A *MISSILE?* SOME SORT OF LUNATIC *ESCAPE* ATTEMPT?
MUST BE PHASE *TWO* OF WHATEVER THIS *ATTACK* IS. GET READY. THIS IS GOING TO BE *ROUGH...*
BLACK, SHOULDN'T WE...?
YES. *DEFINITELY.* BART, YOU GET OVER THERE *NOW.* THE REST OF YOU SCRAMBLE TO THE *TELEPORT* PLATFORM...
WE NEED TO SHUT THIS *DOWN.*
WHAT WAS IT?
NOT WHAT...
WHO...

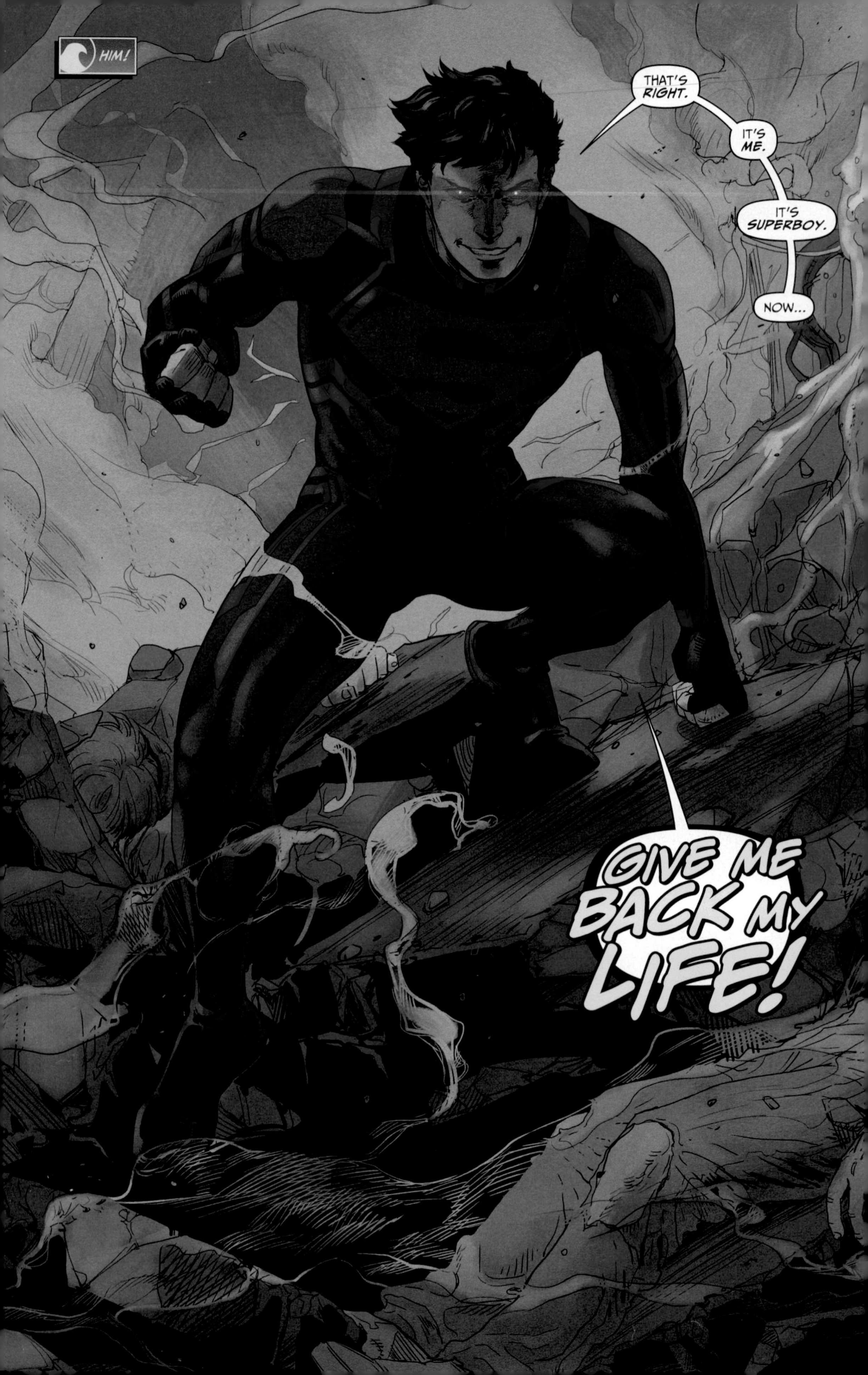
HIM!
THAT'S RIGHT.
IT'S ME.
IT'S SUPERBOY.
NOW...
GIVE ME BACK MY LIFE!

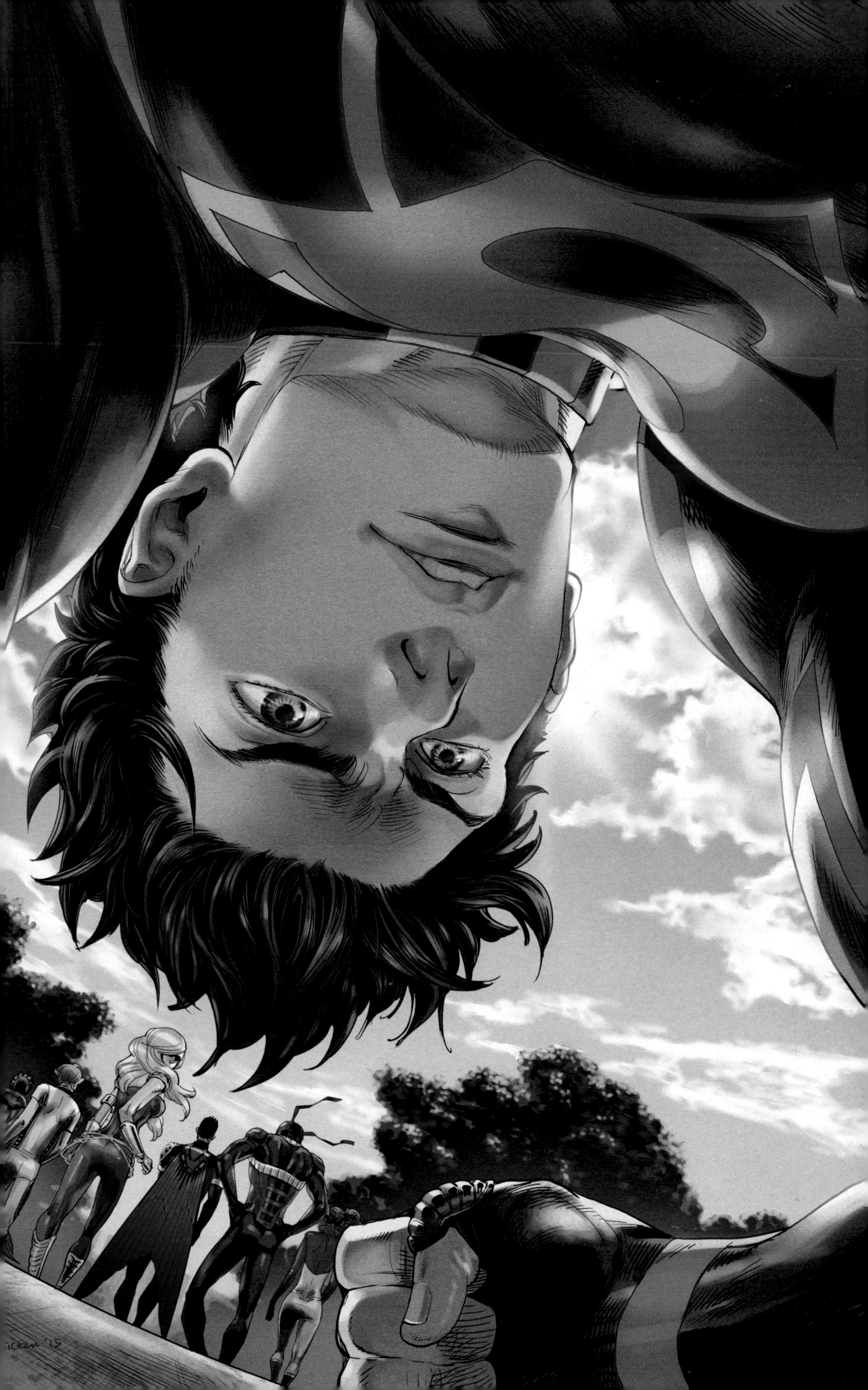

ROGUE TARGETS PART FOUR

SCOTT LOBDELL WILL PFEIFER writers IAN CHURCHILL penciller NORM RAPMUND inker TONY AVIÑA colorist COREY BREEN letterer cover art by RICKEN

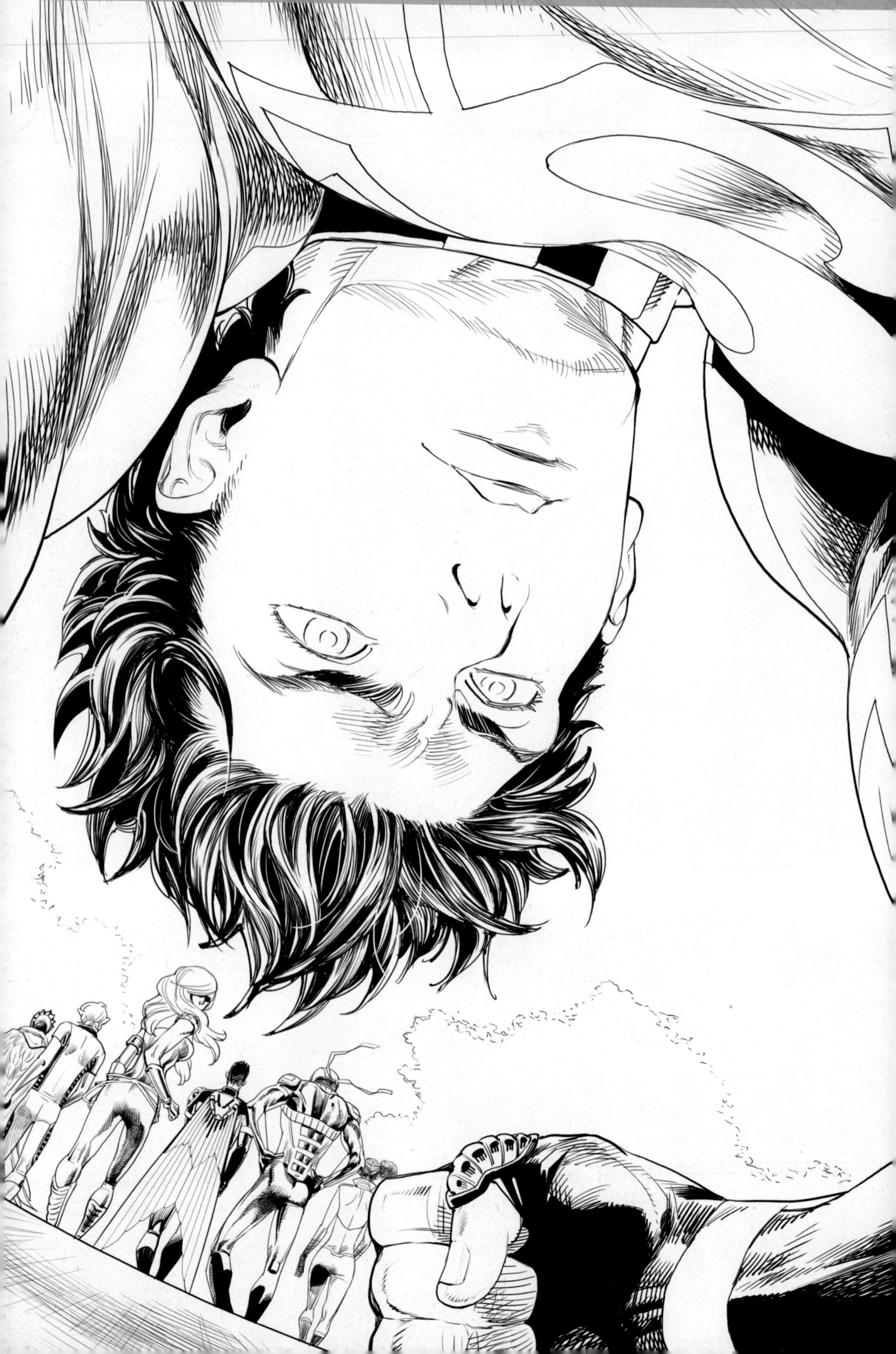

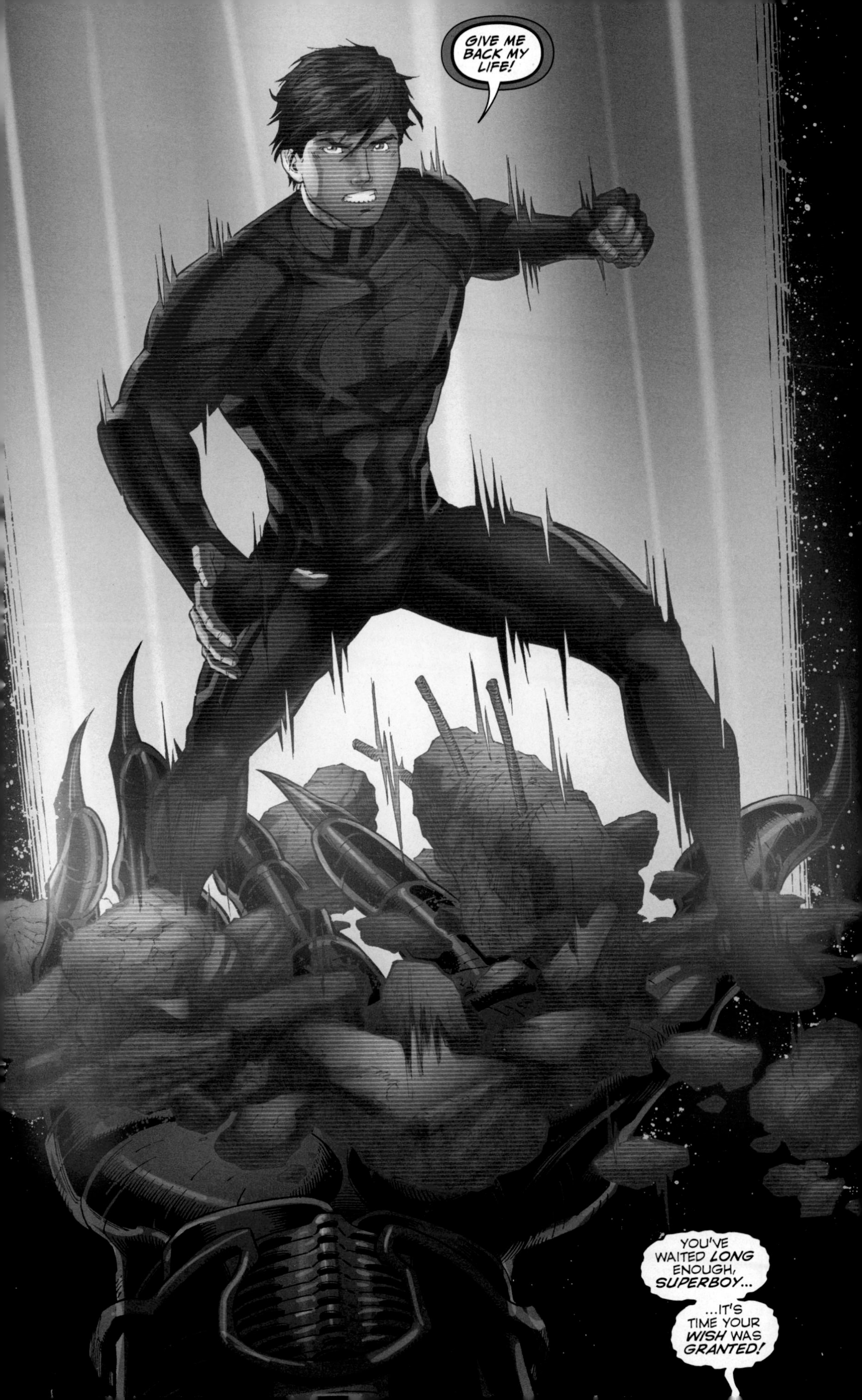
GIVE ME BACK MY LIFE!
YOU'VE WAITED LONG ENOUGH, SUPERBOY...
...IT'S TIME YOUR WISH WAS GRANTED!

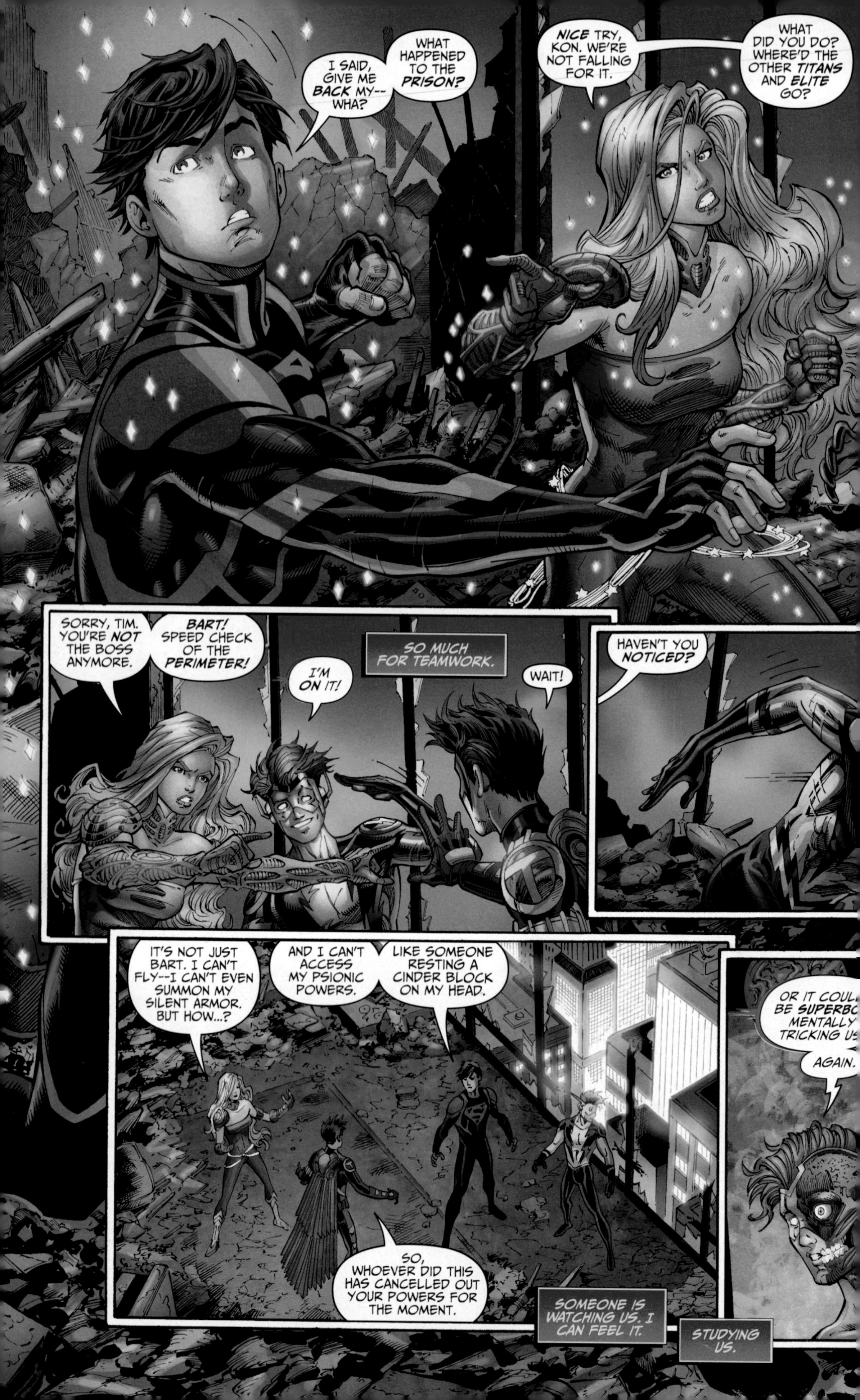

WHAT HAPPENED TO THE PRISON?
I SAID, GIVE ME BACK MY-- WHA?
NICE TRY, KON. WE'RE NOT FALLING FOR IT.
WHAT DID YOU DO? WHERE'D THE OTHER TITANS AND ELITE GO?
SORRY, TIM. YOU'RE NOT THE BOSS ANYMORE.
BART! SPEED CHECK OF THE PERIMETER!
I'M ON IT!
SO MUCH FOR TEAMWORK.
WAIT!
HAVEN'T YOU NOTICED?
IT'S NOT JUST BART. I CAN'T FLY--I CAN'T EVEN SUMMON MY SILENT ARMOR. BUT HOW...?
AND I CAN'T ACCESS MY PSIONIC POWERS.
LIKE SOMEONE RESTING A CINDER BLOCK ON MY HEAD.
SO, WHOEVER DID THIS HAS CANCELLED OUT YOUR POWERS FOR THE MOMENT.
SOMEONE IS WATCHING US. I CAN FEEL IT.
STUDYING US.
AGAIN.

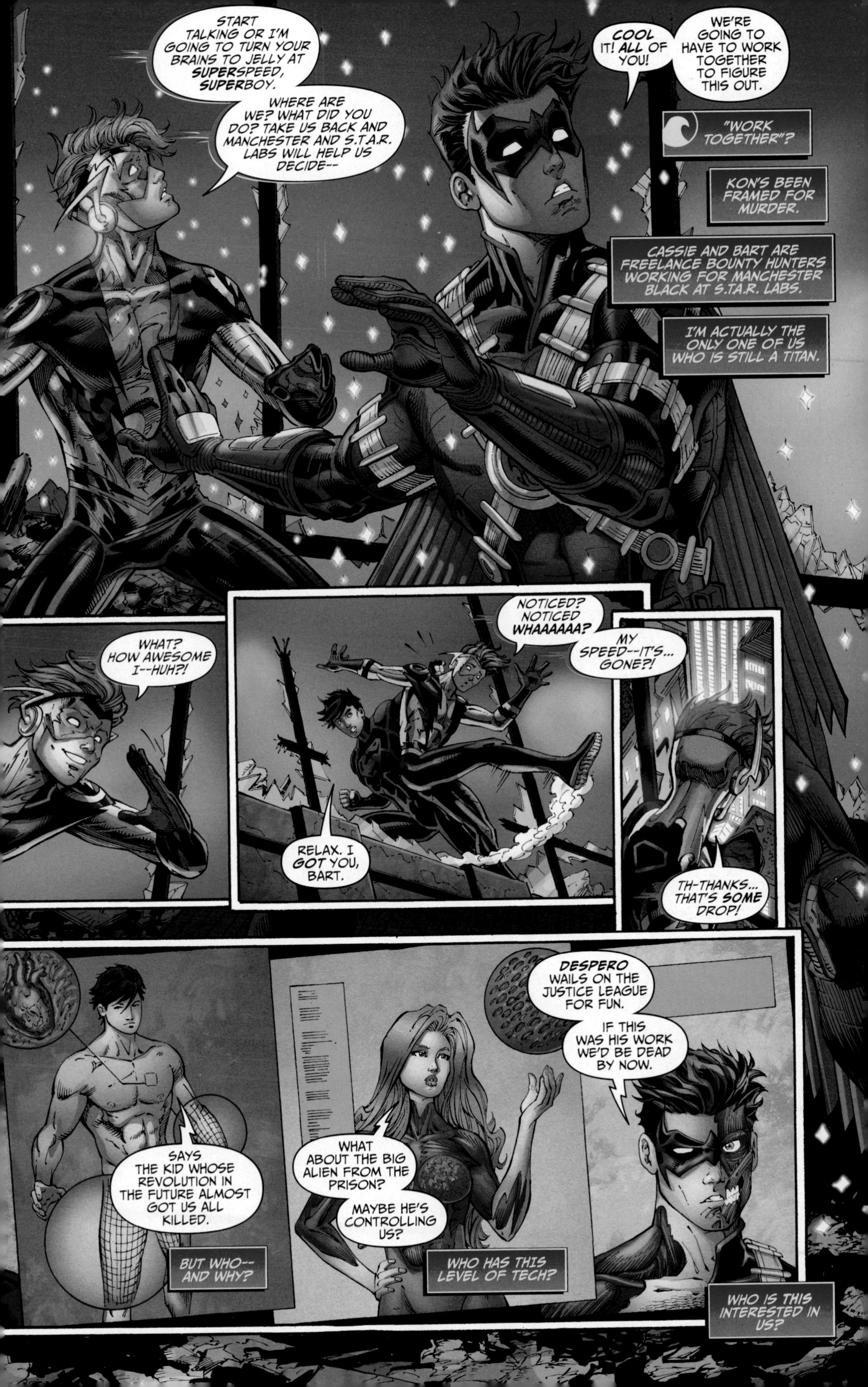
START TALKING OR I'M GOING TO TURN YOUR BRAINS TO JELLY AT SUPERSPEED, SUPERBOY.
WHERE ARE WE? WHAT DID YOU DO? TAKE US BACK AND MANCHESTER AND S.T.A.R. LABS WILL HELP US DECIDE--
COOL IT! ALL OF YOU!
WE'RE GOING TO HAVE TO WORK TOGETHER TO FIGURE THIS OUT.
"WORK TOGETHER"?
KON'S BEEN FRAMED FOR MURDER.
CASSIE AND BART ARE FREELANCE BOUNTY HUNTERS WORKING FOR MANCHESTER BLACK AT S.T.A.R. LABS.
I'M ACTUALLY THE ONLY ONE OF US WHO IS STILL A TITAN.
WHAT? HOW AWESOME I--HUH?!
NOTICED? NOTICED WHAAAAAA?
MY SPEED--IT'S... GONE?!
RELAX. I GOT YOU, BART.
TH-THANKS... THAT'S SOME DROP!
SAYS THE KID WHOSE REVOLUTION IN THE FUTURE ALMOST GOT US ALL KILLED.
BUT WHO-- AND WHY?
WHAT ABOUT THE BIG ALIEN FROM THE PRISON?
MAYBE HE'S CONTROLLING US?
WHO HAS THIS LEVEL OF TECH?
DESPERO WAILS ON THE JUSTICE LEAGUE FOR FUN.
IF THIS WAS HIS WORK WE'D BE DEAD BY NOW.
WHO IS THIS INTERESTED IN US?

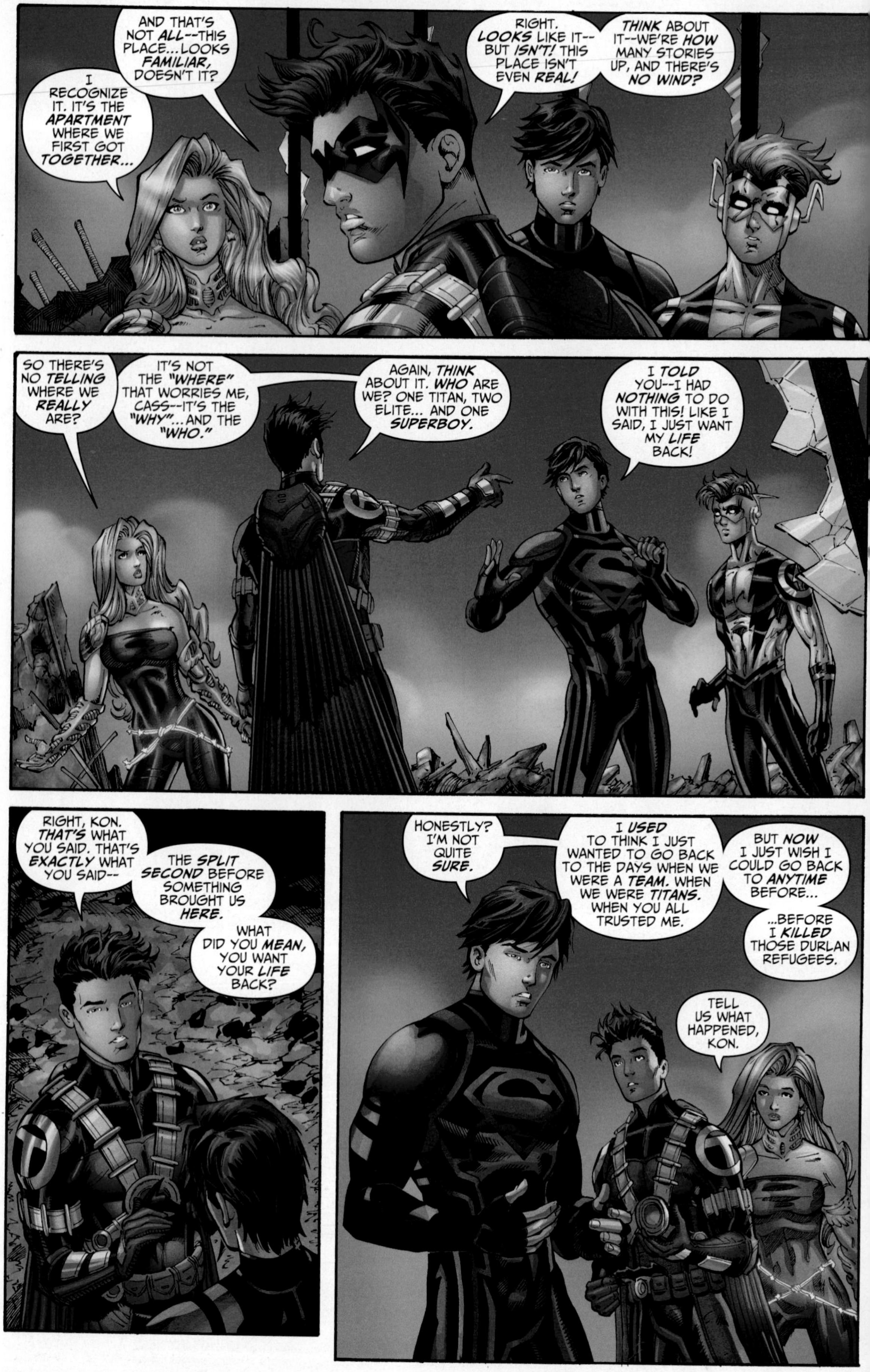

AND THAT'S NOT ALL--THIS PLACE...LOOKS FAMILIAR, DOESN'T IT?
I RECOGNIZE IT. IT'S THE APARTMENT WHERE WE FIRST GOT TOGETHER...
RIGHT. LOOKS LIKE IT--BUT ISN'T! THIS PLACE ISN'T EVEN REAL!
THINK ABOUT IT--WE'RE HOW MANY STORIES UP, AND THERE'S NO WIND?
SO THERE'S NO TELLING WHERE WE REALLY ARE?
IT'S NOT THE "WHERE" THAT WORRIES ME, CASS--IT'S THE "WHY"...AND THE "WHO."
AGAIN, THINK ABOUT IT. WHO ARE WE? ONE TITAN, TWO ELITE... AND ONE SUPERBOY.
I TOLD YOU--I HAD NOTHING TO DO WITH THIS! LIKE I SAID, I JUST WANT MY LIFE BACK!
RIGHT, KON. THAT'S WHAT YOU SAID. THAT'S EXACTLY WHAT YOU SAID--
THE SPLIT SECOND BEFORE SOMETHING BROUGHT US HERE.
WHAT DID YOU MEAN, YOU WANT YOUR LIFE BACK?
HONESTLY? I'M NOT QUITE SURE.
I USED TO THINK I JUST WANTED TO GO BACK TO THE DAYS WHEN WE WERE A TEAM. WHEN WE WERE TITANS. WHEN YOU ALL TRUSTED ME.
BUT NOW I JUST WISH I COULD GO BACK TO ANYTIME BEFORE...
...BEFORE I KILLED THOSE DURLAN REFUGEES.
TELL US WHAT HAPPENED, KON.

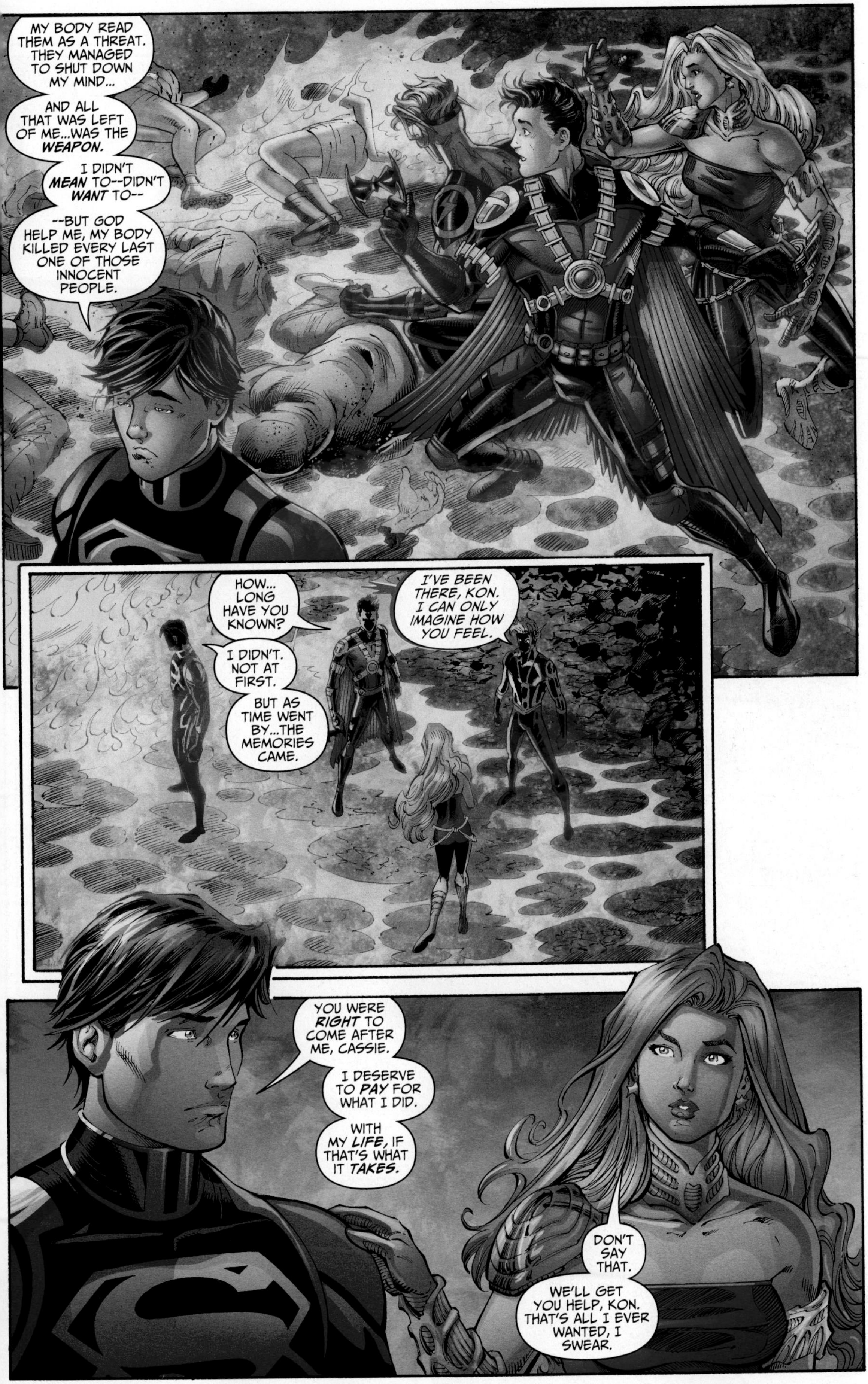
MY BODY READ THEM AS A THREAT. THEY MANAGED TO SHUT DOWN MY MIND...
AND ALL THAT WAS LEFT OF ME...WAS THE WEAPON.
I DIDN'T MEAN TO--DIDN'T WANT TO--
--BUT GOD HELP ME, MY BODY KILLED EVERY LAST ONE OF THOSE INNOCENT PEOPLE.
HOW... LONG HAVE YOU KNOWN?
I DIDN'T. NOT AT FIRST.
BUT AS TIME WENT BY...THE MEMORIES CAME.
I'VE BEEN THERE, KON. I CAN ONLY IMAGINE HOW YOU FEEL.
YOU WERE RIGHT TO COME AFTER ME, CASSIE.
I DESERVE TO PAY FOR WHAT I DID.
WITH MY LIFE, IF THAT'S WHAT IT TAKES.
DON'T SAY THAT.
WE'LL GET YOU HELP, KON. THAT'S ALL I EVER WANTED, I SWEAR.

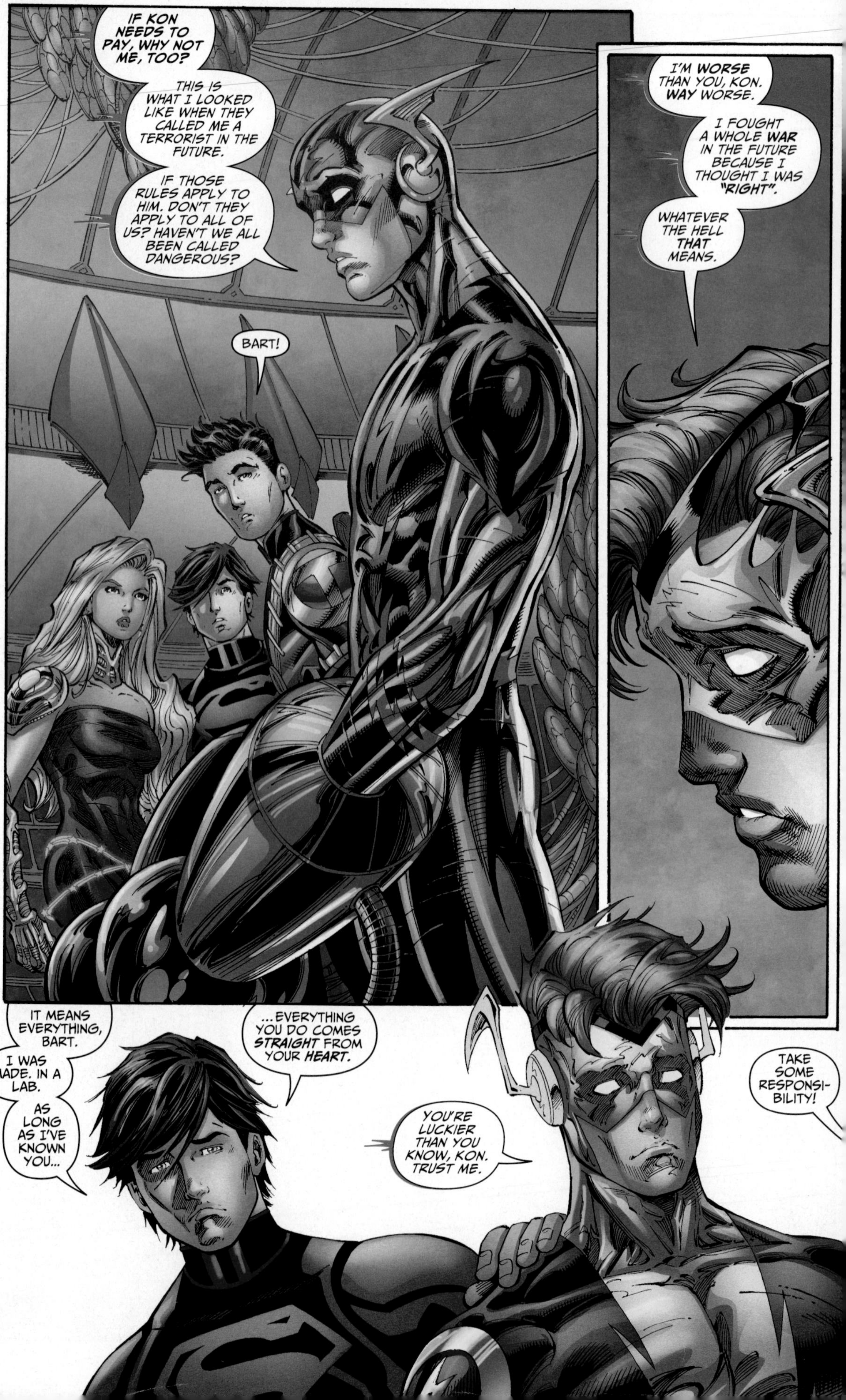
IF KON NEEDS TO PAY, WHY NOT ME, TOO?
THIS IS WHAT I LOOKED LIKE WHEN THEY CALLED ME A TERRORIST IN THE FUTURE.
IF THOSE RULES APPLY TO HIM. DON'T THEY APPLY TO ALL OF US? HAVEN'T WE ALL BEEN CALLED DANGEROUS?
BART!
I'M WORSE THAN YOU, KON. WAY WORSE.
I FOUGHT A WHOLE WAR IN THE FUTURE BECAUSE I THOUGHT I WAS "RIGHT".
WHATEVER THE HELL THAT MEANS.
IT MEANS EVERYTHING, BART.
I WAS MADE. IN A LAB.
AS LONG AS I'VE KNOWN YOU...
...EVERYTHING YOU DO COMES STRAIGHT FROM YOUR HEART.
YOU'RE LUCKIER THAN YOU KNOW, KON. TRUST ME.
TAKE SOME RESPONSI-BILITY!

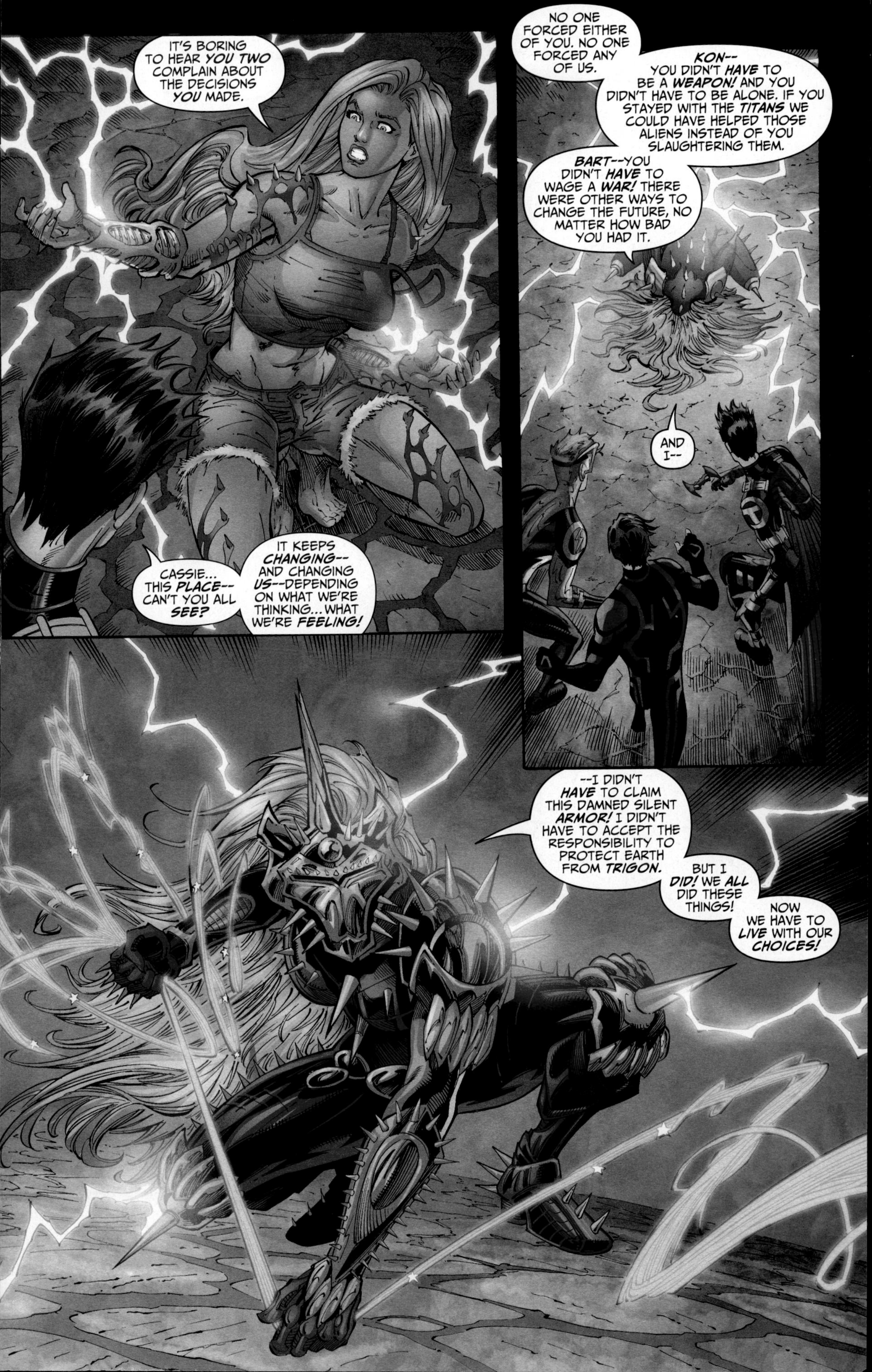
IT'S BORING TO HEAR *YOU TWO* COMPLAIN ABOUT THE DECISIONS *YOU* MADE.
CASSIE... THIS *PLACE*-- CAN'T YOU ALL *SEE?*
IT KEEPS *CHANGING*-- AND CHANGING *US*--DEPENDING ON WHAT WE'RE THINKING...WHAT WE'RE *FEELING!*
NO ONE FORCED EITHER OF YOU. NO ONE FORCED ANY OF US.
KON-- YOU DIDN'T *HAVE* TO BE A *WEAPON!* AND YOU DIDN'T HAVE TO BE ALONE. IF YOU STAYED WITH THE *TITANS* WE COULD HAVE HELPED THOSE ALIENS INSTEAD OF YOU SLAUGHTERING THEM.
BART--YOU DIDN'T *HAVE* TO WAGE A *WAR!* THERE WERE OTHER WAYS TO CHANGE THE FUTURE, NO MATTER HOW BAD YOU HAD IT.
AND I--
--I DIDN'T *HAVE* TO CLAIM THIS DAMNED SILENT *ARMOR!* I DIDN'T HAVE TO ACCEPT THE RESPONSIBILITY TO PROTECT EARTH FROM *TRIGON.*
BUT I *DID!* WE *ALL* DID THESE THINGS!
NOW WE HAVE TO *LIVE* WITH OUR *CHOICES!*

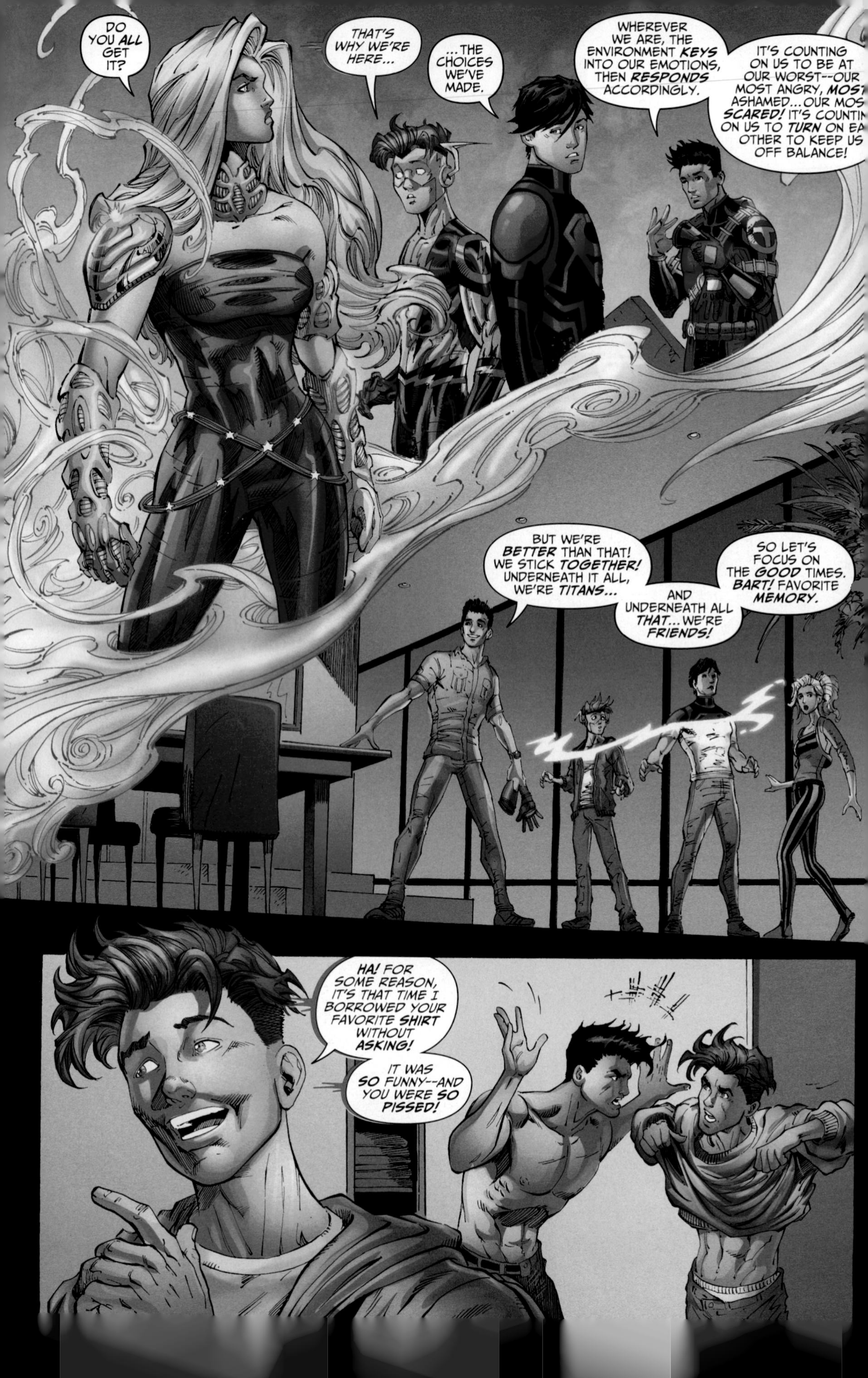
DO YOU ALL GET IT?
THAT'S WHY WE'RE HERE...
...THE CHOICES WE'VE MADE.
WHEREVER WE ARE, THE ENVIRONMENT KEYS INTO OUR EMOTIONS, THEN RESPONDS ACCORDINGLY.
IT'S COUNTING ON US TO BE AT OUR WORST--OUR MOST ANGRY, MOST ASHAMED...OUR MOST SCARED! IT'S COUNTING ON US TO TURN ON EACH OTHER TO KEEP US OFF BALANCE!
BUT WE'RE BETTER THAN THAT! WE STICK TOGETHER! UNDERNEATH IT ALL, WE'RE TITANS...
AND UNDERNEATH ALL THAT... WE'RE FRIENDS!
SO LET'S FOCUS ON THE GOOD TIMES. BART! FAVORITE MEMORY.
HA! FOR SOME REASON, IT'S THAT TIME I BORROWED YOUR FAVORITE SHIRT WITHOUT ASKING!
IT WAS SO FUNNY--AND YOU WERE SO PISSED!

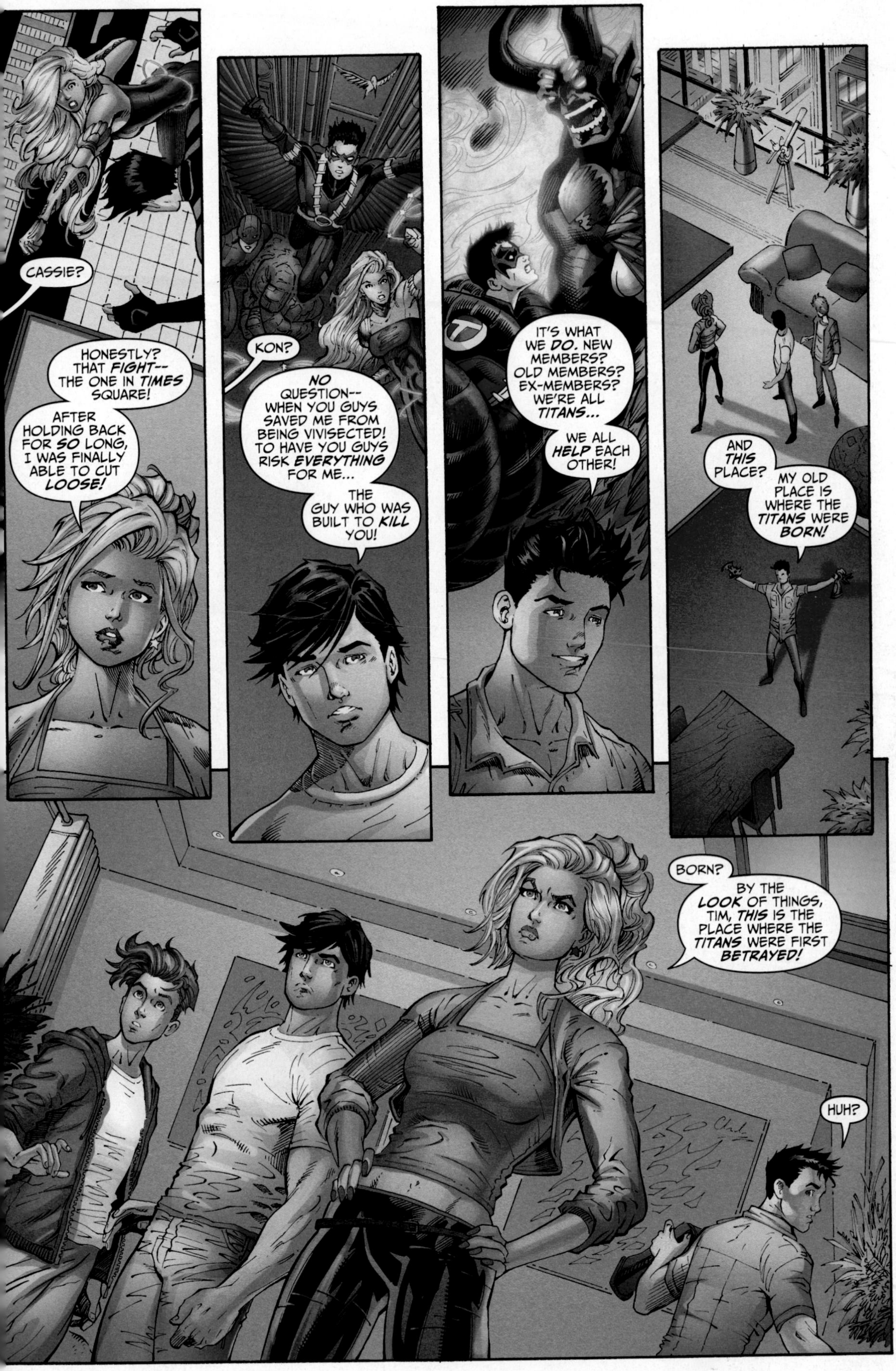

CASSIE?
HONESTLY? THAT FIGHT-- THE ONE IN TIMES SQUARE!
AFTER HOLDING BACK FOR SO LONG, I WAS FINALLY ABLE TO CUT LOOSE!
KON?
NO QUESTION-- WHEN YOU GUYS SAVED ME FROM BEING VIVISECTED! TO HAVE YOU GUYS RISK EVERYTHING FOR ME...
THE GUY WHO WAS BUILT TO KILL YOU!
IT'S WHAT WE DO. NEW MEMBERS? OLD MEMBERS? EX-MEMBERS? WE'RE ALL TITANS...
WE ALL HELP EACH OTHER!
AND THIS PLACE?
MY OLD PLACE IS WHERE THE TITANS WERE BORN!
BORN?
BY THE LOOK OF THINGS, TIM, THIS IS THE PLACE WHERE THE TITANS WERE FIRST BETRAYED!
HUH?

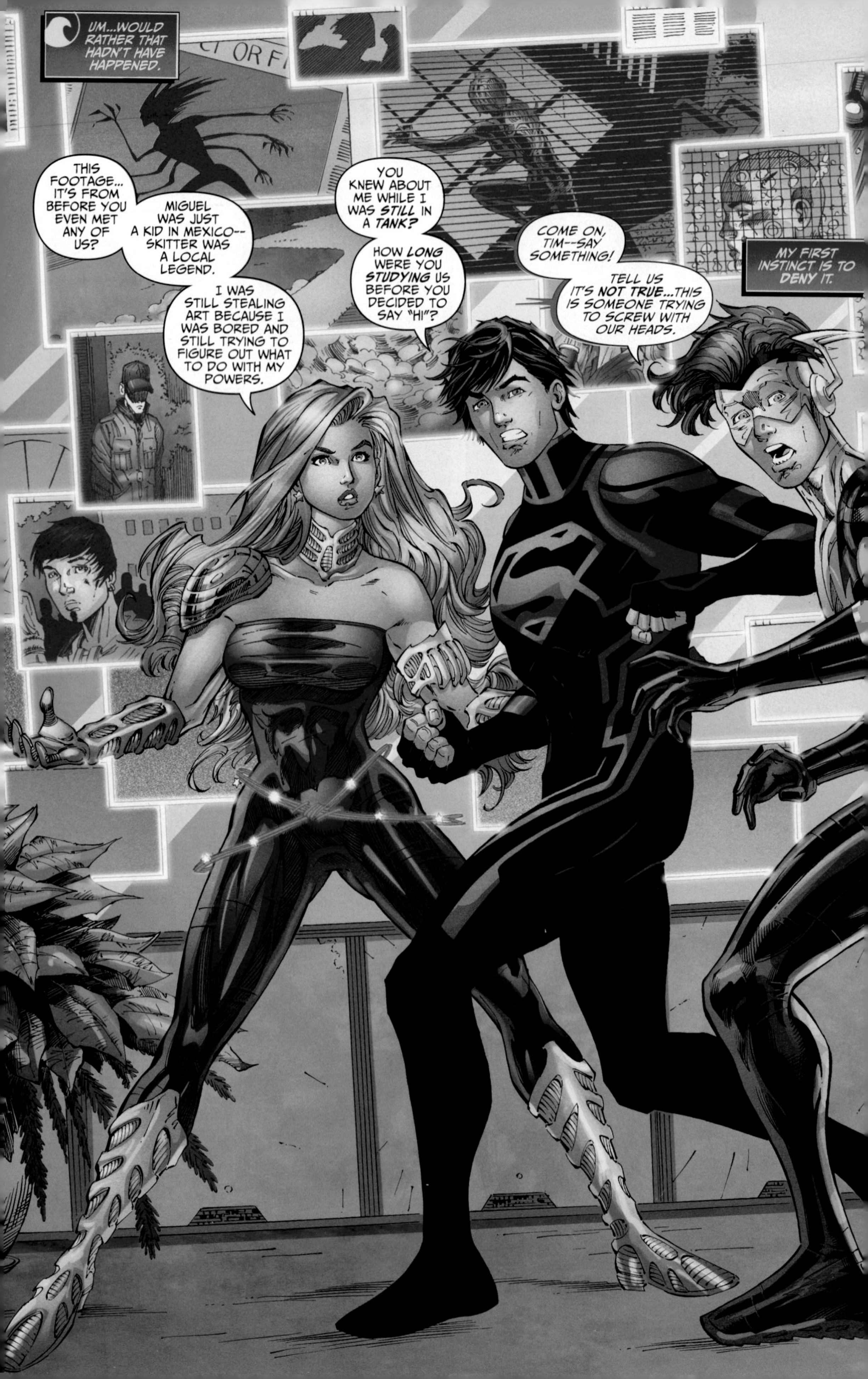
UM...WOULD RATHER THAT HADN'T HAVE HAPPENED.
THIS FOOTAGE... IT'S FROM BEFORE YOU EVEN MET ANY OF US?
MIGUEL WAS JUST A KID IN MEXICO--SKITTER WAS A LOCAL LEGEND.
I WAS STILL STEALING ART BECAUSE I WAS BORED AND STILL TRYING TO FIGURE OUT WHAT TO DO WITH MY POWERS.
YOU KNEW ABOUT ME WHILE I WAS STILL IN A TANK?
HOW LONG WERE YOU STUDYING US BEFORE YOU DECIDED TO SAY "HI"?
COME ON, TIM--SAY SOMETHING!
TELL US IT'S NOT TRUE...THIS IS SOMEONE TRYING TO SCREW WITH OUR HEADS.
MY FIRST INSTINCT IS TO DENY IT.

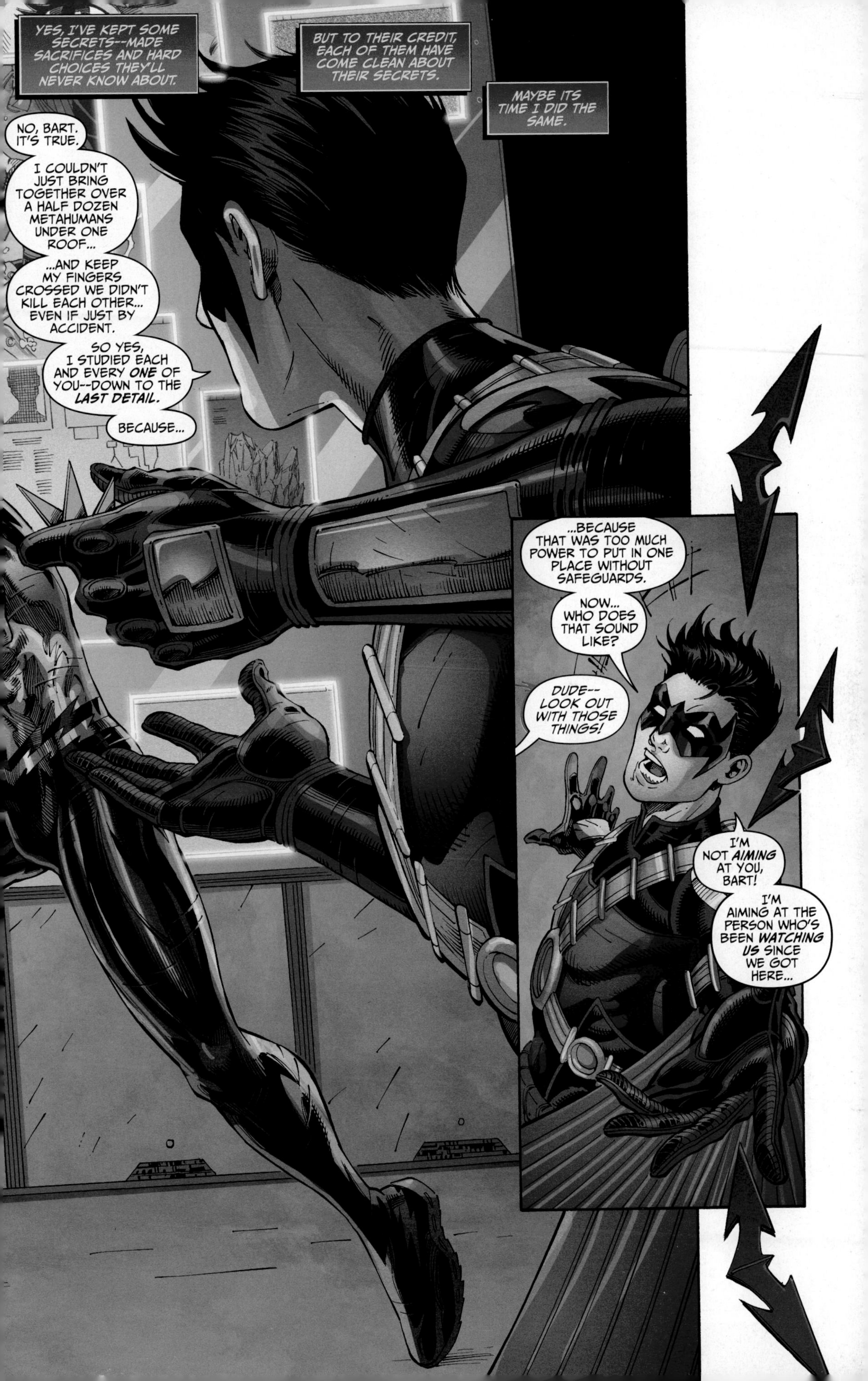
YES, I'VE KEPT SOME SECRETS--MADE SACRIFICES AND HARD CHOICES THEY'LL NEVER KNOW ABOUT.
BUT TO THEIR CREDIT, EACH OF THEM HAVE COME CLEAN ABOUT THEIR SECRETS.
MAYBE ITS TIME I DID THE SAME.
NO, BART. IT'S TRUE.
I COULDN'T JUST BRING TOGETHER OVER A HALF DOZEN METAHUMANS UNDER ONE ROOF...
...AND KEEP MY FINGERS CROSSED WE DIDN'T KILL EACH OTHER... EVEN IF JUST BY ACCIDENT.
SO YES, I STUDIED EACH AND EVERY ONE OF YOU--DOWN TO THE LAST DETAIL.
BECAUSE...
...BECAUSE THAT WAS TOO MUCH POWER TO PUT IN ONE PLACE WITHOUT SAFEGUARDS.
NOW... WHO DOES THAT SOUND LIKE?
DUDE-- LOOK OUT WITH THOSE THINGS!
I'M NOT AIMING AT YOU, BART!
I'M AIMING AT THE PERSON WHO'S BEEN WATCHING US SINCE WE GOT HERE...

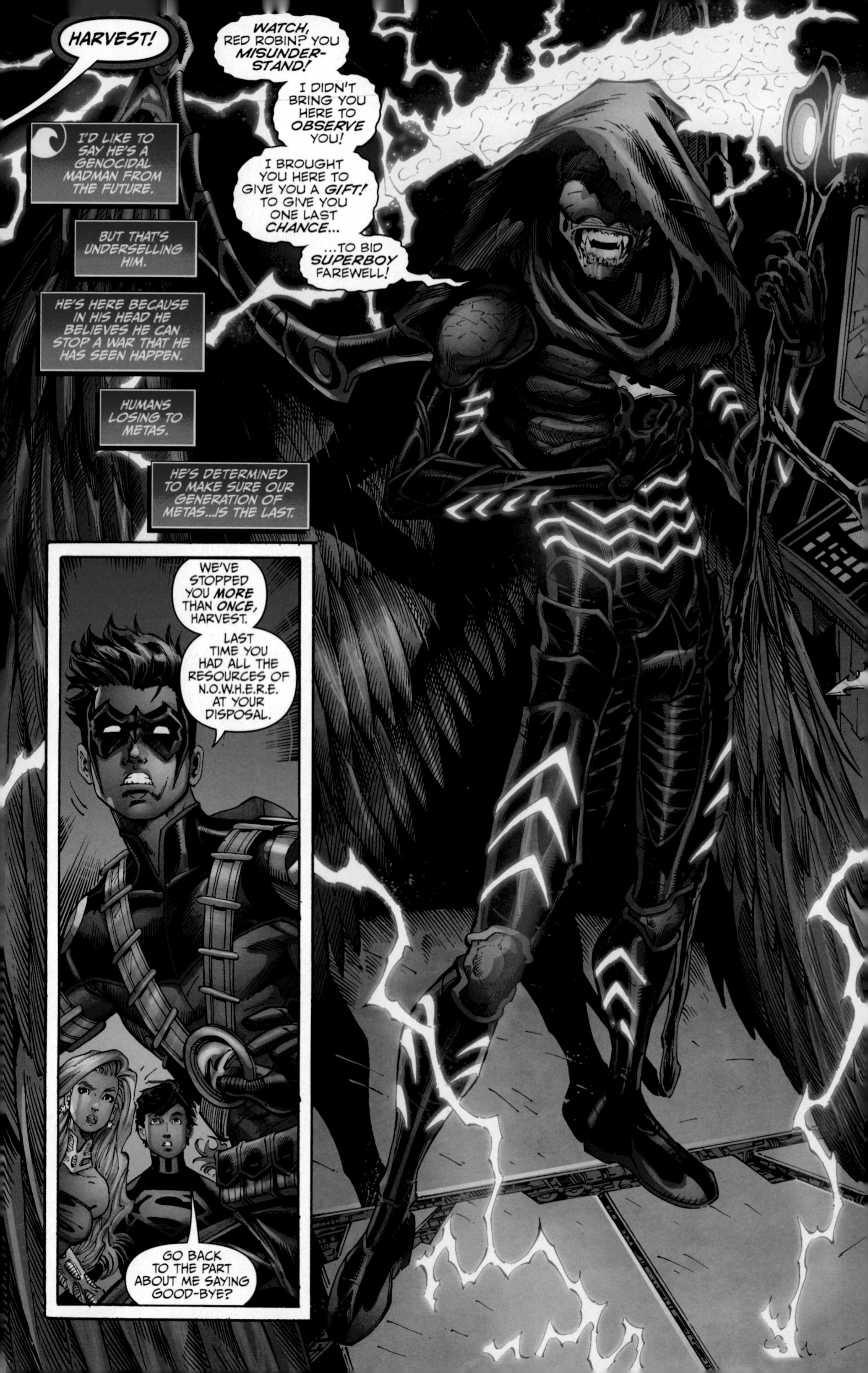

HARVEST!
WATCH, RED ROBIN? YOU MISUNDERSTAND!
I DIDN'T BRING YOU HERE TO OBSERVE YOU!
I BROUGHT YOU HERE TO GIVE YOU A GIFT! TO GIVE YOU ONE LAST CHANCE...
...TO BID SUPERBOY FAREWELL!
I'D LIKE TO SAY HE'S A GENOCIDAL MADMAN FROM THE FUTURE.
BUT THAT'S UNDERSELLING HIM.
HE'S HERE BECAUSE IN HIS HEAD HE BELIEVES HE CAN STOP A WAR THAT HE HAS SEEN HAPPEN.
HUMANS LOSING TO METAS.
HE'S DETERMINED TO MAKE SURE OUR GENERATION OF METAS...IS THE LAST.
WE'VE STOPPED YOU MORE THAN ONCE, HARVEST.
LAST TIME YOU HAD ALL THE RESOURCES OF N.O.W.H.E.R.E. AT YOUR DISPOSAL.
GO BACK TO THE PART ABOUT ME SAYING GOOD-BYE?

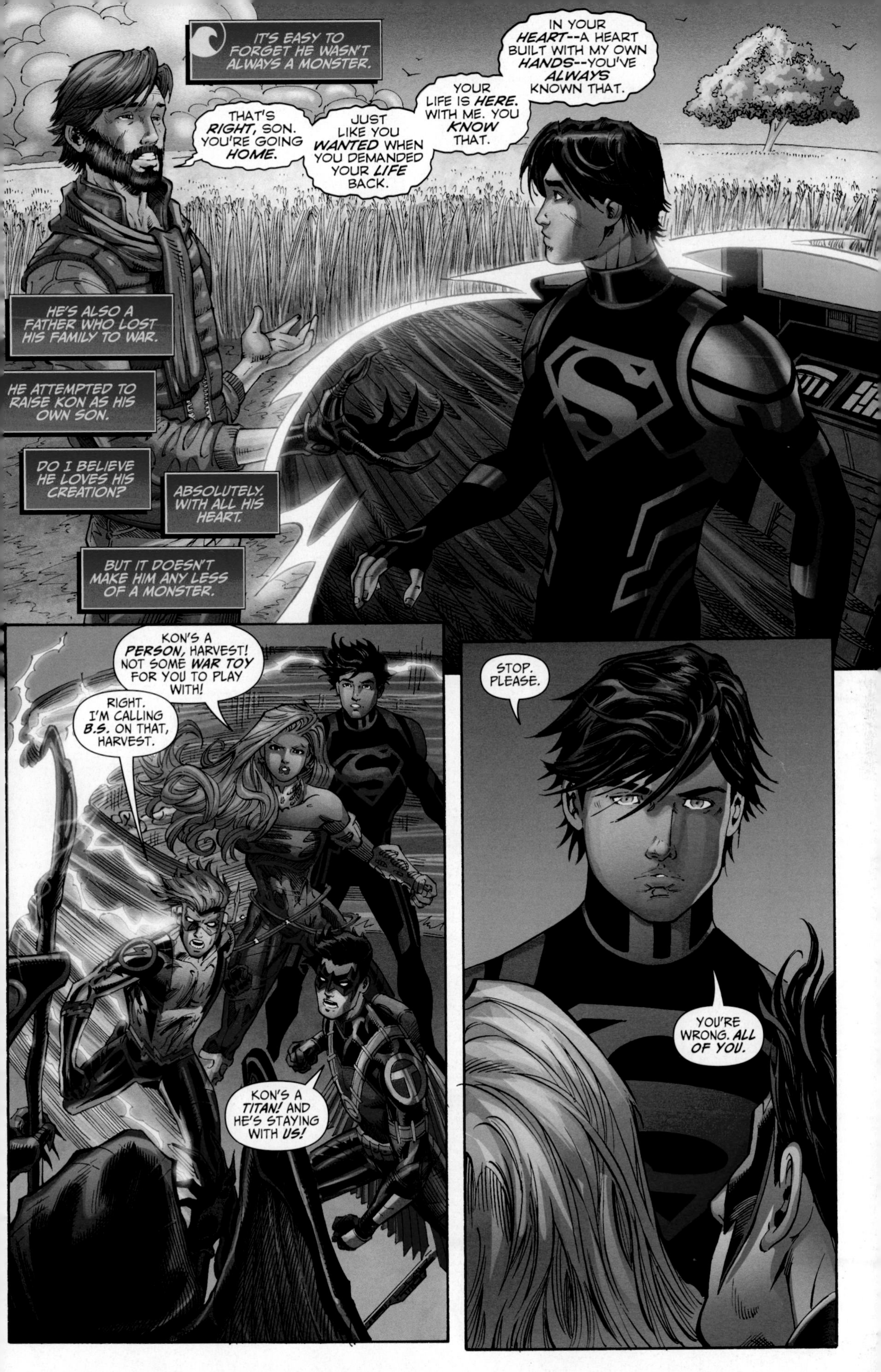
IT'S EASY TO FORGET HE WASN'T ALWAYS A MONSTER.
THAT'S RIGHT, SON. YOU'RE GOING HOME.
JUST LIKE YOU WANTED WHEN YOU DEMANDED YOUR LIFE BACK.
YOUR LIFE IS HERE. WITH ME. YOU KNOW THAT.
IN YOUR HEART--A HEART BUILT WITH MY OWN HANDS--YOU'VE ALWAYS KNOWN THAT.
HE'S ALSO A FATHER WHO LOST HIS FAMILY TO WAR.
HE ATTEMPTED TO RAISE KON AS HIS OWN SON.
DO I BELIEVE HE LOVES HIS CREATION?
ABSOLUTELY. WITH ALL HIS HEART.
BUT IT DOESN'T MAKE HIM ANY LESS OF A MONSTER.
KON'S A PERSON, HARVEST! NOT SOME WAR TOY FOR YOU TO PLAY WITH!
RIGHT. I'M CALLING B.S. ON THAT, HARVEST.
KON'S A TITAN! AND HE'S STAYING WITH US!
STOP. PLEASE.
YOU'RE WRONG. ALL OF YOU.

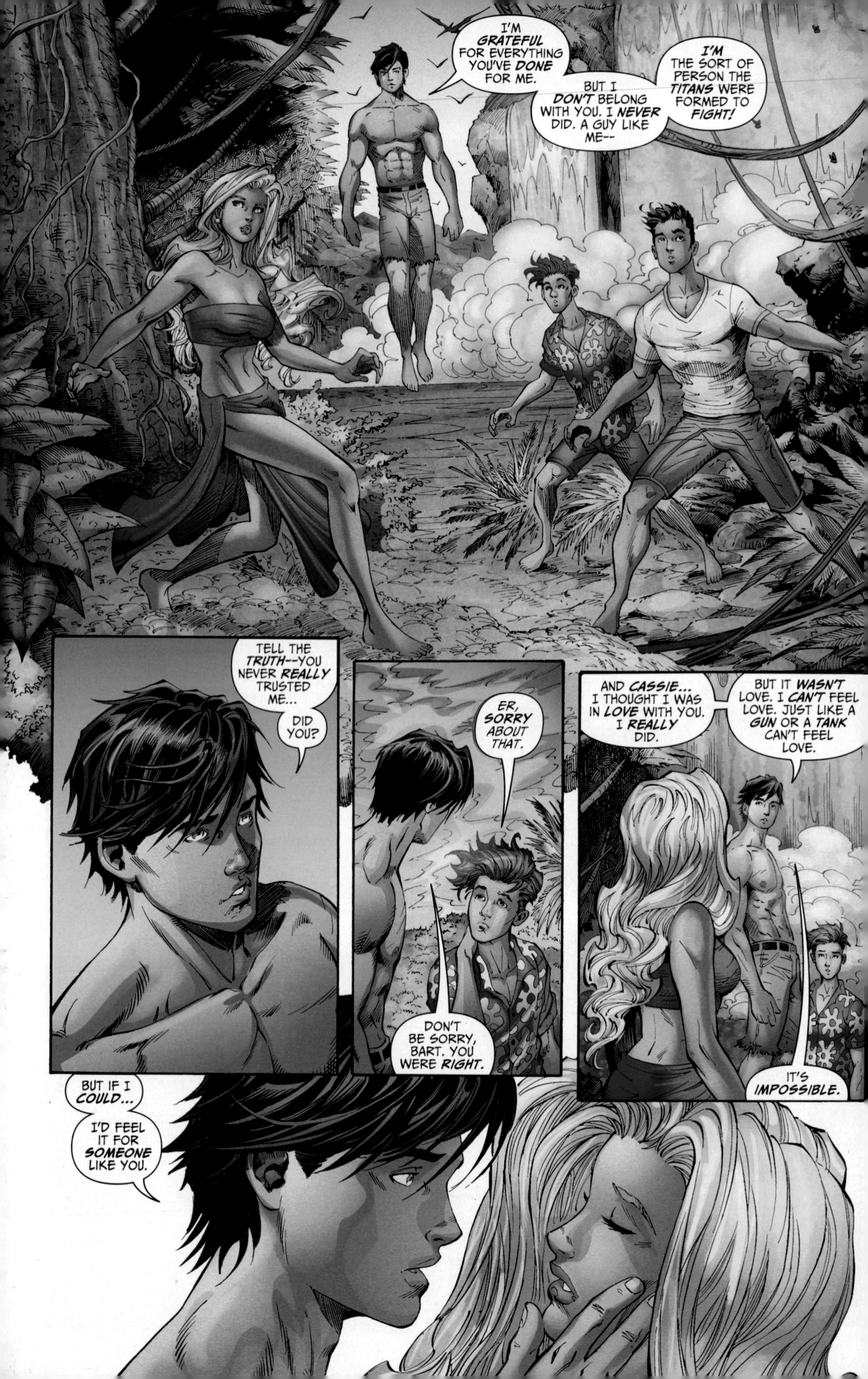
I'M GRATEFUL FOR EVERYTHING YOU'VE DONE FOR ME.
BUT I DON'T BELONG WITH YOU. I NEVER DID. A GUY LIKE ME--
I'M THE SORT OF PERSON THE TITANS WERE FORMED TO FIGHT!
TELL THE TRUTH--YOU NEVER REALLY TRUSTED ME...
DID YOU?
ER, SORRY ABOUT THAT.
DON'T BE SORRY, BART. YOU WERE RIGHT.
AND CASSIE... I THOUGHT I WAS IN LOVE WITH YOU. I REALLY DID.
BUT IT WASN'T LOVE. I CAN'T FEEL LOVE. JUST LIKE A GUN OR A TANK CAN'T FEEL LOVE.
IT'S IMPOSSIBLE.
BUT IF I COULD...
I'D FEEL IT FOR SOMEONE LIKE YOU.

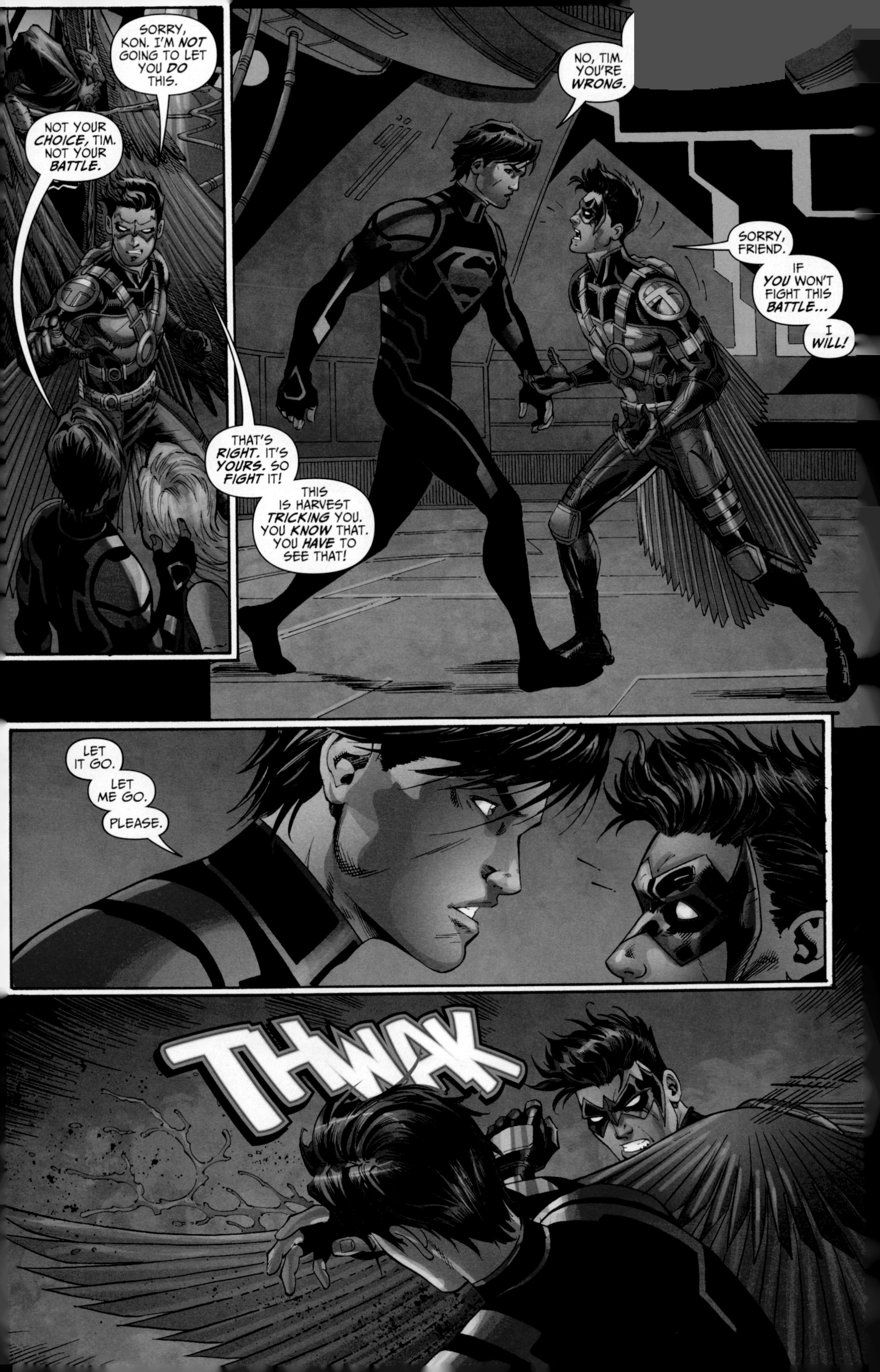
SORRY, KON. I'M NOT GOING TO LET YOU DO THIS.
NOT YOUR CHOICE, TIM. NOT YOUR BATTLE.
THAT'S RIGHT. IT'S YOURS. SO FIGHT IT!
THIS IS HARVEST TRICKING YOU. YOU KNOW THAT. YOU HAVE TO SEE THAT!
NO, TIM. YOU'RE WRONG.
SORRY, FRIEND.
IF YOU WON'T FIGHT THIS BATTLE...
I WILL!
LET IT GO.
LET ME GO.
PLEASE.
THWAK

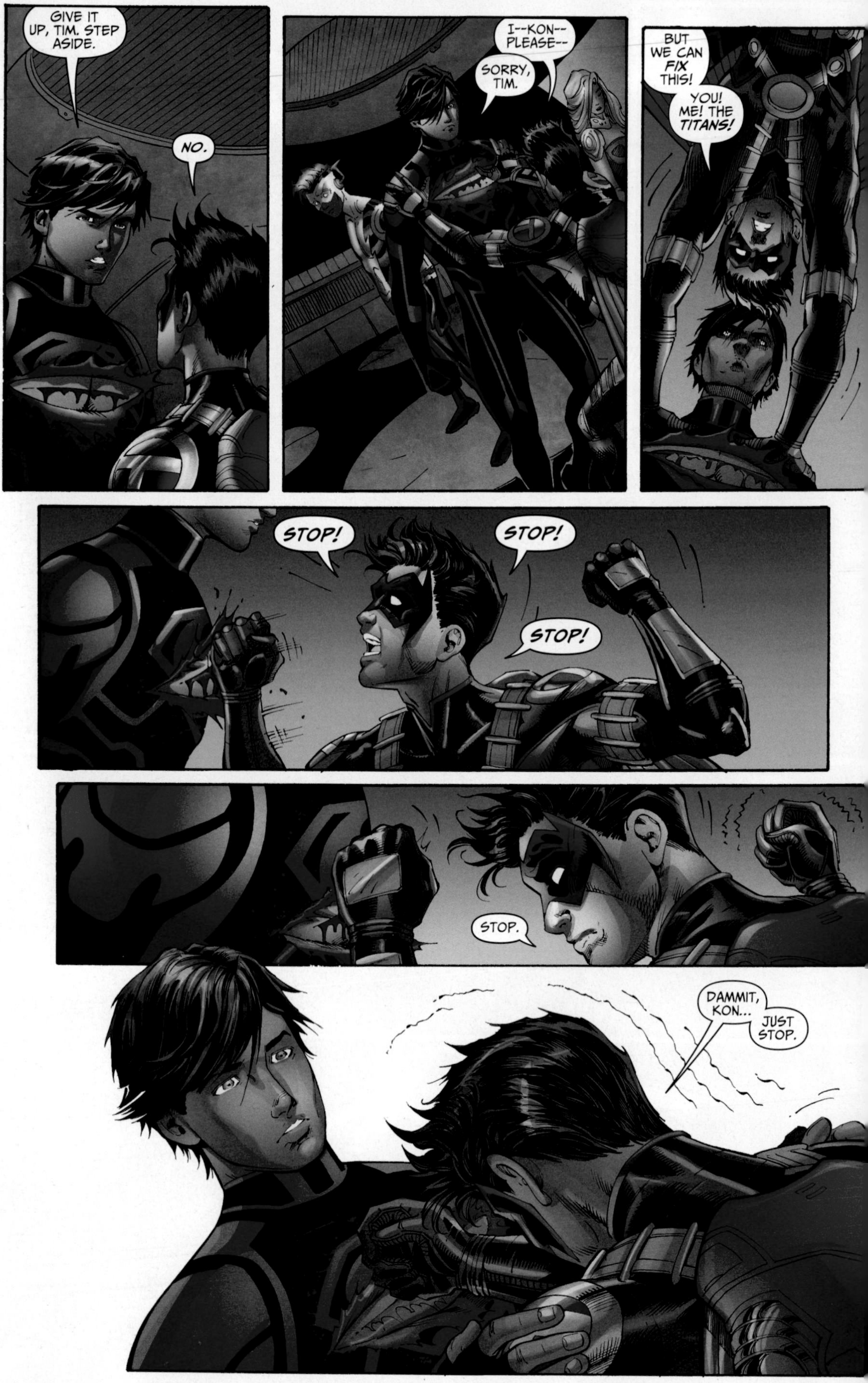
GIVE IT UP, TIM. STEP ASIDE.
NO.
I--KON-- PLEASE--
SORRY, TIM.
BUT WE CAN FIX THIS!
YOU! ME! THE TITANS!
STOP!
STOP!
STOP!
STOP.
DAMMIT, KON...
JUST STOP.

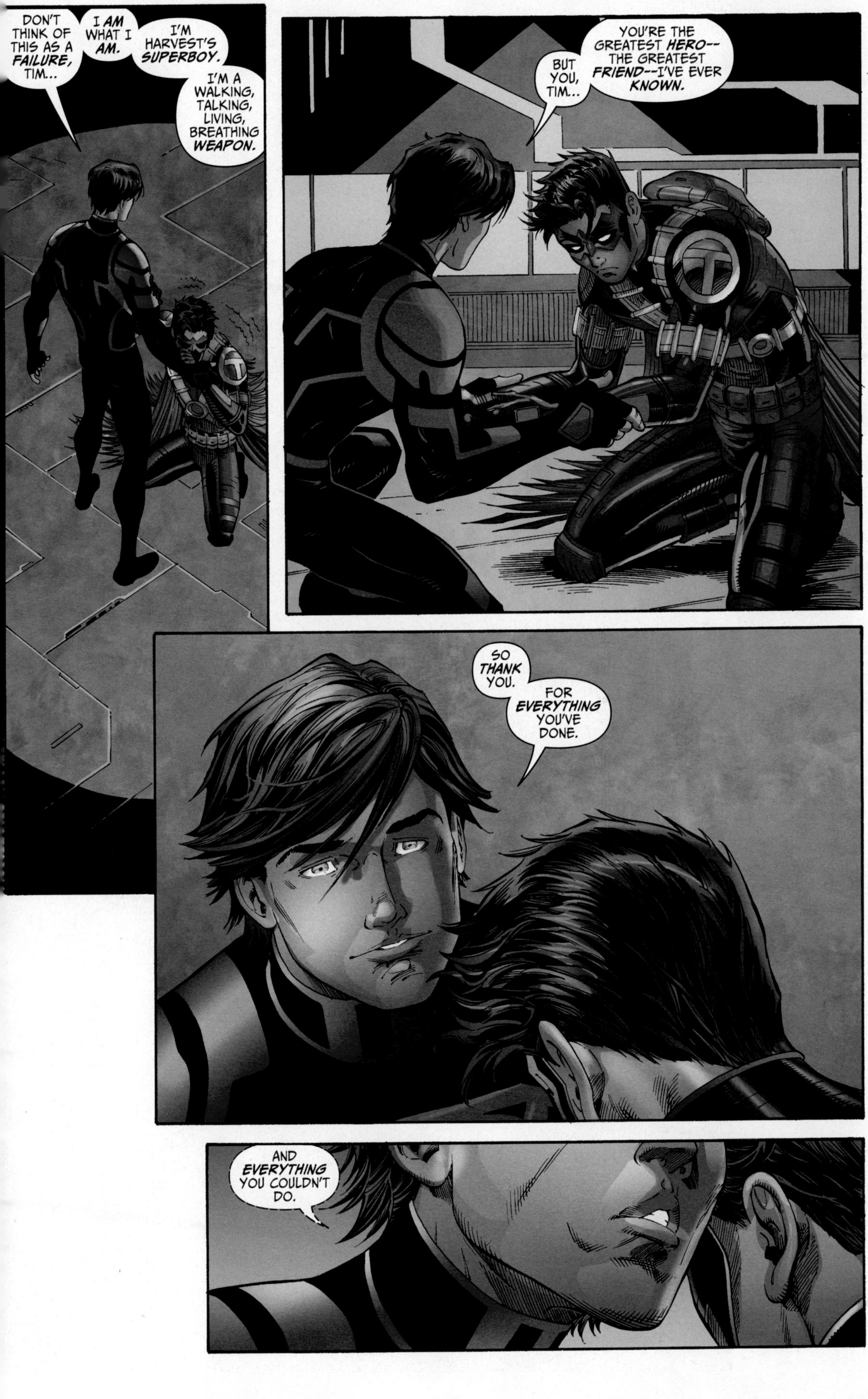
DON'T THINK OF THIS AS A FAILURE, TIM...
I AM WHAT I AM.
I'M HARVEST'S SUPERBOY.
I'M A WALKING, TALKING, LIVING, BREATHING WEAPON.
BUT YOU, TIM...
YOU'RE THE GREATEST HERO--THE GREATEST FRIEND--I'VE EVER KNOWN.
SO THANK YOU.
FOR EVERYTHING YOU'VE DONE.
AND EVERYTHING YOU COULDN'T DO.

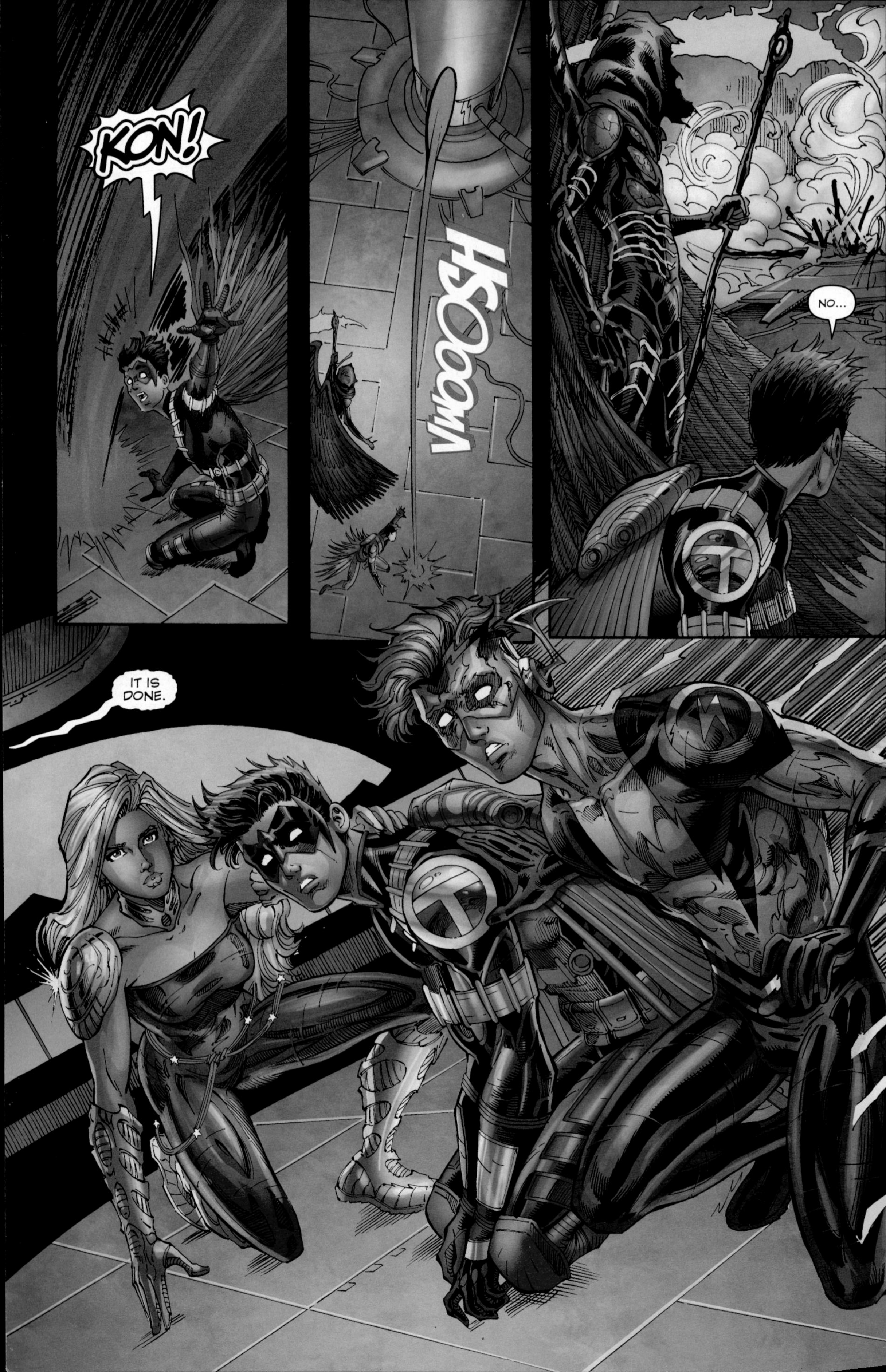
KON!
VWOOOOSH
NO...
IT IS DONE.

DON'T YOU *UNDERSTAND*, CHILDREN? THIS IS DESTINY. *YOUR DESTINY.*

LONG BEFORE ANY OF YOU WERE EVEN *BORN*, THE DIE HAD BEEN *CAST.*

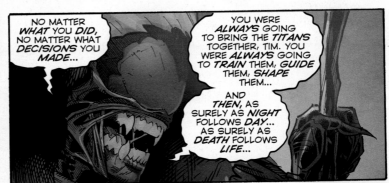

NO MATTER *WHAT* YOU *DID*, NO MATTER WHAT *DECISIONS* YOU *MADE*...

YOU WERE *ALWAYS* GOING TO BRING THE *TITANS* TOGETHER, TIM. YOU WERE *ALWAYS* GOING TO *TRAIN* THEM, *GUIDE* THEM, *SHAPE* THEM...

AND *THEN*, AS SURELY AS *NIGHT* FOLLOWS *DAY*... AS SURELY AS *DEATH* FOLLOWS *LIFE*...

ONE BY *ONE*, YOU WILL JOIN *ME.*

HAVEN'T YOU EVER *WONDERED* WHY I'VE ALLOWED YOU TO *LIVE* THIS LONG? IT'S *SIMPLE.*

IT'S *BECAUSE* YOU WERE BUILDING AN ARMY. *MY* ARMY.

YOU'RE *LYING!*

THE TITANS AREN'T AN *ARMY!* THEY'RE A *TEAM!* A TEAM OF *HEROES!*

I BROUGHT THEM *TOGETHER* TO SAVE THE *WORLD!*

YOU *TELL* YOURSELF THAT, BUT YOU *KNOW* IT'S NOT *TRUE.*

YOU *DIDN'T* BRING THEM TOGETHER OUT OF SOME SENSE OF *ALTRUISM.* YOU BROUGHT THEM TOGETHER OUT OF *FEAR.*

DON'T *DENY* IT-- *EMBRACE* IT!

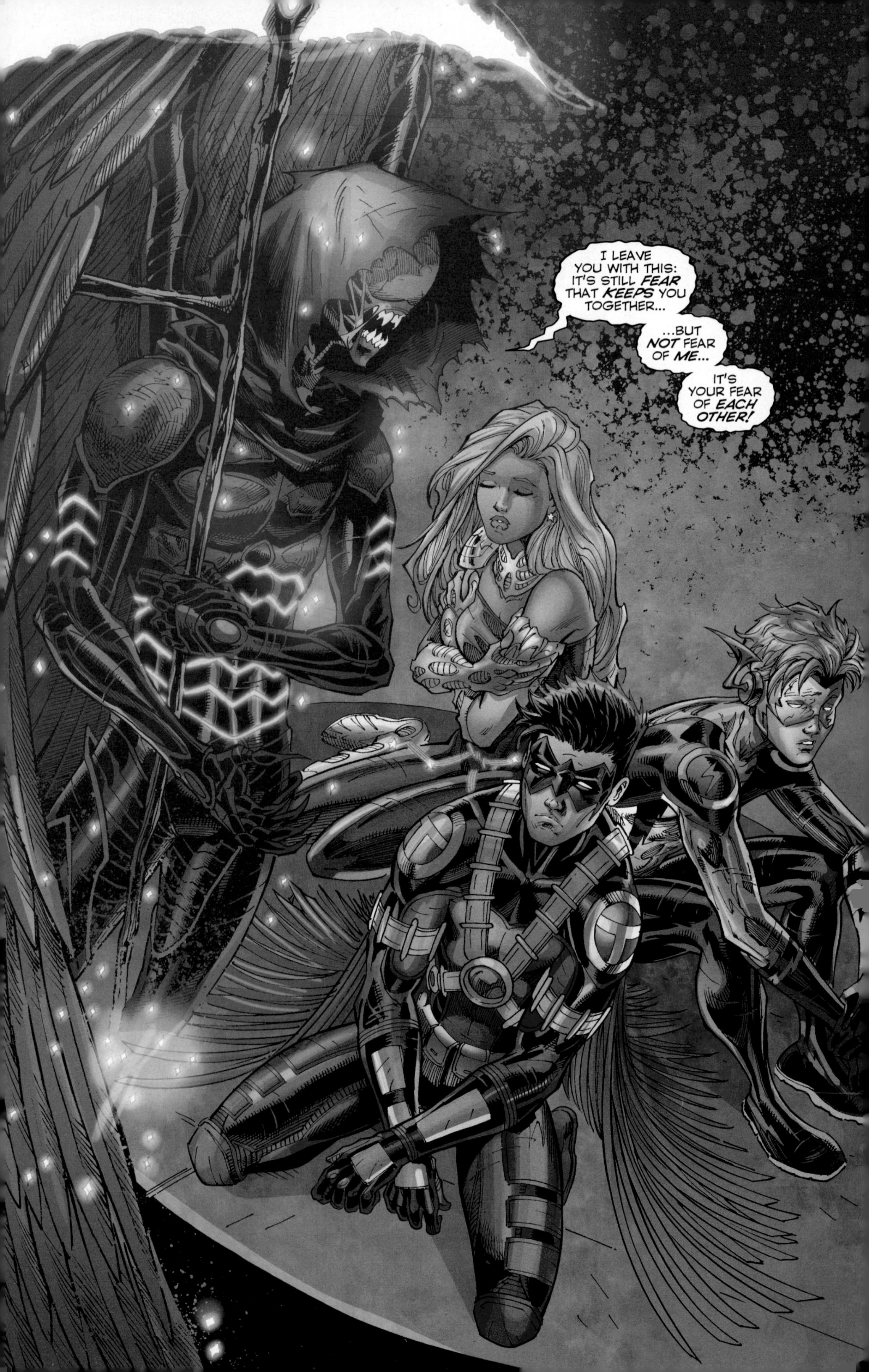

I LEAVE YOU WITH THIS: IT'S STILL *FEAR* THAT *KEEPS* YOU TOGETHER...
...BUT *NOT* FEAR OF *ME*...
IT'S YOUR FEAR OF *EACH OTHER!*

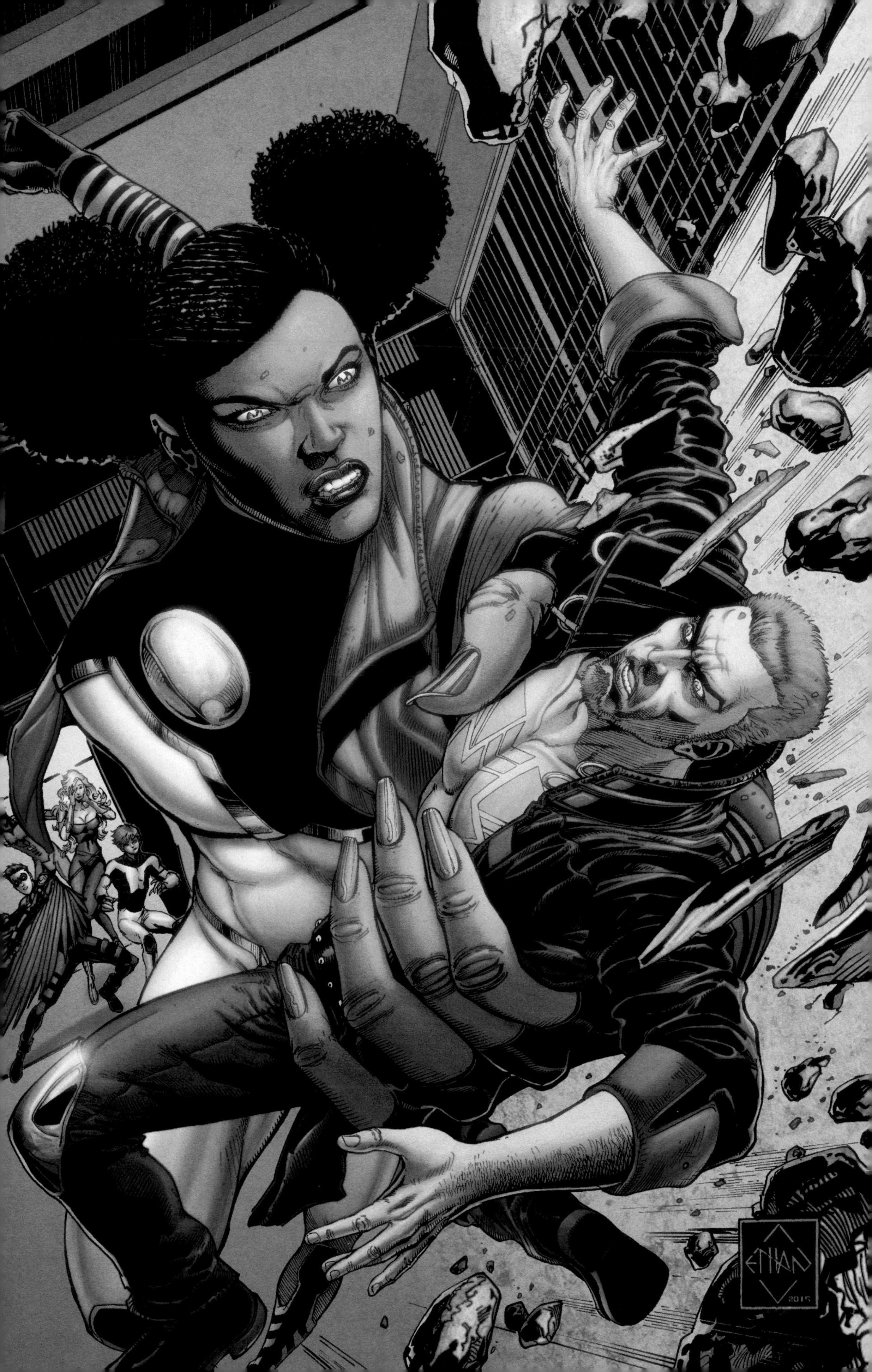
ETHAN
2015

ROGUE TARGETS PART FIVE

WILL PFEIFER writer RICKEN PAOLO PANTALENA NOEL RODRIGUEZ pencillers TREVOR SCOTT JOHNNY DESJARDINS PAOLO PANTALENA inkers RICKEN SCOTT MCDANIEL breakdowns TONY AVIÑA colorist COREY BREEN letterer cover art by ETHAN VAN SCIVER and ANDREW DALHOUSE

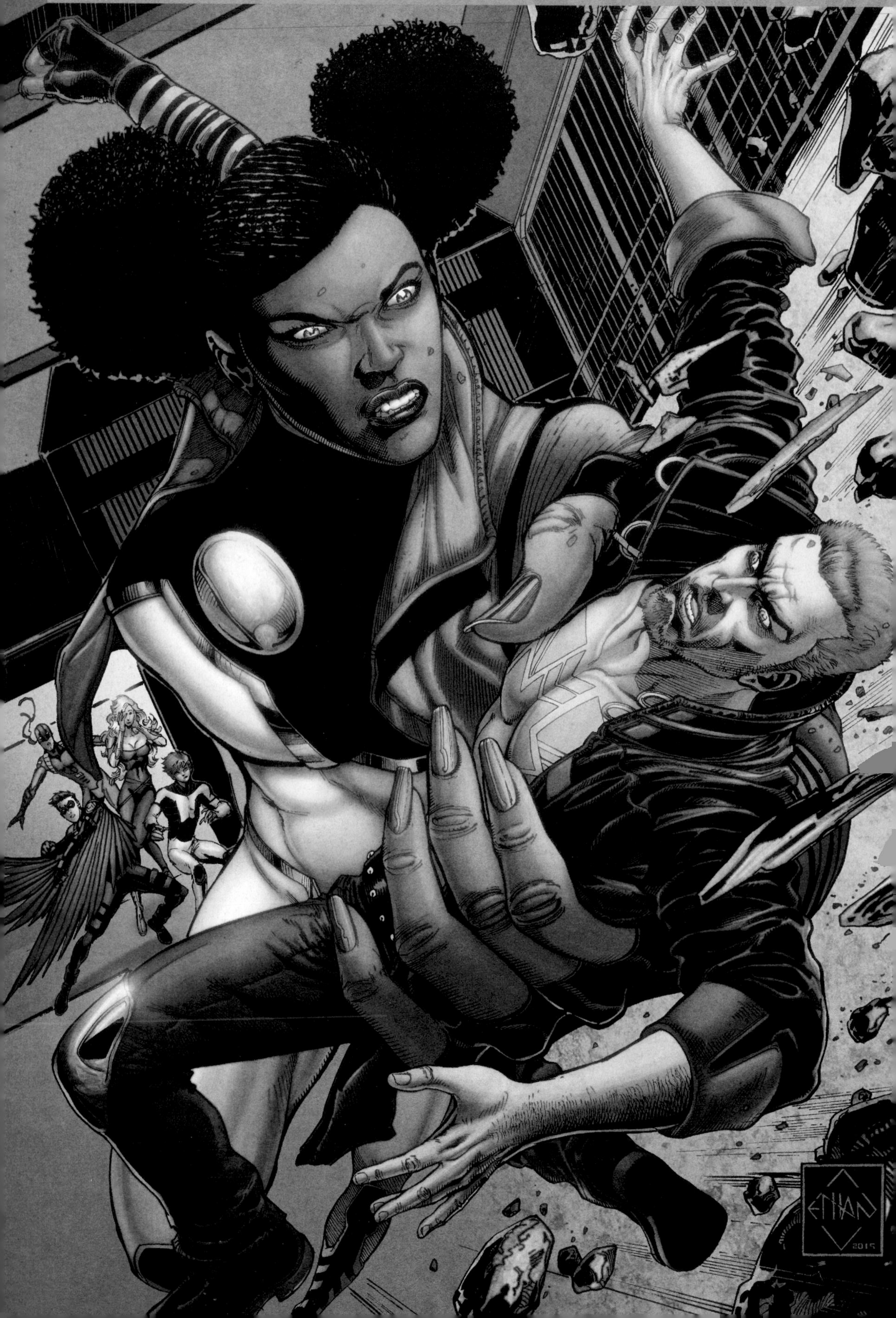

ETHAN
2015

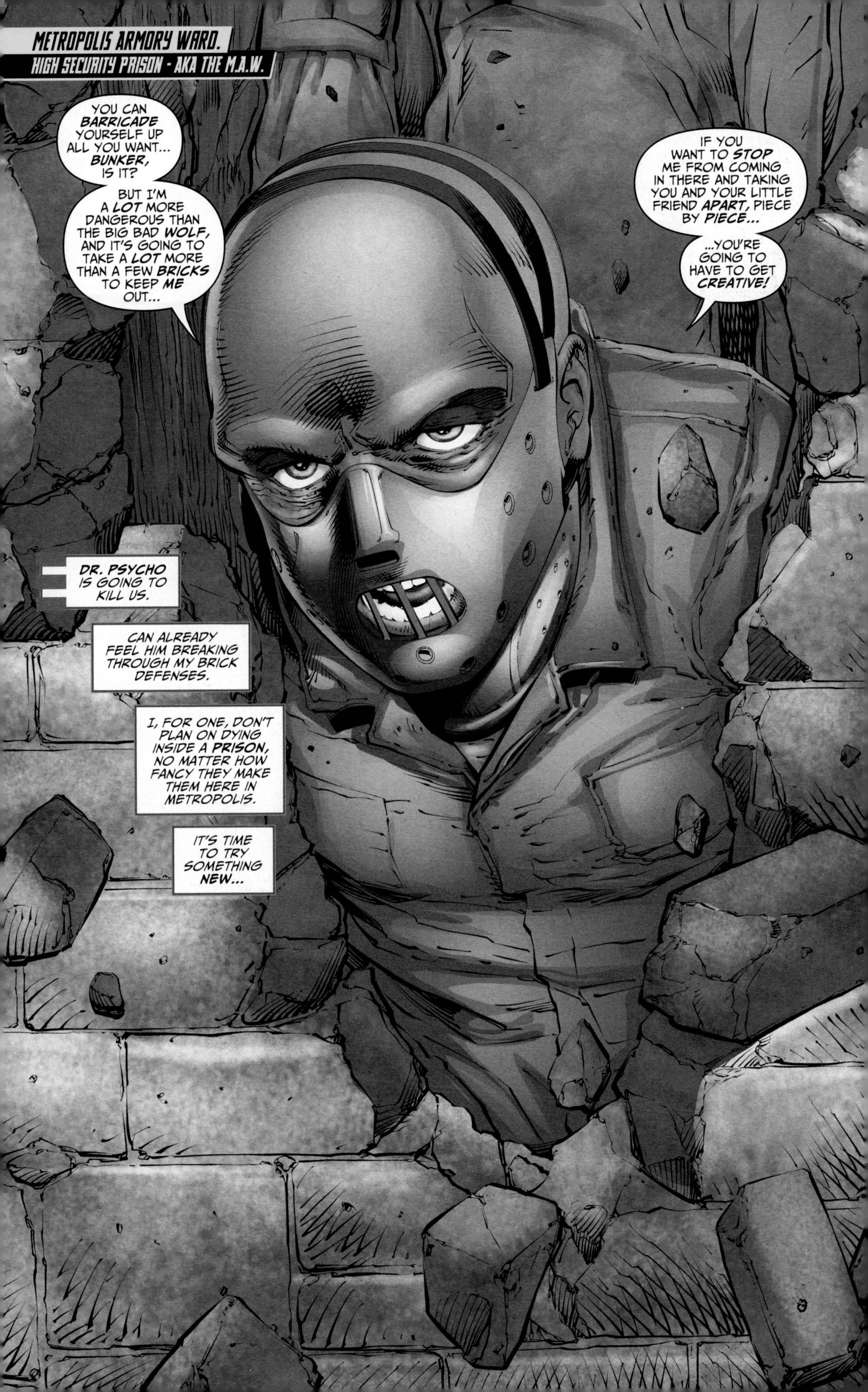
METROPOLIS ARMORY WARD.
HIGH SECURITY PRISON - AKA THE M.A.W.
YOU CAN BARRICADE YOURSELF UP ALL YOU WANT... BUNKER, IS IT?
BUT I'M A LOT MORE DANGEROUS THAN THE BIG BAD WOLF, AND IT'S GOING TO TAKE A LOT MORE THAN A FEW BRICKS TO KEEP ME OUT...
IF YOU WANT TO STOP ME FROM COMING IN THERE AND TAKING YOU AND YOUR LITTLE FRIEND APART, PIECE BY PIECE...
...YOU'RE GOING TO HAVE TO GET CREATIVE!
DR. PSYCHO IS GOING TO KILL US.
CAN ALREADY FEEL HIM BREAKING THROUGH MY BRICK DEFENSES.
I, FOR ONE, DON'T PLAN ON DYING INSIDE A PRISON, NO MATTER HOW FANCY THEY MAKE THEM HERE IN METROPOLIS.
IT'S TIME TO TRY SOMETHING NEW...

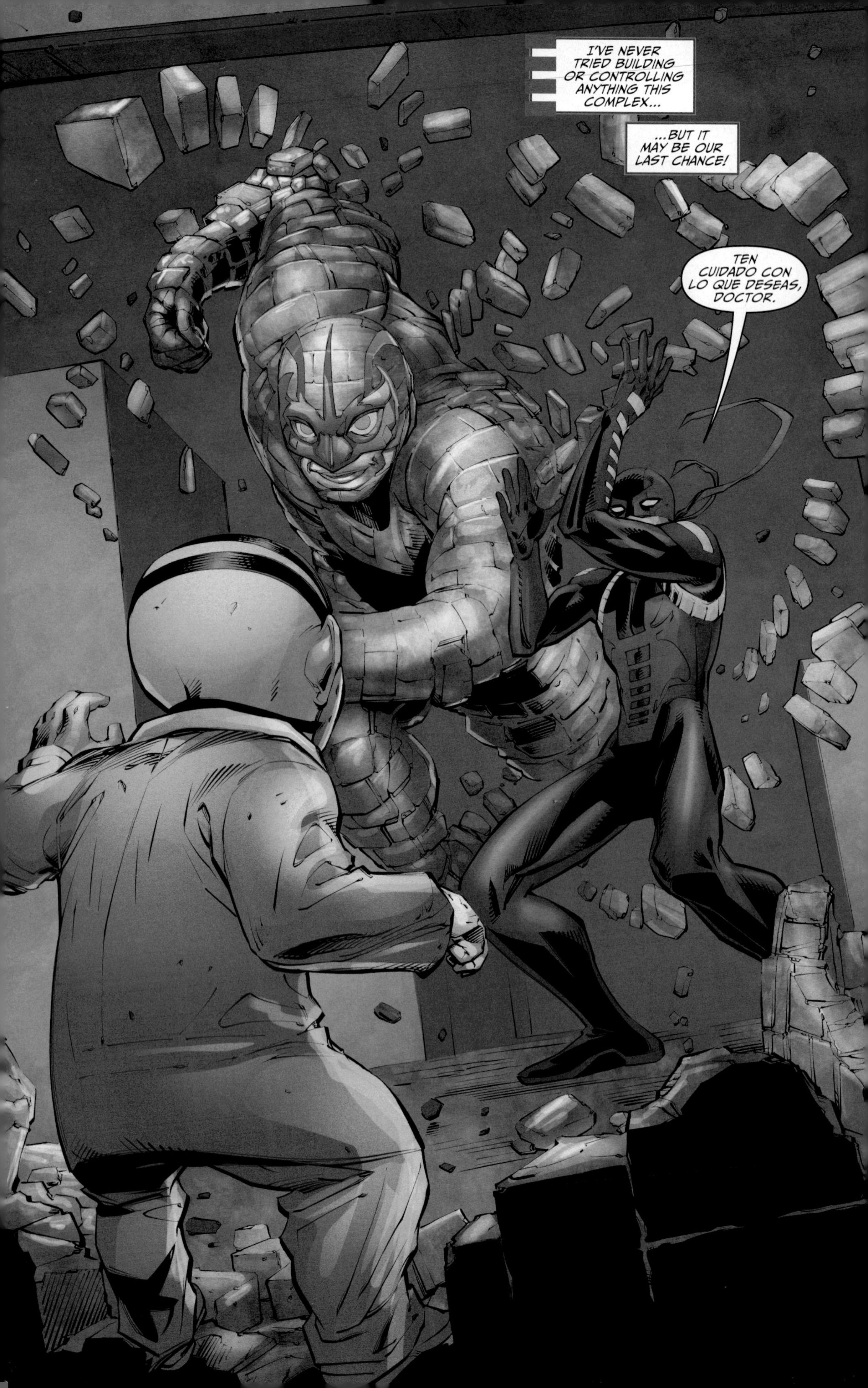
I'VE NEVER TRIED BUILDING OR CONTROLLING ANYTHING THIS COMPLEX...
...BUT IT MAY BE OUR LAST CHANCE!
TEN CUIDADO CON LO QUE DESEAS, DOCTOR.

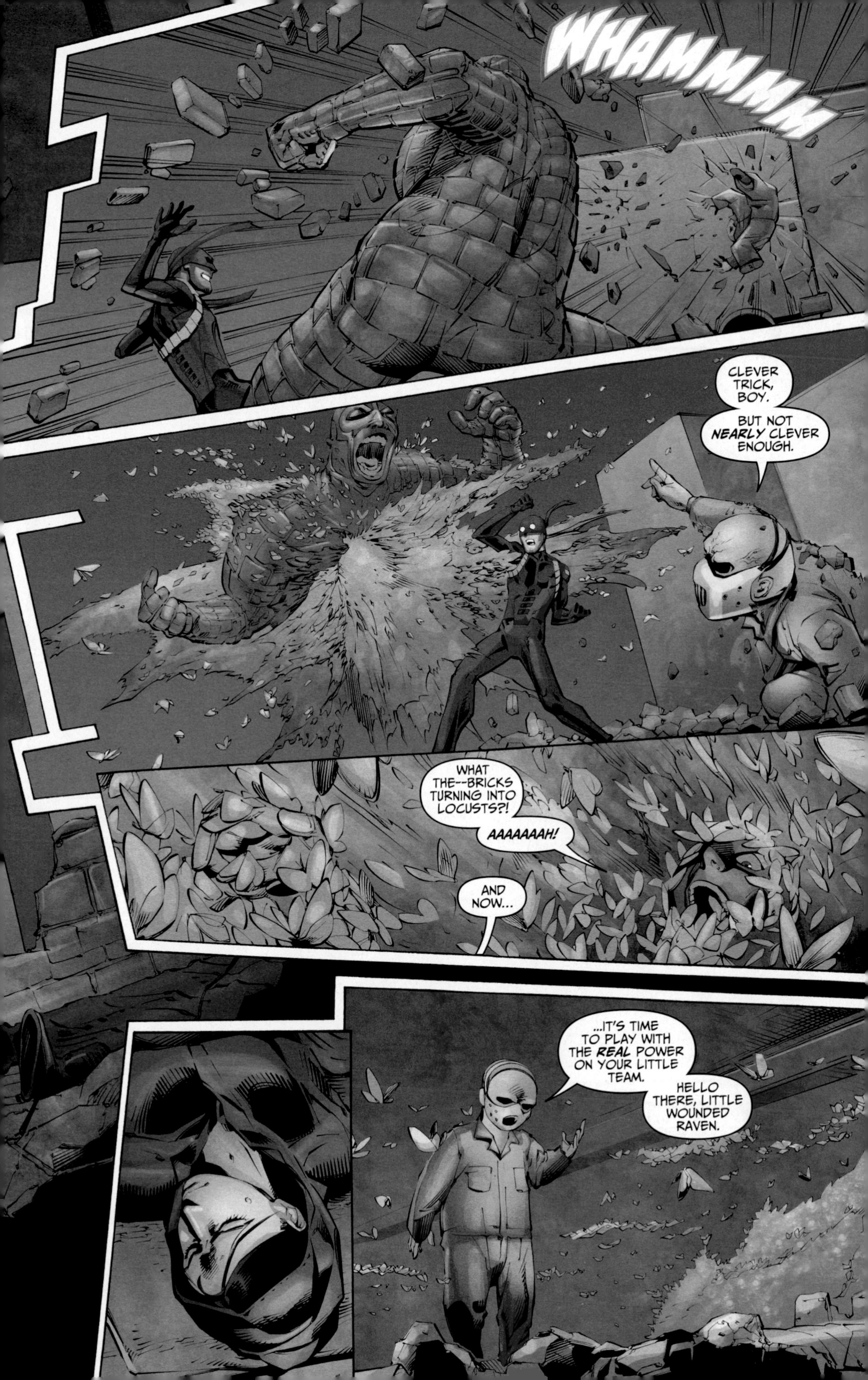
WHAMMMMM
CLEVER TRICK, BOY.
BUT NOT NEARLY CLEVER ENOUGH.
WHAT THE--BRICKS TURNING INTO LOCUSTS?!
AAAAAAAH!
AND NOW...
...IT'S TIME TO PLAY WITH THE REAL POWER ON YOUR LITTLE TEAM.
HELLO THERE, LITTLE WOUNDED RAVEN.

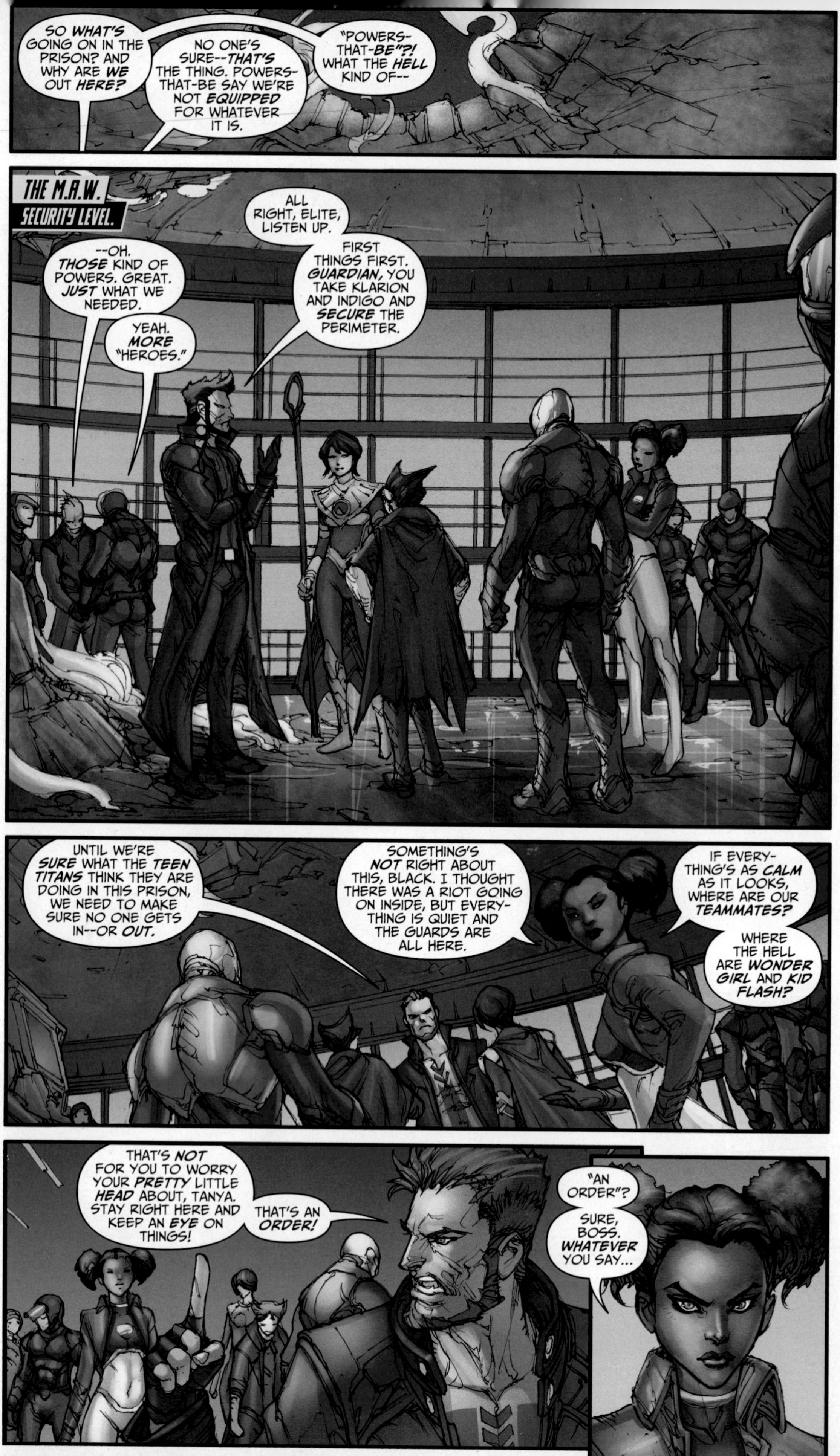
SO WHAT'S GOING ON IN THE PRISON? AND WHY ARE WE OUT HERE?
NO ONE'S SURE--THAT'S THE THING. POWERS-THAT-BE SAY WE'RE NOT EQUIPPED FOR WHATEVER IT IS.
"POWERS-THAT-BE"?! WHAT THE HELL KIND OF--
THE M.A.W.
SECURITY LEVEL.
--OH. THOSE KIND OF POWERS. GREAT. JUST WHAT WE NEEDED.
YEAH. MORE "HEROES."
ALL RIGHT, ELITE, LISTEN UP.
FIRST THINGS FIRST. GUARDIAN, YOU TAKE KLARION AND INDIGO AND SECURE THE PERIMETER.
UNTIL WE'RE SURE WHAT THE TEEN TITANS THINK THEY ARE DOING IN THIS PRISON, WE NEED TO MAKE SURE NO ONE GETS IN--OR OUT.
SOMETHING'S NOT RIGHT ABOUT THIS, BLACK. I THOUGHT THERE WAS A RIOT GOING ON INSIDE, BUT EVERYTHING IS QUIET AND THE GUARDS ARE ALL HERE.
IF EVERYTHING'S AS CALM AS IT LOOKS, WHERE ARE OUR TEAMMATES?
WHERE THE HELL ARE WONDER GIRL AND KID FLASH?
THAT'S NOT FOR YOU TO WORRY YOUR PRETTY LITTLE HEAD ABOUT, TANYA. STAY RIGHT HERE AND KEEP AN EYE ON THINGS!
THAT'S AN ORDER!
"AN ORDER"?
SURE, BOSS. WHATEVER YOU SAY...

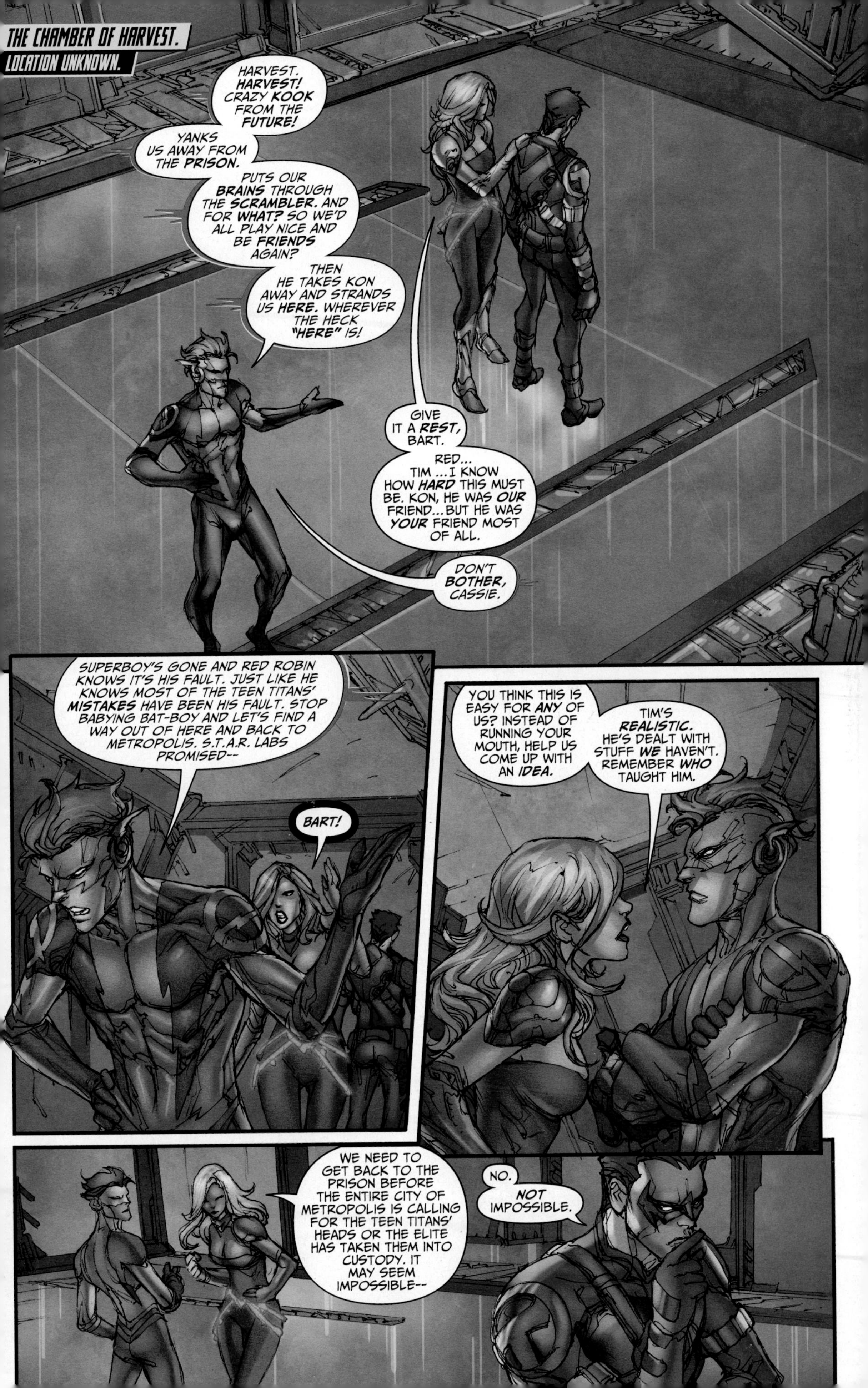

THE CHAMBER OF HARVEST.
LOCATION UNKNOWN.
HARVEST. HARVEST! CRAZY KOOK FROM THE FUTURE!
YANKS US AWAY FROM THE PRISON.
PUTS OUR BRAINS THROUGH THE SCRAMBLER. AND FOR WHAT? SO WE'D ALL PLAY NICE AND BE FRIENDS AGAIN?
THEN HE TAKES KON AWAY AND STRANDS US HERE. WHEREVER THE HECK "HERE" IS!
GIVE IT A REST, BART.
RED... TIM ...I KNOW HOW HARD THIS MUST BE. KON, HE WAS OUR FRIEND...BUT HE WAS YOUR FRIEND MOST OF ALL.
DON'T BOTHER, CASSIE.
SUPERBOY'S GONE AND RED ROBIN KNOWS IT'S HIS FAULT. JUST LIKE HE KNOWS MOST OF THE TEEN TITANS' MISTAKES HAVE BEEN HIS FAULT. STOP BABYING BAT-BOY AND LET'S FIND A WAY OUT OF HERE AND BACK TO METROPOLIS. S.T.A.R. LABS PROMISED--
BART!
YOU THINK THIS IS EASY FOR ANY OF US? INSTEAD OF RUNNING YOUR MOUTH, HELP US COME UP WITH AN IDEA.
TIM'S REALISTIC. HE'S DEALT WITH STUFF WE HAVEN'T. REMEMBER WHO TAUGHT HIM.
WE NEED TO GET BACK TO THE PRISON BEFORE THE ENTIRE CITY OF METROPOLIS IS CALLING FOR THE TEEN TITANS' HEADS OR THE ELITE HAS TAKEN THEM INTO CUSTODY. IT MAY SEEM IMPOSSIBLE--
NO. NOT IMPOSSIBLE.

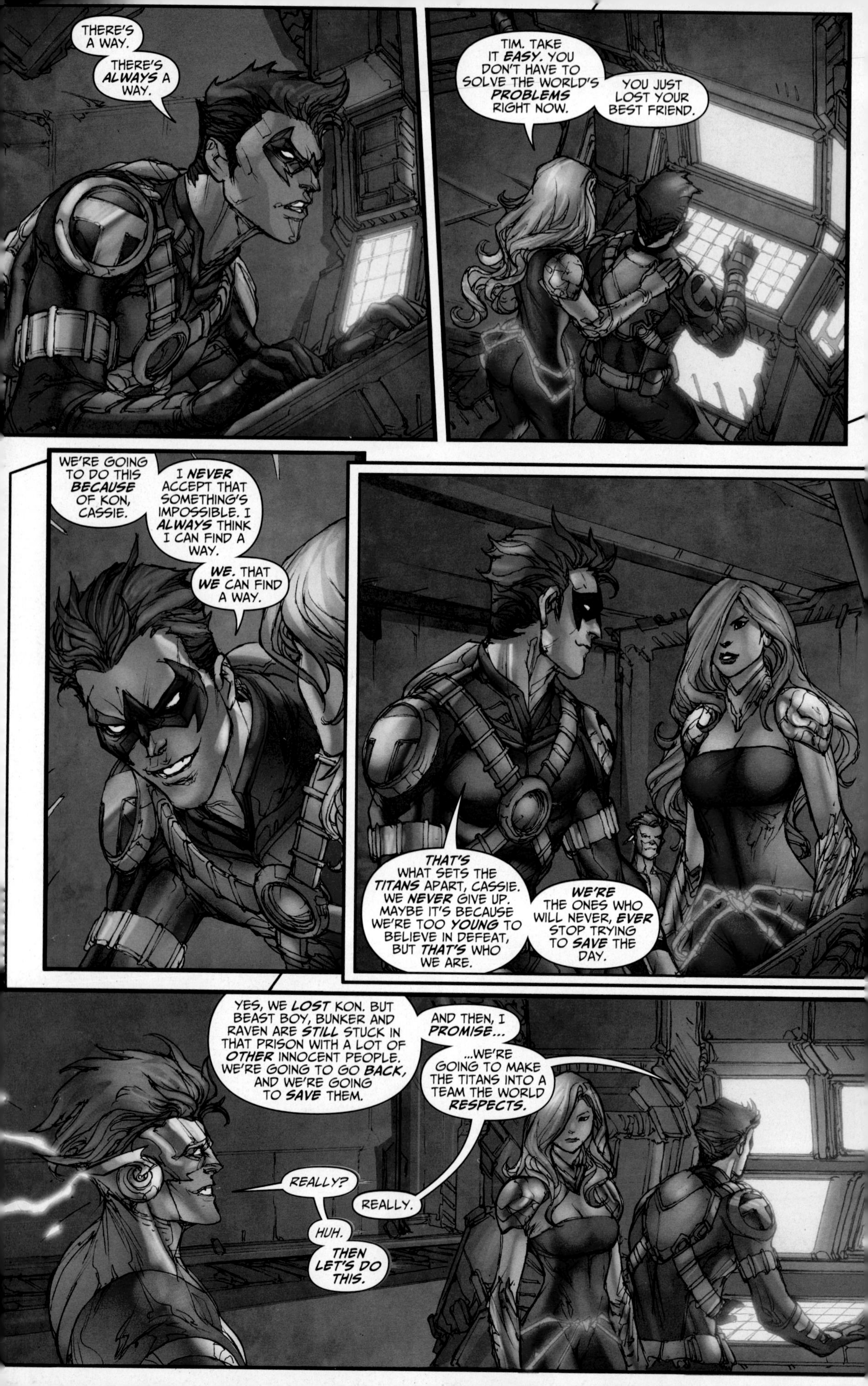
THERE'S A WAY.
THERE'S ALWAYS A WAY.
TIM. TAKE IT EASY. YOU DON'T HAVE TO SOLVE THE WORLD'S PROBLEMS RIGHT NOW.
YOU JUST LOST YOUR BEST FRIEND.
WE'RE GOING TO DO THIS BECAUSE OF KON, CASSIE.
I NEVER ACCEPT THAT SOMETHING'S IMPOSSIBLE. I ALWAYS THINK I CAN FIND A WAY.
WE. THAT WE CAN FIND A WAY.
THAT'S WHAT SETS THE TITANS APART, CASSIE. WE NEVER GIVE UP. MAYBE IT'S BECAUSE WE'RE TOO YOUNG TO BELIEVE IN DEFEAT, BUT THAT'S WHO WE ARE.
WE'RE THE ONES WHO WILL NEVER, EVER STOP TRYING TO SAVE THE DAY.
YES, WE LOST KON. BUT BEAST BOY, BUNKER AND RAVEN ARE STILL STUCK IN THAT PRISON WITH A LOT OF OTHER INNOCENT PEOPLE. WE'RE GOING TO GO BACK, AND WE'RE GOING TO SAVE THEM.
AND THEN, I PROMISE...
...WE'RE GOING TO MAKE THE TITANS INTO A TEAM THE WORLD RESPECTS.
REALLY?
REALLY.
HUH.
THEN LET'S DO THIS.

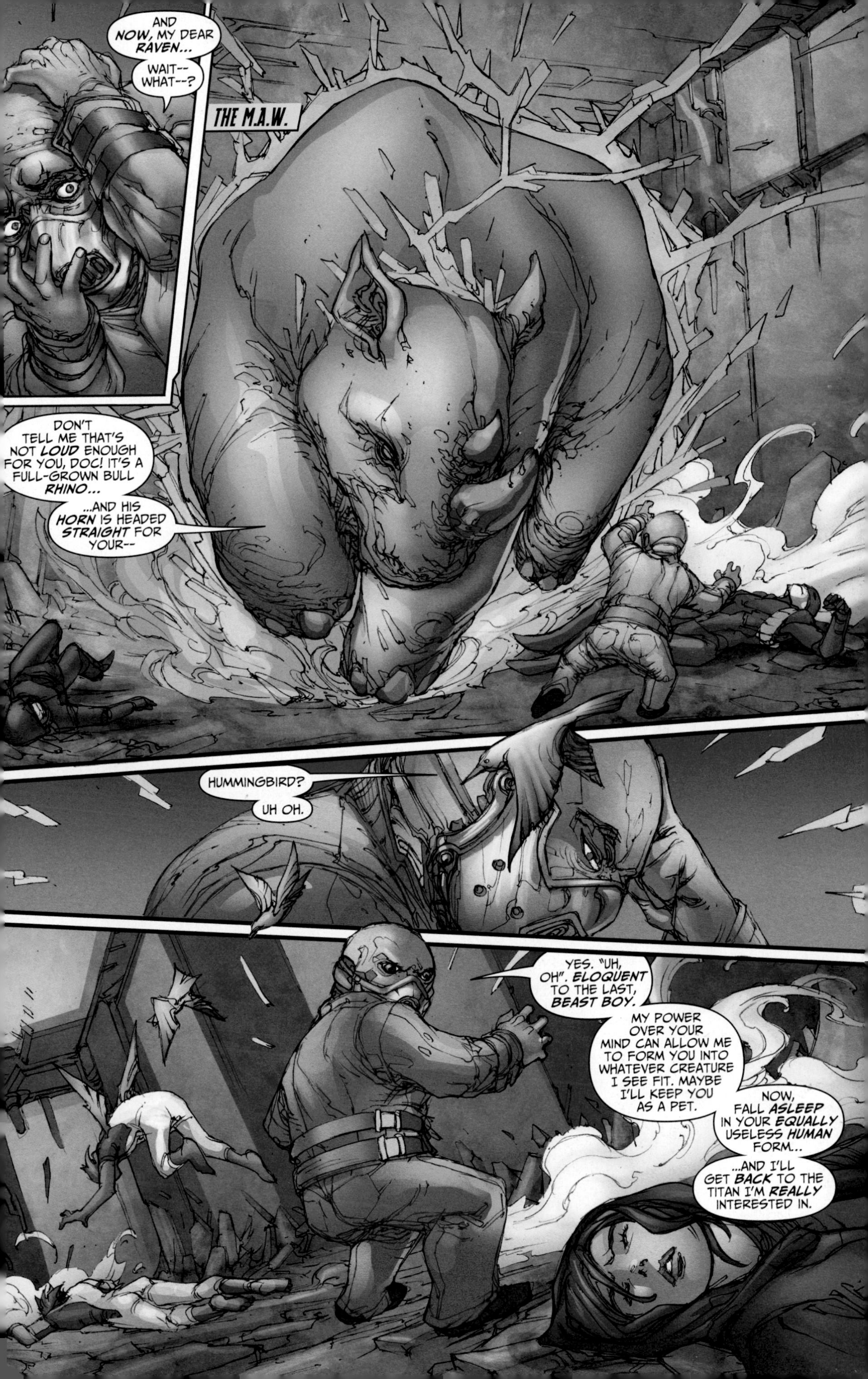
AND NOW, MY DEAR RAVEN...
WAIT-- WHAT--?
THE M.A.W.
DON'T TELL ME THAT'S NOT LOUD ENOUGH FOR YOU, DOC! IT'S A FULL-GROWN BULL RHINO...
...AND HIS HORN IS HEADED STRAIGHT FOR YOUR--
HUMMINGBIRD?
UH OH.
YES. "UH, OH". ELOQUENT TO THE LAST, BEAST BOY.
MY POWER OVER YOUR MIND CAN ALLOW ME TO FORM YOU INTO WHATEVER CREATURE I SEE FIT. MAYBE I'LL KEEP YOU AS A PET.
NOW, FALL ASLEEP IN YOUR EQUALLY USELESS HUMAN FORM...
...AND I'LL GET BACK TO THE TITAN I'M REALLY INTERESTED IN.

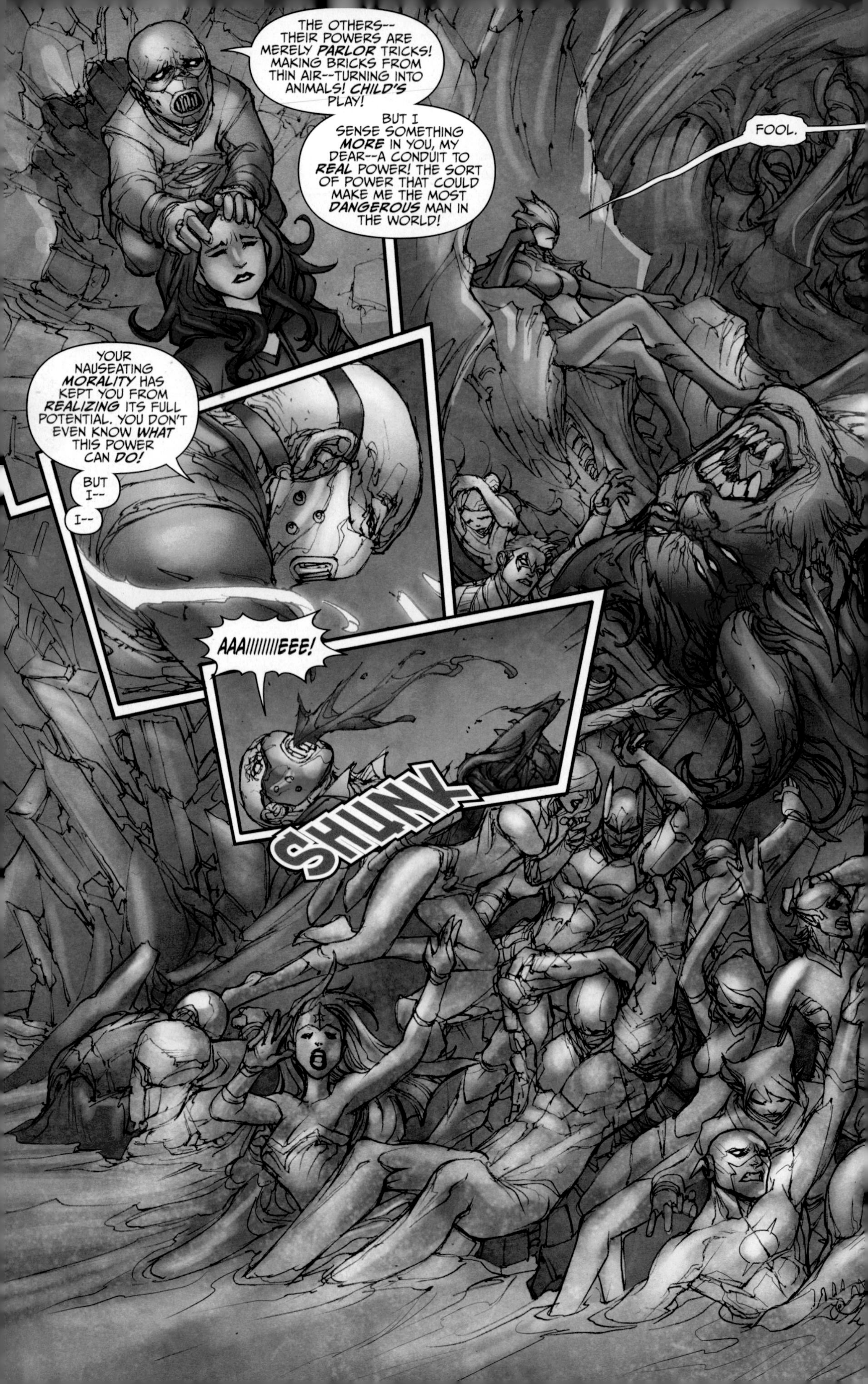
THE OTHERS-- THEIR POWERS ARE MERELY PARLOR TRICKS! MAKING BRICKS FROM THIN AIR--TURNING INTO ANIMALS! CHILD'S PLAY!
BUT I SENSE SOMETHING MORE IN YOU, MY DEAR--A CONDUIT TO REAL POWER! THE SORT OF POWER THAT COULD MAKE ME THE MOST DANGEROUS MAN IN THE WORLD!
FOOL.
YOUR NAUSEATING MORALITY HAS KEPT YOU FROM REALIZING ITS FULL POTENTIAL. YOU DON'T EVEN KNOW WHAT THIS POWER CAN DO!
BUT I--
I--
AAAIIIIIIIIEEE!
SHUNK

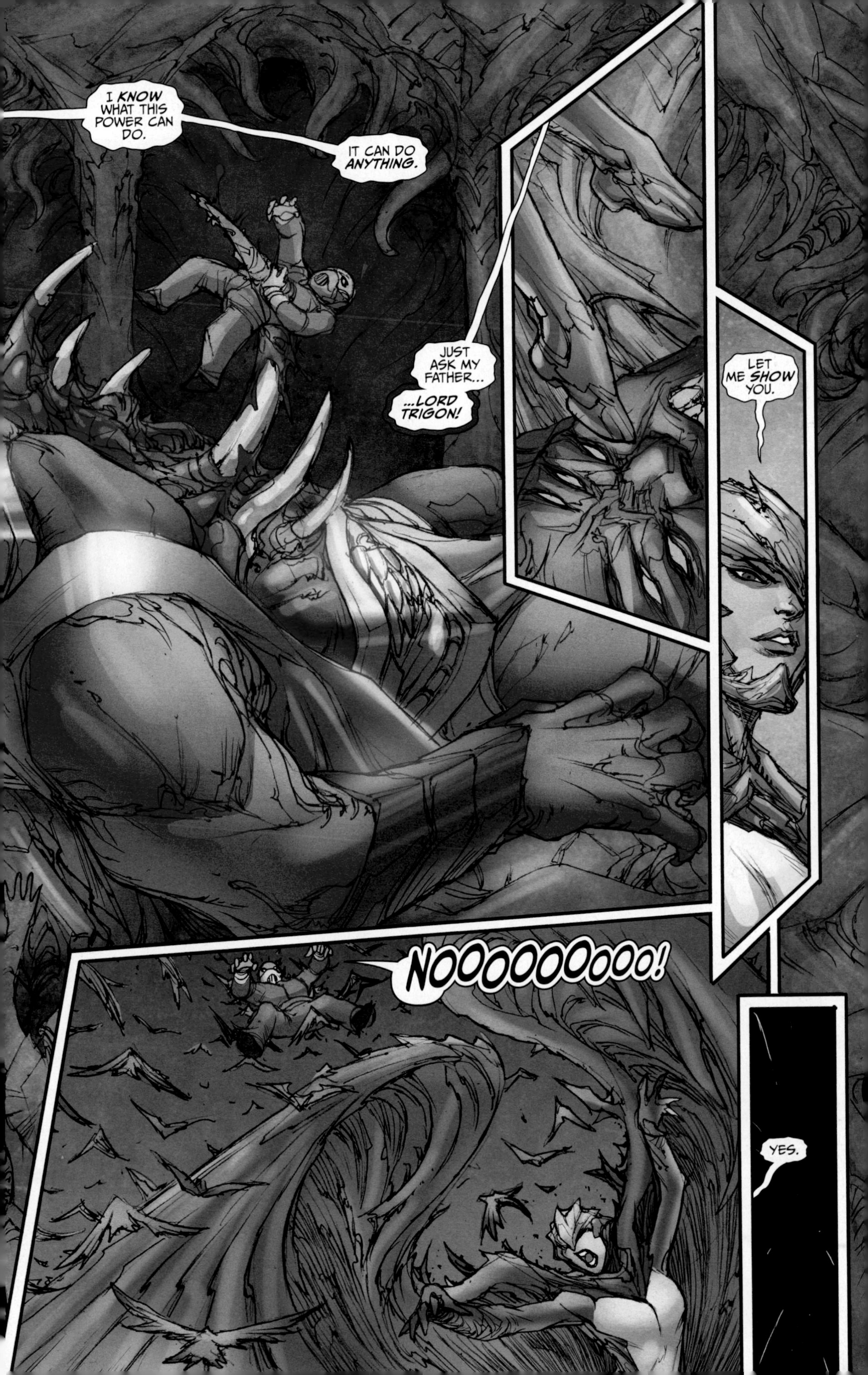
I KNOW WHAT THIS POWER CAN DO.
IT CAN DO ANYTHING.
JUST ASK MY FATHER...
...LORD TRIGON!
LET ME SHOW YOU.
NOOOOOOOOOO!
YES.

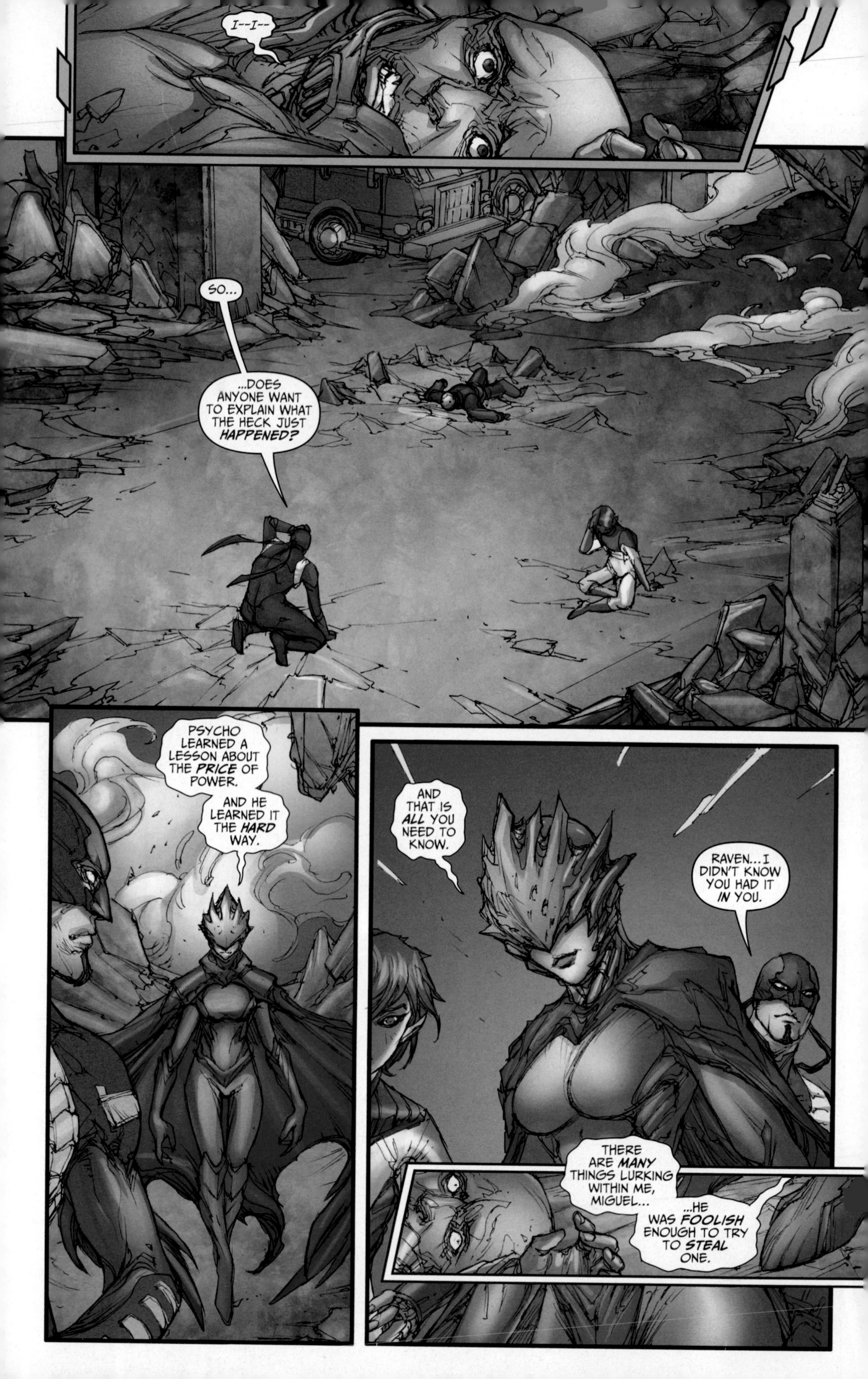
I--I--
SO...
...DOES ANYONE WANT TO EXPLAIN WHAT THE HECK JUST HAPPENED?
PSYCHO LEARNED A LESSON ABOUT THE PRICE OF POWER.
AND HE LEARNED IT THE HARD WAY.
AND THAT IS ALL YOU NEED TO KNOW.
RAVEN...I DIDN'T KNOW YOU HAD IT IN YOU.
THERE ARE MANY THINGS LURKING WITHIN ME, MIGUEL...
...HE WAS FOOLISH ENOUGH TO TRY TO STEAL ONE.

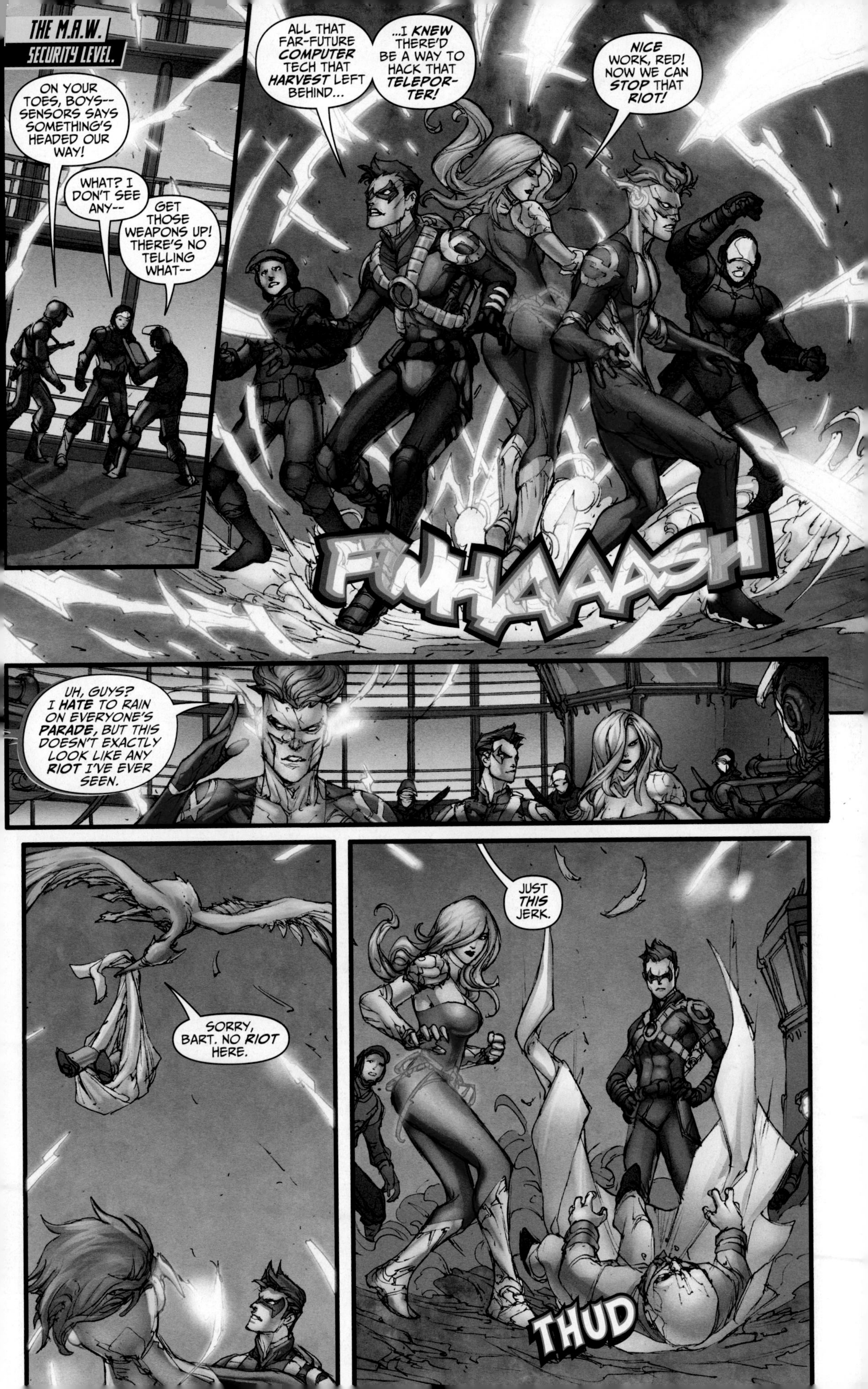
THE M.A.W. SECURITY LEVEL.
ON YOUR TOES, BOYS-- SENSORS SAYS SOMETHING'S HEADED OUR WAY!
WHAT? I DON'T SEE ANY--
GET THOSE WEAPONS UP! THERE'S NO TELLING WHAT--
ALL THAT FAR-FUTURE COMPUTER TECH THAT HARVEST LEFT BEHIND...
...I KNEW THERE'D BE A WAY TO HACK THAT TELEPOR-TER!
NICE WORK, RED! NOW WE CAN STOP THAT RIOT!
FWHAAASH
UH, GUYS? I HATE TO RAIN ON EVERYONE'S PARADE, BUT THIS DOESN'T EXACTLY LOOK LIKE ANY RIOT I'VE EVER SEEN.
SORRY, BART. NO RIOT HERE.
JUST THIS JERK.
THUD

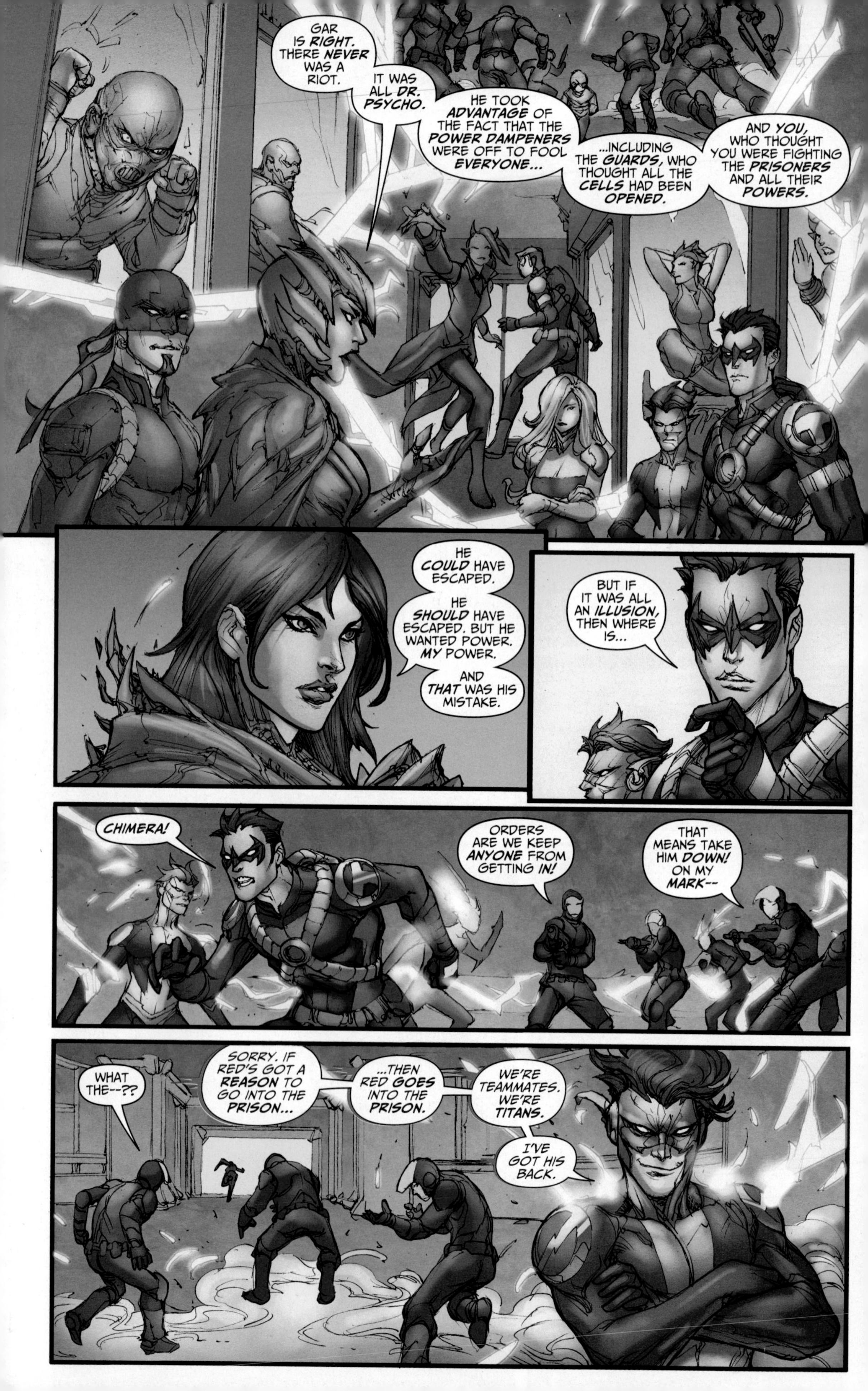

GAR IS RIGHT. THERE NEVER WAS A RIOT.
IT WAS ALL DR. PSYCHO.
HE TOOK ADVANTAGE OF THE FACT THAT THE POWER DAMPENERS WERE OFF TO FOOL EVERYONE...
...INCLUDING THE GUARDS, WHO THOUGHT ALL THE CELLS HAD BEEN OPENED.
AND YOU, WHO THOUGHT YOU WERE FIGHTING THE PRISONERS AND ALL THEIR POWERS.
HE COULD HAVE ESCAPED.
HE SHOULD HAVE ESCAPED. BUT HE WANTED POWER. MY POWER.
AND THAT WAS HIS MISTAKE.
BUT IF IT WAS ALL AN ILLUSION, THEN WHERE IS...
CHIMERA!
ORDERS ARE WE KEEP ANYONE FROM GETTING IN!
THAT MEANS TAKE HIM DOWN! ON MY MARK--
WHAT THE--??
SORRY. IF RED'S GOT A REASON TO GO INTO THE PRISON...
...THEN RED GOES INTO THE PRISON.
WE'RE TEAMMATES. WE'RE TITANS.
I'VE GOT HIS BACK.

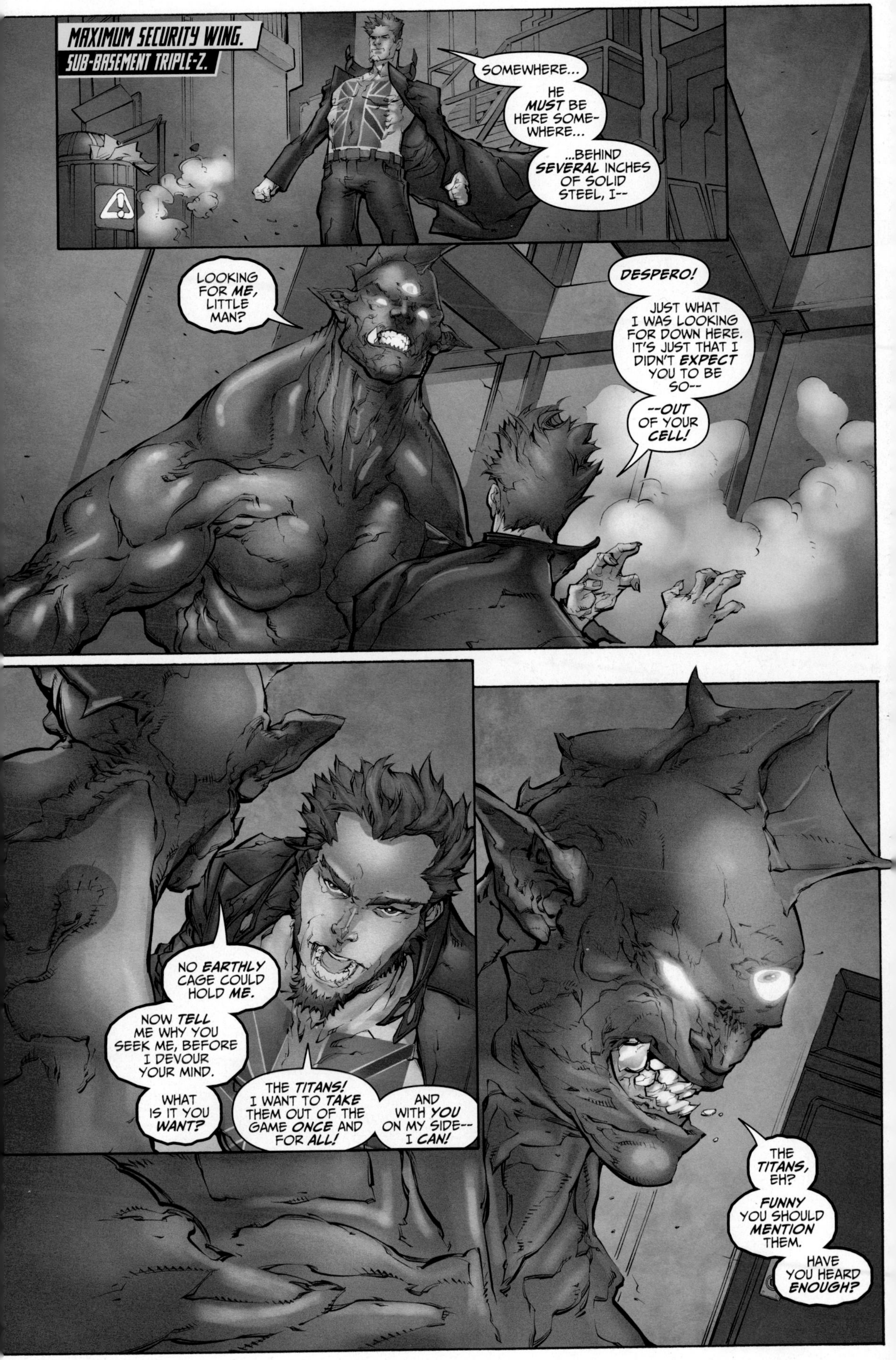
MAXIMUM SECURITY WING.
SUB-BASEMENT TRIPLE-Z.
SOMEWHERE...
HE MUST BE HERE SOME-WHERE...
...BEHIND SEVERAL INCHES OF SOLID STEEL, I--
LOOKING FOR ME, LITTLE MAN?
DESPERO!
JUST WHAT I WAS LOOKING FOR DOWN HERE. IT'S JUST THAT I DIDN'T EXPECT YOU TO BE SO--
--OUT OF YOUR CELL!
NO EARTHLY CAGE COULD HOLD ME.
NOW TELL ME WHY YOU SEEK ME, BEFORE I DEVOUR YOUR MIND.
WHAT IS IT YOU WANT?
THE TITANS! I WANT TO TAKE THEM OUT OF THE GAME ONCE AND FOR ALL!
AND WITH YOU ON MY SIDE-- I CAN!
THE TITANS, EH?
FUNNY YOU SHOULD MENTION THEM.
HAVE YOU HEARD ENOUGH?

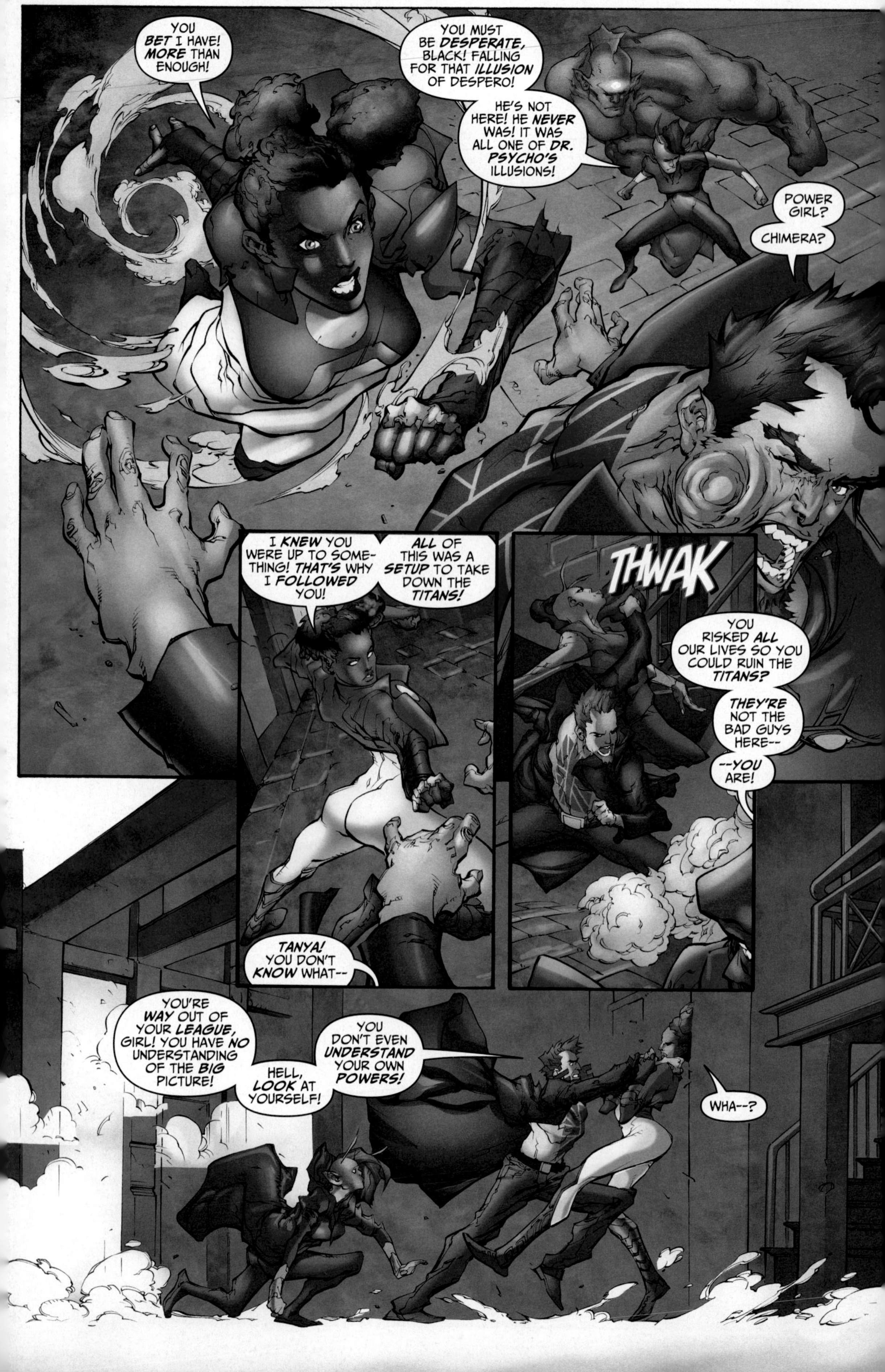

YOU BET I HAVE! MORE THAN ENOUGH!
YOU MUST BE DESPERATE, BLACK! FALLING FOR THAT ILLUSION OF DESPERO!
HE'S NOT HERE! HE NEVER WAS! IT WAS ALL ONE OF DR. PSYCHO'S ILLUSIONS!
POWER GIRL?
CHIMERA?
I KNEW YOU WERE UP TO SOMETHING! THAT'S WHY I FOLLOWED YOU!
ALL OF THIS WAS A SETUP TO TAKE DOWN THE TITANS!
TANYA! YOU DON'T KNOW WHAT--
THWAK
YOU RISKED ALL OUR LIVES SO YOU COULD RUIN THE TITANS?
THEY'RE NOT THE BAD GUYS HERE--
--YOU ARE!
YOU'RE WAY OUT OF YOUR LEAGUE, GIRL! YOU HAVE NO UNDERSTANDING OF THE BIG PICTURE!
HELL, LOOK AT YOURSELF!
YOU DON'T EVEN UNDERSTAND YOUR OWN POWERS!
WHA--?

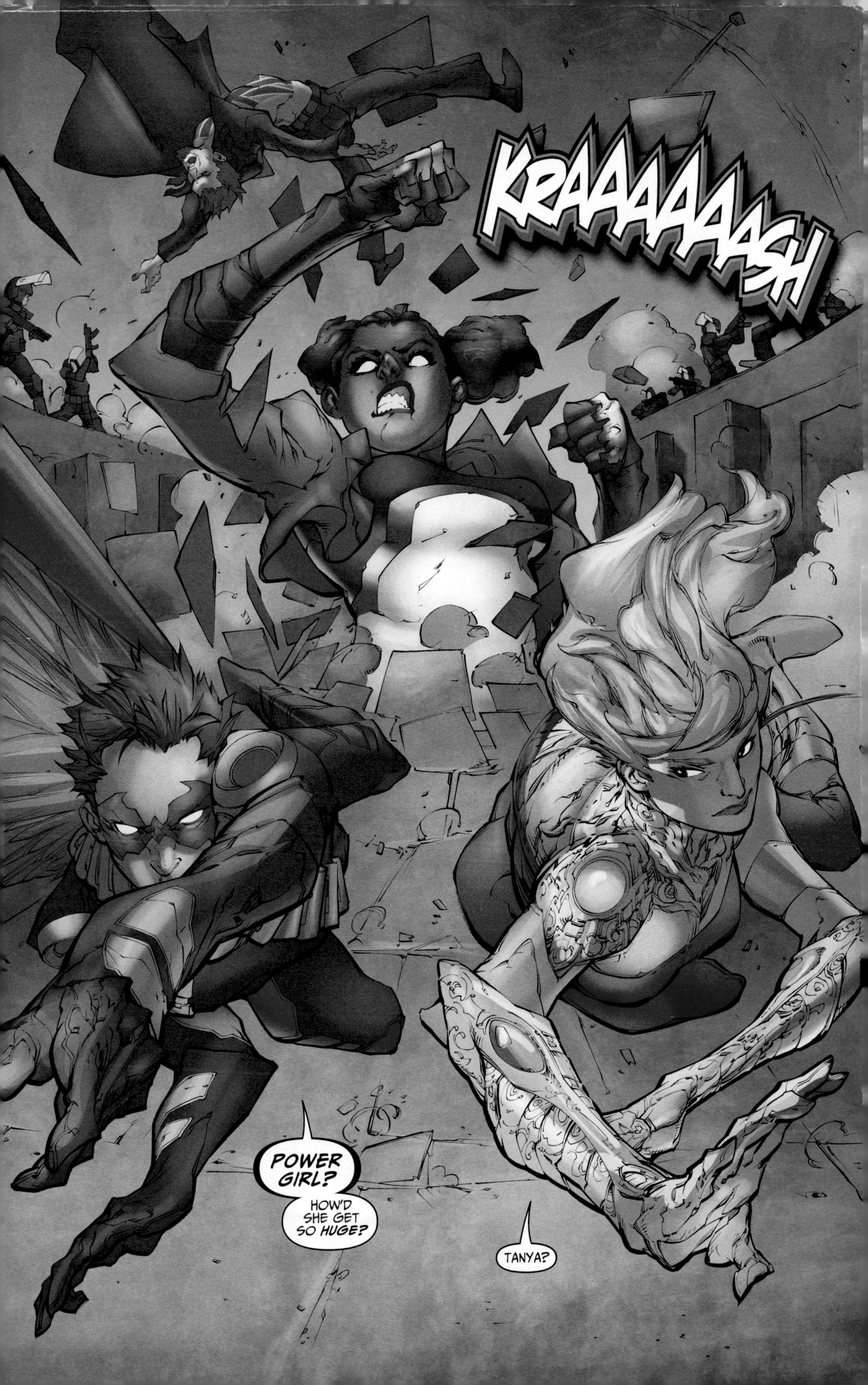
KRAAAAAAASH
POWER GIRL?
HOW'D SHE GET SO HUGE?
TANYA?

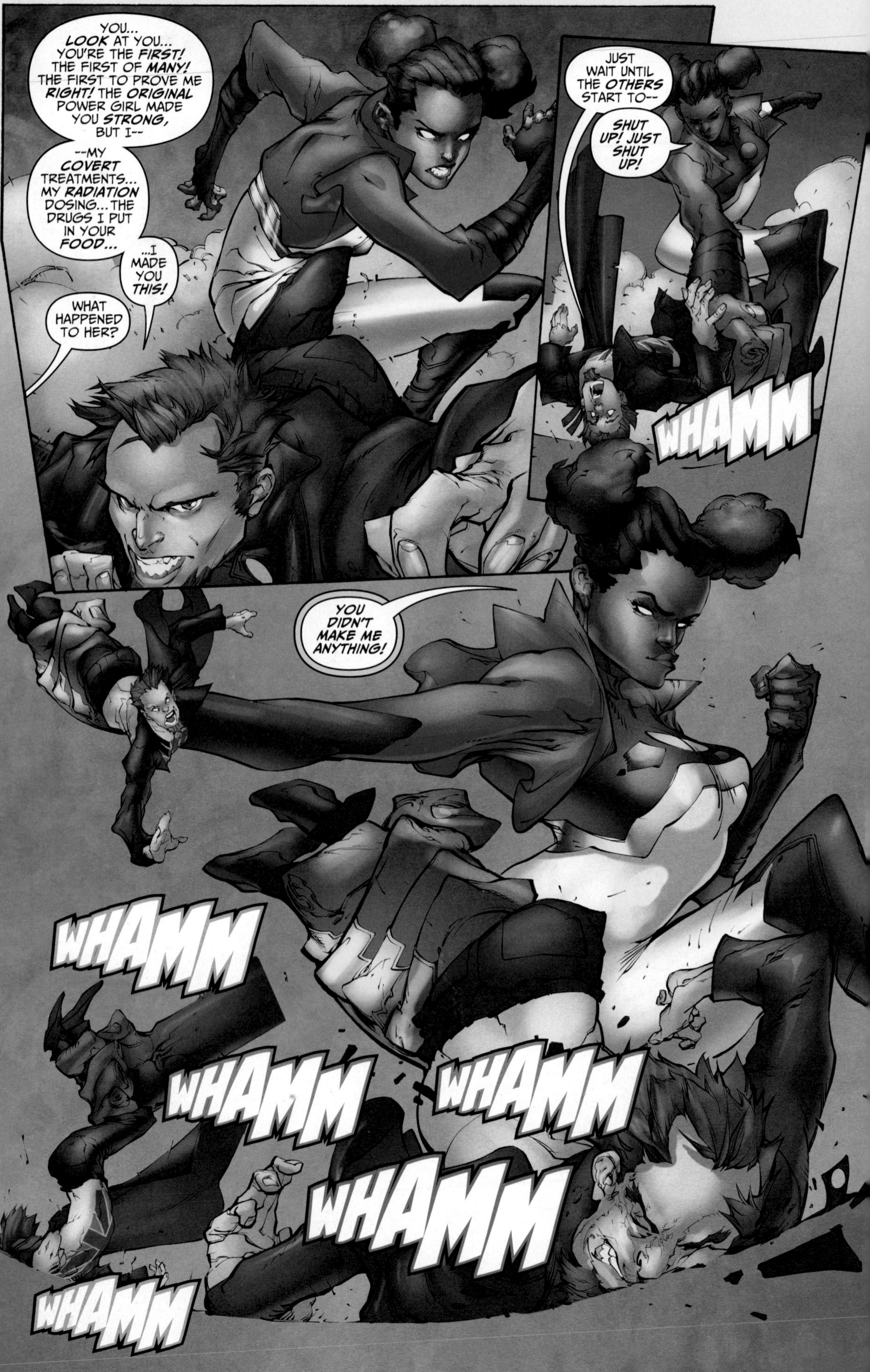

YOU... LOOK AT YOU... YOU'RE THE FIRST! THE FIRST OF MANY! THE FIRST TO PROVE ME RIGHT! THE ORIGINAL POWER GIRL MADE YOU STRONG, BUT I--
--MY COVERT TREATMENTS... MY RADIATION DOSING... THE DRUGS I PUT IN YOUR FOOD...
...I MADE YOU THIS!
WHAT HAPPENED TO HER?
JUST WAIT UNTIL THE OTHERS START TO--
SHUT UP! JUST SHUT UP!
WHAMM
YOU DIDN'T MAKE ME ANYTHING!
WHAMM
WHAMM
WHAMM
WHAMM
WHAMM

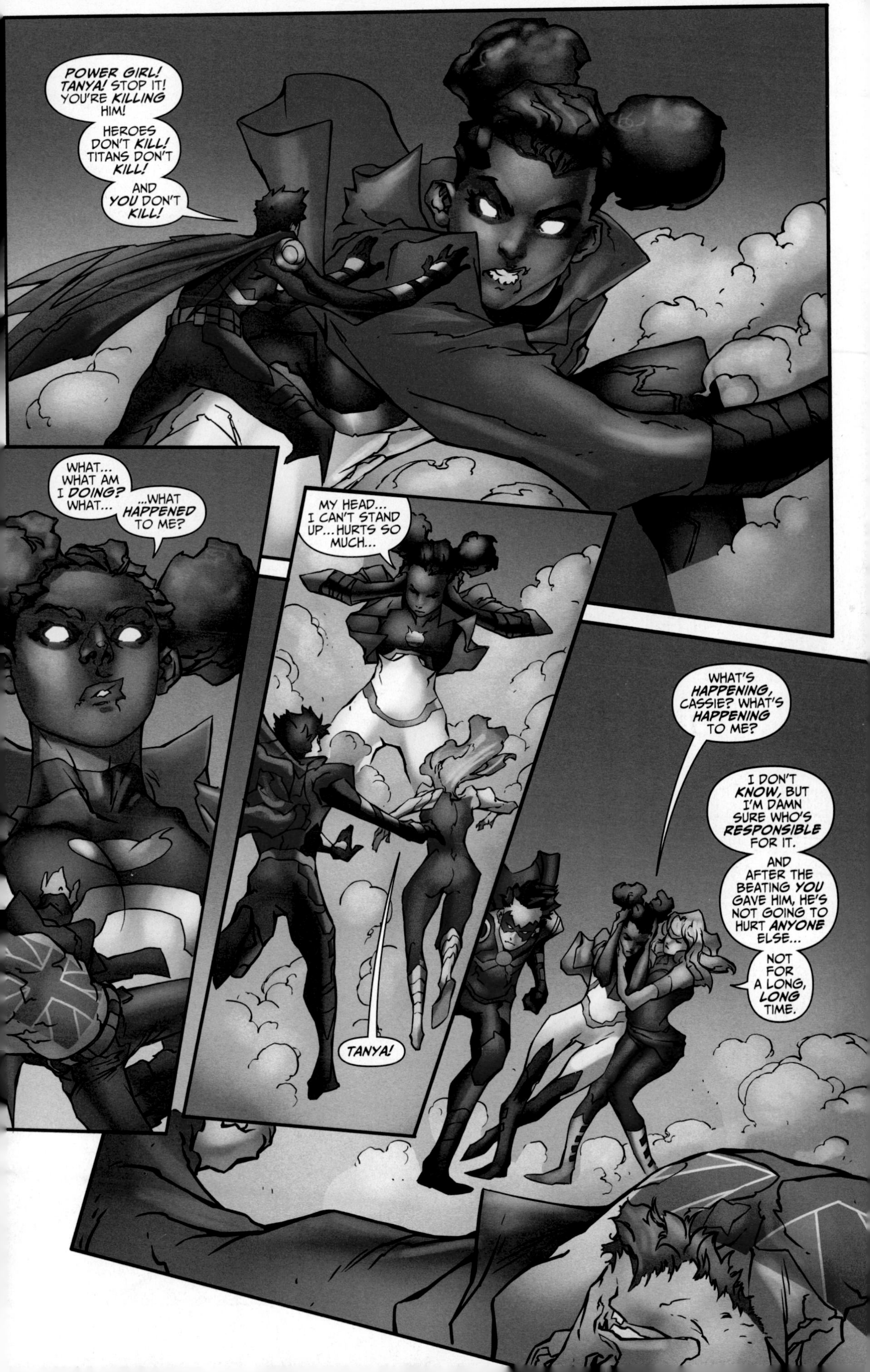
POWER GIRL! TANYA! STOP IT! YOU'RE KILLING HIM!
HEROES DON'T KILL! TITANS DON'T KILL!
AND YOU DON'T KILL!
WHAT... WHAT AM I DOING? WHAT...
...WHAT HAPPENED TO ME?
MY HEAD... I CAN'T STAND UP... HURTS SO MUCH...
TANYA!
WHAT'S HAPPENING, CASSIE? WHAT'S HAPPENING TO ME?
I DON'T KNOW, BUT I'M DAMN SURE WHO'S RESPONSIBLE FOR IT.
AND AFTER THE BEATING YOU GAVE HIM, HE'S NOT GOING TO HURT ANYONE ELSE...
NOT FOR A LONG, LONG TIME.

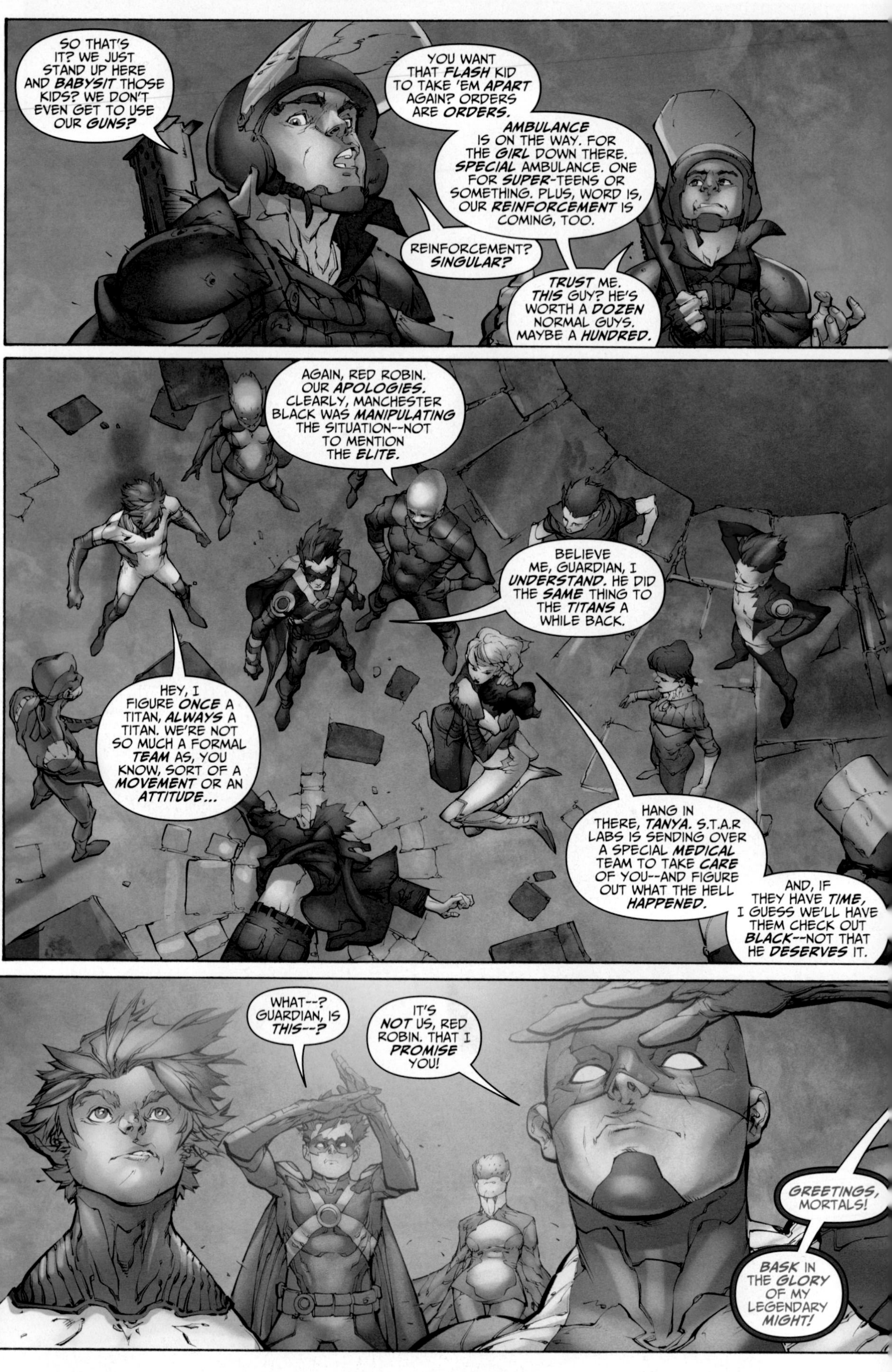
SO THAT'S IT? WE JUST STAND UP HERE AND BABYSIT THOSE KIDS? WE DON'T EVEN GET TO USE OUR GUNS?
YOU WANT THAT FLASH KID TO TAKE 'EM APART AGAIN? ORDERS ARE ORDERS.
AMBULANCE IS ON THE WAY. FOR THE GIRL DOWN THERE. SPECIAL AMBULANCE. ONE FOR SUPER-TEENS OR SOMETHING. PLUS, WORD IS, OUR REINFORCEMENT IS COMING, TOO.
REINFORCEMENT? SINGULAR?
TRUST ME. THIS GUY? HE'S WORTH A DOZEN NORMAL GUYS. MAYBE A HUNDRED.
AGAIN, RED ROBIN. OUR APOLOGIES. CLEARLY, MANCHESTER BLACK WAS MANIPULATING THE SITUATION--NOT TO MENTION THE ELITE.
BELIEVE ME, GUARDIAN, I UNDERSTAND. HE DID THE SAME THING TO THE TITANS A WHILE BACK.
HEY, I FIGURE ONCE A TITAN, ALWAYS A TITAN. WE'RE NOT SO MUCH A FORMAL TEAM AS, YOU KNOW, SORT OF A MOVEMENT OR AN ATTITUDE...
HANG IN THERE, TANYA. S.T.A.R LABS IS SENDING OVER A SPECIAL MEDICAL TEAM TO TAKE CARE OF YOU--AND FIGURE OUT WHAT THE HELL HAPPENED.
AND, IF THEY HAVE TIME, I GUESS WE'LL HAVE THEM CHECK OUT BLACK--NOT THAT HE DESERVES IT.
WHAT--? GUARDIAN, IS THIS--?
IT'S NOT US, RED ROBIN. THAT I PROMISE YOU!
GREETINGS, MORTALS!
BASK IN THE GLORY OF MY LEGENDARY MIGHT!

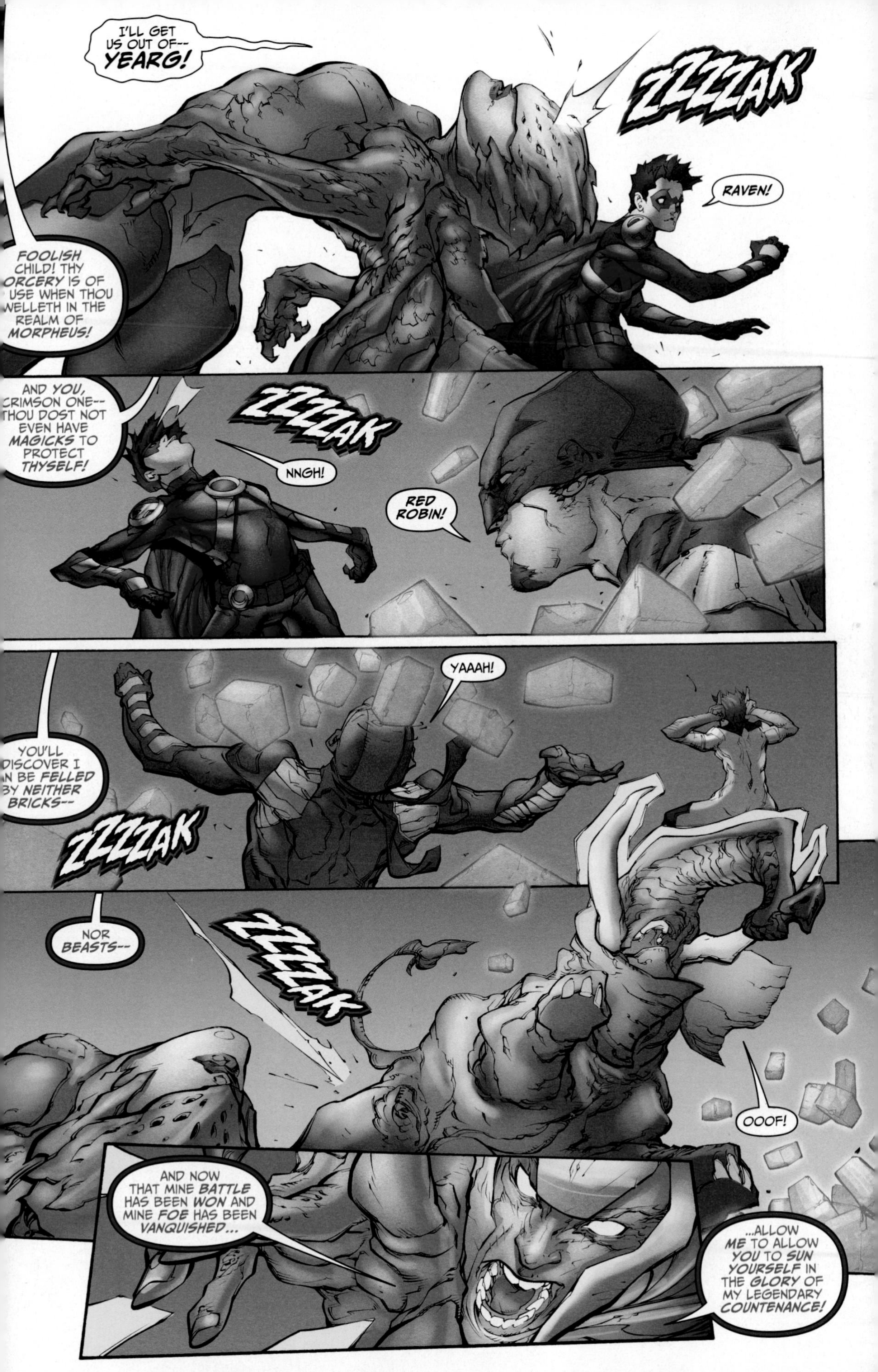

I'LL GET US OUT OF-- YEARG!
ZZZZAK
RAVEN!
FOOLISH CHILD! THY ORCERY IS OF USE WHEN THOU WELLETH IN THE REALM OF MORPHEUS!
AND YOU, CRIMSON ONE-- THOU DOST NOT EVEN HAVE MAGICKS TO PROTECT THYSELF!
ZZZZAK
NNGH!
RED ROBIN!
YAAAH!
YOU'LL DISCOVER I AN BE FELLED BY NEITHER BRICKS--
ZZZZAK
NOR BEASTS--
ZZZZAK
OOOF!
AND NOW THAT MINE BATTLE HAS BEEN WON AND MINE FOE HAS BEEN VANQUISHED...
...ALLOW ME TO ALLOW YOU TO SUN YOURSELF IN THE GLORY OF MY LEGENDARY COUNTENANCE!

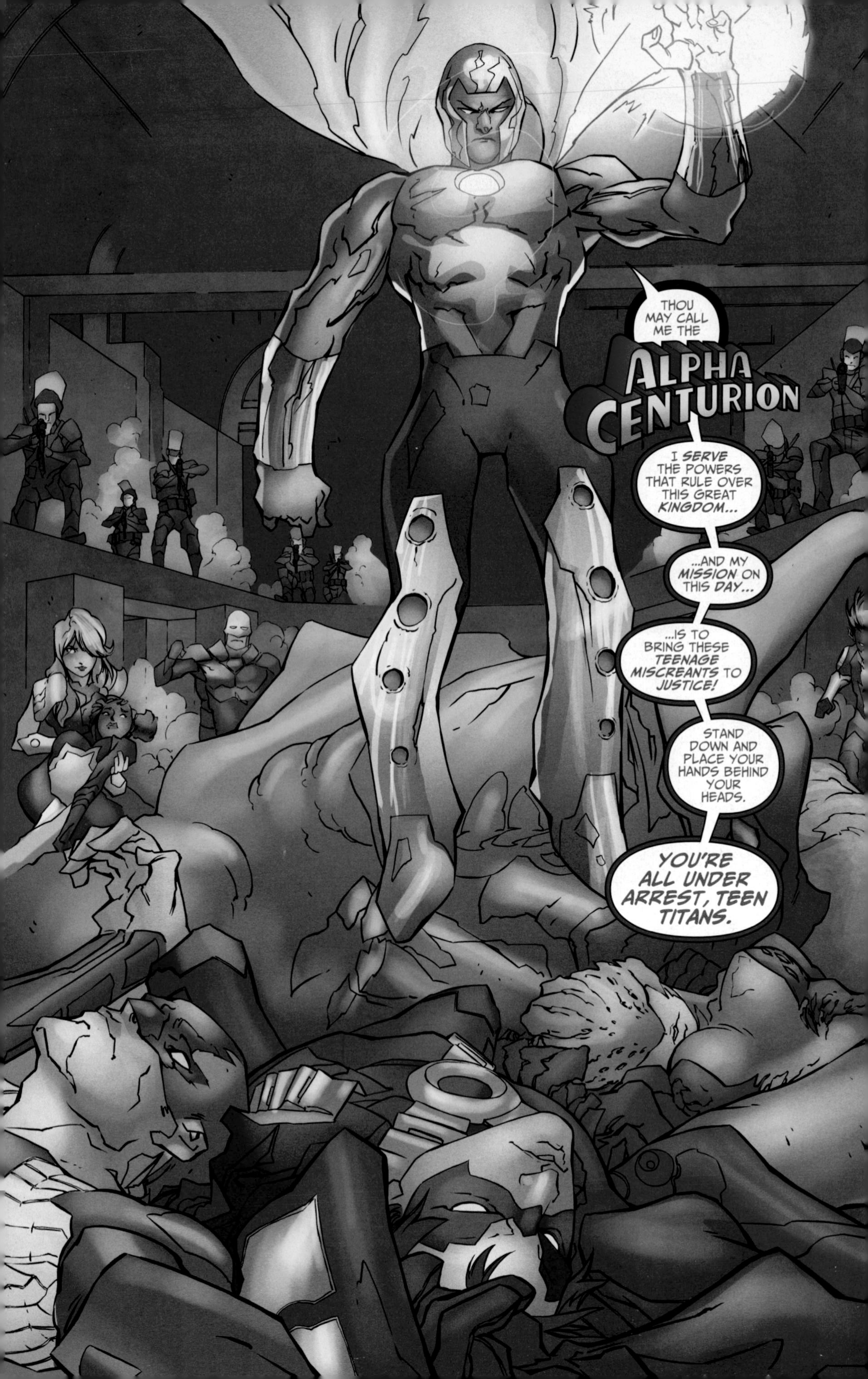
THOU MAY CALL ME THE
ALPHA CENTURION
I SERVE THE POWERS THAT RULE OVER THIS GREAT KINGDOM...
...AND MY MISSION ON THIS DAY...
...IS TO BRING THESE TEENAGE MISCREANTS TO JUSTICE!
STAND DOWN AND PLACE YOUR HANDS BEHIND YOUR HEADS.
YOU'RE ALL UNDER ARREST, TEEN TITANS.

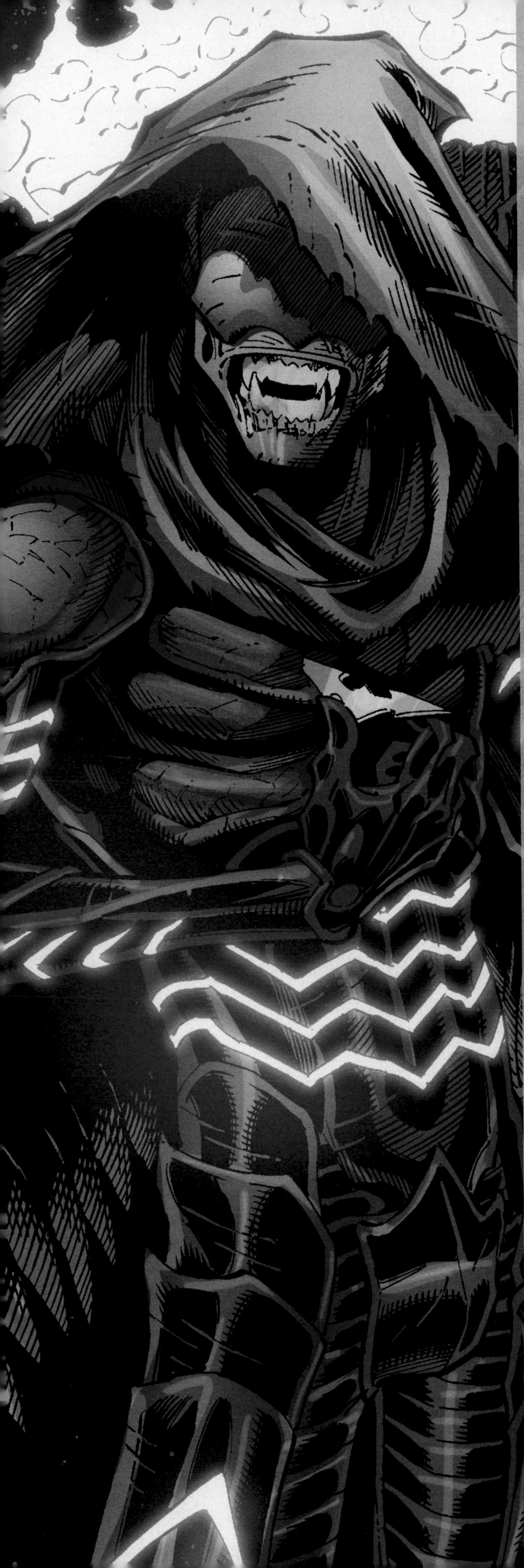

VARIANT COVER GALLERY

TEEN TITANS #8
MOVIE POSTER VARIANT
COVER BY ALEX GARNER

TEEN TITANS #9
JOKER 75TH ANNIVERSARY
VARIANT COVER BY
SCOTT McDANIEL AND
TANYA HORIE

TEEN TITANS #10
TEEN TITANS GO!
VARIANT COVER
BY BEN CALDWELL

TEEN TITANS #11
BOMBSHELLS VARIANT
COVER BY ANT LUCIA

TEEN TITANS #12
GREEN LANTERN
75TH ANNIVERSARY VARIANT
COVER BY MIKE McKONE
AND DAVE McCAIG

TEEN TITANS #13
MONSTER VARIANT COVER
BY AARON LOPRESTI

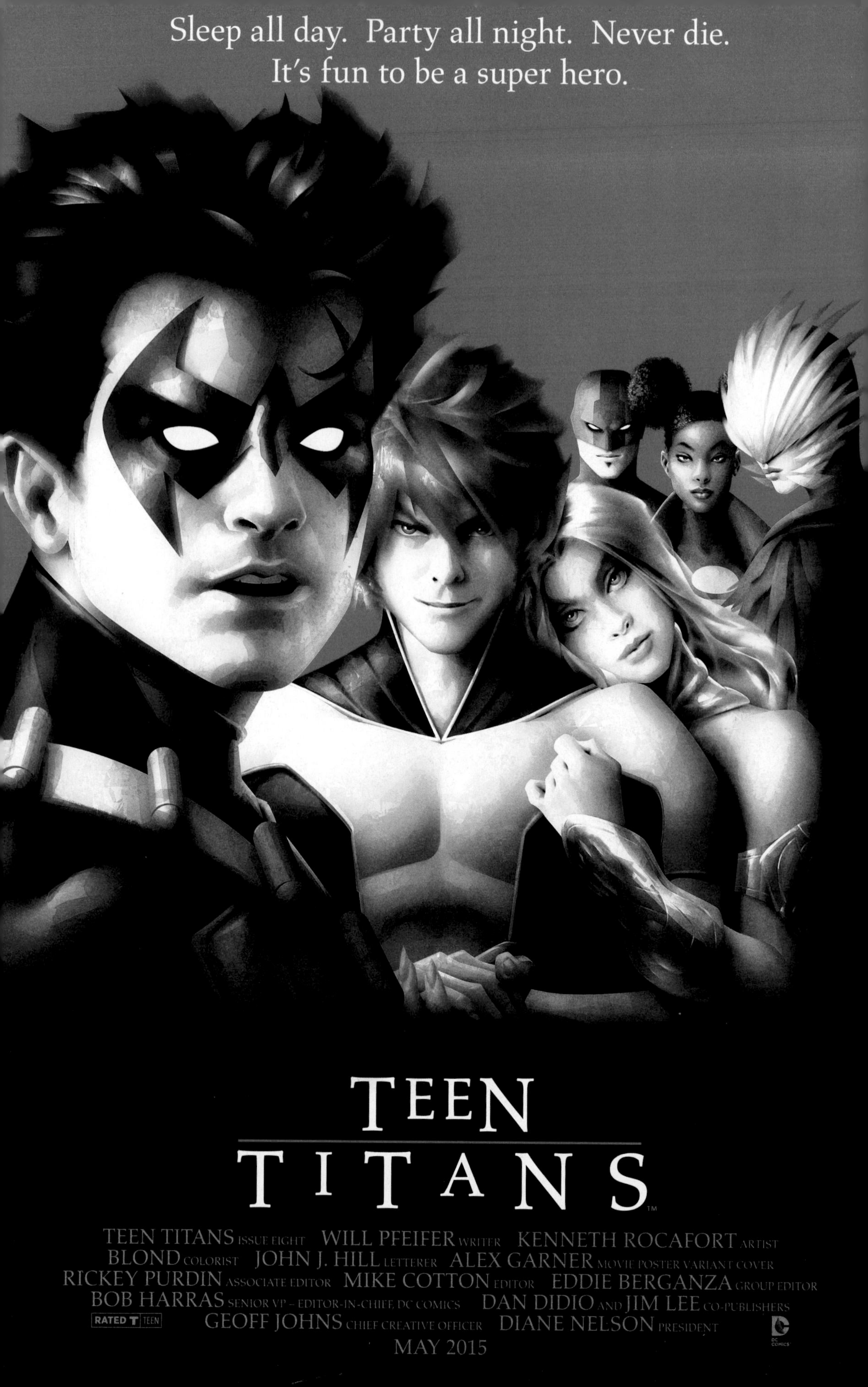

Sleep all day. Party all night. Never die.
It's fun to be a super hero.
TEEN TITANS™
TEEN TITANS ISSUE EIGHT WILL PFEIFER WRITER KENNETH ROCAFORT ARTIST
BLOND COLORIST JOHN J. HILL LETTERER ALEX GARNER MOVIE POSTER VARIANT COVER
RICKEY PURDIN ASSOCIATE EDITOR MIKE COTTON EDITOR EDDIE BERGANZA GROUP EDITOR
BOB HARRAS SENIOR VP – EDITOR-IN-CHIEF, DC COMICS DAN DIDIO AND JIM LEE CO-PUBLISHERS
RATED T TEEN
GEOFF JOHNS CHIEF CREATIVE OFFICER DIANE NELSON PRESIDENT
DC COMICS
MAY 2015

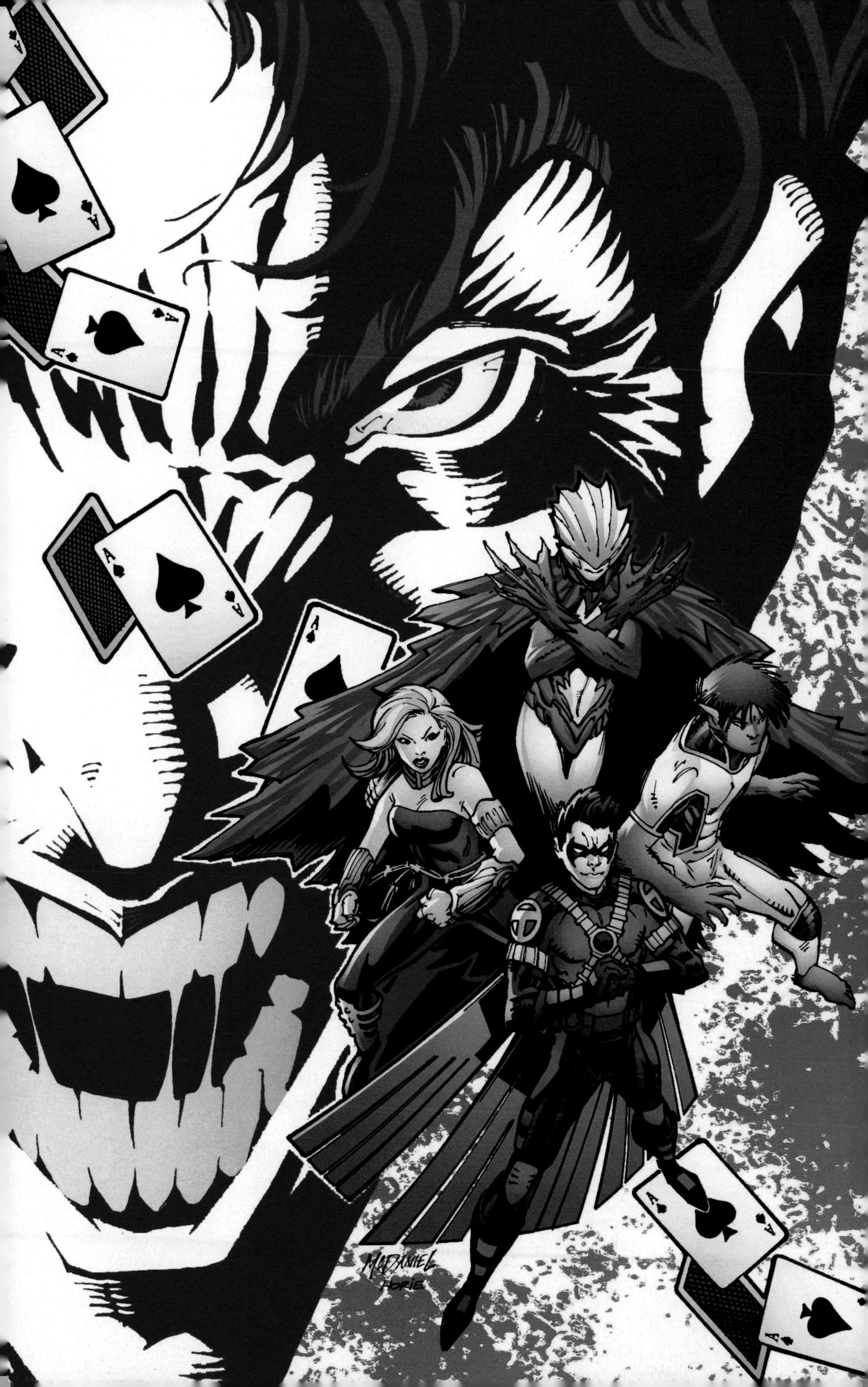
McDANIEL
HORIE

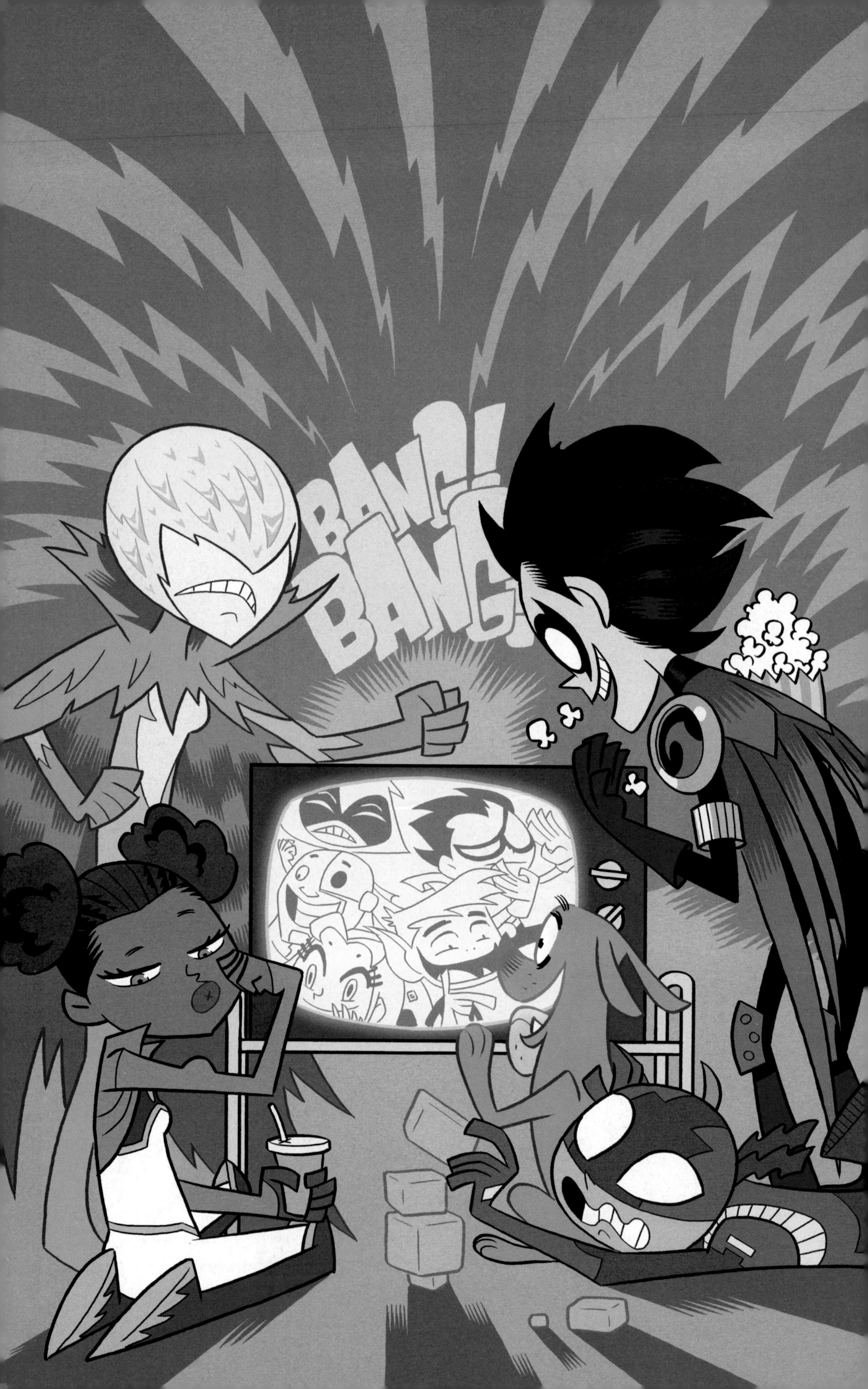
BANG! BANG!

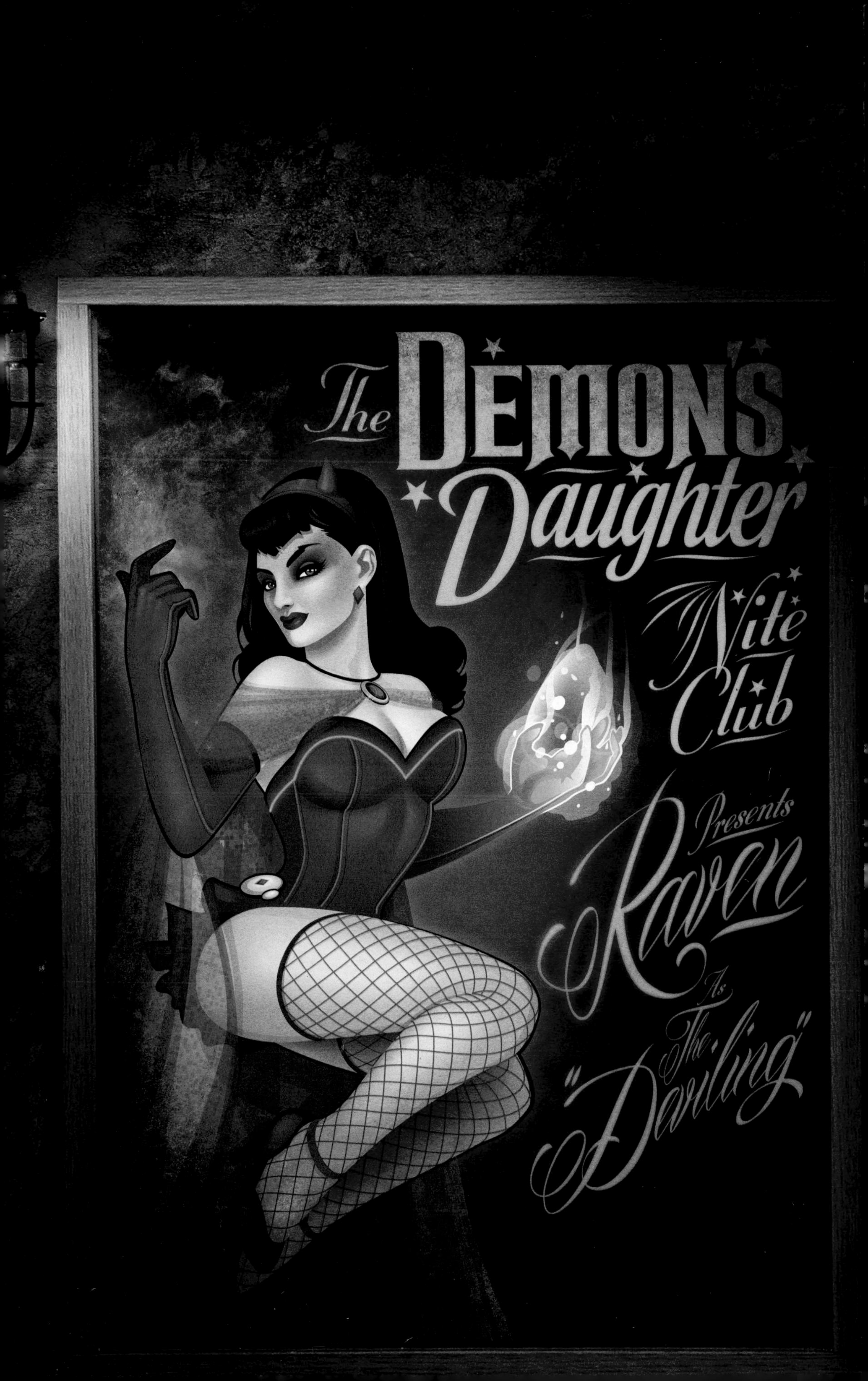
The Demon's Daughter
Nite Club
Presents
Raven
As
The
"Darling"

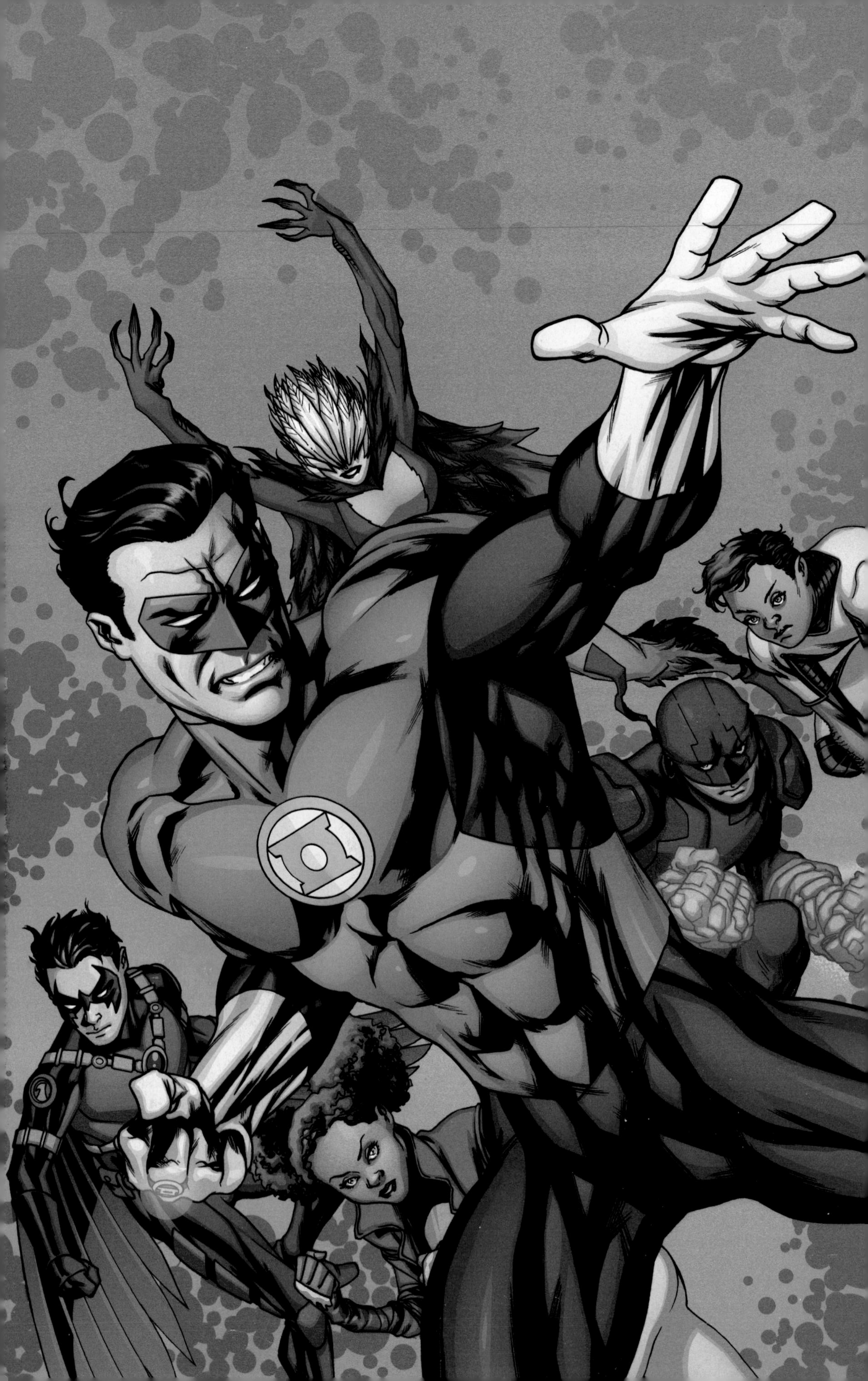

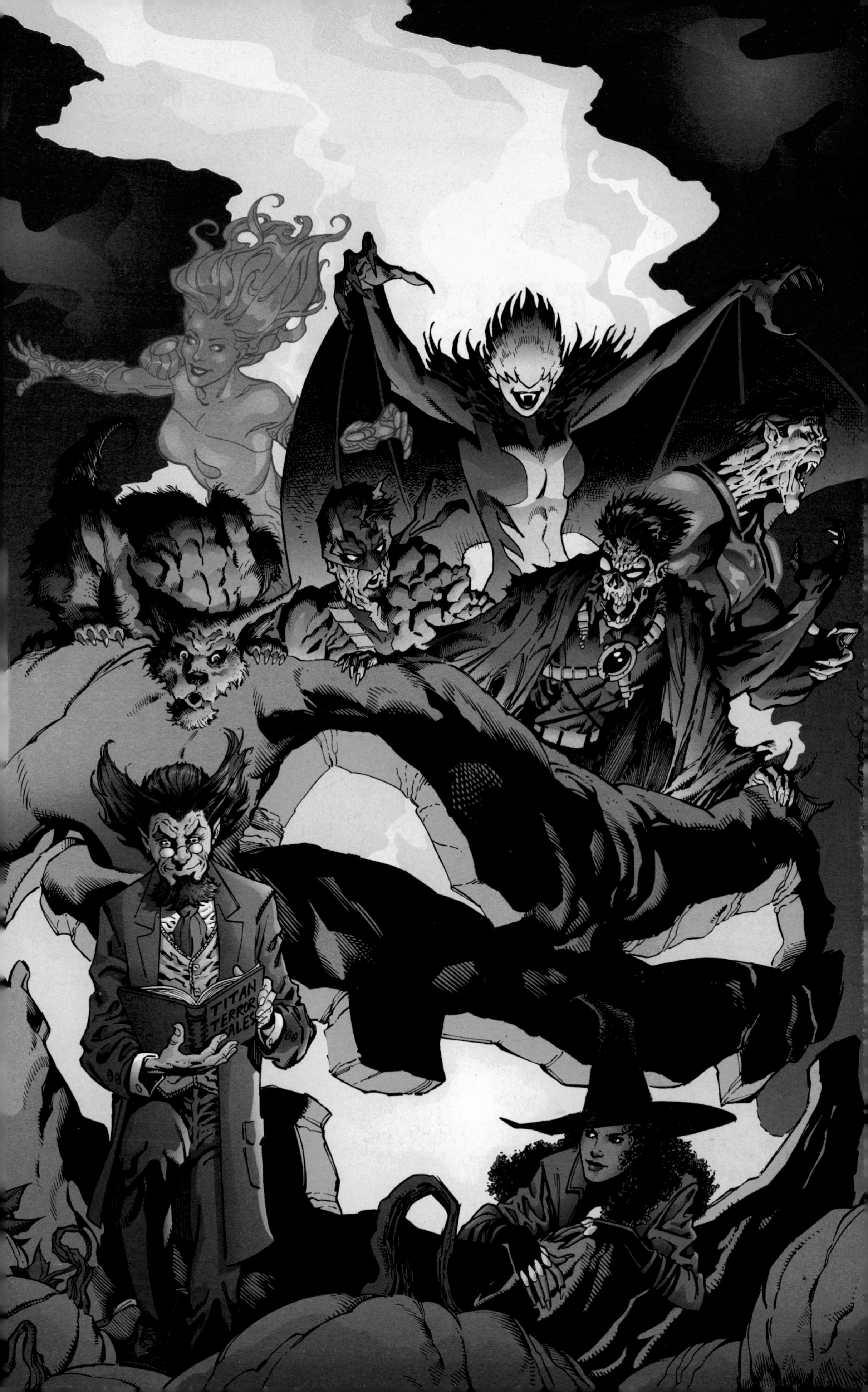
TITAN TERROR TALES

START AT THE BEGINNING!

TEEN TITANS
VOLUME 1: IT'S OUR RIGHT TO FIGHT

**TEEN TITANS
VOL. 2: THE CULLING**

**TEEN TITANS VOL. 3:
DEATH OF THE FAMILY**

**THE CULLING: RISE OF
THE RAVAGERS**

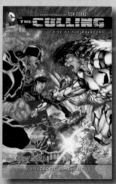

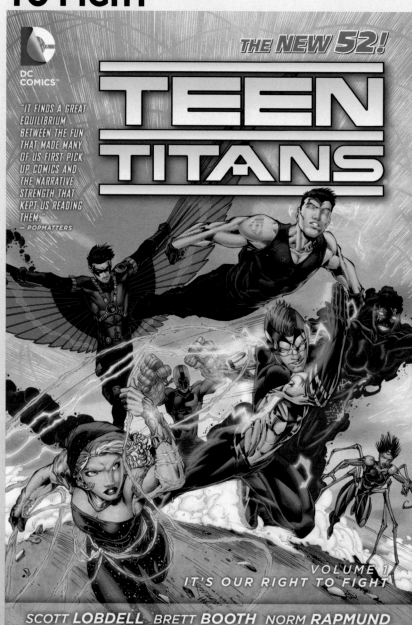

THE NEW 52!

DC COMICS™

TEEN TITANS

*"IT FINDS A GREAT
EQUILIBRIUM
BETWEEN THE FUN
THAT MADE MANY
OF US FIRST PICK
UP COMICS AND
THE NARRATIVE
STRENGTH THAT
KEPT US READING
THEM."*
— POPMATTERS

VOLUME 1
IT'S OUR RIGHT TO FIGHT

SCOTT **LOBDELL** BRETT **BOOTH** NORM **RAPMUND**